RESEARCH IN ORGANIZATIONAL BEHAVIOR

Volume 13 • 1991

RESEARCH IN ORGANIZATIONAL BEHAVIOR

An Annual Series of Analytical Essays and Critical Reviews

Editors: **L. L. CUMMINGS**
Carlson School of Management
University of Minnesota

BARRY M. STAW
School of Business Administration
University of California, Berkeley

Volume 13 • 1991

JAI PRESS INC.

Greenwich, Connecticut   *London, England*

SCHOOL OF
CALIFORNIA
PROFESSIONAL
PSYCHOLOGY
LOS ANGELES

CONTENTS

LIST OF CONTRIBUTORS

Robert A. Baron

Department of Psychology
Renssalaer Polytechnic Institute
Troy, New York

Arthur P. Brief

A. B. Freeman School of Business
Tulane University
New Orleans, Louisiana

Peter Cappelli

The Wharton School
University of Pennsylvania
Philadelphia, Pennsylvania

Janet M. Dukerich

College of Business Administration
The University of Texas
Austin, Texas

Carolyn P. Egri

Faculty of Commerce and Business
    Administration
The University of British Columbia
Vancouver, B. C.
Canada

Peter J. Frost

Faculty of Commerce and Business
    Administration
The University of British Columbia
Vancouver, B. C.
Canada

David B. Greenberger

Department of Management and Human
    Resources
The Ohio State University
Columbus, Ohio

Alice M. Isen

Johnson Graduate School of Management
Cornell University
Ithaca, New York

Roderick M. Kramer

Graduate School of Business
Stanford University
Stanford, California

John W. Meyer

Department of Sociology
Stanford University
Stanford, California

Margaret A. Neale

J. L. Kellogg Graduate School of
    Management
Northwestern University
Evanston, Illinois

Gregory B. Northcraft

Karl Eller Graduate School of Management
University of Arizona
Tucson, Arizona

W. Richard Scott

Department of Sociology
Stanford University
Stanford, California

Peter D. Sherer

The Wharton School
University of Pennsylvania
Philadelphia, Pennsylvania

Stephen Strasser

Graduate Program in Hospital
    Administration
The Ohio State University
Columbus, Ohio

PREFACE

Volume 13 of *Research in Organizational Behavior* covers a broad array of topics ranging from the affective dimensions of behavior in organizations, through structural and situational determinants of organizational processes to an institutional perspective on the development of talent in organizations.

We begin with an essay by Isen and Baron on the role of positive affect in organizations. Attention is given to both the causes and consequences of positive feelings. A wide range of literature is reviewed to argue that positive affect has consequences for both cognitions and behaviors of organizational relevance. Physical working environments, shifts in organizational culture and communication processes are identified as important determinants of positive affect. In turn, positive affect causes pro-social behaviors, improved leader-member relations, more cooperative interpersonal relations in the context of bargaining and task satisfaction.

Cappelli and Sherer argue that individual level studies in organizational behavior would be enhanced if the contexts of individual behavior were given greater attention. They advocate building bridges between micro and macro research by focusing on an intermediate or meso level of analysis. Such research would focus on the environmental determinants of organizational processes and structures; and, in turn, on the individual level consequences of these organizational level phenomena. Special emphasis is given to employment institutions and their role in buffering organizations and employees from external labor markets. The Cappelli and Sherer framework and emphasis fit well with one of the current themes in organizational behavior; namely, the importance of multi and cross level constructs and research designs.

The pervasiveness and roles of personal control in organizations are emphasized in Chapter 3 by Greenberger and Strasser. People are argued to have a general desire for control. Reductions in perceived control are seen as leading to behaviors aimed at enhancing or rebalancing desired and achieved levels of control. The authors present a comprehensive model of situational and dispositional factors related to sensitivity to control as well as behaviors aimed at establishing a sense of personal control. The roles of management in building structures and processes to fit individual control needs are emphasized. Both functional and dysfunctional behaviors, aimed at addressing a control balance, are discussed.

Neale and Northcraft present a framework for understanding two-person bargaining in organizations. Two domains of research are emphasized: (1) research on the effects of context on bargaining behaviors and (2) studies relating characteristics of the bargainer per se to the behavior of bargaining in the dyad. Attention is given to the processes through which bargainers both claim value and create value in the bargaining setting. Several directions for future research are suggested.

The Chapter by Kramer presents a model of intergroup competition that is based on recent social psychological research on social categorization processes and interdependent decisionmaking under conditions of scarce resources. A general model of intergroup relations in organizations is derived from this analysis. Central attention is given to the resource interdependencies that give rise to intergroup competition and to the psychological processes through which such interdependence is interpreted. Implications of the model are drawn for several areas of application; e.g., the resolution of intergroup conflict, the development of intergroup cooperation and the social aspects of decisionmaking in organizations.

Frost and Egri present an analysis of innovation focusing on the political and social processes central to effective innovation in organizations. Focus is on both the objective, observable phenomena associated with innovation as well as the underlying deep, structural assumptions about innovation. Innovators are analyzed as corporate heroes and champions of change. A long term research agenda on innovation is proposed, focusing on both the immediate and longer term technical and social implications of innovation.

Scott and Meyer use institutional analyses to explore the determinants and origins of training programs within organizational contexts. Similarities and differences between education and training are analyzed using this institutional framework. Explanations of four types are offered for the growth and diversity of training endeavors; i.e., a technical perspective, a social control perspective, a polity or political membership perspective, and a set of specific institutional explanations. The roles of both institutional agencies and processes are examined as they relate to the growth and diversification of training programs.

Finally, Brief and Dukerich make a case for not utilizing usefulness when evaluating theoretical perspectives in organizational behavior. They argue that attempts to make a theory useful are likely to impede the development of sound theory. The analysis invites several questions of central relevance to the organizational scholar.

- At what stage in theory development is usefulness a legitimate criteria?
- How can theory builders and action researchers co-exist within the same domain?
- Is practicality to be interpreted as irrelevant to the advancement of organizational behavior?

It is concluded that good theory has practical value as a guide to the development of applications and expansions of theory; i.e., it is a practical tool for the theoretician.

L. L. Cummings
Barry M. Staw
Series Editors

POSITIVE AFFECT AS A FACTOR IN ORGANIZATIONAL BEHAVIOR

Alice M. Isen and Robert A. Baron

ABSTRACT

Positive affect, defined as pleasant feelings induced by commonplace events or circumstances, has been found to exert significant effects on several aspects of social behavior. For example, positive affect usually increases a person's tendency to help others and reduces overt aggression. Positive affect also facilitates recall of material in memory with a positive affective tone, increases efficiency in making some types of decisions, broadens the range of material individuals think about in response to stimuli, and promotes innovation and creative problem solving. Such effects, in turn, are relevant to—and play a role in—many aspects of organizational behavior. Growing evidence suggests that even relatively mild shifts in positive affect (induced through diverse procedures) can influence such important organizational processes as face-to-face bargaining, preference for various modes of resolving interpersonal conflicts (e.g., collaboration rather than avoidance), evaluations of ratees (both in job interview and performance appraisal contexts), and task perception and satisfaction. Other, less direct evidence, indicates that positive affect may also play a role in pro-

Research in Organizational Behavior, Volume 13, pages 1–53.
ISBN: 1-55938-198-1

1

social organizational behavior (e.g., citizenship behaviors), leader-member relations, and cognitive processes that may relate to the escalation-of-commitment phenomenon. The influence of positive affect on these processes is often—but not necessarily always—beneficial to individuals and organizations. Enhanced positive affect can be induced in organizational settings through such techniques as improvements in several aspects of physical working environments, shifts in organizational culture, and enhanced communication.

INTRODUCTION

As students of organizational behavior, we seek to understand the factors that influence the functioning of organizations and life in these formal groups, in hopes of finding ways of developing more effective, beneficial, and enlightened organizations in society. Recent research indicates that positive affect can influence processes fundamental to organizational functioning, from decision-making and innovation to group cohesiveness and interpersonal processes, and thus can play an important role in many aspects of organizational life. The purpose of this chapter is to bring these effects into focus and explore their implications.

Recent investigations suggest that mild, positive affect states induced by seemingly minor, everyday events can have significant effects on social behavior and cognitive processes that can be important for the functioning of organizations. These effects frequently have a beneficial influence on the organization and help it to function optimally. But under some circumstances the processes to which good feelings give rise may interfere with performance of the tasks required to accomplish the organization's goals. For example, people in whom positive affect has been induced have been found to be more sociable, cooperative, and helpful to others than are members of a control group. It would usually seem desirable to foster these kinds of social processes in organizational settings, since they seem likely to contribute to smooth functioning, pleasant atmosphere, helpfulness, and thus efficiency in the organization. However, under some circumstances, people in positive feeling states have also been found to behave in ways that might seem more independent or guided by principle; and sometimes the behavior of people who are feeling happy reflects a desire to maintain those positive feelings. These tendencies may sometimes be helpful in achieving organizational goals, but they may not always be so. Thus, clear understanding of the circumstances under which positive affect is likely to have one type of influence vs. another, and the range of situations in which those influences will promote the organization's goals vs. complicate the process of accomplishing them, can be helpful to those who wish to create effective and humane organizations.

In addition, this same kind of positive affect has been shown to influence memory, judgment, and decision-making, and to result in improved creative-problem-solving ability and originality, as reflected by task performance. Originality and ability to solve complex problems in creative ways are important skills for both personal life and organizational functioning. Thus, in still another way, positive affect appears able to make a major contribution to the development of organizations and of the individuals within them. Again, however, there may be circumstances under which the processes associated with positive affect may interfere with achievement of organizational goals, unless this possibility is recognized and addressed. Therefore, in order to make use of the potential benefits that can come from positive affect, and to control any interference with organizational functioning that affect may introduce, students of organizational behavior will need to be familiar with these effects.

These sorts of social and cognitive processes may often be overlooked as factors contributing to organizational functioning, but actually they are of central importance, potentially playing a role both directly and indirectly in the tone of daily life and in the success of the organization's mission. Through influence on these factors, the *affect* that is generated through daily events and situations can play an important role in the life of the organization. The atmosphere and overriding goals of organizations may be influenced by the affective tone that predominates and the interpersonal and cognitive effects that this tone fosters. Further, these factors can also play a role in shaping specific organizational processes such as leadership style, communication patterns and styles, group and interpersonal structures and orientations, and decision-making processes and innovation, all of which are recognized as crucially important in determining the level and nature of functioning of the organization. Thus, the purpose of this chapter is to discuss ways in which feelings may influence the behavior and thought processes of people in organizational settings, so that researchers and students of management can consider in more detail the impact of feelings on organizational processes.

The plan for this chapter is first to provide a bit of background information that will help to clarify the focus of the empirical work to be discussed and the methods that have been used to gather these data. Then, we present an overview of the major effects of positive feelings on cognition and social behavior that have been obtained in the program of research conducted by Isen and her associates. Some of these effects, like the ones on helping and problem solving, or even on decision-making, will immediately seem relevant to organizational behavior; other effects of feelings that will be discussed, like those on memory, may at first seem less relevant to organizational behavior. Nonetheless, these more fundamental findings may also help us to understand more complex relationships between affect and cognition and social behavior, and thus they are presented as well. Following this, the chapter focuses more specifically, and in greater detail, on consideration of how the effects of feelings on cognition and behavior might be relevant to organizational behavior topics that we believe are informed by the more basic problem-solving and interpersonal processes discussed. These include leadership styles, group processes, communication, conflict resolution and negotiation, job satisfaction, productivity, and change and development.

Background

Let us focus briefly first on certain aspects of the research itself: (1) The type of affect state studied, and (2) the means of inducing affect and verifying its role in the outcome of the studies.

Research on the influence of positive affect on social interaction and cognitive processes indicates that happiness or mild elation, induced in a variety of simple ways, can increase helping and generosity, can promote sociability and friendliness, and can facilitate integrative bargaining so that both parties are more likely to obtain the optimal outcome from negotiation. In one series of studies people who had received information that they had performed well on a test of perceptual-motor skills donated more money to a charity collection can, were more likely to initiate a conversation with a stranger, and were more willing to aid a third party in need of assistance with what she was carrying, than were others who had not received the positive feedback about performance on this task (Isen, 1970). A follow-up series of studies revealed that people in whom positive affect had been induced, by means of being offered cookies while studying in the library, by means of getting their money back in the coin-return slot of a public telephone in a shopping mall (Isen & Levin, 1972), or by means of receiving a small free-sample packet of stationery at their front doors from someone posing as a company representative giving out samples door-to-door (Isen, Clark, & Schwartz, 1976), were more likely to help a stranger in need of assistance or more likely to volunteer to help, but not to annoy, others who were studying. In the shopping-center study, in which affect had been induced by finding money in the coin-return of a telephone, the helping task involved no request for aid, but rather assessed the subject's likelihood of spontaneously offering to help a woman who dropped the papers that she was carrying. (The helping opportunity was presented after a subject had completed his/her call, of course.) In the library study, in which affect was induced by offering subjects cookies as they studied at individual carrels, the helping task involved volunteering time to serve as an experimenter's assistant who would aid subjects to obtain the highest score possible on a task. This was contrasted with conditions in which the proposed task was depicted as one in which the volunteer assistant would annoy subjects who were trying to study. In the at-home study, in which affect was induced by means of the free sample at the door, the helping task involved responding to a telephoned request for aid that came a few minutes after the subject had been contacted at the front door by the confederate; it required subjects to look up a telephone number and make a call for the anonymous caller who, reportedly, had just used her last change and had reached the wrong number (the subject). In different conditions of the study, calls came at different amounts of time following receipt of the free sample, and thus the study also provided an indication of the duration of the behavioral impact of the affect induction. This study showed that the observed effect of feelings on helping measured in this way lasted approximately 20 minutes (Isen et al., 1976).

These same kinds of simply-induced affective states can influence cognitive processes such as memory, judgment, and decision-making. For example, mild positive affect has been shown to facilitate recall of positive material in memory, and to influence judgments regarding neutral material. In one study, conducted in a shopping mall, people were unaware that they were subjects in an experiment were approached and given a small free-sample note pad or nail clipper (males received nail clippers; females, note pads). Subsequently, when these subjects encountered a different person taking a consumer-opinion survey and participated in that survey, they evaluated the performance and service records of their major consumer products more positively than did a control group whose members had not been given the free sample (Isen, Shalker, Clark, & Karp, 1978).

Likewise, in several studies, using various means of affect induction, from victory on a computer game (Isen et al., 1978) to reading the Velten (1968) Positive Mood Induction procedure (Teasdale & Fogarty, 1979), it has been found that positive affect can serve as a retrieval cue for positive material in memory, making recall of that material easier and more likely (Isen et al., 1978); Laird, Wagner, Halal, & Szegda, 1981; Nasby & Yando, 1982; Teasdale & Fogarty, 1979).

In particular, these studies indicate that positive material is more accessible to people who are feeling good. For this reason, it has been suggested that the influence of happiness on social behavior may be, in part, *attributable* to its influence on memory and judgment. Thus, fundamental cognitive processes have been identified as factors possibly contributing to the impact of feelings on social behavior and more complex cognitive activity.

The Type of Affect Studied. Two things should be noted about the kind of affect state studied in this research. First, most of this work has concentrated on positive, pleasant feelings rather than on negative, unpleasant feelings such as anxiety or anger or depression. Much of the earlier psychological literature addressing the influence of feelings or emotional states on social behavior and intellectual performance has focused primarily on unpleasant states. For example, there are large bodies of work on the influence of frustration or anger on aggression, and on the relationship between anxiety and performance. There has also been considerable research on sadness or depression. Negative affect manipulations have sometimes been included in the studies to be presented here, but a major focus in this work has been on discovering what happens to people's thought processes and social interaction when they feel good.

In this context, it should also be noted that in this body of literature on the influence of affect on social behavior and cognitive processes, the effects of positive and negative affect have not always been found to be parallel or symmetrical. For example, while positive affect has been found to promote sociability and helpfulness over a wide range of situations, negative affect has not always been found to reduce the occurrence of those behaviors. Sometimes people in whom negative affect has been induced help less than control subjects, but research has found that sometimes they help more, and sometimes negative affect and control groups do not differ (see Isen, 1984, 1987 for discussion).

Likewise, the lack of symmetry between the two kinds of states has been noted in the literature on affect and *cognition*. For example, as noted, a growing body of research indicates that positive affect facilitates retrieval of positive material in memory. However, most of the studies that report such effects, and that attempt simultaneously to investigate the influence of comparable sadness on recall of negative material, report non-symmetrical effects of sadness and happiness. That is, sadness either fails to facilitate the recall of negative material, or its facilitative effect is less than that of positive feelings on positive material (see Isen, 1984; 1985; for discussion of this issue).

It has been suggested that this asymmetry may result from motivational or cognitive structural factors, or both (Isen, 1985; 1987; 1990). That is, negative affect may not be seen to facilitate accessibility of negative material because people may voluntarily try to counter any such tendency, in an effort to improve their feeling states. Another possibility is that negative material, or at least some types of negative material, may be structured in the mind more specifically or narrowly than positive material is. Consequently, any given negative feeling state may not be as effective a retrieval cue for negative material in general as positive states seem to be for positive material in general. Thus, it may be that negative states may be more focused and may cue only very specifically related material, whereas positive states appear to cue a wider range of positive material. These possibilities are under investigation (e.g., see Isen, 1990).

It is interesting to think about why this situation may exist, but for our present purposes the point that needs to be made is only that one should not assume that negative affect will necessarily have the inverse effect of positive. It may, but it may not; and this is one area in which additional research is needed.

Work on negative affect is undoubtedly important, but, as is becoming more and more clear, so is the understanding of positive feelings. Positive feelings seem capable of bringing out our "better nature" socially and, as we will see, our creativity in thinking and problem solving. Thus, they are a potential source of interpersonal cooperativeness and organizational effectiveness, as well as of personal well being, growth, and development. This chapter, like the research on which it is based, will focus primarily on the effects of positive feelings.

Second, regarding the type of affect state studied, the research to be described has dealt with low-level, "everyday" feelings states, rather than with relatively intense, dramatic, focused episodes of emotion. It is well known that powerful emotion can interrupt and influence behavior, but growing evidence indicates that even low-level general feeling states are potentially quite influential in directing thought and influencing both social behavior and task performance or problem-solving strategy. Because these states are relatively subtle, and because (being mild or induced by small things) they may occur frequently, the effects that they have on social interaction and cognitive processes may be quite pervasive and important to study. Thus, in summary, the kinds of affect studied in this research are common positive feelings of happiness, well-being, competence, good fortune, or enjoyment, induced by everyday events.

Methods of Affect Induction. This research has demonstrated that an affective state sufficient to influence social behavior and cognitive processes can be induced by surprisingly small things. This brings us to the second general background point mentioned at the outset of this section, our methods of affect induction and their verification. In this research the positive-affect subjects experience some small pleasure, and, as noted, it has been found that this can influence their social behavior and certain cognitive processes. For example, the kinds of things that have been shown to affect social behavior and cognitive processes as described include finding a dime in the coin return of a public telephone, receiving a free-sample note pad, nail clipper, or package of stationery (valued at about $.29) from a manufacturer's representative, receiving a cookie, being offered refreshments (juice and cookies) at the experimental session, winning a computer game, hearing positive feedback about one's performance on a task of perceptual-motor skills, receiving a coupon for a free fast-food hamburger, receiving a tablet of paper, seeing five minutes of a comedy film, or receiving a small bag of wrapped hard candies (e.g., Carnevale & Isen, 1986; Isen, 1970; Isen, Daubman, & Nowicki, 1987; Isen & Geva, 1987; Isen & Gorgoglione, 1983; Isen, Johnson, Mertz & Robinson, 1985; Isen & Levin, 1972; Isen & Patrick, 1983; Isen et al., 1976; Isen et al., 1978).

One point that should be considered, then, is the validity of these manipulations as ways of inducing affect. Are these small things effective in inducing feelings, and do they they bring on the affect intended by the researchers? This kind of question—regarding verification of the success of an attempt to induce some internal state—is a difficult one, and it might be helpful to focus on it briefly here.

This question is often addressed experimentally by means of so-called "manipulation-checks." In a typical manipulation check, subjects are asked to fill out one or more questionnaires describing, for example, their feelings or opinions, in order for the experimenter to be able to tell whether certain perceptions were generated or, as in the present case, feelings induced.

The problem with this kind of manipulation-check, for purposes of verifying affect induction in our experiments, is twofold: First, such measures are *themselves* of unknown validity. That is, it is not clear to what extent subjects are able (or willing) to express their feelings as ratings on a scale, and therefore the correspondence between actual feelings and rated feelings is not known. Second, in most instances this method of assessment is too reactive. That is, it is likely to focus people's attention on their feeling states, or on the experimenter's interest in their feeling states. This may preclude obtaining natural responses on either the manipulation check itself or the subsequent dependent measure, or both. In many instances, the studies are specifically designed with ecological validity (realistic responding) in mind, and it would be counter-productive to introduce this note of artificiality into the studies. In addition, use of such direct inquiries about affect might produce additional problems if the request for these ratings creates in subjects suspicion about the experimenter's intent. This might be especially likely, for example, in studies involving gifts to subjects. An inquiry about feelings following a gift might lead subjects to question the motives and genuineness of the giver, and thus the inquiry might serve to undermine the positive-affect induction.

Consequently, for the most part, this program of research has tended not to use affect check-lists or other affect self-report devices, or has tended not to rely on them alone. Instead, it has tried to use a variety of methods to verify that affective state was varied as intended. Some may view these other methods of assessment as more indirect than affect scales or check-lists, but as suggested above, responses on an affect check-list are also only indirect indicators of affect; ratings of felt affect are not a direct reflection of feeling, but rather are statements about feelings, subject to the factors that influence statements. Therefore, self-report of feelings should be seen as only one, and not necessarily the best one in all circumstances, of several possible ways of determining whether affect has been induced as intended.

These problems, that affect can be verified only indirectly, and that under some circumstances self-report of feelings can undermine the objectives of the study, have been addressed in two ways in this research: First, the studies have used a variety of methods, including self-report of affect in some instances, to verify the accuracy of the affect inductions; and second they have used the conceptual tool of converging operations "triangulating" on the desired affective state. The end result is that in most cases one can feel a substantial degree of confidence that the appropriate affect state has been induced and is responsible for the observed effects.

Let us briefly describe how these methods have been used in this program of research. In some instances, it is plausible to obtain subjects' ratings of how the affect-induction procedure made them feel (e.g., Isen et al., 1987; Isen & Gorgoglione, 1983). For example, in studies using films as the means of affect induction, subjects were told the films were being pre-tested for use in a future study, and thus participants could quite naturally be asked to indicate the effect that seeing the film had on them without arousing suspicion about the experimenter's intent or genuineness in inducing affect, and without placing the dependent measure in jeopardy because of such suspicion. In another, similar, variant of this technique, subjects may be asked to evaluate the affect-inducing film or to write a few words describing how the film made them feel, and then raters indicate the affect apparent in the descriptions. As noted, however, if this technique is to be used, it would be beneficial to employ, as well, an additional means of verification of the affective state induced, because the self-report of feelings is open to response-bias factors such as "experimenter demand." It also may serve to focus subjects' attention on their affective states, which could influence the dependent measure and/or limit the generalizability of the findings to situations in which feelings are made focal. Sometimes these kinds of problems associated with direct questions about the affect generated can be mitigated, or at least monitored, by using an experimental design in which only half of the subjects receive the manipulation-check (affect) questionnaire. In this way, responses of the two halves of the sample (those who received the manipulation-check questionnaire and those who didn't) on the dependent measure can be compared, in order to see whether responding on the manipulation check has influenced subsequent responses.

Another technique that has been used is subjects' ratings of the pleasantness of ambiguous neutral material (e.g., Forest, Clark, Mills, & Isen, 1979; Isen & Nowicki, 1981; Isen & Shalker, 1982; Isen et al., 1985). This technique is based on data indicating that induced positive affect can influence the ratings of ambiguous or neutral material (e.g., Isen et al., 1978; Schiffenbauer, 1974).

Even though ratings have thus been used, the conceptual tool of converging operations is the more convincing. It has been the primary method that has been used in this program of research to verify the affect induction. Using converging operations to validate the intervening variable involves triangulating or converging on the concept of affect experimentally, over the studies as a group, by inducing affect in several different ways and seeing these methods converge as they produce similar effects on relevant dependent measures. It relies on the realization that, without the hypothesized, unseen, intervening variable (feelings), there would be no reason to expect the divergent events, such as succeeding on a task, receiving a free gift, and laughing at a comedy film, to produce the same or theoretically compatible effects. This method also provides assurance that the effects observed are not attributable to some other factor unexpectedly covarying with one of the affect inductions. Any such factor accompanying one method of inducing affect would not likely be present when a different affect induction were used. Some of these studies have also provided for discriminant validation, in that the authors predicted differential effects of an affect induction on different dependent measures (Isen & Levin, 1972; Isen & Simmonds, 1978). That is, a positive-affect induction was predicted to influence one dependent measure but not another, or to influence a given dependent measure under one set of circumstances but not under another. Take, for example, the study in which the authors expected people in whom positive affect had been induced, compared with control subjects, to volunteer more time to help, but less time to distract or annoy, fellow students who were studying (Isen & Levin, 1972). In that study, positive-affect subjects' willingness to volunteer to help cannot be attributed to a global, non-specific factor such as pressure from the experimenter to comply with the request, because an interaction was obtained between type of request and affect condition (and the experimenters did not know the affect condition of subjects as they interacted with them). And it suggests that the influence of positive affect is specifically on helpfulness rather than on just any activity. This kind of design provides further conceptual validation of the authors' hypotheses.

These kinds of conceptual validation offer support across the studies as a group, rather than for each experiment looked at individually; and they provide a strong conceptual tool for drawing conclusions regarding unseen, intervening variables such as induced feelings. As noted above, by using diverse ways of inducing affect and of collecting the dependent measure, the studies as a group render any particular alternative interpretation of the findings less plausible than the hypothesized induced affective state, as the cause of the observed effect. (See Campbell & Fiske, 1959; Garner, 1954; Garner, Hake, & Eriksen, 1956, for discussion of this and related issues.)

Moreover, this research has been conducted naturalistically, in an attempt to reduce the potential for alternative influences such as "experimenter demand" or other experimental artifacts. Many of the studies described above were carried out in shopping malls, libraries, railroad stations, and street corners, using subjects who did not know that they were subjects in an experiment. This, too, increases confidence in the validity of this program of research. All of this in the aggregate leads us to believe that it is affect that has been influenced by the small manipulations and that has produced the observed effects on social behavior and cognition.

OVERVIEW: EFFECTS OF POSITIVE FEELINGS ON SOCIAL BEHAVIOR AND COGNITIVE PROCESSES

In this section we describe the results of studies that demonstrate effects of feelings on processes relevant, directly or indirectly, to organizational functioning.

Social Behavior

A substantial body of literature indicates that positive affect can influence social behavior in a number of ways that can be very constructive in the organizational context. In particular, positive affect has been found to promote helpfulness and generosity to others (e.g., Aderman, 1972; Batson, Coke, Chard, Smith & Taliaferro, 1979; Cunningham, 1979; Fried & Berkowitz, 1979; Isen, 1970; Isen & Levin, 1972; Levin & Isen, 1975; Moore, Underwood, & Rosenhan, 1973; Weyant, 1978); cooperativeness and graciousness toward others (Gouaux, 1971; Griffitt, 1970; Veitch & Griffitt, 1976); and a problem-solving, less hostile and less competitive orientation in face-to-face negotiation with others (Carnevale & Isen, 1986).

In these studies, affect has been induced in a large variety of ways, ranging from receiving a free sample or getting one's coin back in the coin-return of a public telephone or being offered a cookie while working, to success on a task or to listening to music or thinking about positive events that had occurred in the past. Thus, these effects appear robust and something of a general response to positive affect. For example, it was shown that persons who had found a dime in the coin-return of a public telephone were more likely to help a stranger who had dropped papers that she was carrying (Isen & Levin, 1972); likewise, randomly selected persons who had received information that they had succeeded on a battery of perceptual-motor tasks subsequently were more generous in donating to charity and were more helpful to a stranger who dropped her books (Isen, 1970). The general conclusion that can be drawn from this work is that feeling good tends to make one more likely to help others.

However, it should be noted that, as might be expected, this effect is not completely general and unqualified: Under some circumstances positive affect may not promote helpfulness and may even reduce a person's willingness to volunteer assistance. For example, in one study in which affect had been induced by means of the offer of cookies while studying, and in which the volunteer task involved annoying an innocent third party, persons in whom positive affect had been induced were less likely than control subjects to volunteer (Isen & Levin, 1972). In that same study, the positive-affect group helped more than controls where the volunteer task was one that would benefit the third party. Subjects in whom positive affect had been induced appeared more sensitive to the potential harm or unpleasantness to the victim and tended to speak out against it, as well as withholding the harmful action. This study thus suggests that positive affect promotes specifically helping behavior, not just any activity.

However, there is also evidence that not even all clearly helpful behavior will be performed by persons in whom positive affect has been induced. In another study, subjects who had found a dime in the coin return of a public telephone were more likely than those in a control condition to help someone by reading and evaluating statements that they were told would put themselves in a good mood, but positive-affect subjects were *less* likely than those in a control group to help by reading statements they were told would put them in a *bad* mood. This suggests that a person who is feeling good may actually be less willing to help than someone in a neutral state, if she or he has reason to believe that engaging in the helping task will destroy his/her own positive feeling state (Isen & Simmonds, 1978). This finding indicates that positive affect may also promote a tendency to maintain that state (Isen & Simmonds, 1978). Thus, for themselves as well as for others, persons in whom positive affect has been induced appear more sensitive than control subjects to un-pleasant outcomes and more motivated to avoid them. A similar finding, involving the distinction between liked and disliked causes, indicated that subjects in whom positive affect had been induced helped a liked cause more, but a disliked cause less, than did controls (Forest et al., 1979). This, togeth-er with the other two studies described, suggests that people who feel good may be more likely to behave as they please, helping more when they want to help, but helping less when there is a reason that they do not want to help.

This, in turn, suggests that positive affect may have separately identifiable influences—a tendency to increase the likelihood of helping in general but tendencies toward affect state protection, social responsibility, and possibly one also toward personal freedom or independence. Under some circumstances, but not necessarily always, the latter may override the increased likelihood of behavior such as helping. Consequently, attempts to utilize the impact of positive affect on helping in organizational settings will need to take these other factors in consideration as well.

Not only is affect likely to increase helping and generosity and promote sociability and friendliness, as described, but there is also evidence that people in whom positive affect has been induced may show less hostile aggressiveness (Baron, 1964; Baron & Ball, 1974) and may be more cooperative in negotiation (Carnevale & Isen, 1986).

One context in which reduced aggressiveness has been found to be helpful is in negotiation. In that context, especially in integrative bargaining situations, studies suggest that adoption of a problem-solving orientation also contributes to improved outcomes (e.g., Pruitt, 1981). Interestingly, research has shown that positive affect can influence both of these processes. It has been found to reduce hostile aggressiveness in face-to-face negotiation and to promote the adoption of a problem-solving orientation in an integrative bargaining situation (Carnevale & Isen, 1986).

An integrative bargaining task or problem situation is one in which the parties to the negotiation have different pay-off possibilities for each of several issues about which they are bargaining, and must make trade-offs in order to reach the optimal agreement. Reaching agreement in such a task involves seeing a large number of alternatives and thinking flexibly about how they might be combined. Integrative solutions are contrasted with "compromise," in which concessions are made to a middle ground on some one obvious dimension. An often-used illustration of the difference between compromise and an integrative solution is as follows: Two persons are quarreling over an orange that is in their joint possession. They cut it in half and share it equally (compromise), only to discover that one drinks the juice from his half and throws the rind away, while the other cuts the rind from his half to use in making a cake and throws the juice away. If they had negotiated integratively, they would have discovered their real needs and each obtained more of what he was seeking. Integrative solutions are also contrasted with "yielding," in which one party lowers his/her aspirations and seeks very little. Like compromise, this negotiation strategy can be seen as inferior to an integrative one, because it results in lower overall joint benefit than is possible to achieve in the situation. (For greater detail, see, for example, Pruitt, 1983.)

Pruitt (1981) has noted that the use of contentious tactics interferes with the discovery of integrative solutions and that problem-solving tactics tend to facilitate this process. Thus, for both interpersonal (lessened aggressiveness) and cognitive (discovery of integrative solutions) reasons, positive affect might be expected to improve the process and outcome of negotiation or dispute resolution. And, as mentioned, a recent study has found that, whereas in a control condition negotiators who bargained face-to-face were likely to become hostile and to break off negotiation without reaching agreement, persons in whom positive affect had been induced were more cooperative in orientation and in fact were more likely to obtain optimal outcomes than the control negotiators (Carnevale & Isen, 1986).

In this study, persons in whom positive affect had been induced by means of a small free gift (a tablet of paper) and the reading of a few cartoons, and who then bargained face-to-face with another person on an integrative bargaining task, were significantly more likely than comparable control subjects, in whom positive affect had not been induced but who bargained face-to-face, to reach agreement, to reach the optimal agreement (i.e., achieve the highest possible joint and individual outcomes), and to have positive evaluations of the situation and of the other participant. In addition, there was a near-significant tendency among positive-affect subjects to have greater under-standing of the other player's payoff matrix (priority preferences among 3 items about which negotiation was centered), the one piece of information that was not allowed to be communicated directly.

The latter suggests that people in the positive-affect condition had a better understanding of the overall situation than control subjects and possibly went about the task differently, trying to figure out what the other person's goals and strategies were. The other findings, especially the outcome measure, are also compatible with this interpretation. The task is not one in which simple yielding would result in the optimal, or even an acceptable, outcome for either party (Pruitt, 1981). Thus, the results that were obtained cannot be attributed to a greater tendency on the part of positive-affect subjects to yield to the other party, say, for example, on account of greater liking for the other or increased desire to avoid conflict. People who are feeling happy may like others better, but desire to yield or avoid conflict because of this cannot account for the results, because simple yielding is not effective in this task. Something more creative must be undertaken. (The impact of positive affect on creative or innovative responding will be examined in detail in the next section, but, to preview that material, it will just be noted here that positive affect has been shown to give rise to cognitive flexibility and innovativeness.) Thus, positive affect has been found to facilitate face-to-face negotiation and to promote the understanding of a complex interpersonal situation. In fact, improved understanding of the situation may even mediate the positive social outcomes that occurred (successful negotiation, liking for the other party, and enjoyment of the activity).

Some studies suggest that positive affect may also lead to greater receptiveness to persuasive communication (Gallizio & Hendrick, 1972; Janis, Kaye, & Kirchner, 1965), although there is reason to believe that this may not hold true under all circumstances. In particular, if persons are already negatively disposed toward a target, positive affect may not promote cooperativeness or receptiveness toward it (Forest et al., 1979). As described in the section on helpful behavior, there is also some evidence that under certain circumstances positive affect may promote a sense of personal freedom, and people who are feeling good may act more in accord with their own wishes and principles than at other times.

Cognitive Processes

As noted in the introduction, it has also been found that these same kinds of simply induced affective states can influence cognitive processes that can have important implications for behavior in organizations. These include memory and judgment, decision-making, risk preference, problem solving, innovation, and, in general, cognitive organization.

Memory and Judgment. Affect has been found to influence memory and judgments made from memory (e.g., Isen et al., 1978; Laird et al., 1982; Nasby & Yando, 1982; Teasdale & Fogarty, 1979). In particular, mild positive affect has been found to facilitate recall of positive material in memory, and to influence judgments regarding neutral material (Isen & Shalker, 1982; Isen et al., 1978).

The effect on memory most consistently reported, over a variety of affect inductions, is one of positive affect at time of *retrieval* (attempted recall). That is, a person in whom positive affect has been induced at time of attempted recall shows improved recall of material with a positive affective tone, relative to other material and relative to other persons (e.g., Isen et al., 1978; Laird et al., 1982; Nasby & Yando, 1982; Riskind, 1983; Teasdale & Fogarty, 1979). This effect has been obtained with several different affect inductions and therefore appears rather general.

Other effects on memory have been reported, but less frequently or reliably and over a smaller range of affect inductions. For example, an effect at time of *encoding* (learning) has been reported by some authors. (This effect has been called "mood congruent learning" by Bower and his colleagues.) That is, some studies have found that people who have been made to feel happy (by means of hypnosis or of thinking about positive events) at the time they learn material, later show better recall of positive than negative material from the corpus presented at time of learning, regardless of their affective state at time of recall (e.g., Bower, Gilligan, & Montiero, 1981; Nasby & Yando, 1982). This suggests that positive material may be better learned by people who are feeling happy. (Bower et al., 1981, also reported this effect for the feeling state of sadness, suggesting that learning, and later recall, of material related to sadness was likewise facilitated by sadness at time of learning. But Nasby & Yando, 1982, failed to find the parallel effect of sadness.) A series of recent studies indicates that the encoding effect may be more likely to occur with hypnotic mood induction than with others (Buchwald, 1988). This suggests that something about the hypnotic, and hypnotic-like, inductions (perhaps the instruction to retain the mood at its initial level of intensity) may promote the effect of feelings at time of encoding. The precise mechanism remains to be investigated; however, the findings of Buchwald (1988) suggest that the *encoding* (mood-congruent *learning*) effects reported in the literature may depend on factors specific to particular ways of inducing affect.

A third type of memory effect of feelings, the *state-dependent-learning* effect, has also been reported in the literature by a few authors (e.g., Bartlett & Santrock, 1979; Bower, Montiero, & Gilligan, 1978). (Again, Bower and colleagues reported the effect for both happiness and sadness, but Bartlett and colleagues report it only for positive affect, failing to find the parallel effect with sadness.) In this effect, it has been reported that people show better recall of material (any material, regardless of its affective content) that was learned and recalled in the same affective state than of material learned and recalled during nonmatching states. However, this effect appears to be unreliable. It has more frequently not been found (e.g., Isen et al., 1978; Laird et al., 1982; Nasby & Yando, 1982), and most recently it has been called "unreliable" by Bower and his colleagues, formerly among its strongest proponents, after repeated failures to obtain it with any affect state (Bower & Mayer, 1985). A state-dependent-learning effect of strong and distinctive physiological states has been reported and is thought to be reliable, though *small*. This means that material learned while intoxicated, for example, would show a small advantage in memory over material learned while sober, if the recall were to take place when the person were again intoxicated. It has been suggested that state-dependent learning might be most likely to occur where the state is distinctive and focal in the person's attention, and where there is no better memory device for a person to use than his/her state (Eich & Birnbaum, 1982; Isen et al., 1978). This, in turn, suggests that state-dependent learning may tend to occur when stimuli are particularly devoid of meaning or structure, or when the person's cognitive capacity is limited or reduced so that encoding and retrieval strategies cannot be developed. The relative weaknesses of state-dependent-learning effects of feelings on memory suggest that the influence of feelings on memory is usually not best understood as an automatic process of association, but rather is usually mediated by processes of meaning and interpretation (see Isen, 1984, 1987; Isen & Diamond, 1989, for discussion of this issue).

Decision-making. In addition to an influence on memory and judgment, positive affect has also been seen to influence decision-making, problem solving, and risk preference. First, mild positive affect has been shown to promote simplification of complex tasks, under some circumstances (Isen & Means, 1983; Isen, Means, Patrick, & Nowicki, 1982). It should be noted that this can lead to either impaired or improved task performance, depending on the situation and the requirements of the task.

In one series of studies (Isen et al., 1982) for example, subjects in whom good feelings had been induced either by giving them a small gift or by placing them in especially comfortable surroundings, complete with refreshments, were found to be more likely to use an intuitive solution and a heuristic in solving two different types of problems (a physics timer-tape problem used to study time-rate-distance relationships, and a relative frequency judgment). In these problems, simplifying the situation and using a heuristic or an intuitive answer led to incorrect answers, and therefore a subject's performance was impaired by the presence of positive affect. In other situations, however, it may be that being able to find a heuristic to use on an otherwise unsolvable task, might improve performance. Moreover, additional aspects of the task situation, such as the absence of performance feedback, may have played a role in the impaired performance that was observed.

Furthermore, other studies have shown that persons who were made to feel happy performed better or more efficiently than control subjects. For example, in a complex decision-making task involving choice of a car for purchase from among six alternatives differing along each of nine dimensions, subjects in whom positive affect had been induced (by report of success on an unrelated task) were more efficient in reaching a decision than were control subjects (Isen & Means, 1983). The cars chosen by the two groups did not differ on average, but the experimental subjects reached a decision in 11 minutes, as contrasted with the control group's mean of 19 minutes. In addition, protocol analysis indicated that people in the positive-affect condition engaged in significantly less rechecking of information already considered and tended significantly more than people in the control condition to eliminate unimportant dimensions from the material to be considered. (The dimensions eliminated by positive-affect subjects may be said to be "unimportant" because they were those rated by control subjects, who as a group did not eliminate them, at least important, in a questionnaire following the task.)

The findings of the car-choice study are entirely compatible, in terms of the process that they imply, with those of the experiments that found increased use of heuristics in problem solving as a function of positive affect, even though the two types of studies revealed different effects on performance. Together they suggest that people who are feeling happy tend to simplify at least some types of decision or problem-solving situations; as can be seen, sometimes this tendency may impair performance, and sometimes it may facilitate it, depending on the task and the circumstances. It should be noted that different types of affect induction were employed in these various studies—success on a task of perceptual-motor skill, presence of refreshments at the experimental setting, and receipt of a small gift, and that therefore the effects observed cannot be attributed to any possible extraneous effect of any particular method of affect induction used.

One important aspect of the situations in which these effects were observed, however, may be that these tasks were complex ones, not readily solved or answered. The car-choice problem, for example, was one that involved a large amount of information to be managed, and subjects who did not simplify the problem became bogged down in it. Thus, the observed tendency for positive-affect subjects to simplify decision tasks, may apply only to complex, otherwise unmanageable, situations.

Factors such as degree of importance of the task or expertise among the decision-makers may also play a role in the tendency of positive affect to promote task simplification. The car-choice task, on which this simplification was observed, involved a hypothetical choice among hypothetical alternatives. A recent follow-up study, in which the same procedure was used to observe the influence of positive affect on the decision-making processes employed by third-year medical students reasoning about a diagnosis, revealed compatible but importantly different results (Isen, Rosenzweig, & Young, 1990). Here again it was found that decision-makers in whom positive affect had been induced reached the required decision more efficiently than controls. However, in this situation, they did not stop working when the decision was made (and therefore their total time on task or protocol length was not less than that of controls), and they did not completely eliminate any dimensions from consideration. Instead what these positive-affect subjects did, to a significantly greater extent than controls, was to reach a decision regarding the assigned task earlier and then go on to analyze the materials more fully: They considered diagnoses for the other patients after they had identified the patient most likely to have the target diagnosis, which had been the only task assigned. Moreover, their protocols revealed significantly less evidence of confusion during the process and significantly greater evidence of configural, integrative thinking or combining of dimensions in reasoning about the cases. This suggests, compatibly with the results of the car-choice study, increased efficiency and a tendency to integrate or "simplify" the materials and the task, on the part of positive-affect subjects, but without any actual elimination of dimensions (or shorter time devoted to the project overall) as had occurred in the earlier study.

A second effect of feelings on cognitive processes related to decision-making is on decisions in situations of risk or uncertainty. Positive affect has been found to promote risk-taking in *hypothetical* situations or where chance of winning is high and salient while possibility of real loss is limited or unapparent; but, in contrast, it has been shown to lead to increased sensitivity to loss, and to behaviors that protect against loss (such as cautiousness), in situations in which meaningful loss is possible and salient. For example, in one study, in which subjects were given the opportunity to gamble with chips representing fractions of their credit for participating in the experiment (a real loss), and in which the only bet open to them was a high-risk one (17 percent chance of winning), those in whom positive affect had been induced (by receipt of a coupon for a free hamburger) bet less than control subjects (Isen & Patrick, 1983). Similarly, in another study, in which the dependent measure was an acceptable probability level for placing a predetermined bet of 1, 5, or 10 chips (again, representing fractions of participation credit), subjects in whom positive affect had been induced (by receipt of a small bag of candy), relative to controls, required a higher probability of winning before they were willing to bet 5 or 10 chips (but not for 1 chip). In these conditions, they also expressed a higher percentage of thoughts about losing than control subjects, in a thought-listing task (Isen & Geva, 1987). These findings, like the previous, suggest that positive-affect subjects tend to be cautious where the potential for meaningful loss is high.

Likewise, another series of studies highlights the importance of focus upon possible loss in the relationship between positive affect and cautiousness (Arkes, Herren, & Isen, 1988). Those studies indicate that, in a hypothetical situation inquiring about purchase of lottery tickets, people in whom positive affect has been induced report willingness to pay more than do control subjects, at higher levels of payoff and probability of winning, but that the positive-affect subjects are also willing to pay more for insurance than are control subjects, especially at higher levels of potential loss. While willingness to purchase lottery tickets indicates risk-proneness, willingness to purchase insurance indicates risk-aversion. An important difference between these two tasks was thought to be that consideration of the purchase of insurance involves focus upon potential losses. (A third study in the series indicated that it was not simply willingness to purchase anything that was influenced by positive affect.)

Most recently, another study has indicated that positive affect influences the subjective negative utility of losses, making them loom larger (seem worse) than they normally might (Isen, Nygren & Ashby, 1988). This study used a procedure devised by Davidson, Suppes, and Siegel (1956) to estimate perceived utility while holding probability constant, by having subjects indicate their preferences over a series of gambles. Results indicated that potential losses held greater negative utilities (impact) for subjects who had received a small gift than for those in a control condition. Changes in subjective *probability* (likelihood) have been hypothesized to influence the risk preferences of persons in affective states, and Johnson and Tversky (1983) found positive affect to reduce people's subjective *probability* of negative events occurring. However, the results of the study of utilities show that, independent of any effect that positive feelings may have on the subjective probability of negative events occurring, negative *utilities* are affected—that is, possible negative events seem *more aversive* to persons who are feeling good.

This finding is compatible with those showing increased conservativeness among positive-affect subjects, and it suggests that the effect may be mediated by an impact on perceived utility, independent of any influence of affect on subjective probability of an event's occurrence. Moreover, because this study showed heightened negative utilities specifically for losses among positive-affect subjects, it goes one step further in suggesting a mechanism behind the increased conservatism observed: It indicates that for people who are feeling happy, avoidance of loss may be a factor in decisions involving risk and potential loss. In this, it is also compatible with the research in the area of social behavior described earlier, which indicates that maintenance of a positive state may become an important motive of people who are feeling happy. Recall, for example, the study that found that, although positive affect normally facilitates helpfulness and generosity, it may not do so if the helping task is one which promises to interfere with the person's good feeling state (Isen & Simmonds, 1978).

Cognitive Organization and Creativity. Induced good feelings have also been observed to influence categorization, to result in more unusual first associates to neutral words, and to facilitate creative problem solving as represented by tasks such as Duncker's (1945) candle task and the Mednicks' (1964) Remote Associates Test. These results suggest that cognitive organization—patterns of association and perceived interrelatedness of ideas—may be influenced by affective state.

For example, persons in whom positive affect has been induced tend to categorize a wider range of neutral stimuli together, as indicated by a rating task and by a sorting task (Isen & Daubman, 1984). The rating task was similar to that used by Eleanor Rosch (1975) to study prototypicality. Subjects were asked to rate, on a scale from 1 to 10, the degree to which they felt an item was a member of a category. On this task, people in whom positive affect had been induced rated fringe exemplars (that is, words like "purse," "ring," and "cane" in the category "clothing") more as members of the category than did people in a control condition. Likewise, in a sorting task in which subjects were asked to sort the stimuli into groups of items that could be grouped together, people in whom positive affect had been induced made larger groupings—that is, said more items could go together—than did control subjects. In a more recent study, preliminary evidence suggests that, if given *multiple* trials and asked how many *different* ways the items could be organized, positive-affect subjects sort stimuli into more *different* groupings. These subjects identify more different dimensions along which to sort the stimuli, and combine the items in more different ways. All of these results together suggest that persons who are feeling happy are more cognitively *flexible*—more able to make associations, to see dimensions, and to see potential relations among stimuli—than are persons in a neutral state.

This suggestion is also supported by studies of word association and creative problem solving. Several recent studies show, for example, that persons who are happy, compared with controls, give more unusual and more diverse first associates to neutral (but not to positive or negative) stimulus words (Isen et al., 1985). For example, to the stimulus word, "house," whose most common associate is "home," people in positive-affect conditions tended more than control subjects to respond with related but uncommon words such as "residence" or "apartment." In those studies positive affect was induced in four different ways—being offered refreshments, giving associates to positive words, viewing a short comedy film, and receiving a bag of candy. For another example, to "carpet" positive-affect subjects tended to give responses such as "plush," "living room," and "texture" instead of the most common associate, "rug." These examples illustrate that the unusual responding of persons in the positive-affect conditions was not an artifact of their giving unrelated positive words (that is, responding only to their positive feelings), but rather, that, as a group, these people's associations to the target words were more far-ranging and their thoughts more flexible. The fact that their responses were more *diverse* than those of control subjects also suggests that this interpretation is appropriate, because the diversity measure indicates the variety of responses within each group, independent of any standard norms for the word associations typical of a given word. This means that, within the positive-affect group, to a greater extent than within the control group, subjects responded with more *different* associates to a given word, as well as more unusual associates.

Given the findings just described, it is not surprising that positive affect has also been found to promote creativity and creative problem solving ability. The measures used to study creativity in these studies have been the Mednicks' Remote Associates Test (Mednick, Mednick, & Mednick, 1964) and Duncker's (1945) candle task (Isen, Daubman, & Nowicki, 1987). Most recent conceptualizations define "creativity" as the useful combining of elements that are not usually related (e.g., Koestler, 1964; Mednick, 1962), and these measures are in keeping with such a definition. These studies indicate that persons in whom positive affect has been induced, by receipt of a small bag of candy or by watching 5 minutes of a comedy film, are better able to solve these tasks, which are usually considered to require creativity.

The "candle task" is the one used by Karl Duncker (1945) in his demonstrations of what he called "functional fixedness." In this task the subject is presented with a box of tacks, a candle, and book of matches, and is asked to attach the candle to the wall so that it will be able to be lit and burn without dripping wax on the table or floor. This problem can be solved if the box containing the tacks is emptied, tacked to the wall, and used as a platform for the candle.

In studies using this task, subjects in whom positive affect had been induced by means of a comedy film (5 minutes of "bloopers" from old television shows) performed significantly better (about 67 percent got the correct answer) than those exposed to 5 minutes of a control film, "Area Under a Curve" (20 percent), and better than those in a no-manipulation control condition (12 percent, not different from those exposed to the control film). The positive-affect subjects also performed better than subjects exposed to "arousal" conditions. "Arousal" was represented in two ways, in one condition by physical exercise, and in another by exposure to 5 minutes of an upsetting film, "Night and Fog," which is a French documentary of the Nazi death camps. These two methods were used because there is disagreement about the meaning of the concept of arousal, and in this way a sampling of the definitions people think are appropriate was included. Clearly, one of these methods involves negative affect, but some people believe that "arousal" means just that—upset or distress. The other is more affectively neutral, conveying only physiological activation. Some researchers propose that this captures the essence of "arousal." Resolution of the issues surrounding the concept of arousal is beyond the scope of this chapter, but readers might want to be aware that some dispute as to the utility of the general concept exists (e.g., Lacey, 1979; Lacey, Kagan, Lacey, & Moss, 1967). In any case, rates of solution in these two conditions (about 27 percent) were not significantly different from those of controls and were significantly different from that of the comedy-film condition (Isen et al., 1987).

The second task used to examine the influence of positive affect on creative problem solving or cognitive flexibility was based on the Mednicks' (1964) Remote Associates Test. The test, based on Sarnoff Mednick's (1962) theory that creativity involves the combination of elements that are remotely associated, was designed to be an individual-difference measure of creativity. In this test, each item consists of three words and a blank line, and subjects are asked to provide, in the blank, a word that relates to each of the three words given in the item. An example of a Remote Associates Test item is the following:

MOWER   ATOMIC   FOREIGN   _____*

*The answer may be found on the last page of this chapter.

Using items of moderate difficulty (such as the example above), two studies indicated that positive affect improved people's performance on this measure of creativity or cognitive flexibility. Again, subjects in whom positive affect had been induced, either by means of the comedy film or by means of a gift of a bag of candy, scored significantly better than those in a no-manipulation control condition or an "arousal" group which had been asked to exercise (the step test) for two minutes. These four studies, then, involving two affect manipulations and two measures of creativity or cognitive flexibility, indicate that positive affect tends to promote cognitive flexibility. Since they included examination of the effects of arousal and negative affect, they also suggest that there is something specific to good feelings that promotes this ability to think creatively or flexibly.

In actuality, there is no reason to have expected arousal to have facilitated creative or unusual responding, because arousal is thought to facilitate a person's dominant response, not an unusual one (e.g., Matlin & Zajonc, 1968; Zajonc, 1965). However, it is often suggested informally, on an apparently intuitive basis, that positive affect's influence is one that comes from "arousal." As noted above, the concept of "arousal" is a complex and controversial one, and full discussion of it is beyond the scope of this chapter. However, the studies described do address this matter to some extent and indicate that positive affect has an influence on creativity that the two types of "arousal" studied do not. It should also be noted, however, that the studies discussed do not preclude the possibility that some other affective states, possibly including negative affective states, may also facilitate creative responding under certain circumstances. As noted earlier in the chapter, negative and positive affect do not always have opposite effects. At this point, however, this remains to be investigated.

In summary, then, of this overview of the effects of positive feelings on social behavior and cognitive processes, the evidence indicates that positive affect is associated with increased cooperativeness, helpfulness, benevolence to self and others, decreased hostility, a productive, problem-solving orientation in negotiation and a tendency to take other people's perspectives and to take, in general, a broader view of situations. In addition, good feelings have been found to influence memory and judgment, and to promote a tendency toward risk taking where no meaningful loss is possible, but toward conservativeness and sensitivity to loss, where real loss threatens. Moreover, positive affect is associated with problem-simplification and/or increased efficiency in complex decision-making (sometimes improving, and sometimes impairing, performance), and with increased creative-problem-solving ability and cognitive flexibility, reflected in the ability to take others' perspectives, to make unusual or remote associations, and to see potential relations among ideas.

POSITIVE AFFECT AND ORGANIZATIONAL BEHAVIOR: RESEARCH FINDINGS

Taken as a whole, then, existing evidence strongly suggests that positive affect exerts significant influence upon several aspects of social behavior and a wide range of cognitive processes (cf., Isen, 1987). In recent years, many researchers have turned their attention to the issue of whether such effects have a direct bearing on important aspects of organizational behavior (e.g., Dipboye, 1985; Cardy & Dobbins, 1986; Tsui & Barry, 1986). The results of their investigations point to the conclusion that positive affect does indeed exert appreciable effects upon many aspects of behavior in work settings. Specifically, positive affect has been found to influence such important organizational processes as performance appraisal (e.g., Tsui & Barry, 1986), interviews (Baron, 1987a), decision-making (Isen & Geva, 1987; Isen & Means, 1983), conflict (Baron, 1984), and negotiation (Carnevale & Isen, 1986). In addition, other evidence suggests, at least indirectly, that positive affect may also play a role in prosocial organizational behaviors (Brief & Motowidlo, 1988; Organ, 1988), in certain aspects of job satisfaction (e.g., Oldham & Fried, 1987), and in aspects of leadership (Wakabayashi, Graen, Graen, & Graen, 1988). Evidence pointing to such conclusions will now be reviewed.

Positive Affect and Conflict

Conflict is a serious matter for most organizations. Surveys of practicing managers reveal that many spend a considerable portion of their time dealing with conflict or its aftermath (Baron, 1989; Thomas & Schmidt, 1976). Given this fact, and the waste of precious human resources it implies, effective management of organizational conflict seems to represent an important task for managers and organizations alike (Thomas, in press). Several considerations suggest that positive affect is relevant to this important process, and can sometimes play a useful role both in reducing existing conflict and in preventing its emergence.

First, conflict in work settings often involves strong, negative feelings on the part of the individuals involved. Anger, resentment, hostility—all are hallmarks of persistent and costly organizational conflicts (Thomas, in press). Countering or at least reducing such feelings might be a useful initial step toward resolving many conflict situations. Considerable evidence suggests that the induction of positive affect can often be successful in reducing anger and open hostility (cf., Baron, 1983). Indeed, one technique for the reduction of anger and aggression that has been found to be quite effective in reducing such feelings (and also subsequent aggression) in a wide range of settings is one based on the induction of affective states incompatible with anger or frustration (the incompatible response strategy; Baron, 1977).

In one experiment specifically designed to examine the impact of positive affect on conflict in organizations (Baron, 1984), male and female subjects played the role of executives in a large organization and discussed two issues currently facing their company: should it move to the Sunbelt, and should it invest heavily in a new product (a portable phone suitable for use in airplanes). One of the two persons present during each session was actually an accomplice of the experimenter, specially trained to disagree with whatever views the real subject happened to adopt. The style in which he or she disagreed, however, was systematically varied. In one condition, the accomplice disagreed in a calm and reasonable fashion (e.g., "I can see why you feel that way, but I guess I disagree.") In a second condition, in contrast, the accomplice disagreed in a highly condescending manner (e.g., "Oh come on, you've got to be kidding! How could *anyone* hold such views?") A second aspect of the investigation—the one most directly related to the impact of positive affect—took place after the discussion of both issues was complete. The experimenter left the room (ostensibly to get some needed forms), and during this time, the accomplice either sat quietly or engaged in one of three actions designed to induce positive affect in the subject. The accomplice either offered him/her a small snack (a cherry candy), explained that he or she was very tense because of several important exams (a plea for sympathy), or asked him/her to help choose the funniest of several cartoons for use in a class project. Previous studies indicated that all three actions would induce positive affect among subjects (feelings of gratitude, sympathy, and amusement, respectively; Baron, 1983). Subjects in a no-treatment control group were not exposed to any actions on the part of the accomplice designed to induce positive affect.

When the experimenter returned, participants completed a questionnaire on which they rated the accomplice on several dimensions (e.g., likability, pleasantness) and indicated how they would handle future conflicts with this person—through competition, avoidance, compromise, accommodation, or collaboration (cf., Thomas, 1976; in press). Results indicated that subjects assigned lower ratings to the accomplice and reported stronger likelihood of handling future conflicts through competition or avoidance when this person had behaved in a condescending manner than in a reasonable one. More germane to the present discussion, subjects also reported greater willingness to solve future conflicts through collaboration when they had been exposed to any of the positive-affect inducing (negative-affect reducing) treatments than when they had not. It should be noted that in this study the treatments employed may have exerted their effects not only by inducing positive affect but also by reducing the negative feelings generated by the accomplice's earlier behavior.

Another study, mentioned earlier, showed that positive affect can help to avoid the development of conflict in a negotiation situation (Carnevale & Isen, 1986). In that study, the participants were not initially provoked in any manner. However, the bargaining situation itself provided a context in which conflict often arises. Results indicated that under control conditions (no induction of positive affect), hostility quickly developed. Those who bargained face-to-face in the no-affect-induction (control) condition had difficulty reaching a satisfactory agreement. In fact, the modal outcome for those pairs was to break off negotiation and reach *no* agreement. Moreover, in this condition, participants engaged in hostile verbal and facial interactions. In contrast, those in whom situationally-unrelated positive affect had been induced were significantly less likely to display hostility and more likely to reach a mutually satisfactory—indeed, the optimal—agreement. They were also more likely to take the other person's point of view and to adopt a constructive, problem-solving orientation in the negotiation. This suggests that positive feelings unrelated to one's opponent can not only promote more mutually beneficial negotiation strategies and outcomes, but can also help to avoid the emergence of conflict in situations in which it would otherwise be likely to occur. These results, and those of Baron (1984), point to the conclusion that the induction of positive affect or the reduction of negative affect among parties to a conflict can contribute to the constructive resolution of such disputes. Not only can positive affect help to dispel anger and hostility, but it can also help to avoid their development under some circumstances.

The relevance of improved face-to-face negotiation skills for life in organizations is clear. And it is helpful to know that easily-induced positive affect can facilitate both the social and cognitive processes conducive to improved negotiating. Positive-affect inductions such as refreshments, exchange of gifts, pleasant conversation, or introductory humorous comments might serve to improve the outcome of negotiation sessions. (Needless to say, the more sincere and effective the positive-affect induction is in influencing *feelings*, the more it may facilitate negotiation. Since the goal of these preliminary actions is to influence feelings in a positive direction, routinized traditions or obviously insincere comments that appear to be positive-affect inductions but that don't actually work may not have the desired effect on negotiation either.)

One might wonder about application of these findings to real-life organizational settings, because negotiation situations would seem to be inherently tense. The bargaining situation in the study described was realistic, and subjects appeared to get involved and take the task seriously. In the control group quite a bit of hostility developed between subjects engaged in face-to-face negotiation, and the most common result was for the bargainers to break off negotiation and not reach any agreement on the task. Thus, there is reason to believe that the induced positive affect insulated the participants against such effects in a relatively realistic situation. Nonetheless, it is not clear how positive affect might be maintained in the face of some rather tense and hostile real-life organizational bargaining situations or situations in which negotiation is required. That is, there may be some organizational contexts in which conditions are similar to those in the study described—a relatively neutral relationship between the participants at the outset and a situation capable of good resolution. But there may be others in which the stakes are too high (or seem so), or in which additional, complicating situations and relationships exist simultaneously, making it difficult to induce, or sustain, positive affect. In such situations, the good feelings may have to be induced in a different way (to be discussed below).

Together, then, the findings obtained by Baron (1984) and Carnevale & Isen (1986) suggest that the induction of positive affect may sometimes be helpful from the point of view of reducing the intensity or duration of ongoing conflicts, and may initiate strategies and orientations that may also prove useful in preventing the development of conflict.

Positive Affect and Prosocial Organizational Behavior

All individuals who work within a given organization are interdependent, at least to a degree. If the organization prospers, there are more resources to be divided among employees. Conversely, if the organization experiences negative outcomes, the persons working within it, too, are likely to suffer the consequences. In view of these basic facts, a high level of *prosocial behavior* among organizational members seems desirable. In short, actions by one or more members which benefit one or more others are, generally, to be encouraged. Such prosocial behavior can take many different forms (Brief & Motowidlo, 1986). For example, individuals who work together often assist one another with job-related or even personal matters. They pitch in and help those who have been absent, assist those experiencing especially heavy work loads, and seek to protect or enhance their organization's resources. When such actions involve the performance of tasks and responsibilities that are not formally part of employees' jobs, they are termed "citizenship behaviors" (Brockner, 1988; Organ, 1988). Of course, these can be valuable to an organization, contributing to its productivity in important ways. An additional form of prosocial behavior involves providing services and help to people outside the organization, such as important customers or suppliers.

Finally, helping behavior often takes the form of mentoring in work settings (Kram, 1985). Mentors are older, more experienced organization members who advise, counsel, and otherwise contribute to the personal and career development of younger, less experienced persons. While mentor-protege relationships might, at first glance, seem to be one-way arrangements in which mentors provide aid to proteges and receive little in return, research on mentoring suggests that in fact, it is very much a reciprocal arrangement, providing advantages to both parties and to the organization. Mentors supply emotional support and guidance to their proteges, and also help to advance their careers by nominating them for promotions, by suggesting useful strategies for reaching major goals, and by calling them to the attention of top management (Burke, 1984). In return, proteges offer loyalty, support, and hard work on assigned tasks to their mentors. Their success is often attributed, at least in part, to their mentors' efforts, and mentors may also gain status and approval for their efforts to nurture and develop young talent.

However, there are also potential negative outcomes for both parties. Mentors must invest considerable time and effort in the tasks of helping proteges, with no guarantee that these persons will succeed. By the same token, proteges, may suffer if their mentors leave the organization or experience a political reversal. And their close relationship with the mentor may provide them with a limited or distorted view of the organization (Hurley, 1988). Moreover, beyond such "political" kinds of drawbacks, to the extent that mentors come to expect or demand loyalty and support from those they sponsor, a rather stultifying influence on young people's independence or innovativeness may develop. Nonetheless, mentoring may often avoid these pitfalls, and at its best it can contribute to the development of young talent and to the continued health of organizations in which it flourishes.

Does positive affect play a role in these diverse forms of prosocial behavior? As noted previously in this chapter, a substantial body of evidence suggests that positive affect often facilitates helping and related actions (Isen, 1970; Isen, 1987). While this research was not generally conducted in work settings, there appear to be no strong grounds for questioning its generalizability to organizations and organizational behavior. Some of these studies were conducted in laboratory settings, but some were performed in natural settings such as shopping centers, railroad stations, or subjects' own homes (cf., Isen, 1987). Thus, the findings appear generalizable over a wide range of settings, and there is a basis for assuming that they would be applicable in work environments as well. In addition, the results of a study conducted by Puffer (1987) provide at least indirect support for the hypothesis that positive affect among employees increases their tendencies to engage in various forms of prosocial behavior.

In this investigation, managers in a chain of retail furniture stores rated the frequency with which salespersons engaged in various prosocial actions (e.g., assisting other sales personnel, keeping product displays and catalogs tidy, attaching sales tags to merchandise). The salespersons completed questionnaires designed to assess a number of personal characteristics and work-related attitudes. Included among these were measures of their satisfaction with material job-related rewards (e.g., pay), as well as trust and confidence in current management. Not surprisingly, results indicated that the higher the salespersons' satisfaction and confidence, the more frequently they engaged in prosocial behaviors on the job. If it is assumed that higher levels of satisfaction and confidence with one's bosses reflect higher levels of positive affect, these findings can be interpreted as evidence for the hypothesis that positive affect enhances prosocial behavior in work settings, as it does elsewhere (cf., Organ, 1988).

Given that this research was correlational in nature, this conclusion should be viewed as only tentative, because the direction of causation is not known. That is, it is possible that, as suggested, positive affect led to the increased prosocial behavior observed. But another possibility is that the higher levels of prosocial behavior in the organization studied produced the higher levels of satisfaction noted, or that some third factor in the situation promoted both of these. However, the conclusion that positive affect gives rise to prosocial behavior in the organization is consistent with the findings of a large number of controlled experiments conducted in both laboratory and naturalistic settings, as noted above, that indicate that positive affect increases tendencies toward helping. Research specifically focused on the ways in which positive affect at work may promote prosocial behavior in organizational settings, and the conditions under which such effects are most likely to occur, would add importantly to our understanding of these topics.

Additional support for the role of positive affect in prosocial actions in organizations is provided by evidence concerning the initiation and development of mentor-protege relationships (Kram, 1985). Such relationships do not form at random. Rather, mentors seem to select proteges from among many potential candidates on the basis of initial affective reactions: they choose those persons they find pleasant or attractive, while avoiding those they find unpleasant or unattractive. Further, as the relationship develops, mentors appear to be more willing to exert effort to assist proteges toward whom they have strong, positive feelings than ones toward whom such reactions are weaker (Kram, 1983). Evidence concerning these relationships is relatively informal (e.g., based on retrospective reports by mentors and proteges). However, it is consistent with the view that positive affect can facilitate several forms of helping in organizational settings. It is also possible that mentoring relationships may be more likely to develop or thrive in organizations in which positive relationships between supervisors and subordinates exist, and favorable rather than unfavorable working relationships predominate. The positive feelings generated by such conditions might be conducive to the development of an overall tone or "culture" of helpfulness within the organization and, further, might enhance the process of relationship formation by enabling both the mentor and the protege to avoid feeling threatened by, or competitive with, one another. Research on these possibilities and, in general, the factors that promote helpfulness within organizations, seems warranted.

Positive Affect and Decision-Making

Earlier in this chapter, we noted that positive affect can influence several types of decision-making, including complex choices among alternatives differing on multiple dimensions (Isen and Means, 1983; Isen et al., 1990) and situations involving risk (Arkes, Herren, and Isen, 1988; Isen and Geva, 1987; Isen & Patrick, 1983). Here, we wish to note that positive affect may also play a role in a phenomenon known as "escalation of commitment" (Staw, 1981; Staw & Ross, 1987; Staw & Ross, 1989) or the "sunk-costs" effect. This can be observed in situations in which one sees that persons who have made an initial decision stick to it in the face of mounting evidence that it was a poor one, and despite increasing costs for such intransigence. Thus, instead of reducing commitment to a failing venture, these people keep putting resources into it or increase their commitment to it. Several different explanations for this effect have been suggested, but perhaps the one that has received most attention to date emphasizes the role of *self-justification* (Staw, 1976; Staw & Ross, 1987). This interpretation indicates that once decisionmakers have made initial investments in a course of action, they find it extremely difficult to "cut their losses" and withdraw, because doing so would rule out any possibility of justifying the costs already incurred. Moreover, admitting that their initial decision was a poor one is inconsistent with their own largely favorable self-image.

Support for these suggestions has been obtained in several studies (e.g., Bazerman, Giuliani, & Appelman, 1984; Schoorman, 1988), so it appears that pressures toward self-justification do indeed play a role in the escalation of commitment. For example, in the study by Bazerman and his colleagues (1984), only individuals who felt responsible for a previous, failing decision demonstrated a tendency to stick with it. Those who felt it was not their responsibility did not demonstrate escalation of commitment. It seems possible, however, that other cognitive and affective factors may also play a role in this phenomenon. For example, being able to take a broader perspective on the situation, or being able to think of alternative ways to accomplish one's goals, may enable people to cut loose from failing projects. Persons who are responsible for failing decisions may be less able to take these perspectives.

If this is the case, then positive affect may enhance decision-making with regard to such situations, because, as noted previously, positive affect has been found to promote cognitive flexibility, integration of information, and the generation of more alternatives. Several previous studies indicate that persons experiencing positive affect are more likely than persons not experiencing positive affect to generate more diverse associations to neutral stimulus words, to see connections among ideas not usually noted (Isen & Daubman, 1984; Isen et al., 1985). Similarly, persons experiencing positive affect are better than those in a more neutral affective state in performing tasks requiring the generation of novel strategies (Isen et al., 1987), and in taking an innovative, problem-solving approach in negotiation (Carnevale & Isen, 1986). Based on these results, it seems possible that persons experiencing positive affect might generate and consider more diverse and perhaps more novel and integrative alternatives in some decision-making situations. As a result, their probability of choosing an ineffective strategy might be reduced and their probability of taking a broader perspective that allows them to see the larger picture might be enhanced. Further, given their greater cognitive flexibility, persons experiencing positive affect might be more likely to generate strategies that *do* permit them to "cut their losses" and escape from initial poor decisions with their "face" and reputations intact. At the present time, no direct evidence concerning these suggestions exists. However, the fact that positive affect has been found to influence several aspects of decision-making suggests that research designed to extend such effects to escalation or "sunk costs" situations might prove well worthwhile.

Positive Affect and Performance Appraisal

Performance appraisal is widely recognized as one of the most important processes occurring in organizations (cf., Ilgen & Feldman, 1983). Such ratings play a central role in decisions concerning personnel (e.g., determination of merit raises, promotions). Recent conceptualizations of performance appraisal take note of the fact that it is a highly complex process, influenced by many factors other than ratees' past performance (Bernardin & Villanova, 1986). Among these are many cognitive processes, including various aspects of memory and the operation of several heuristics such as accessibility or representativeness (Feldman, 1981). Consequently, given that positive affect has been found to exert important effects upon cognitive processes, it seems reasonable to expect that it might also have an impact upon performance appraisal. The results of a number of recent studies suggest that this is indeed the case (e.g., Cardy & Dobbins, 1986; Tsui & Barry, 1986).

In several of these investigations, positive affect has been manipulated in a different manner from that in much of the research reviewed earlier in this chapter. Specifically, participants in these studies were first induced to like or dislike one or more strangers, and then were asked to rate the performance of those persons on various tasks. A clear example of such procedures is provided in a study conducted by Cardy (1987).

In this study, business school students received written information suggesting that several persons whom they observed on videotapes (Borman, 1977) were either likable, neutral, or dislikable. This information consisted of descriptions of the target persons' behavior in informal settings (a luncheon, a cocktail party). The likable person was described as having a good sense of humor and as being helpful while, in contrast, the dislikable person was described as engaging in various actions that would embarrass himself and others (e.g., complaining, spilling a pitcher of water).

Subjects first read the behavioral descriptions and then watched videotapes in which the three persons took part in an appraisal interview. They then rated the performance of these target persons along several dimensions. Results indicated that subjects assigned the highest ratings to the likable target and lowest rating to the unlikable target. Moreover, subjects' ratings were less accurate (as compared to true performance scores) in judging the likable than the neutral or dislikable individuals.

Similar findings have been reported in several additional studies (Cardy & Dobbins, 1986). The results of these investigations suggest that liking for subordinates significantly increases such rating errors as leniency and halo, while the negative affect studied (mild feelings of sorrow, dislike for the person) tends to exert weaker effects on such judgments and decisions, and to reduce such errors (Sinclair, 1988; Tsui & Barry, 1986). This difference between negative and positive affect, however, may be due at least in part to the direction in which the evaluation would be driven by the affect. That is, the anticipated consequences of acting upon one's negative impulses (i.e., rather arbitrarily harming someone) may be such as to inhibit such action, whereas the anticipated consequences of relatively arbitrarily benefiting someone may not be as constraining.

It is important to note that in the investigation described, positive affect was not manipulated directly; rather, characteristics of the persons rated were varied to induce high or low levels of liking for them. Thus, the results observed in these studies may have more to do with the way people have learned to respond to those they like or dislike, or to people possessing certain characteristics. However, since liking is generally associated with positive affect and disliking with negative affect, it may be that these findings are similar to those that might be expected to occur when people experience positive or negative affect because of some extraneous event. However, this remains to be seen. The results of studies on positive-affect induction, in particular, suggest that the effects of such procedures may interact in a complex manner with other factors in the situation (for example, feedback regarding performance on the task, importance of the task, etc.). Thus, it may be that induced affect will not always produce the same influence on performance appraisal. However, these findings suggest an impact of affective states, or at least feelings about people, upon aspects of performance appraisal. They further suggest that additional research is required to understand the extent and limits of such effects.

Positive Affect and Job Interviews

Related research has examined the impact of positive affect on the ratings assigned to applicants in employment interviews (Baron, 1987a; Williams & Keating, 1987; Williams, Alliger, & Pulliam, 1989). In general, the results of these investigations suggest that, under some circumstances, positive affect tends to elevate evaluations of job applicants and at the same time can increase the magnitude of halo and other rating errors.

Several of the experiments performed to investigate such effects have been laboratory simulations. In one such study, Baron (1987b) had undergraduate students interview a same-sex stranger (actually an accomplice of the researcher) for an entry-level management position. Prior to conducting these interviews, participants worked on several problems and received either positive, neutral, or negative feedback concerning their performance. During the simulated interviews (which followed a relatively structured format) accomplices offered identical responses in each of the three induced-affect conditions. When the interviews were completed, participants rated the applicants (i.e., accomplices) on a number of work-related (e.g., motivation, talent, potential as a future employee) and personal (e.g., attractiveness, likableness, friendliness) dimensions.

Results indicated that among males, those in the positive affect condition assigned higher ratings on both sets of items than those in the neutral or negative mood conditions. A similar pattern of findings was obtained for females, but did not attain customarily accepted levels of significance and therefore cannot be considered reliable. This, of course, suggests that, at least for males, affect can interfere with objective evaluation or at least can influence it. Additional findings indicated that subjects of both sexes recalled more affect-consistent information than affect-inconsistent information, a finding compatible with some of the research cited previously. Finally, male subjects in the positive affect condition reported using an inclusive strategy for processing information about the accomplice—one in which all information about this person was combined—to a greater extent than did subjects in the negative or neutral feeling conditions.

This finding is compatible with those described earlier, indicating that positive affect promotes the use of more integrative decision-making strategies (e.g., Isen & Daubman, 1984; Isen et al., 1985; Isen & Means, 1983; Isen et al., 1990), and suggests that under certain circumstances (e.g., when complex judgments requiring processing of large amounts of information are performed) positive feelings can contribute in a beneficial way to the evaluation process. Of course, the results overall are also compatible with the suggestion that positive affect promotes a positive bias or generalized halo. However, in a follow-up investigation (Baron, 1990[c]), it was found that the influence of positive affect was maximal under conditions in which applicants' qualifications for the job in question were ambiguous. Such effects were significantly reduced when the qualifications of the applicants were either excellent or very poor. This finding is in keeping with those in the affect-and-cognition literature indicating that the impact of affect on other judgments is greatest for ambiguous stimuli (Isen & Shalker, 1982; Schiffenbauer, 1974). This suggests that any halo effects generated by positive affect will be limited to some extent. Additional research is needed to identify the conditions under which affect is most likely to influence evaluation, and to determine the circumstances under which positive affect will facilitate or interfere with efforts to evaluate job applicants and others accurately.

In addition to the studies reporting simulation procedures (Baron, 1987a,

1989b), other investigations have been conducted in the context of actual interviews. These have yielded similar results to those of the simulation studies. For example, in a recent study by Williams, Alliger, and Pulliam (1989), interviewers in a leadership training program rated their own affective states after each of a series of interviews. Results indicated that the more positive these states, the greater interviewers' tendencies toward leniency in their ratings. Of course, such studies do not establish the direction of cause or the causative agent, because respondents were not randomly assigned to conditions. Moreover, interviewers may have liked the interviewees, or thought them particularly appropriate for the positions, and this might have generated both the positive affect and the good ratings. However, to the extent that these findings are compatible with results of controlled experiments, these studies may help to complete the picture concerning the overall influence of affect.

Taken together, these and related studies suggest that positive affect may significantly influence hiring and other decisions based upon interviews. From one perspective, then, affective states may be construed as yet another source of bias of "noise" in job interviews (some others that have been studied, for example, include race, sex, age, and attractiveness of applicants; Arvey & Campion, 1982). It should be noted, however, that some studies show a facilitative effect of positive feelings on decision-making (e.g., Isen, 1987). Therefore, additional research seems warranted, to investigate the circumstances under which positive affect may improve, versus those under which it may impair, decision-making and judgments in work settings.

Positive Affect and Job Satisfaction

Job satisfaction is generally defined, in the field of organizational behavior, as positive or negative attitudes held by individuals toward their jobs (Locke, in press). As an attitude, job satisfaction involves several basic components: specific beliefs about one's job, behavior tendencies (intentions) with respect to it, and feelings about it. The last of these components is clearly linked to affective states. Studies concerned with acquisition of attitudes suggest that this affective component can sometimes derive from a process resembling classical conditioning (Lohr & Staats, 1973). That is, when individuals experience positive affect in the presence of some object, individual, or event, they may acquire positive affective reactions to the object through a process of association. Such effects have been observed for a wide range of attitudinal objects, including other persons (Byrne, 1971).

To the extent that this mechanism operates in work settings, and influences reactions to abstract entities such as jobs, it would be anticipated that conditions serving to induce positive affect among employees while on the job might lead to the development of more favorable work-related attitudes. Indirect support for this view is provided by the results of diverse studies not specifically designed to assess this potential link between positive affect and job satisfaction. One such investigation was conducted by Oldham and Fried (1987). These researchers were concerned with the impact of physical aspects of work settings on job satisfaction. To obtain evidence on this issue, they asked full-time clerical employees at a large university to complete a questionnaire designed to measure their job satisfaction. In addition, Oldham and Fried assessed several characteristics of the physical settings in which these people worked. Included were social density (the number of persons in each office), level of illumination, number of enclosures (partitions affording privacy), and interpersonal distance (the distance from one desk to another). Results indicated that all four factors were significantly related to participants' reported job satisfaction. Satisfaction was higher under conditions of low rather than high social density, high rather than low illumination, more rather than fewer enclosures, and larger versus smaller interpersonal distance. Similar effects were also reported with respect to discretionary withdrawal (the extent to which employees took their breaks out of the office) and office turnover.

Positive affect is relevant to this discussion because many previous investigations indicate that environmental conditions exert strong effects upon individuals' affective states (e.g., Fisher, Bell, & Baum, in press). Moreover, the conditions found by Oldham and Fried (1987) to enhance job satisfaction and reduce turnover and discretionary withdrawal, are ones previously shown to induce relatively positive affect (e.g., Baum & Valins, 1977). Thus, the findings reported by Oldham and Fried can be interpreted as indirect evidence for a link between positive affect at work and job satisfaction.

Additionally, results of a recent study provide evidence of a direct influence of positive affect on aspects of job satisfaction (although not exactly as traditionally measured) and on the way in which people may view their jobs and working conditions (Kraiger, Billings & Isen 1989). That study indicated that positive affect, induced by exposure to non-hostile humor, may promote a tendency among people to see their tasks as being more motivating and richer (e.g., Hackman & Oldham, 1975; 1976), at least under conditions where the task is reasonably rich to begin with, and as more satisfying, as measured by rating scales. Positive-affect subjects reported greater satisfaction with working conditions, in particular, a somewhat ambiguous or neutral aspect of the job situation. This finding is compatible with those reported earlier which emphasized that the influence of positive affect tends not to be one of gross distortion, but rather appears greatest on ambiguous or neutral material. This study indicates, then, that positive affect unrelated to the job or actual working conditions can influence people's perceptions of their jobs and plays a role in their reported satisfaction with some aspects of their jobs.

Positive Affect and Leader-Member Relations

According to one theory of leadership, the Vertical-Dyad Linkage Model, leaders do not have identical relations with all members in their groups (Dansereau, Graen, & Haga, 1975). On the contrary, the nature of their dyadic exchanges with individual subordinates varies greatly. At one extreme are persons toward whom leaders hold highly positive views. These subordinates enjoy a considerable amount of support and assistance from the leader, are part of his or her "in-group," and are generally in his or her confidence across a wide range of contexts. At the other extreme are subordinates toward whom leaders hold highly negative views. Such persons receive little support and assistance and are definitely not in their leaders' confidence.

Such differences in dyadic exchanges are compatible with the effects of liking and disliking on performance appraisal, discussed earlier. That they can exert important effects on individuals' careers is suggested by the results of a study of Japanese managers conducted by Wakabayashi, Graen, Graen, and Graen (1988). These investigators followed the careers of eighty-five male managers, to determine what factors influenced their selection for the "fast" or "slow" career tracks, respectively, in their companies. Results indicated that many factors played a role in this process, but that one of the most important was the quality of the young managers' relations with their bosses. The better these were, the more likely the managers were to enter the "fast" track in their organizations. Put another way, the findings reported by Wakabayashi et al. (1988) suggest that the more the young managers were liked by their bosses, and the more rapidly they developed good working relationships with them, the more likely they were to advance rapidly in their careers. Thus, one type of positive affect on the part of bosses seems to play an important role in the subsequent careers of organizational newcomers. It seems possible, in addition, that individuals who enjoy good relations with their bosses may experience positive reactions to their favored treatment and feel happier at work. These reactions, in turn, may enhance their confidence, self-efficacy, and actual performance, and thus further contribute to excellent achievement (Bandura, 1986).

In addition, certain leadership styles may promote positive affect and contribute to both employee morale and job satisfaction. For example, it is known that a consultative style often enhances employee satisfaction (e.g.,

Heilman et al., 1984; Muczyk & Riemann, 1987). Similarly, employee satisfaction is higher in the context of democratic rather than autocratic leadership style (Tjosvold, 1984). More generally, the concept of "manager as helper" is receiving growing recognition as an important orientation that promotes optimal functioning in organizations. This orientation contrasts with the more traditional view of "manager as instructor" or "task master," and flows from the assumption that the manager's goal is to help his/her subordinates grow and develop, be independent, and fulfill their potential (Gutteridge, 1986).

Positive Affect and Ingratiation In Organizations

Several studies have suggested that when individuals succeed in inducing positive affect in important others in their work settings, they may reap many significant benefits. Such persons are evaluated more favorably in performance appraisals, are more likely to be hired after a job interview, are more likely to obtain concessions from opponents in bargaining contexts, are more likely to obtain needed help from other organization members, and are more likely to develop favorable working relations with their bosses. Clearly, then, the capacity to induce positive affective reactions among others can be a major "plus" in organizational settings.

Sometimes, individuals induce positive affect in others as a side-effect of doing a good job or of enthusiasm for their work. In other instances, however, people may adopt this goal strategically, in order to achieve specific desired ends or favors. In other words, they may engage in attempts at *ingratiation*. Liden and Mitchell (1988) have offered an insightful analysis of this process as it occurs in organizations.

In their review, Liden and Mitchell define ingratiation as behaviors employed strategically by an individual to make himself or herself more attractive to one or more others for a purpose (Liden & Mitchell, p. 573; Wortman & Linsenmeier, 1977). They note that individuals engage in efforts at ingratiation for several different reasons. However, primary among these are the desire to defend oneself against criticism or negative feedback and the desire to obtain the benefits of being liked by others. The former comes into play in situations in which individuals may receive negative feedback on their work (Baron, 1988). The latter motivation is most likely to be activated under conditions in which individuals are highly dependent on others for completing assigned tasks, when resources are scarce, and when criteria for appraisals of job performance are largely subjective. In such cases, individuals seek to be liked by other members of their organization as a kind of insurance against future negative outcomes; after all, popular persons rarely receive less than their fair share when any division of available resources takes place.

Research on the process of how individuals attempt to ingratiate themselves to others points to numerous strategies (Jones, 1964; Tedeschi & Melburg, 1984). First, and most directly, they may engage in efforts to induce positive affect in the target person through flattery and related menas. Second, they may attempt to present themselves in a favorable light, by laying claim to desirable characteristics (e.g., efficiency, excellent performance, sincerity, modesty). A third set of strategies involves agreeing with target persons, engaging in self-disclosure (i.e., revealing personal information), or requesting advice and help.

To the extent such efforts succeed, high levels of positive affect and liking will be induced among the targets of ingratiation. However, often such efforts are transparent and backfire when their targets sense the true purpose of the maneuvering (Jones, 1964). Even when successful, moreover, such strategies are not likely to enhance an organization's over-all climate, because the costs they exact can be considerable. For one thing, an ingratiating individual's co-workers may recognize what is happening even if the target of the flattery does not. Consequently, organizational morale may suffer. Second, as noted previously, liking and positive affect may exert important effects upon key decisions involving personnel which should, in fact, be made on other bases (i.e., past performance). Thus, while successful efforts at ingratiation may benefit the individuals who perform them, their over-all impact upon achievement and upon attainment of procedural and distributive fairness (justice) within an organization may be quite negative (cf., Greenberg, in press).

Moreover, attempts at ingratiation, even if successful in inducing increased levels of liking, may simultaneously generate other, unwanted feelings or expectations, which, in turn, might produce undesired effects. For example, consider an employee who frequently requests help or advice from his supervisor. Initially, such requests may increase liking for this person. Beyond some point, however, repeated requests for help may generate annoyance on the part of the supervisor, or serious question about the employee's competence and abilities. Clearly, such reactions can have serious repercussions for the requester's career. In sum, while positive feelings at work can have facilitative effects on many aspects of performance and relationships in the organization, attempts at ingratiation, especially if perceived as insincere, may be counter-productive. Research on the unanticipated (and undesired) "side-effects" of various tactics of ingratiation in organizational settings should be conducted to clarify such possibilities.

Positive Affect and Other Aspects of Organizational Behavior: Stress and Perceived Fairness

Interest in the impact of positive affect on various aspects of organizational behavior is relatively new. Consequently, many potential effects of this factor have not as yet been investigated. At this point, however, it seems useful to mention additional aspects of organizational behavior and organizational processes that may also be influenced by positive affect.

Stress.   Work-related stress poses a serious problem for countless individuals and the organizations in which they work. Growing evidence suggests that prolonged exposure to high levels of stress can exert adverse effects upon personal health (Frese, 1985; Motowidlo, Packard, & Manning, 1986), and task performance (Keinan, 1987). Moreover, it can ultimately lead to *burnout*—a psychological state in which individuals lose motivation and interest in their jobs, and their effectiveness at work all but disappears (Maslach & Jackson, 1984).

A number of different techniques have been found to be effective in mitigating such effects (e.g., Davis, Eshelman, & McKay, 1983). Among these are several that involve the induction of positive affect among persons undergoing stress. For example, one such procedure involves engaging in activities designed to induce positive feelings incompatible with the negative ones that often accompany stress. Such actions include muscle relaxation, purposely speaking in a calm, modulated manner (rather than shouting or speaking rapidly), and even imagining scenes and events that are pleasant and calm (cf., Holmes, 1984). Another tactic involves "planning for pleasure"—identifying enjoyable activities and then taking active steps to build them into one's schedule. Some findings suggest that participation in such positive-affect generating activities (e.g., various hobbies, vacations) significantly reduces self-reported stress, even among individuals identified as especially competitive and hard-driving by some measures, so-called "Type A's" (Roskies, 1987). These and related procedures for managing stress clearly involve the induction of positive affect among people experiencing the negative impact of work-related stress. Thus, positive affect may prove quite valuable in efforts to reduce costly stress-induced effects.

Perceived Fairness.   If there is one thing that induces negative reactions among individuals at work it is the perception that they are somehow being treated unfairly by others or by their organization (Greenberg, 1987). According to equity theory, which focuses on such reactions, individuals regularly compare the ratio of their own outcomes and inputs (what they provide to their organizations and the benefits they receive) with the same ratio for other persons.

If these ratios appear to be approximately equal, a state of equity exists: the persons involved conclude that existing conditions are reasonably fair. If, instead, the ratios appear to differ (and especially if they are unfavorable for the persons in question), then inequity exists. In such cases, individuals perceive that they are being treated unfairly and react in predictable ways— with unhappiness, anger, and annoyance. They may then engage in various actions designed to redress the imbalance, such as demanding larger rewards (outcomes) or devoting less effort to their work (i.e., reducing their inputs).

Other efforts to cope with inequity involve shifts in perceptions or other psychological reactions, some counterproductive, some potentially constructive. For example, individuals who perceive that they are receiving less than they deserve, given their inputs, may change the way in which they think about the situation. Sometimes this may involve cognitive distortions—for example, distorting others' inputs, so that these appear larger than they actually are, or convincing themselves that others' higher outcomes are deserved because of special factors (e.g., extra training or experience, personal background). But sometimes the redefinition of the situation may involve realistic reappraisals of other's or their own inputs.

It is with respect to such psychological reactions to inequity that positive affect seems most relevant. Based on what is known about positive affect, there is no reason to expect people who are experiencing positive affect to distort reality—recall that it is mainly for ambiguous material that positive affect has been found to exert an influence on evaluation (e.g., Baron, 1990; Isen & Shalker, 1982; Kraiger, et. al., 1989; Schiffenbauer, 1974). However, we might expect them to conceptualize the situation more broadly and integrate more features of it into their thinking (Isen, 1987), and to be more likely to take the other person's perspective (Carnevale & Isen, 1986). Moreover, if individuals encountering feelings of inequity can be made to experience positive affect, then, as suggested by previous research on positive affect and memory, positive events or features of their jobs and organization should more readily come to mind and be expressed (Isen, 1987; Kraiger et al., 1989). To the extent that this is accomplished, the kind of psychological shifts effective in realistically and constructively countering feelings of inequity may also be facilitated. (At the same time, however, if realistic appraisal of the situation continues to suggest inequity, even when a lot of relevant information is broadly and integratively conceived, then, as described earlier, there is reason to anticipate that people who are experiencing positive affect will be more assertive in efforts to alter the situation; Isen, 1987.) No direct evidence on such possibilities in organizations currently exists, but several studies concerned with equity as an aspect of work motivation suggest that cognitive restructuring effects such as those just described may indeed occur (e.g., Greenburg & Ornstein, 1983).

In one study concerned with the impact of inequity, Greenburg and Ornstein (1983) asked student participants in a laboratory investigation to do some extra work. One group was asked to do this extra work without receiving any additional benefits. In contrast, another group was given a high-status title. Results indicated that those in the latter condition were more productive on the extra tasks than those not compensated with a title. Since the title was chosen (through pre-testing) to be one subjects found attractive, it seems reasonable to assume that this title enhanced participant's affective states (i.e., generated increased positive affect). In a related field investigation (Greenburg, 1988), life insurance underwriters were temporarily assigned to new offices. (This was necessitated by construction activities in their building.) Some were assigned to the offices of persons higher in status than themselves, some to the offices of persons lower in status than themselves, and some to offices of equal-status persons. (These assignments were made at random.) Measures of their subsequent performance indicated that performance of those transferred to the offices of higher status persons increased, while that of persons transferred to the offices of lower-status persons decreased. It seems reasonable to assume that those in the former group, enjoying the benefits of a larger, plusher office, experienced higher levels of positive affect than those transferred to smaller, less desirable offices. If this was the case, then positive affect, not simply efforts to cope with inequity by increasing output, may have contributed to the observed rise in employees' productivity.

Of course, additional research specifically designed to examine the role of positive affect in situations related to feelings of equity or inequity is necessary. However, given that the feeling of inequity has been shown to be quite negative in nature (Adams, 1965), and that positive affect has been found to influence not only prosocial behavior but also memory and cognitive structure and perception of the richness of one's own tasks and job situation (Isen, 1987; Isen & Levin, 1972; Isen et al., 1978; Kraiger et al., 1989), it seems quite possible that positive affect may play an important mediating role with respect to reactions to perceived unfairness.

TECHNIQUES FOR INDUCING POSITIVE AFFECT IN ORGANIZATIONAL SETTINGS

Taken as a whole, the diverse body of research reviewed in this paper suggests that positive affect exerts robust effects upon behavior and cognitive processes, and that such effects, in turn, may play an important role in organizational settings. Moreover, several findings point to the conclusion that the induction of positive affect can have beneficial effects with respect to several key organizational processes (e.g., prosocial behavior, conflict management). How, then, can such reactions be enhanced? What steps can organizations or individuals take to increase positive affect in work places? Several possibilities appear to exist.

First, such efforts might focus on the physical environment. Some of the earliest research on organizational behavior was concerned with such effects (e.g., Roethlisberger & Dickson, 1939), and recent findings have served to underscore the importance of environmental factors in shaping employees' attitudes, motivation, and performance (e.g., Baron, 1987b; Oldham & Fried, 1987). A number of different variables appear to be important in this respect (e.g., temperature, workspace, lighting, air quality). Indeed, even the presence of pleasant aromas has been found to influence several forms of organizational behavior, including negotiation, preferred modes for resolving interpersonal conflict, and self-set goals (Baron, 1990[a]). Providing employees with physical work environments that are pleasant and comfortable may involve some investment on the part of organizations; however, the positive affect induced and the benefits that may follow from such reactions (e.g., increased motivation and productivity) suggest that the return may well be worth the initial investment.

Other steps that may serve to enhance positive affect among employees might focus on "organizational culture" (Schein, 1985). Such shared beliefs, values, and expectations exert strong effects upon organization members, influencing their actions and attitudes about themselves and others in pervasive and often subtle ways (Akin & Hopelain, 1986; Saffold, 1988). For example, in many organizations the existing culture contains attitudes about employees that may expose them to unnecessary levels of stress, interfere with effective communication, and generally convey the message that subordinates are not to be trusted, or are not competent, and that managers are present to check up on them and goad them into doing their jobs. Not all organizations have such cultures, of course, but many do possess at least some of these negative features.

In contrast, a culture that fosters a positive attitude toward employees and complimentary expectations about their motives and competencies may lead to actually enhanced affect among the work force. Positive attitudes towards employees may help reduce the frequency of inappropriate (destructive) negative feedback (Baron, 1988, 1990[b]; Larsen, 1989), and may also foster increased emphasis on and acknowledgement of employees' strengths and accomplishments. This, in turn, can contribute to creating the kind of atmosphere in which employees can do their best. With respect to the first of these points, recent findings indicate that the delivery of negative feedback that is harsh in tone, general rather than specific in content, and that makes internal attributions for failure induces strong negative reactions among recipients, reduces their motivation, and undermines their feelings of self-efficacy (Baron, 1988). Clearly, the elimination of such inappropriate, destructive feedback can be a useful step toward enhancing positive affect among employees.

Explicating key aspects of an organization's culture is a difficult task; and producing changes in it may require even more effort. Still, careful examination of shared beliefs and values within an organization—its often unstated assumptions about people and appropriate ways of doing business—would seem to be beneficial from the point of view of identifying those aspects that are inducing negative reactions among employees and some that may promote positive feelings.

For example, one often encounters the situation in which organization members' successes are ignored, while their failures or difficulties are emphasized. Sometimes this may occur unintentionally, since errors must be corrected and are therefore attention-getting, while successes simply result in the smooth flow of work and projects. But often the practice is intentional, and stems from beliefs on the part of managers that negative affect "motivates" workers. Also, one sometimes sees the intentional creation of a tense atmosphere within an organization through competition, again in the interest of enhanced "motivation." Many managers accept the view that competition will improve performance, through incentive and pressure.

In contrast, much of the work reviewed in this chapter would suggest that such conditions may detract from, rather than facilitate, some important organizational processes or employees' problem-solving skills. As a result, individuals working in a tense, competitive atmosphere may indeed work very hard but may produce only routine and mundane ideas and products. In addition, they may suffer the effects of stress and burn-out noted previously. This suggests that a work environment which emphasizes pressure, competition, and hostility may well prove counter-productive, especially where creative, integrative ideas are sought. Certainly such factors should not just be assumed to be beneficial. In this context, it might be useful to investigate the influence of various forms of negative affect, such as tension or anger, or factors such as competition (which might tend to promote a negative, hostile atmosphere), as well as positive affect, on processes important to organizational functioning. Alleviation of such negative aspects of the culture may often go a long way toward encouraging higher levels of positive affect among many if not all organization members.

Additional steps that may prove useful in attaining this goal include the enhancement of communication within an organization, and changes in what might be viewed as more structural aspects of the organization such as greater participation by organization members in decisions that affect their jobs. Recent findings suggest that most individuals strongly prefer having a voice in decisions that affect their work (Heilman, et al., 1984). Moreover, this appears to be true even in situations where existing theories (Vroom & Yetton, 1973) suggest that more autocratic or manager-centered decision-making procedures would be preferable (Heilman, et al., 1984). Thus, shifts toward a more participative style of decision-making and leadership may be helpful in inducing positive affect among organization members in a wide range of contexts (Crouch & Yetton, 1987). Of course, the changes described above also produce many effects in addition to positive affect, such as feelings of empowerment.

In sum, the induction of positive affect among individuals in an organization may, under appropriate circumstances, yield important and general benefits. Certainly, this will not always be true; as noted previously, high levels of positive affect may discourage (or encourage) risk taking under some circumstances (e.g., Arkes et al., 1988; Isen & Geva, 1987; Isen et al., 1988; Isen & Patrick, 1983), and may, under some conditions, lead to decision-making strategies in which heuristic processes are used and details are overlooked or ignored (e.g., Isen & Means, 1983). It may also lead to a positive bias in judgment of ambiguous cases. In situations in which such outcomes might occur (and these should be investigated), however, it is possible that appropriate steps designed to lessen their likelihood can be implemented. For example, providing individuals with feedback about their performance may eliminate tendencies to use heuristic or simplified processing, or tendencies to allow positive bias to occur in the evaluation of borderline cases.

The potential benefits of positive affect seem sufficient in scope and magnitude to warrant close consideration of it as a potential means for enhancing several organizational processes. Where positive feelings may result in unwanted effects, various interventions may be available to control these. Thus, it appears that good feelings can contribute favorably in many respects to the ways in which people think and behave at work. And this, in turn, may enhance the productivity and efficiency of the organizations to which they belong.

This last point raises an issue which is a crucial one for research concerning the role of positive affect in organizations and organizational behavior: The possibility of a link between enjoyment at work or enjoyment of specific jobs (or aspects of them) and productivity. Such a relationship is certainly plausible. Its existence is consistent with, but not synonomous with, the view that *job satisfaction* is related to (and perhaps predictive of) task performance (cf., Locke, in press) and productivity. This, however, is a topic that has received a lot of attention in the literature but little clear confirmation.

While existence of a link between job satisfaction and productivity has frequently been suggested, it has proven difficult to demonstrate. Some studies report that job satisfaction is indeed related to productivity (e.g., Miller and Monge, 1986), but others have failed to confirm this relationship. Indeed, in many cases, job satisfaction has been found to have little if any impact on task performance (cf., Locke, in press; Porter & Lawler, 1968). Several factors may be responsible for this puzzling pattern.

First, in many work settings, there is little room for gross change in performance. Jobs are structured so that the persons holding them keep busy most if not all of the time and must maintain at least some minimal level of performance. If they do not, they cannot retain their jobs. Further, there is often little leeway for exceeding these minimum standards. One result of such a restricted range of performance is that there is little opportunity for job satisfaction to influence observable output, quality, or related measures (cf., Baron & Greenberg, 1990), at least in the short run.

A second reason for the absence of consistent and compelling evidence for the existence of a link between job satisfaction and task performance may derive, at least in part, from the fact that measures of job satisfaction often focus primarily on formal aspects of jobs (e.g., salary, fringe benefits, status). Typically, they do not include measures of employees' actual job *enjoyment* or happiness at work. However, it may be that such affective reactions, rather than beliefs about one's job or organization, play a crucial role with respect to productivity. While formal aspects of jobs are undoubtedly important and should not be underemphasized, still they may not completely determine job enjoyment. Job enjoyment may depend on other factors such as the climate or atmosphere on a job, the extent to which employees are made or allowed to feel comfortable, to feel effective and contributing, to feel part of a team, or to feel good about themselves and their abilities. Research on factors such as these might be informative. It may well be job enjoyment, affected by factors such as these, and thus more specifically related to everyday affect on the job, that enhances productivity.

Finally, positive affective reactions to one's work may well influence performance, but in ways that are not readily assessed by traditional measures of productivity. Enjoyment of one's work may facilitate creativity and other forms of cognitive flexibility—positive outcomes, the effects of which are not directly assessed by the short-term volume or quality of work, or by low rates of absenteeism and of voluntary turnover (e.g., Carsten and Spector, 1987), but rather may be more apparent over the longer term. Research specifically designed to assess these possible long-term effects of work-generated positive affect would shed additional light on the relationship between positive affect and productivity. Additionally, since long-term measures have not typically been used in the investigation of the link between traditionally assessed job satisfaction and productivity either, such research might help to explicate the relationship between traditional measures of job satisfaction and such task performance, as well.

In sum, then, we have seen that positive feelings can have important beneficial effects in organizations. They can facilitate various forms of prosocial behavior and can promote the development of innovation and creative problem solving. The challenge for managers is to foster the development of work environments that give rise to pleasant feelings and that enhance and maintain the positive effects of good feeling states, while minimizing or eliminating any potential untoward consequences. Considerable research will be needed to elucidate the major conditions necessary for accomplishing this task. Given the potential benefits for both individuals and organizations that might result, however, there appear to be strong grounds for placing such investigation high on the research agenda of our field.

*   *   *

Answer to the Remote Associates Test item presented on p. 23: POWER.

REFERENCES

Adams, J. S. (1965). Inequity in social exchange. In L. Berkowitz (Ed.) *Advances in Experimental Social Psychology*, Vol 2, 267–299. New York: Academic Press.

Aderman, D. (1972). Elation, depression and helping behavior. *Journal of Personality and Social Psychology, 24,* 91–101.

Akin, G., & Hopelain, D. (1986). Finding the culture of productivity. *Organizational Dynamics, 7,* 19–32.

Arkes, H. R., Herren, L. T., & Isen, A. M. (1988). The role of potential loss in the influence of affect on risk-taking behavior. *Organizational Behavior and Human Decision Processes, 42,* 181–193.

Arvey, R. D., & Campion, J. E. (1982). The employment interview: A summary and review of recent research. *Personnel Psychology, 35,* 281–322.

Bandura, A. (1986). *Social foundations of thought and action: Social cognitive theory.* Englewood Cliffs, NJ: Prentice-Hall.

Baron, R. A. (1977). *Human aggression.* New York: Plenum.

Baron, R. A. (1983). The control of human aggression: An optimistic overview. *Journal of Social and Clinical Psychology, 1,* 97–119.

Baron, R. A. (1984). Reducing organizational conflict: An incompatible response approach. *Journal of Applied Psychology, 69,* 272–279.

Baron, R. A. (1987a). Mood interviewer and the evaluation of job candidates. *Journal of Applied Social Psychology, 17,* 911–926.

Baron, R. A. (1987b). Effects of negative air ions on cognitive performance. *Journal of Applied Psychology, 72,* 131–137.

Baron, R. A. (1988). Negative effects of destructive criticism: Impact on conflict, self-efficacy, and task performance. *Journal of Applied Psychology, 73,* 199–207.

Baron, R. A. (1989a). Applicant strategies during job interviews. In G. R. Ferris & R. W. Eder (Eds.). The employment interview: *Theory, research, and practice.* Newbury Park, CA: Sage.

Baron, R. A. (1989b). Personality and organizational conflict: The Type A behavior pattern and self-monitoring. *Organizational Behavior and Human Decision Processes, 44,* 281–296.

Baron, R. A. (1990c). Interactive effects of interviewers' current moods and applicants' qualifications on the outcome of job interviews. Unpublished manuscript, Rensselaer Polytechnic Institute.

Baron, R. A. (1990b). Countering the effects of destructive criticism: The relative efficacy of four interventions. *Journal of Applied Psychology, 75,* 235–245.

Baron, R. A. (1990a). Environmentally-induced positive affect: Its impact on self-efficacy, and task performance, negotiation, and conflict. *Journal of Applied Social Psychology, 20,* 368–384.

Baron, R. A., & Ball, R. L. (1974). The aggression-inhibiting influence of non-hostile humor. *Journal of Experimental Social Psychology, 10,* 23–33.

Baron, R. A., Fortin, S., Frei, R., Hauvner, L., & Shack, M. (1990). Reducing organizational conflict: The potential role of socially-induced positive affect. *International Journal of Conflict Management, 1.*

Baron, R. A., & Greenberg, J. (1990). *Behavior in Organizations,* 3rd edition, Boston, MA: Allen & Bacon.

Bartlett, J. C., Burleson, G., & Santrock, J. W. (1982). Emotional mood and memory in young children. *Journal of Experimental Child Psychology, 34,* 59–76.

Bartlett, J. C., & Santrock, J. W. (1979). Affect-dependent episodic memory in young children. *Child Development, 50,* 513–518.

Batson, C. D., Coke, J. S., Chard, F., Smith, D., & Taliaferro, A. (1979). Generality of the "Glow of goodwill": Effects of mood on helping and information acquisition. *Social Psychology Quarterly, 42,* 176–179.

Baum, A. & Valins, S. (1977). *Architecture and social behavior: Psychological studies of social density.* Hillsdale, NJ: Erlbaum.

Bazerman, M. H., Guiliani, T., & Appleman, A. (1984). Escalation of commitment in individual and group decision-making. *Organizational Behavior and Human Performance, 33,* 141–152.

Bernardin, H. J., & Villanova, P. (1986). Performance appraisal. In E. A. Locke (Ed.), *Generalizing from laboratory to field settings,* (pp. 200–211). Lexington, MA: Lexington Books.

Borman, W. (1977). Consistence of rating accuracy and rating errors in the judgment of human performance. *Organizational Behavior and Human Performance, 20,* 238–252.

Bower, G. H. (1981). Mood and memory. *American Psychologist, 36,* 129–148.

Bower, G. H., Gilligan, S. G., & Montiero, K. P. (1981). Selectivity of learning caused by affective states. *Journal of Experimental Psychology: General, 110,* 451–473.

Bower, G. H., & Mayer, D. (1985). Failure to replicate mood-dependent retrieval. *Bulletin of the Psychonomic Society, 23,* 39–42.

Bower, G. H., Montiero, K. P., & Gilligan, S. G. (1978). Emotional mood as a context for learning and recall. *Journal of Verbal Learning and Verbal Behavior, 17,* 573–585.

Brief, A. P., & Motowidlo, S. J. (1986). Prosocial organizational behaviors. *Academy of Management Review, 4,* 710–725.

Brockner, J. (1988). *Self-esteem at work: Research, theory and practice.* Lexington, MA: Lexington Books.

Buchwald, A. (April, 1988). Paper presented at the meeting of the Midwestern Psychological Association, Chicago.

Burke, R. J. (1984). Mentors in organizations. *Group and Organization Studies, 9,* 353–372.

Byrne, D. (1971). *The attraction paradigm.* New York: Academic Press.

Campbell, D. T., & Fiske, D. (1959). Convergent and discriminant validation. *Psychological Bulletin, 56,* 81–105.

Cardy, R. L. (1987). Liking as a source of level bias in performance ratings. Paper presented at the 1987 meetings of the Society of Industrial and Organizational Psychology, Atlanta, GA.

Cardy, R. L., & Dobbins, G. H. (1986). Affect and appraisal accuracy: Liking as a integral dimension in evaluating performance. *Journal of Applied Psychology, 71,* 672–678.

Carnevale, P. J. D., & Isen, A. M. (1986). The influence of positive affect and visual access on the discovery of integrative solutions in bilateral negotiation. *Organizational Behavior and Human Decision Processes, 37,* 1–13.

Carsten, J. M., & Spector P. E. (1987). Unemployment, job satisfaction, and employee turnover: A meta-anlytic test of the Muchinsky model. *Journal of Applied Psychology, 72,* 734–381.

CRM film (1979). Helping, a growing dimension of management.

Crouch, A., & Yetton, P. (1987). Manager behavior, leadership style, and subordinate performance: An empirical extension of the Vroom-Yetton conflict rule. *Organizational Behavior and Human Decision Processes, 39,* 384–396.

Cunningham, M. R. (1979). Weather, mood, and helping behavior: Quasi-experiments in the sunshine Samaritan. *Journal of Personality and Social Psychology, 37,* 1947–1956.

Dansereau, G., Graen, G., & Haga, B. (1975). A vertical dyad linkage approach to leadership within formal organizations: A longitudinal investigation of the role making process. *Organizational Behavior and Human Performance, 13,* 45–78.

Davidson, D., Suppes, P., & Siegel, S. (1956). *Decision making: An experimental approach.* Stanford: Stanford University Press.

Davis, M., Eshelman, E. R., & McKay, M. (1983). *The relaxation and stress reduction workbook.* Oakland, CA: New Harbinger Publications.

Dipboye, R. L. (1985). Some neglected variables in research on discrimination in appraisals. *Academy of Management Review, 10,* 116–127.

Duncker, K. (1945). On problem-solving. *Psychological Monographs, 58,* Whole No. 5.

Easterbrook, J. A. (1959). The effect of emotion on cue utilization and the organization of behavior. *Psychological Review, 66,* 183–201.

Eich, J. E., & Birnbaum, I. M. (1982). Repetition, cueing and state-dependent memory. *Memory and Cognition, 10,* 103–114.

Feldman, J. M. (1981). Beyond attribution theory: Cognitive processes in appraisals. *Academy of Management Review, 10,* 116–127.

Fisher, J. D., Bell, P. A., & Baum, A. S. (in press). *Environmental psychology,* 3rd ed. New York: Holt, Rinehart, & Winston.

Forest, D., Clark, M. S., Mills, J., & Isen, A. M. (1979). Helping as a function of feeling state and nature of the helping behavior. *Motivation and Emotion, 3,* 161–169.

Forgas, J. P., Bower, G. H., & Krantz, S. E. (1984). The influence of mood on perceptions of social interactions. *Journal of Experimental Social Psychology, 20,* 497–513.

Frese, M. (1985). Stress at work and psychosomatic complaints: A causal interpretation. *Journal of Applied Psychology, 70,* 314–328.

Fried, R., & Berkowitz, L. (1979). Music hath charms . . . and can influence helpfulness. *Journal of Applied Social Psychology, 9,* 199–208.

Galizio, M., & Hendrick, C. (1972). Effect of musical accompaniment on attitude: The guitar as a prop for persuasion. *Journal of Applied Social Psychology, 2,* 350–359.

Garner, W. R. (1954). Context effects and the validity of loudness scales. *Journal of Experimental Psychology, 48,* 218–224.

Garner, W. R., Hake, H. W., & Eriksen, C. W. (1956). Operationism and the concept of perception. *Psychological Review, 63,* 149–159.

Gouaux, C. (1971). Induced affective states and interpersonal attraction. *Journal of Personality and Social Psychology, 20,* 37–43.

Greenberg, J. (1987). A taxonomy of organizational justice theories. *Academy of Management Review, 12,* 9–22.

Greenberg, J. (1988). Equity and workplace status: A field experiment. *Journal of Applied Psychology, 73,* 606–613.

Greenberg, J., & Ornstein, S. (1983). High status job title as compensation for underpayment: A test of equity theory. *Journal of Applied Psychology, 68,* 285–297.

Griffitt, W. B. (1970). Environmental effects on interpersonal affective behavior: Ambient effective temperature and attraction. *Journal of Personality and Social Psychology, 15,* 240–244.

Gutteridge, T. G. (1986). Organizational career development systems: The state of the practice. In D. T. Hall & Assocs. (Eds.), *Career Development in Organizations* (pp. 50–94). San Francisco: Jossey-Bass.

Hackman, J. R., & Oldham, G. R. (1975). Development of the job diagnostic survey. *Journal of Applied Psychology, 60,* 159–170.

Hackman, J. R., & Oldham, G. R. (1976). Motivation through the design of work: Test of a theory. *Organizational Behavior and Human Performance, 16,* 250–279.

Heilman, M. E., Hornstein, H. A., Cage, J. H., & Herschlag, J. K. (1984). Reactions to prescribed leader behavior as a function of role perspective: The case of the Vroom-Yetton model. *Journal of Applied Psychology, 69,* 50–60.

Holmes, D. S. (1984). Meditation and somatic arousal reduction. *American Psychologist, 39,* 1–10.

Hurley, D. (1988). The mentor mystique. *Psychology Today, 22*(5), 38–43.

Ilgen, D. R., & Feldman, J. M. (1983). Performance appraisal: A process focus. In L. L. Cummings & B. M. Staw (Eds.), *Research in organizational behavior,* Vol 5 (pp. 141–197). Greenwich, CT: JAI Press.

Isen, A. M. (1970). Success, failure, attention and reaction to others: The warm glow of success. *Journal of Personality and Social Psychology, 15,* 294–301.

Isen, A. M. (1975). Positive affect, accessibility of cognitions, and helping. Paper presented as part of the symposium, "Directions in theory on helping behavior" (J. Piliavin, Chair), Eastern Psychological Association Convention, New York.

Isen, A. M. (1984). Toward understanding the role of affect in cognition. In R. Wyer & T. Srull (Eds.), *Handbook of social cognition* (pp. 179–236). Hillsdale, NJ: Erlbaum.

Isen, A. M. (1985). The asymmetry of happiness and sadness in effects on memory in normal college students. *Journal of Experimental Psychology: General, 114,* 388–391.

Isen, A. M. (1987). Positive affect, cognitive processes, and social behavior. In L. Berkowitz (Ed.), *Advances in experimental social psychology,* vol. 20 (pp. 203–253). New York: Academic Press.

Isen, A. M. (1990). The influence of positive and negative affect on cognitive organization: Some implications for development. In N. Stein, B. Leventhal, & T. Trabasso (Eds.), *Psychological and Biological Approaches to Emotion* (pp. 75–94). Hillsdale, NJ: Erlbaum.

Isen, A. M., Clark, M., & Schwartz, M. F. (1976). Duration of the effect of good mood on helping: "Footprints on the sands of time." *Journal of Personality and Social Psychology, 34,* 385–393.

Isen, A. M., & Daubman, K. A. (1984). The influence of affect on categorization. *Journal of Personality and Social Psychology, 47,* 1206–1217.

Isen, A. M., Daubman, K. A., & Nowicki, G. P. (1987). Positive affect facilitates creative problem solving. *Journal of Personality and Social Psychology, 51,* 1122–1131.

Isen, A. M., & Diamond, G. A. (1989). Affect and automaticity. In J. Uleman & J. Bargh (Eds.), *Unintended thought* (pp. 124–152). NY: Guilford.

Isen, A. M., & Geva, N. (1987). The influence of positive affect on acceptable level of risk: The person with a large canoe has a large worry. *Organizational Behavior and Human Decision Processes, 39*, 145–154.

Isen, A. M., & Gorgoglione, J. M. (1983). Some specific effects of four affect-induction procedures. *Personality and Social Psychology Bulletin, 9*, 136–143.

Isen, A. M., Johnson, M. M. S., Mertz, E., & Robinson, G. (1985). The influence of positive affect on the unusualness of word associations. *Journal of Personality and Social Psychology, 48*, 1413–1426.

Isen, A. M., & Levin, P. F. (1972). The effect of feeling good on helping: Cookies and kindness. *Journal of Personality and Social Psychology, 21*, 384–388.

Isen, A. M., & Means, B. (1983). The influence of positive affect on decision-making strategy. *Social Cognition, 2*, 18–31.

Isen, A. M., Means, B., Patrick, R., & Nowicki, G. (1982). Some factors influencing decision-making strategy and risk-taking. In M. S. Clark & S. T. Fisk (Eds.), *Affect and cognition: The 17th Annual Carnegie Symposium on Cognition*. Hillsdale, NJ: Erlbaum, 243–261.

Isen, A. M., Nygren, T. E., & Ashby, F. G. (1988). The influence of positive affect on the subjective utility of gains and losses: It's not worth the risk. *Journal of Personality and Social Psychology, 55*, 710–717.

Isen, A. M., Rosenzweig, A. S., & Young, M. J. (1990). The influence of positive affect on clinical problem solving. Manuscript.

Isen, A. M., & Shalker, T. E. (1982). Do you "accentuate the positive, eliminate the negative" when you are in a good mood? *Social Psychology Quarterly, 45*, 58–63.

Isen, A. M., Shalker, T., Clark, M., & Karp, L. (1978). Affect, accessibility of material in memory and behavior: A cognitive loop? *Journal of Personality and Social Psychology, 36*, 1–12.

Isen, A. M., & Simmonds, S. F. (1978). The effect of feeling good on a helping task that is incompatible with good mood. *Social Psychology* (now *Social Psychology Quarterly*), *41*, 345–349.

Janis, I. L., Kaye, D., & Kirschner, P. (1965). Facilitating effects of "eating while reading" on responsiveness to persuasive communications. *Journal of Personality and Social Psychology, 11*, 181–186.

Janis, I. L., & Mann, L. (1977). *Decision making*. NY: Free Press.

Johnson, E., & Tversky, A. (1983). Affect, generalization and the perception of risk. *Journal of Personality and Social Psychology, 45*, 20–31.

Jones, E. E. (1964). *Ingratiation*. New York: Appleton-Century-Crofts.

Keinan, G. (1987). Decision making under stress: Scanning of alternatives under controllable and uncontrollable threats. *Journal of Personality and Social Psychology, 52*, 638–644.

Koestler, A. (1964). *The act of creation*. New York: Macmillan.

Kraiger, K., Billings, R. S., & Isen, A. M. (1989). The influence of positive affective states on task perception and satisfaction. *Organizational Behavior and Human Decision Processes, 44*, 12–25.

Kram, K. E. (1985). *Mentoring at Work: Developmental Relationships in Organizational Life*. Glenview, IL: Scott, Foresman.

Laird, J. D., Wagener, J. J., Halal, M., & Szegda, M. (1982). Remembering what you feel: The effects of emotion on memory. *Journal of Personality and Social Psychology, 42*, 646–657.

Larson, J. R., Jr. (1989). The dynamic interplay between employees' feedback-seeking strategies and supervisors' delivery of performance feedback. *Academy of Management Review, 14*, 408–422.

Lazarus, R. S., Kanner, A. D., & Folkman, S. (1980). Emotions: A cognitive phenomenological analysis. In R. Plutchik & H. Kellerman (Eds.), *Theories of emotion* (Vol. I of *Emotion: Theory, research and experience*). NY: Academic Press.

Levin, P. F., & Isen, A. M. (1975). Something you can still get for a dime: Further studies on the effect of feeling good on helping. *Sociometry, 38,* 141–147.

Liden, R. C., & Mitchell, T. R. (1988). Ingratiatory behaviors in organizational settings. *Academy of Management Review, 13,* 572–587.

Locke, E. A. (in press). The nature and causes of job satisfaction. In M. Dunnette (Ed.), *Handbook of Industrial and Organizational Psychology,* 2nd ed. Palo Alto, CA: Consulting Psychologists Press.

Lohr, J. M., & Staats, A. W. (1973). Attitude conditioning in Sino-Tibetan languages. *Journal of Personality and Social Psychology, 26,* 196–200.

Maslach, C., & Jackson, S. E., (1984). Burnout in organizational settings. In S. Oskamp (Ed.), *Applied social psychology annual, H,* vol. 5 (pp. 135–154). Beverly Hills: Sage.

Matlin, M. W., & Zajonc, R. B. (1968). Social facilitation of word associations. *Journal of Personality and Social Psychology, 10,* 455–460.

Mednick, M. T., Mednick, S. A., & Mednick, E. V. (1964). Incubation of creative performance and specific associative priming. *Journal of Abnormal and Social Psychology, 69,* 220–232.

Mednick, S. A. (1962). The associative basis of the creative process. *Psychological Review, 69,* 220–232.

Miller, K. L., & Monge, P. R. (1986). Participation, satisfaction, and productivity: A meta-analytic review. *Academy of Management Journal, 29,* 727–753.

Moore, B. S., Underwood, W., & Rosenhan, D. L. (1973). Affect and altruism. *Developmental Psychology, 8,* 99–104.

Motowidlo, S. J., Packard, J. S., & Manning, M. R. (1986). Occupational stress: Its causes and consequences for job performance. *Journal of Applied Psychology, 71,* 618–629.

Muczyk, J. P., & Reimann, B. C. (1987) The case for directive leadership. *Academy of Management Executive, 1,* 301–311.

Nasby, W., & Yando, R (1982). Selective encoding and retrieval of affectively valent information. *Journal of Personality and Social Psychology, 43,* 1244–1255.

Oldham, G. R., & Fried, Y. (1987). Employee reactions to workplace characteristics. *Journal of Applied Psychology, 72,* 75–80.

Organ, D. W. (1988). *Organizational citizenship behavior: The good soldier syndrome.* Lexington, MA: Lexington Books.

Porter, L. W., & Lawler, E. E., III (1968). *Managerial Attitudes and Performance.* Homewood, IL: Dorsey.

Pruitt, D. G. (1981). *Negotiation behavior.* New York: Academic Press.

Pruitt, D. G. (1983). Strategic choice in negotiation. *American Behavioral Scientist, 27,* 167–194.

Puffer, S. M. (1987). Prosocial behavior, noncompliant behavior, and work performance among commission salespeople. *Journal of Applied Psychology, 72,* 615–621.

Riskind, J. H. (1983). Nonverbal expressions and the accessibility of life experience memories: A congruence hypothesis. *Social Cognition, 2,* 61–86.

Rosch, E. (1975). Cognitive representations of semantic categories. *Journal of Experimental Psychology: General, 104*(3), 192–233.

Roskies, E. (1987). *Stress management for the healthy type A: Theory and practice.* New York: Guilford.

Saffold, G. S., III. (1988). Culture traits, strength, and organizational performance: Moving beyond "strong" culture. *Academy of Management Review, 13,* 546–558.

Schiffenbauer, A. (1973). Effects of observer's emotional state on judgments of the emotional state of others. *Journal of Personality and Social Psychology, 30,* 31–36.

Schoorman, (1988). Escalation bias in performance appraisals: An unintended consequence of supervisor participation in hiring decisions. *Journal of Applied Psychology, 73,* 58–62.

Sinclair, R. D. (1988). Mood, categorization breadth, and performance appraisal: The effects of order of information acquisition and affective state of halo, accuracy, information retrieval, and evaluations. *Organizational Behavior and Human Decision Processes, 42,* 22–46.

Staw, B. M. (1976) Knee-deep in the big muddy: A study of escalating commitment to a course of action. *Organizational Behavior and Human Performance, 16,* 27–44.

Staw, B. M. (1981). The escalation of commitment to a course of action. *Academy of Management Review, 6,* 577–587.

Staw, B. M., & Ross, J. (1987). Behavior in escalation situations: Antecedents, prototypes, and solutions. In L. L. Cummings & B. M. Staw (Eds.), *Research in Organizational Behavior,* vol. 9 (pp. 39–78). Greenwich, CT: JAI Press.

Staw, B. M., & Ross, J. (1989). Understanding behavior in escalation situations. *Science, 246,* 216–220.

Teasdale, J. D., & Fogarty, S. J. (1979). Differential effects of induced mood on retrieval of pleasant and unpleasant events from episodic memory. *Journal of Abnormal Psychology, 88,* 248–257.

Teasdale, J. D., Taylor, R., & Fogarty, S. J. (1980). Effects of induced elation-depression on the accessibility of memories of happy and unhappy experiences. *Behavior Research and Therapy, 18,* 339–346.

Tedeschi, J. T. & Melburg, V. (1984). Impression management and influence in the organization. In S. B. Bacharach & E. J. Lawler (Eds.)., *Research in the sociology of organizations,* vol. 3 (pp. 31–58). Greenwich, CT: JAI Press.

Thomas, W. K. (1976). Conflict and conflict management. In M. Dunnette (Ed.), *Handbook of industrial and organizational psychology.* Chicago: Rand McNally.

Thomas, W. K. (in press). Conflict and negotiation processes. In M. Dunnette (Ed.), *Handbook of industrial and organizational psychology,* 2nd ed. Chicago: Rand McNally.

Tjosvold, D. (1984). Effects of leader warmth and directiveness on subordinate performance on a subsequent task. *Journal of Applied Psychology, 69,* 222–232.

Tsui, A. S., & Barry, B. (1986). Interpersonal affect and rating errors. *Academy of Management Journal, 29,* 586–599.

Veitch, R. & Griffitt, W. (1976). Good news—bad news: Affective and interpersonal effects. *Journal of Applied Social Psychology, 6,* 69–75.

Wakabayashi, M., Graen, G., Graen, M., & Graen, M. (1988). Japanese management progress: Mobility into middle management. *Journal of Applied Psychology, 73,* 217–227.

Weyant, J. M. (1978). Effects of mood states, costs, and benefits of helping. *Journal of Personality and Social Psychology, 36,* 1169–1176.

Williams, K. J., & Keating, C. W. (1987). Affect and the processing of performance appraisal information. Paper presented at the meetings of the Society of Industrial and Organizational Psychology, Atlanta, GA.

Williams, K. J., Alliger, G. M., & Pulliam, R. (1989). Interviewer affect and ratings: Evidence for the moderating effects of perceived competence. Manuscript submitted for publication, SUNY-Albany, Albany, NY.

Wortman, C. B., & Linsenmeier, J. A. (1977). Interpersonal attraction and techniques of ingratiation in organizational settings. In B. M. Staw & G. R. Salancik (Eds.), *New directions in organizational behavior* (pp. 133–178). Chicago: St. Clair Press.

Zajonc, R. B. (1965). Social facilitation. *Science, 149,* 269–274.

THE MISSING ROLE
OF CONTEXT IN OB:
THE NEED FOR A MESO-LEVEL APPROACH

Peter Cappelli and Peter D. Sherer

ABSTRACT

We argue that recent research in organizational behavior has ignored the potential influence of the external environment on the responses of individuals because of underlying philosophical assumptions concerning the nature of the
objective environment. Empirical results from a variety of fields, however,
suggest that the external environment has an important influence on individuals,
especially employees whose relationship with labor markets outside their organizations affects their responses within those organizations. The absence of a
role for context in organizational behavior not only leads to inadequate explanations for individual attitudes and behavior but also makes it impossible to
develop a common paradigm for micro and macro organizational research:
There is no way at present to relate the individual-based explanations of individual behavior in micro research to the environment-based explanations of

Research in Organizational Behavior, Volume 13, pages 55–110.
Copyright © 1991 by JAI Press Inc.
All rights of reproduction in any form reserved.
ISBN: 1-55938-198-1

organizational characteristics in macro research. In addition to examining the
relationship between the environment external to organizations and the responses of individuals within them, we argue that the best way to build bridges
between micro and macros research is to focus on an intermediate or meso level
of analysis between individuals and the external environment. Such research
would examine the characteristics of organizations (which are shaped by the
external environment) and explain how those characteristics affect the responses
of individual employees. The most important organizational characteristics are
the employment institutions that buffer employers and employees from external
labor markets.

INTRODUCTION

We argue that micro organizational behavior (OB)[1] has ignored the influence
of the external environment in its explanations of the responses of individuals.
This is especially so for employees because they have attachments and relationships not only to their employer's organization but also to the labor market
outside of those organizations. As a result, labor market developments and
organizational practices that buffer labor market pressures may affect a wide
range of employee responses within organizations. By ignoring the external
environment and the broader context in which individuals function, research
in OB encounters a series of problems. Perhaps the most important is that OB
cannot be related to organizational theory and a common paradigm for organizational studies cannot be developed because there is at present no way to
relate the individual-based explanations of individual behavior in micro research to the environment or context-based explanations of organizations in
macro research. One way to develop a common paradigm is for OB to develop
bridge statements that identify relationships between organizational characteristics (which macro research explains using the external environment) and
individual responses. These relationships constitute a mesoscopic or intermediate level of analysis between traditional macro and micro research. The
most important of these relationships may center on employment institutions
such as internal labor markets that buffer employers and employees from the
pressures of external labor markets.

   The term "context" refers to the surroundings associated with phenomena
which help to illuminate that phenomena, typically factors associated with
units of analysis above those expressly under investigation. The context for
most OB research with its focus on individual behavior is therefore the environment external to the individual, and this includes characteristics of the
organization to which the individual belongs and of the environment external

to the organization, the focus here.[2] Arguments that individual behavior is shaped by context or "embedded" in the circumstances external to the individual go back at least to Aristotle and are especially important components of historical and sociological explanations; they have recently received more attention in fields such as sociology (Granovetter, 1985) and political science (Sprague, 1982). The experience of OB is somewhat unique, however, in that the dominant approaches to many OB topics have moved away from earlier research traditions where contextual issues were given more explicit roles. They also tend to ignore contemporary research in related fields which finds empirical support for relationships between traditional OB issues and context. The explanation for this development lies in underlying but unstated epistemological assumptions about OB research, especially the need to be consistent with developing theories in psychology, the most important of which are cognitive models which downplay the importance of an objective environment. Others have argued for a role for contextual issues in specific OB topics, but we believe our contribution lies in explaining the reasons for the systematic exclusion of the external environment from OB research, the consequences associated with that exclusion, and in suggesting a general way forward.

REVIEWING THE LITERATURE

The first section of the paper reviews research on three topics central to OB research; job attitudes, absenteeism, and turnover.[3] It reviews contemporary and older research in OB as well as studies from related fields such as economics and sociology and finds important relationships between individual employee responses and the external environment, a relationship that operates through the attachment that individuals have to the outside labor market. Despite this empirical evidence, contextual factors are absent from virtually all contemporary OB research. The explanation for the decline of context in OB therefore seems based on systematic changes that underlie the field, changes we examine in the next section.

Job Attitudes

Job attitudes have been a major focus of OB research, arguably the topic most central to OB research in part because they were thought to be related to job performance, but the absence of clear relations between the two has been understood for some time now (e.g., Schwab & Cummings, 1970). The behaviors that job satisfaction best predicts, for example, are externally-oriented behaviors such as turnover and absenteeism and not internal organizational matters such as performance (see reviews such as Dunham & Smith, 1979). The focus on job attitudes seems best explained by the concern that OB has with psychological states, a concern that reflects the interests of its parent disciplines in psychology. Models of job attitudes, especially satisfaction, are discussed below, and they illustrate the absence of a consideration of context in OB research and its potential importance.

Congruence: Locke's (1976) survey of job satisfaction suggested that there were about 3000 job satisfaction studies by the mid-1970s, and it seems reasonable that there may be as many as 4000 by 1990. Most satisfaction studies, as Schneider (1985) notes, are based on a model of congruence between individual characteristic and the job situations, although virtually all examine only one side of the match. The majority of the studies in the congruence tradition examine situational and demographic characteristics of the individual, such as age, tenure, etc., as proxies for expectations or needs and predict higher satisfaction where these needs are lower (see Locke, 1976 for a review). Studies of job characteristics such as Hackman and Oldham (1976) represent the other side of the match. These are typically need fulfill-ment models where satisfaction varies directly with how well a job's charac-teristics address a predetermined set of individual needs.

Arguments that both sides of the match need to be examined have been around for some time (e.g., Pervin, 1968), but studies that actually examine both sides simultaneously constitute a very small proportion of satisfaction studies (exceptions include O'Reilly, 1977; Granrose & Portwood, 1987).[4] Instead, the implicit assumption in most satisfaction studies is that one side of the match is constant and can be ignored. While this is unrealistic, it persists because it saves the paradigm from having to confront an issue that it cannot comfortably address; the characteristics of these matches are shaped by fac-tors external to the individual.

The notion of congruence implies that the individual issues of needs and job characteristics do not by themselves explain satisfaction; workers with low expectations in poor jobs can be just as satisfied as are workers in good jobs who have high needs and expectations. Instead, it is their combination—the match—that is the determining factor. Understanding satisfaction therefore requires understanding how "good" matches get made, and that requires examining extra-individual behavior and institutions such as the labor market where job-worker matches are made. The tacit assumption that one side of the match can be ignored prevents researchers from having to address these extra-individual issues which are uncomfortably outside the paradigm. Yet there is important variance in the quality of matches which in turn affects satisfaction. And factors external to the individual—indeed, to the organization—affect the quality of matches, issues we explore in more detail below with the discussion of turnover.

The characteristics of jobs, one half of the match, are external to the individual and are by definition part of the external environment.[5] Yet the dominant approaches to examining jobs rely on individual perceptions. This helps the arguments conform to the dominant cognition-response model, but the relationship between actual job characteristics and perceptions of them is not always strong, a problem we return to below, and the explanatory power of these models is less than overwhelming (see, e.g., Roberts & Glick, 1981). There is also evidence that attitudes are affected by aspects of jobs that are not associated with the actual workplace. Drory and Shamir (1988) find, for example, that the appreciation and support that the external community gives occupations are among the best predictors of jobs satisfaction. Finally, none of the dominant congruence models which examine only one side of the match have performed particularly well in empirical tests, explaining relatively small proportions of the total variance in attitudes, and that is perhaps the most important criticism of them.

Externally-Based Explanations: The remaining branches of the job satisfaction literature have more of a social than an individual perspective, and perhaps because their unit of analysis has not been the individual, they have been much less popular in OB. These include comparison-based theories such as relative deprivation, equity theory, and social comparisons. All of these theories suggest that satisfaction is a *relative* concept that depends not on intrinsic individual needs or individual job characteristics but a social phenomena—how one perceives themselves relative to some referent.

Of the comparison approaches, equity theory has been the focus of the most empirical research. Equity-based explanations have had considerable support in the past (see Walster et al., 1978 for a survey), and studies continue to find support for the basic arguments. Berkowitz et al. (1987), for example, find that equity considerations are the best predictors of satisfaction in their data. But the trend in research has been away from equity-based studies. And much of the equity theory research limits itself to within-organization comparisons which unfortunately designs-away the ability to observe comparisons outside the organization. Cosier and Dalton (1983) note that laboratory research, which constitutes the bulk of equity studies, ignores the context in which equity is judged. They argue that history—past perceived inequities including those with other organizations—is the crucial factor in determining inequity, and that history is ignored in laboratory studies.

Intra-individual comparisons are also a potentially important influence on employee attitudes as Austin (1980) observed and have also been neglected.

However, it is important to think carefully about what is actually being measured with intra-individual comparisons. These comparisons are based on how the individual was treated previously, often within different organizations. What they may really measure, therefore, is not an individual characteristic but perceptions of previous organizational practices. These perceptions are proxies for prevailing practices in employment relationships which are shaped by the external labor market. As such, it might be more useful to examine such practices explicitly, for example, by identifying situations where organizational rules were changed.

As Staw (1984) suggests, research based on equity theory has suffered from two problems. First, the choice of comparisons plays a crucial role in determining whether inequity is perceived, and the existing OB research offers little guidance as to which comparisons will be chosen.[6] Arguments about job choices in economics, which go back to Adam Smith (1776), do provide such guidance. They are very similar to equity theory in positing that comparisons determine attitudes toward one's current job, but here the choice of comparisons is explicit: The comparisons that really matter are those with other job opportunities in the market. These comparisons are more salient because they are real opportunities that offer choices. And as Salancik and Pfeffer (1978) argue, choices have an important effect on attitudes. This suggests an a priori theory for comparisons; they should be most important for referent jobs that represent real alternatives. And there is research support for this view. Dornstein (1988) finds, for example, that the most important external comparisons are within the same occupation where alternative employment is most likely, that is, within the same labor market.

The second problem is that equity theory suggests a range of alternatives through which perceived inequity can be addressed but offers no arguments as to which ones will be selected in a given setting. But such arguments can easily be fashioned by considering the external environment. Cappelli and Chauvin (forthcoming) find, for example, that where the external labor market makes leaving one's job costly (e.g., high unemployment and lower outside wages), workers are more inclined to use alternative mechanisms such as grievance procedures to address their problems. Rusbult et al. (1988) also find that increased employee investment, which makes leaving difficult, increases the use of "voice" mechanisms for solving problems as opposed to quitting.

Relative deprivation theories have perhaps the longest pedigree of equity-based research and have been applied successfully in political models, for example, of satisfaction with governments (see Martin, 1981; & Crosby, 1984; for reviews). They seem better oriented toward predicting actual behavior than most theories, but as Staw (1984, p. 637) notes, "little of this type of research has yet appeared in the organization literature, although it would seem to present a major means of revitalizing work on equity and job satisfaction."

Adaptation-level arguments are also related to equity issues and suggest that individuals are concerned with the distribution of rewards within their organizations and communities. Brickman (1975) finds, for example, that the satisfaction of individual respondents varied with the distribution of rewards within their groups. The resurgence of interest on questions of distributive justice and their effects on psychological variables (e.g., Greenberg & Cohen, 1982) suggests that the structure of rewards in the external community plays an explicit role in shaping attitudes.

OB research during the 1960s explored some of the effects of community on job attitudes. Studies by Turner and Lawrence (1963), Blood and Hulin (1967), Hulin and Blood (1968) suggested that characteristics of the community where one works and also where one lives can shape attitudes toward jobs. The argument was that community characteristics are mediated through psychological variables such as reference groups and adaptation levels to influence attitudes. Workers living in poorer communities, for example, tend to be more satisfied with a given job and pay level. On the basis of these studies, Hulin (1969) argued that it was futile to search for general explanations of attitudes where the relevant factors lie entirely within individuals and their jobs. Similar studies found a relationship between job attitudes and family communities (albeit in more complicated ways; see Kanter, 1977) and with the extent of participation in nonwork activities (Staines & Pagnucco, 1977). Some of this research tradition continues (e.g., Martinson & Wilening, 1984), although as Near, Rice, and Hunt (1986) note in their survey, it no longer appears to be an important theme in OB research.

Social information processing models of attitudes have perhaps the most explicit role for factors outside the individual. They suggest that satisfaction and related attitudes are influenced by the social cues or signals given about jobs, the way they are labelled, and other information about jobs that individuals perceive from the environment (Salancik & Pfeffer, 1978). (There is a parallel literature in economics noted below.) Laboratory studies (O'Reilly & Caldwell, 1979) and field studies (Griffin, 1983) find that such information does affect attitudes. These models also suggest that the extent and quality of alternative opportunities has a powerful effect on attitudes. Pfeffer and Lawler (1980) find, for example, that job attitudes are significantly lower where respondents have more alternative jobs. Yet as Schnieder (1985) observes, the social information processing approach has yet to really catch on.

There is an older body of research on job satisfaction now outside of the mainstream OB paradigm which suggested an explicit and important role for the labor market in determining employee attitudes. For example, Hoppock (1935) conducted one of the first studies of job satisfaction during the Depression and found much greater levels of satisfaction than expected. He explained the results by appealing to the external environment: "Millions were unemployed. Presumably anyone who had a job was grateful for it and anxious to keep it. Perhaps . . . in 1933 they felt contented only because they saw so many who had no jobs at all" (Hoppock, 1935 p.10). This argument is consistent both with social comparisons (i.e., unemployed referents were much worse off) and with social information processing (i.e., no alternatives raised satisfaction). Similarly, the widely-reported job dissatisfaction of the late 1960s has been interpreted in part as the result of a rapidly expanding economy and tight labor markets: satisfaction fell as referents did better and opportunities elsewhere increased (e.g., Flanagan, Ulman, & Strauss, 1974). Arguments in industrial relations suggested that attitudes especially toward pay were shaped by institutionally-based comparisons—competition between unions (e.g., Ross, 1948) or where long-standing pay comparisons created common wage practices or "wage contours" (Dunlop, 1957).

More recent economics-based studies have also applied these arguments to explain the satisfaction of individuals. Hamermesh (1977) explains job satisfaction with a human capital-based estimate of an individual's wage in alternative jobs. The more their current wage exceeds that alternative, the greater is their satisfaction. Cappelli and Sherer (1989) identify alternative wages for airline employees in their respective labor markets and find that these wages explain elements of satisfaction even when controlling for the employee's own wage—in other words, the greater their wage relative to the labor market, the greater their satisfaction. They also found that the awareness individuals have of these market comparisons had a significant and independent effect on satisfaction.

Some OB studies have worked to identify relationships between the external environment and job attitudes where the environment is an integral part of the characteristics of the job. This relationship is especially clear in Schneider's (1973) study where the organization's customers are part of the external environment and the characteristics of those customers (e.g., whether they are pleasant) also become an important part of the job. Sutton and Rousseau (1979) and Green et al. (1983) also find relationships between the organization's environment and job attitudes presumably through some intermediary step involving the organization's response to that environment. (We examine mechanisms through which that relationship could operate below.) There has been little research on this relationship since these studies.

Overall, social and externally-based models of job satisfaction have had surprisingly little influence on contemporary OB research, especially given their long history in the field. Indeed, one could argue that OB has purged itself of earlier externally-based explanations for job attitudes. It is not obvious why this should have occurred. There was no body of empirical research refuting these externally-based studies. And when comparing these social and external models with the dominant congruence model, it is certainly not obvious that empirical support is greater for the latter. Nor is it the case that the dominant model is superior in terms of theory, especially given the atheoretical nature of many current studies and the poor application of congruence arguments to most tests. Certainly the current approach is easier to use because data only need to be collected about individuals, rather than about the environment as well, and because that data can be collected directly from the respondents with survey instruments that are common across situations. (Hackman & Lawler, 1971 note these advantages in examining job characteristics.) But ease of data collection should not be an acceptable argument for a theoretical approach. The rise of the current individual-oriented approach to attitudes, which relies at best on perceptions of the environment, and the decline of environmental and context models requires a different explanation which we return to in the next section.

Absenteeism

Traditional approaches to the study of work attendance examine it as a form of withdrawal behavior. Perhaps the most comprehensive model is by Steers and Rhodes (1978) who consider attendance as a function of ability and motivation to attend where the latter is driven by attitudes such as job satisfaction and to a lesser extent organizational commitment (Steers & Rhodes, 1978; Mowday, Porter, & Steers, 1982). Yet as Fichman (1984) concludes, the empirical support for these relationships in prior studies has not been strong, and these traditional studies using attitudes as antecedents are in his words "not informative."

Other factors such as personal characteristics (Ilgen & Hollenback, 1977) and characteristics of the job (Garrison & Muchinsky, 1977) are sometimes considered, although as Clegg's (1983) survey makes clear, these considerations appear rarely and when they do are not examined per se but are typically used as control variables. The finding that absenteeism varies widely across organizations (e.g., Chadwick-Jones et al., 1983) certainly suggests that some organization-level factors should be important, but these have not been pursued, either.

Alternative specifications never seem to extend to factors outside the organization even though the theoretical arguments lead in that direction. For example, Steers and Rhodes (1978) note that job expectations are crucial to satisfaction-based explanations, yet none of the research in their review looks at factors outside the workplace that might influence those expectations. Similarly, they survey some studies that emphasize the role of norms concerning behavior on absenteeism, but those studies never look beyond the workgroups for the determination of norms; even issues such as work ethics are treated as individual variables, an example of what Johns and Nicholson (1982) describe as misguided efforts in the attendance literature to understand essentially social behavior by aggregating information about individuals. Perhaps the most common example of such confusion are the results noted in most surveys that absenteeism is higher among women with children. Unfortunately, these results are generally interpreted as a situational characteristic—that women have more demands outside of work (at home)—when, of course, those "demands" are driven by cultural norms: In the last decade, for example, absenteeism among women with children has begun to decline while it has risen for men with children, reflecting changing social norms about child care responsibilities. In other words, women's attendance patterns are driven by the social context.

Rational Decisionmaking: Studies like Morgan and Herman (1976), which examine how potential costs of absenteeism might affect attendance, and Staw and Oldham (1978), which consider the potential benefits for the worker of absenteeism, see the process differently, as a rational decision where individuals weigh the costs and benefits of being absent. This development is important because the factors that affect the costs and benefits of an individual's decision on any issue, including whether to attend work or not, may include factors from the totality of their experiences and are certainly not limited to considerations within the confines of the workplace. This is especially so for the Staw and Oldham (1978) argument which relies on the match between worker and job characteristics; to understand these matches requires examining the selection process through which workers enter from the outside, an issue we examine below. Assessments of the costs and benefits of absenteeism have been pursued in greater detail by economists who find substantial support for the role of factors outside the individual. Winkler (1980) and Jacobson (1989), for example, find that absenteeism is higher where pay is not lost and lower where bonuses are paid for better attendance. Gafni and Peled (1984) find that workers who are aware of shortened life expectancy due to hypertension are absent more than are workers with identical health problems who are unaware of their condition because the former now value leisure more. But so far, efforts to examine these costs and benefits have been limited to such things as demands from nonwork activity (e.g., Chadwick-Jones, Brown, & Nicholson, 1973). The failure to pursue these factors from the external environment are consistent with the critique made by

Clegg (1983) of this literature and stand in the way of efforts to explore the rational decision approach to absenteeism.

There is explicit evidence from studies outside the current OB paradigm that the context within which work occurs helps shape absenteeism. For example, Turner and Lawrence (1965) found attendance differences between urban and rural areas in part because of differences in community and religious norms governing the importance of work. Dalton and Perry (1981) note that relationships between labor and management, expressed in collective bargaining agreements, can have a strong effect on absenteeism by creating norms (e.g., acceptable levels of absence). Absenteeism rates vary dramatically by country, presumably reflecting different cultural norms concerning work. Rising absenteeism like poor attitudes was an important component of the worker dissatisfaction/productivity crisis associated with the entrance of "baby boom" workers in the late 1960s and their alleged higher expectations (e.g., Flanagan, Strauss, & Ulman, 1974; *Work in America*, 1973).

Absenteeism also is related to labor market factors. Taylor (1979) suggests that the decline in absenteeism in the late 1970s was attributed to rising unemployment. Leigh (1985) pursues this issue econometrically and finds that for a national sample, absenteeism is lower when unemployment rates are higher. His results find that this is due not only to the fact that those laid off when unemployment rises tend to be those with higher absenteeism, an artifact, but also that those who remain employed reduce their absenteeism.[7] Allen (1981) finds that absenteeism is lower where wages are higher and for older workers. Results from the Cappelli and Chauvin (forthcoming) grievance study also suggest that absenteeism is lower at plants within the same firm where wage premiums over the outside market are higher and where a greater proportion of workers are on layoff.

Steers and Rhodes (1978) and others acknowledge the potential role that unemployment plays in absenteeism but interpret it along neoclassical, economic lines; workers are less likely to be absent when unemployment rises because they are more afraid of being fired. But there are institutional reasons for believing that a more behavioral explanation is in order. Firms deal with downturns by laying off workers, not by firing them for cause, and most firms have explicit decision rules for layoffs that are specified well in advance. The most common of these, present in most firms and virtually all unionized shops, is seniority. Increased absenteeism therefore does not affect the probability of layoff. In the Cappelli and Chauvin (forthcoming) study, for example, layoffs are by seniority, all the employees know it, and yet they still find that unemployment lowers absenteeism. It is unlikely that the reduction was caused by fear of job loss.[8]

In theory, firms that need to get rid of workers could tighten their performance standards for dismissal in order to get rid of "bad" performers—

lowering the standards for absenteeism, e.g.—but in practice such policy revisions may be hard to do. Most firms explicitly allow a certain amount of absenteeism through "personal days," sick days, etc., and only absenteeism beyond that threshold would cause problems in any case. But there is no evidence that firms reduce the quota of sick days and other allowed absences before layoffs. Even firms that want to crack down on absenteeism often do so by instituting rewards for attendance rather than penalties for absence which the Steers and Rhodes (1978) survey suggests have better results than punitive measures.

It is easier to interpret the relationship with the outside labor market in the context of a comparison-based, behavioral explanation, much as Hoppock (1935) interpreted job satisfaction during the depression. When conditions worsen outside (i.e., higher unemployment, lower wages) the sense of equity and satisfaction with one's own job may rise relatively not only because alternatives have declined but also because the experience of referents worsened as many become unemployed. Arguments suggesting that attendance may be related to an informal psychological contract where such equity considerations play a role have been around for some time in OB (e.g., Gibson, 1966) but have generally not been advanced. Allen (1981) presents some evidence supporting an equity-based explanation of absence in the context for economic study. He finds, for example, that absence is higher where working conditions are more dangerous than average, suggesting that workers may be reacting to the perceived inequity associated with poorer conditions by withdrawing (absenteeism).

The OB literature typically acknowledges the potential role of these outside factors, albeit in passing, but never seems able to get around to using them in their arguments. (One important exception is the review by Forrest et al., 1977.) Johns and Nicholson (1982) argue that there has been in OB "a profound lack of interest exhibited by researchers in the extra organizational factors that may influence absence" and suggests that this is because adherence to unstated axioms are drawing inappropriate boundaries around models of research. Chadwick-Jones et al. (1982) also note that the social context is ignored in part because research tends to accept the assumptions of previous studies without confronting alternative explanations. The arbitrary boundaries around models and the tendency to conform to previous results are problems that we examine more formally below.

Turnover:

Turnover has been the subject of extensive research in economics as well as in OB, and the external environment plays a central role in economics studies. Because much of the OB research on turnover has its roots in the rational individual decision-making approach associated with March and Simon (1958), it is closer in argument and spirit to environmentally-based approaches like economics than is perhaps any other issue in organizational behavior.

The basic March and Simon view suggests that satisfaction with one's current job and factors measuring the perceived ease of movement determine turnover. Since the very notion of turnover implies leaving the organization and moving outside, it seems obvious that an explicit consideration of the environment outside the organization would be an important criterion in the decision, and March and Simon devote approximately half of their discussion to the economic environment. This is perhaps the biggest difference between absenteeism and turnover; turnover explicitly involves the attractions of alternative jobs while absenteeism at most involves only the attractions of non-work activities.[9] Indeed, March and Simon (1958, p. 100) argue that "the most accurate single predictor of labor turnover is the state of the economy." Yet Mobley's (1982) account of the development of OB theories of turnover shows that over time these theories have not only grown more complex but systematically reduced the role for the external environment. The survey of turnover reviews by Steers and Mowday (1981) suggests that the 1000 or more turnover studies focused primarily on job attitudes, presented some evidence for the role of personal characteristics, and generally ignored information about external issues such as prospective jobs. Similarly, Clegg's (1983) survey of the empirical turnover literature finds no behavioral studies with any context variables.

The literature in other fields suggests quite strongly that factors outside of the organization play a crucial role in turnover and that turnover is shaped by factors other than individually-based attitudes and personal characteristics.[10] For example, even more so than with absenteeism, the quit rate varies directly with the business cycle; it was high in the 1960s when labor markets were tight and then dropped off substantially with the recessions in the 1970s. This is true in other countries as well (Jones & Martin, 1986). As Akerlof, Rose, and Yellen (1988) argue, one reason for this is that as some workers leave for better jobs when the economy is expanding, they create vacancies—a "vacancy chain"—which then creates opportunities for other workers to switch jobs.[11] Public policy can also play a role as, for example, wartime manpower policies did in reducing quits in the United States (Burton & Parker, 1969). The treatment by public policy of quits, as opposed to dismissals or layoffs, can also play a role. For example, workers who are laid off or dismissed are typically eligible for unemployment insurance payments while those who quit are not, making it more desirable for employees in difficult work situations to wait until they are laid off or fired rather than quit.[12]

We also know, for example, that the quit rate varies widely by industry and by job, reflecting not only characteristics of the work but also of labor markets and employment relationships (see Stoikov and Raimon, 1968; Price, 1977 for a survey). These are clearly aspects of the external environment. For example, blue collar jobs have higher quit rates—as high as 4.9 percent *per month* in manufacturing (Parsons, 1985)—than do exempt, white collar jobs. Construction jobs have among the highest quit rates because the craft labor market creates workers with interchangeable skills, and hiring halls make it possible to swap jobs and workers; government employment has the lowest quit rate not only because of large pensions which encourage attachment (see Ippolito, 1987 below) but presumably also because of the nature of the employment relationship which, among other things, makes the demands and rewards from work very stable. More generally, we also know that quits vary significantly across countries. They are, for example, very low in Japan compared to the United States not only because of cultural differences but also because of labor market institutions which help tie workers to their firms (see Taira, 1970).

Characteristics of individual workers as they are valued by the market, such as training and age, also affect the quit rate. We know that it is concentrated among inexperienced and younger workers: the probability of eventually quitting a job is 70 percent for workers with less than ten years of experience but only 5 percent for those over 40 with more than 10 years on the job (Mincer & Jovanovic, 1979). Similar results prevail in other countries (Main, 1982). Price's (1977) survey concludes that unskilled workers have higher turnover while better educated and managerial workers have much lower turnover. These worker characteristics are associated with types of employment relationships, the former with the "secondary" labor market of Doeringer and Piori's (1971) dual labor market model and the latter with the primary labor market. We return to the association between behaviors and dual labor markets in section IV.

Within an organization, the single strongest and most consistent predictor of firm-level turnover appears to be the wage level. Price (1977), a sociologist, surveys the economics and behavioral literature on turnover and concludes that higher wages and also increases in wages (other things equal) reduce turnover; more recent studies continue to support this conclusion (Antel, 1988). There appears to be more evidence for the relationship with wages than for any other variable, yet as Price (1977) notes, behaviorally-oriented reviews of the literature tend to ignore it.

Perhaps the second strongest and most consistent predictor of individual turnover in Price's survey is opportunity elsewhere. Recent studies also continue to support this relationship: Lakhani (1988), for example, finds that combat soldiers have a lower quit rate from the army than do other soldiers in part because their skills (thankfully) do not translate to alternative employment. Weiss (1984) finds that alternative opportunities increase quits when controlling for satisfaction with one's current job. Yet Steers and Mowday (1981) note that behavioral studies of turnover have tended to ignore information about prospective jobs. Since then, Youngblood and Mobley (1983) call very explicitly for greater attention to opportunities outside the organization in turnover studies and find in their own study that the expected utility of alternative civilian careers influences turnover from the military.

The basic tenets of most turnover models are quite similar and focus on the net advantages of leaving one's current job versus staying. Because workers are by definition moving from the firm to the outside environment, the importance of context to turnover should be obvious. Certainly the ability to move at all is largely constrained by the economic environment; whether workers can afford to quit depends on their alternatives outside of the organization. Price (1977) notes that the failure to consider opportunities in many studies may explain the lack of relationship between satisfaction and turnover; dissatisfied workers stay because they can't leave. Muchinsky and Morrow (1980) and Hulin, Roznowski, and Hachiya (1985) also argued that dissatisfaction should provide a better prediction of quit rates when alternative jobs are plentiful, and Carsten and Spector (1987) reanalyze previous turnover research with a meta analysis and find support for this hypothesis. Jacofsky and Peters' (1983) results, for example, show that expectations predict movement within a firm much better than movement from the firm; the labor market context, which is not in their model, is much less relevant for moves within the firm yet crucial for moves outside the firm, so it is no surprise to find that a study which does not include context is much less successful at predicting outside moves. Considering moves within a firm as an alternative to quitting helps explain Stoikov and Raimon's (1968) observation that large organizations have lower turnover, because more internal moves are possible and act as a substitute for quits. It also helps explain why Brett and Riley (1988) find a particularly strong relationship between attitudes and the decision to take a new job within a company at another location (transfers); the labor market was not a factor because all of the subjects by definition had alternative jobs available within the firm. Yet these arguments have not influenced the mainstream of turnover research.

The "side bets" literature (Becker, 1960) is also an argument about constraints on leaving. Rusbutt and Farrell (1983) argue that investments in the job that are lost in moving provide important costs that restrict turnover. The portability of many of these investments, such as housing or skills, are determined by the outside market. There is extensive support for this position in economics where the notion of organization-specific skills has long been used to explain lower quit rates (e.g., Mincer, 1981).

The external environment also shapes attitudes and expectations, as noted in the above sections, influencing the assessment of one's current job and subsequent turnover. Telly, French, and Scott (1971) for example, find a relationship between equity arguments and turnover which can easily be extended to incorporate referents from the external environment. Overall, then, the external environment plays an absolutely central role in determining employee turnover.

Job Matches and Search: As noted earlier, an important issue implicit in congruence models of satisfaction is the notion of the "match" between one's expectations and the characteristics of the current job. For similar reasons, matches are also a crucial issue for turnover, but as Steers and Mowday (1981) note, this is another area that behavioral research on turnover has ignored. Not all matches are equally good, and the implication for turnover is that workers with a poor fit between expectations/needs and their job will be the most inclined to quit. There are many aspects of jobs that candidates cannot know until they get in them, and it possible to see at least some components of turnover as an information gathering exercise. Economists argue that this explains why younger workers have higher quit rates, because they have not done enough sampling yet to find a good match (e.g., Hirshleifer, 1973).[13] There is also evidence that external factors can improve the quality of matches and, in turn, improve job satisfaction. For example, Elstrom, Freeberg, and Rock (1987) find that participants in youth employment programs which increase their ability to find permanent jobs report higher job satisfaction in subsequent employment.

Economists point to the higher satisfaction scores of more senior workers in behavioral studies as evidence that senior workers must have better matches. An alternative, more behavioral explanation might be that as Wanous (1976) argues, younger workers simply have higher, perhaps unrealistic expectations and that those expectations are revised downward over time. This suggests a straightforward empirical test between the two explanations: do workers who have had more jobs (and therefore have more information and presumably a better match) report higher satisfaction after controlling for the length of job experience?

Of course, a more efficient way to learn about at least some aspects of jobs is to search in the labor market before taking a job. There are few labor markets so competitive that workers can quit and immediately find a new job. Yet as Mattila (1974) discovered, most workers who quit move directly to new jobs, suggesting that they began searching for alternative jobs before they quit. As Jovanovic (1983) points out, workers have an incentive to search, provided the costs are low (e.g., reading the classified ads); even if they are satisfied with their current job, they would leave if they find one that is better on balance. Akerlof et al. (1988) calculate that only 15 percent of those who quit are without a new job and are searching for a new one (i.e., count as unemployed). The remaining 85 percent either have new jobs as soon as they quit or withdraw from the labor force (e.g., retire). It would be an important exercise for behavioral scholars to examine separately turnover by cause, especially the difference between those who quit to take alternative jobs and those who quit to continue or perhaps begin searching, and identify what determinants, if any, are different in their decision. Presumably alternative jobs play less of a role for the latter group, almost by definition, and dissatisfaction with current jobs should play a proportionately greater role.

The most obvious case where alternative jobs are less important is early retirement (as opposed to mandatory retirement which is not voluntary). Voluntary retirement is an especially important issue for organizations where manpower planning is crucial and also in those seeking to downsize. The constraint provided by job vacancies, a key factor in seeking new jobs, is obviously less of a factor in an individual's retirement decision. One might therefore expect the traditional OB concerns with individual characteristics and situational factors to play more of a role in retirement decisions than where workers quit for other jobs. Filer and Petri (1988) find, for example, that retirement is earlier from jobs that are more difficult and less pleasant, suggesting withdrawal behavior.[14] Yet there is evidence even here that the outside environment helps shape retirement decisions: alternative opportunities for paid employment (Mitchell & Fields, 1984) make retirement more likely; living costs relative to pension entitlements and the prospects for social security payments (Lazear, 1985) shape retirement decisions as do life expectancies which affect the relative value of leisure retirement (Hamermesh, 1984).

In the process of analyzing turnover separately by cause, behavioral research might contribute substantially to our understanding of some key labor market and economics questions. For example, a relatively small number of workers account for a disproportionate amount of aggregate turnover and, more importantly, for unemployment (i.e., they have long spells of unemployment). Antel (1988) finds, for example, that workers who quit are likely to have had higher quit rates in previous jobs. There is considerable debate and speculation as to whether the explanation lies with dispositions (i.e., lazy workers) or situational characteristics (e.g., lack of resources), and this is a question for which behavioral research is uniquely suited to address.

Because most workers quit only when they have another job, presumably one they believe, on balance, is preferable, then the employee's search while on-the-job is a crucial element in determining whether they quit. The better one's search, the more likely that they will find a better job and leave, independent of how they feel about their current job. Behavioral models of turnover ignore the role that search plays in the turnover process.[15] We know from other literatures, however, that there are important differences across individuals in the extent and effectiveness of search. Situational characteristics, for example, play a role in determining the effectiveness of search. Gronau (1971) finds that older workers, who have shorter careers left until retirement, search less, possibly because the returns from search are less (i.e., fewer years in the new job). Danforth (1979) finds that workers with more personal wealth can afford more thorough searches. These workers could, for example, quit in order to search without yet having a job. Similarly, we might also expect employee attitudes to affect search behavior. Employees with greater attitudinal commitment to their current organization may find it more difficult to search, possibly seeing it as an act of disloyalty that creates dissonance. Presumably dispositional issues such as personality (e.g., extroversion) may also affect the ease of search.

The external environment plays an important role in determining search behavior. In general, the problem of search can be seen as balancing the costs against the expected benefits of getting additional information (Stigler, 1961). How much search one is willing to undertake depends on one's expectations about success, and those expectations are shaped by the environment. The "discouraged worker" effect, for example, causes unemployment rates to decline slightly in the depth of recessions when job prospects are very poor; some workers give up job searches and are therefore dropped from the ranks of the unemployed. Granovetter (1972) finds that the more successful searches are those conducted through informal channels such as family and friends. It would be reasonable to hypothesize, therefore, that the quit rate would be lower among workers who lack these informal channels, such as workers who have just moved to a new community. Tobin (1972) pointed out that search is less effective when the market is "congested," when many other people are looking (e.g., when unemployment is higher). It also suggests why previous behavioral studies found lower quit rates in rural areas: It is more difficult to search in rural areas because jobs are spread-out over larger areas, across communities, and information about them may therefore be harder to obtain. The presence of search or "headhunting" firms are also an important part of the external environment and should increase turnover because they assist workers with information on alternative jobs, making search easier and less costly (see Bull et al., 1984). It is also important to note that search may affect attitudes and behaviors other than turnover. For example, additional search time may take the form of increased absenteeism, and the additional information about the availability and desirability of alternative jobs should affect job attitudes—negatively if lots of desirable jobs are available.

Selection: The above arguments about the importance of search and match quality in outcomes such as turnover and satisfaction focus attention on the issue of selection which is the organizational side of the search process. The revival of interest in dispositional arguments (e.g., Staw et al., 1986) highlights the importance of the attitudes and characteristics that members bring to organizations and enhances the role for selection. Understanding selection requires examining the explicit relationship with the external environment, in this case, the labor market.

Potential candidates may have information about some of their characteristics that are of interest to the organization. The problem for the organization is then to get the candidates to reveal that information, a problem sometimes referred to as "asymmetric information." In many cases, the candidates have an incentive to lie about these characteristics—to say that they are hardworking, e.g.—so revealing the information accurately is no small accomplishment. The clearest and perhaps most effective ways of revealing that information truthfully involve self-selection. Here, the organization might design a job or position such that only workers with the appropriate characteristics are attracted to apply for it. The most obvious of such self-selection devices involve compensation arrangements. For example, low base pay and high commission pay for sales jobs attract candidates who believe they have what it takes to sell; those who do not have no incentive to apply for the job because they will not earn much money (low base pay). The realistic job previews that Wanous (1979) argues for can be seen (in part) as an effort to assist the self-selection mechanism. Cappelli and Sherer (1990) find, for example, that workers who self-selected into the 'B' tier of a two-tier wage plan appear to have lower expectations, consistent with those lower wages, than do workers who entered the organization with higher wages.

The characteristics of jobs as they relate to their respective labor markets are important factors in the self-selection process. For example, studies have shown that where jobs are better than average, the length of the queue for job applicants is longer (Boskin, 1982; Krueger, 1988). The biographical characteristics of job candidates vary systematically across jobs (Heckman & Sedlacek, 1985; Blau, 1985). Filer (1986) has shown that standard personality test scores are strongly associated with occupational choices. In other words, jobs with certain characteristics tend to attract workers with similar characteristics.

Organizations may try to create situations where potential job candidates undertake actions that signal their characteristics to the outside market. This "signalling" argument (Spence, 1973) suggests, for example, that candidates might signal to employers that they can work hard under pressure by completing a rigorous MBA program. The importance of the degree, in this case, is not simply an indication of skills acquired but of underlying dispositions and characteristics. This general argument is sometimes known as the "screening hypothesis" when viewed from the employer's perspective. Miller and Volker (1984) present some interesting evidence for screening by noting that employers paid more for educational credentials even where the skills associated with the credentials were irrelevant to the job requirements. Similarly, both workers and organizations are concerned about their reputations which help them secure favorable matches. For workers, this concern might lead to more positive behaviors in order to prevent losing the investment they have made in the form of a good reputation from being lost (see Parsons, 1985 p. 800 for evidence). Some behaviors, therefore, may be attempts to send signals to the outside market.

Selection arguments may also help explain why jobs take the form that they do. Selection operates through the interaction of supply and demand, so employers adjust those job characteristics within their control—especially pay—in accordance with the supply of candidates from the outside environment. We know, for example, that jobs with higher probabilities of layoff pay premiums over other jobs (Abowd & Ashenfelter, 1981), that occupations with greater variance in earnings, indicating greater risk, tend on average to pay a premium (King, 1984), that more dangerous jobs pay premiums (Viscusi, 1980), etc. As Adam Smith (1776) first argued, pay and other job characteristics within the control of the organization are adjusted by management to compensate for characteristics that are more difficult to adjust in order to equate the supply of workers to the organization's demands. The extreme version of this argument would suggest that all jobs are equally desirable when a full accounting is taken of factors such as training costs, status, etc. While this is certainly unrealistic, we know, and as Krueger and Summers (1986) have shown, wages vary considerably across identical jobs in common labor markets, we also know that organizations are intensely interested in the pay and other conditions of jobs equivalent to theirs in organizations elsewhere and adjust those conditions according to changes in the outside market. This suggests another issue: The need to examine the patterns of attitudes and job behaviors as they relate to their respective labor markets. For example, job satisfaction may be more similar across jobs in the same labor market than across jobs in different labor markets even when the latter are within the same organization. It also suggests one mechanism through which events in the external environment affect the attitudes and behaviors of workers within an organization: Organizations may make systematic changes in their jobs in response to changes in outside labor markets.

Other Effects of the External Environment

The focus on job attitudes, absenteeism, and turnover should not suggest that the effects of the external environment are limited to these issues. We know, for example, that relative absence of alternative jobs with comparable wages is associated with lower discipline problems (Cappelli & Chauvin, forthcoming) and with higher performance levels (Raff & Summers, 1987), relationships sometimes referred to as "efficiency wages." Labor market conditions such as unemployment rates also affect levels of stress, suicide rates, and aspects of worker's physical and psychological health (see Jackson et al., 1983 for a brief survey); demographic trends such as the baby boom have powerful effects on a range of work issues, such as job and earning opportunities, as well as on nonwork-like experiences (Easterlin, 1980); factors such as religion (Tomes, 1984), ideology and culture (Schneider & Bonjean, 1983), and historical and cultural events (see Sewel, 1988 for a survey) also shape workplace behavior; even the way leadership can be exercised (Ford, 1981) is shaped by environmental constraints. Yet these contextual explanations have in general not been incorporated into the paradigm of OB research. As Near, Rice, and Hunt (1980 p. 416) conclude, hypotheses concerning the relationship between work responses and phenomena outside of one's job "have received little modern attention."

Summary

The arguments above suggest that the responses of individual employees are affected by the external environment, particularly developments in the labor market, in part because individuals in their role as workers maintain an attachment to the outside labor market in case they need to enter it. Employers may fail and dismiss their employees, workers may need to change jobs for family and nonwork reasons, and individuals are interested in and are always free to pursue job opportunities that are superior to those they currently have. Conditions in the labor market affect turnover directly, through the attractions of superior jobs, and indirectly through the effects of social comparisons, etc. on attitudes and on search. They also affect responses within the workplace such as expectations and attitudes, attendance, performance, etc. Clearly, these relationships vary depending on the degree of attachment that employees have to the external labor market. There is certainly a cultural component to that attachment: workers in feudal societies or even those in Japan who work in systems with lifetime employment norms are likely to have much less attachment to the outside labor market and to be less affected by it than are those in the United States where attachment to employers appears to be less. And, as will be argued in Section IV, attachment also varies across and within organizations depending on the nature of the employment relationship.

The arguments below consider the more complicated question as to why research in OB has abandoned consideration of contextual matters and the problems that raises for the field.

REASONS FOR THE ABSENCE OF CONTEXT

The research reviews outlined above suggest that the external environment plays an important role in determining individual behavior and that research in OB often ignores that role. In many cases, the development of research in the field has over time actually removed considerations of context from previous research traditions. The fact that this development occurred across a range of topic suggests that it was not due to random factors. As Roberts et al. (1978, p. 28) argue, "that some variables are systematically missing without explicit explanation is itself an interesting social phenomenon." This development is disturbing because it conflicts with what many would like to believe about how research paradigms advance—that theories are tested against the world as revealed through observation, are replaced by those that provide better explanations of the empirical world, and that current theories are therefore in some sense better than those that came before. Our arguments suggest that OB research has followed almost the reverse process, that by abandoning important explanations for individual behavior, research in OB may actually have gotten worse over time, at least by the standard of predictive power. This can happen because there are a range of criteria in addition to predictive power that govern the development of research, and competition between these criteria make it possible for all fields, including OB, to sacrifice empirically important arguments for the pursuit of other ends. The willingness to do so, however, depends on often unstated philosophical assumptions that may not be in the long-run interest of the field.

Paradigms as a Conservative Force

How could a scientific field like OB ignore relevant contextual arguments? Historians of science point out that many old theories now discarded, such as the philogistic theory of chemical compounds, were not thought during their reign to be contradicted by empirical observations, yet they now seem so obviously in conflict with the facts as to appear often laughable. These theories endured not so much because of the inability to develop empirical tests as because of the conservative role that existing paradigms play in scientific research. Paradigms can be defined as sets of questions, laws (well-accepted explanations), ontological commitments (i.e., what kind of things exist), and associated methods which operate within a broader topic area or discipline, as Newton's studies of mechanics are a paradigm within the field of physics. Thomas Kuhn (1970) describes how normal science which operates through paradigms resists change in part by limiting the field of relevant questions. "Relevant" questions include identifying new facts, such as the boiling points of materials in chemistry or correlates of job satisfaction in OB, and the subsequent efforts to measure them more carefully; efforts to resolve ambiguities in the paradigm and flesh it out with discoveries, for example, of physical constants such as the rate of acceleration in physics or the role of growth needs strength in need-based theories of job satisfaction; and finally, identifying empirical evidence to test the paradigm's laws.[16] Kuhn (1970, p. 25) refers to the empirical work that constitutes the majority of normal science as "mopping-up" work. Developing new or alternative explanations is not included in its set of relevant questions. As Roberts, Hulin, and Rousseau (1978, p. 26) assert, the OB paradigm "seriously limits the number and kind of variables studied or even considered." The limited set of acceptable topics for OB research to which some observers have objected (e.g., Staw & Oldham, 1978; Staw, 1984) and the subsequent lack of success in expanding that set are perfectly consistent with the resistance of paradigms to change.

Beyond limiting the list of relevant questions, the philosophical rules for assessing theories and determining their worth are perhaps the most important source of resistance to changes in paradigms. These rules are typically referred to as justification principles and can be though of as criteria for justifying the continued use of a theory or the acceptance of a new one. It is fair to say that there is no consensus about the relative importance of various justification principles, but there are several that have exerted a powerful influence on science (see Hempel, 1964 for the clearest statement of these justification principles).

The justification principle that is perhaps best known, at least implicitly, in the social sciences is that of falsification: paradigms should be developed so that they can be tested empirically by comparing it with observation.[17] By this view, theories fall into disrepute only when new facts are turned up which contradict their predictions, the third part of Kuhn's mopping up work, and it would seem difficult for existing paradigms like OB's to endure if they left out important parts of explanations. One difficulty with this position, however, is that normal science is unlikely to uncover facts that contradict the paradigm precisely because it is not looking for such facts. In Popper's phrase, all empirical work is "soaked in theory"—guided so thoroughly by theory that it is unlikely to seek out counterinstances which challenge that theory. Further, scholars are unlikely to notice such facts even if they trip over them without some framework to let them know what to look for. For example, there is considerable evidence that several scientists had produced oxygen before Lavoisier and Priestly, refuting the philogistic theory, yet these scientists had no reason to believe that "air" had any subcomponents and, as a result, ignored the findings or explained them away. Writing about the social psychology theories that also forms the basis of most OB research, McGuire (1969) argues that research was designed to produce the theorized relationships, not test them: When experimental results appeared to falsify theories, researchers typically found some error in the experimental design and redid the study to produce the desired effect. And in field studies, the goal was to find the right case that would produce the desired effect.

The second problem with the falsificationist view is that, in practice, it is often conveniently ignored when it threatens existing paradigms. Feyerabend (1988, Ch. 5) points out that the fundamental works in modern science— Copernicus's view of the solar system, Bohr's atomic model, Einstein's theory of relativity—have instances where they are clearly at odds with observed reality, and yet no one in these fields suggests throwing these theories out, which is the solution demanded by the falsification principle. Further, he argues that "there is not a single interesting theory that agrees with all the known facts in its domain" (p. 21). Instead, as McGuire (1969) notes about social psychology, what typically happens is that these conflicts are treated as anomalies and assumed to be uninteresting, externally invalid, etc. rather than as counterinstances which challenge the paradigm. If needed, various ad hoc hypotheses are added to address the complication. The approximations in Newtonian mechanics arose for exactly this reason, and Ptolemaic astronomy grew increasingly complicated as ad hoc explanations were added to deal with the contradictions in it that were uncovered by Copernicus.[18]

There is ample evidence in the OB research surveyed above that the lack of empirical support for theoretical approaches has not always influenced the direction of subsequent research. Gergen (1973) argued that the explanations offered for empirical results in the social psychology models underlying much of the OB paradigm were so inconsistent that what researchers were really doing was not science but history—a different explanation for each situation. Steiner (1986) finds that the consistency of results has not improved much in the period since Gergen wrote. Nor did poor results necessarily lead to new models. Fichman (1984) argues that the lack of support for the dominant satisfaction-based models of absenteeism led not to a search for new models but instead to a search for constraints that may have been preventing the satisfaction models from working. Roberts et al. (1978, Ch. 5) provide one of the best examples of the abandonment of falsification as a criterion, noting that models of selection based on individual attributes have a predictor validity of approximately zero once initial skills have been learned, and that no progress has been made in this area in 40 years. Yet they point out that new theories and arguments in selection have mainly been "tinkering" within the existing approaches. With respect to our arguments above, the fact that many OB studies failed to confirm existing theories when examined across organizational settings not only should have challenged the existing theories but should have suggested that context is an important factor that should be incorporated into OB theories. The lack of empirical support and the associated criticisms of theories had little effect on the paradigm. Even the most ambitious reforms generally amount to controlling for contextual effects, including them as limiting conditions (rather than examining them) so that the underlying models will provide better explanations. As Staats (1983, p. 128) argued in a broader discussion, "the criticism has had little effect. Psychology continues on its way, doing the same things it has always done. . . ."

The reason that paradigms are not abandoned when evidence refuting them is presented is that if they were thrown out, science would not know how to operate: Paradigms serve as a kind of road map for research, and until a new map is found, science proceeds with the old one even if a few roads turn out to be in odd places. As Roberts et al. (1978, p. 15) assert, we do not want to abandon what we have accepted as true simply because part of it turns out to be wrong (although that is what falsification demands). Only where a new theory arises and makes a competition with the existing paradigm possible are old paradigms likely to be replaced with new ones. Kuhn (1970) argues that even then, the old paradigm is overthrown only if the new version can demonstrate that there are big anomalies between the old version and reality. [19] For example, it was not until rationalization and information processing theories provided an alternative to the rational individual decision models that non-rational behavior—presumably always in abundance—was finally "discovered" in OB research. One could make similar arguments about the rise of behavioral intentions in OB models. [20] (Feyerabend (1988) cites J. S. Mill as describing this process more cynically in ecological terms: New paradigms take hold only after the supporters of the old ones die.)

The Consistency Condition

The most important justification principle for explaining the development of OB research and, in particular, the declining role of the external environment, is the consistency condition. In brief, this justification principle says that all new theories should be consistent with what is already known and accepted—with existing laws.[21] On its face, this condition makes perfect sense: it seems silly to take a new theory seriously if it has implications that we believe to be wrong. This view of scientific development, that progress is made through the steady accumulation of knowledge and ideas that build upon older work, is a very common and powerful view in science. Through its operation, however, the consistency condition exerts a powerful conservative influence on the development of research because it demands that new developments build on and be consistent with the existing paradigm.

The obvious difficulty with the consistency condition is that, looking historically, most of the accepted theories and knowledge to which new theories would be required to conform have turned out to be false: The Copernican view would never have come into being if it had been forced to be consistent with the accepted Ptolemaic theory nor would relativity if it had been made to conform to Newtonian mechanics. As Feyerabend (1988) points out, consistency gives an enormous amount of support to those theories that simply happened to turn up first: If the new theory had been thought of first, then the consistency condition would require the refutation of the old theory.[22] Indeed, it seems obvious that old theories could never be refuted and science could never progress if the consistency condition were strictly applied. Further, many currently accepted theories within the same paradigms have elements that are inconsistent with each other, that is, suggest contradictory explanations (see Dunheim, 1962). This implies, as Kuhn (1970, p. 96) notes, that "science does not tend toward the ideal that our image of its cummulativeness has suggested."

The reliance on the consistency condition as a justification principle helps explain why OB has found it increasingly difficult to incorporate an understanding of the external environment into its research. The first researchers in many of the now-traditional OB topics came from a variety of disciplinary backgrounds (indeed, many were not psychologists by training), and perhaps the only unifying theme in their research was the tendency to approach these topics nonparadigmatically in part because many of their studies were case-based, fact-gathering exercises where the ability to discover new relationships, including those associated with context, was not designed-away.[23] After World War I, however, psychology had much of the field to itself. The government had given psychology a big role in developing selection procedures for the military that gave it a head start on influencing manpower decisions in industry after the war (see, e.g., Jacoby, 1985, 1988).[24]

With little competition from other disciplines, psychology gradually began to mold the study of employment topics and the field of OB according to its paradigm. The disciplinary roots of OB are in social and personality psychology and industrial/organizational psychology, but it is clear that both social and I/O psychology have borrowed their theories very heavily from other areas of psychology and that their theoretical roots are virtually identical.[25] Staats (1983) outlines a hierarchy of fields within psychology in terms of the extent to which their theories build on each other with organizational issues at the top—viewed either as the least fundamental or the top of the food chain, depending on one's perspective. The difficulty is that the evolving paradigm in psychology, with which OB was striving to be consistent, saw a decreasing role for context and the external environment in its explanations for the reasons outlined below.

The Role of Individual and Cognitive Arguments

Certainly the main building block of the OB paradigm, which is common to virtually all psychology, is the focus on the individual as the unit of analysis. Allport's (1968) history of the psychology paradigm suggests that initial experiments with broader units of analysis eventually were abandoned in favor of the individual. Even in social psychology, where groups are an explicit focus, some researchers have taken this position to its extreme—methodological individualism—which argues that only the individual is real; "there is no group" (Konecni, 1979 p. 88).[26] All appearances of "social" or group behavior are really nothing but aggregations of individual behavior. Sampson (1977) suggests that the individual focus may be largely driven by cultural attitudes and may be an artifact of American research; specifically, that the focus of American values on individualism leads to a research focus on individuals.

Using the individual as a unit of analysis simply suggests that data on individuals becomes the dependent variable in research, and there is nothing in that formulation per se that would exclude a consideration of the external environment as independent variables. Indeed, founding scholars in OB like Lewin (1959, p. 100) argued that the external environment was a crucial part of the "psychological environment." The behavioralist paradigm explicitly focuses on individuals and their behavior as the response or dependent variable and the environment external to them as the stimulus or independent variables. But as reviewers such as Cartwright (1979) and Markus and Zajonc (1985) conclude, the behavioralist paradigm has in recent years given way in psychology to a cognitive paradigm. [Landman and Manis (1983) describe the development of cognitive approaches in psychology and its later arrival in OB.]

The rise of a cognitive paradigm in psychology and the efforts of OB researchers to be consistent with that paradigm represent the most important reason why OB has found it increasingly difficult to address the external environment. In addition to methodological individualism, cognitive arguments involve what Sampson (1981, p. 731) calls a subjectivist reduction where "The knower's psychological states, the ideas in his or her head, are held to be more important, more knowable, and more certain than any . . . objective properties of the stimulus situation." In such a model, as Ilgen and Klein (1989, p. 329) conclude, "the nature of the environment to which the individual responds is at least partially constructed by that individual." And it is not a great leap to suggest that objective accounts of the environment are therefore irrelevant. As Steiner (1986) notes, it is now rarely the case that research ever includes data from anything but participating observers—that is, data in the form of perceptions—despite the fact that more objective data have been proven useful in a wide range of previous research. This is in sharp contrast to earlier scholars of organizational issues who were suspicious of subjective judgments—"treacherous things to work with" as Homans (1950, p. 38) described them—and who preferred to use objective measures whenever possible.

Cummings (1981) argued that OB during the 1980s could draw either from social psychology or sociology for new theories and argued convincingly that OB would benefit from a more radical shift in the OB paradigm that would, for example, borrow from sociology to give a broader role to context. But he predicted, accurately, that OB would follow the former path because it would avoid challenges and conflicts with the underlying OB paradigm—an explicit application of the consistency principle. Cummings rightly describes this development as conservative and representing a cumulative view of how science develops. And Ilgen and Klein's (1989) review suggests that the individualist, cognitive paradigm from social psychology is now well on the way to being established in OB.

It is easy to see how the rise in OB of even implicit aspects of this cognitive paradigm could lead to a sharp reduction in concern with the external environment in OB research. If individuals construct their own images of the environment which vary across individuals, then why bother with the objective environment? The gradual rise of this paradigm in OB documented by Ilgen and Klein (1989) coincides closely with the gradual erosion in the role for context in OB research. Perhaps the best illustration of the application of the individualistic, cognitive paradigm in OB research comes with the limited discussion of organizational context, as close as OB typically gets to a consideration of the environment. When measures of the organizational environment such as climate are included in analyses, they typically are not measured directly but are included only through the perceptions of individuals. Certainly this makes for a messy measure—because of common method variance with responses such as satisfaction, because it is not clear whether the measure is an attribute of individuals, organizations, or some interaction of the two, etc. Roberts, Hulin, and Rousseau (1978, p. 32) explain why the practice continues: "the use of individual perceptions of environments is more consistent with past practices than use of more objective data referring to entities larger than individuals." In other words, despite being a poor measure, it is consistent with the paradigm.

Scholars in other areas of psychology have been sharply critical of the individualist, cognitive paradigm which, when pushed to its extreme, leads to very limited and often inappropriate approaches to research. House (1977) argues that excessive focus on individuals has inhibited efforts to reexamine group behavior while Steiner (1986) observes that it has helped eliminate the "social" concern in social psychology and, in turn, that field's uniqueness; Ross (1977) says that the neglect of contextual factors often leads this research to falsely attribute contextual effects to individuals (the "fundamental attribution error"); Steiner (1986) argues that the cognitive focus leads researchers to ignore less proximal but important influences on responses such as continuing events and relationships. Many scholars such as Cartwright (1979) and Sampson (1981) have argued that the neglect of the objective environment in cognitive approaches is a crucial omission because that environment not only provides the information for cognition but also helps structure the process of cognition which is not independent from the social and historical context in which the individual operates.

What makes OB distinct from other topics in psychology is that behavior and attitudes are influenced by membership in an organization, influenced by that context, and there is ample empirical evidence of such influence. The cognitive solution is to consider context, if at all, by measuring it as the perceptions of the participant. But perceptions are a poor measure of the external environment for a variety of reasons whose philosophical roots run deep.

The Problem of Phenomenalism

Philosophers at least since Bishop Berkeley have recognized that our perceptions, what philosophers refer to as sensa, are not always accurate representations of objective reality or even consistent representations over time and across individuals (see Hirst, 1959 for a critical review). Optical illusions helped establish that point in the study of perception. The great problem with the position that perceptions are not identical to objective reality, which is known as phenomenalism, is that it is very difficult to understand much about the nature of that external reality. In the extreme version, held by Berkeley and

other idealists, all that is real is our senses; our environment is completely
constructed by individual perceptions. But if this is so, then that environment
ceases to exist when we are not observing it. This view faces obvious empirical difficulties when, for example, closing our eyes fails to stop a speeding
Buick from hitting us.[27]

Linguistic phenomenalism more accurately represents the position of cognitive psychology; the external reality exists independently from our perceptions of it, but we can only know that reality through our perceptions (see
Ayer, 1940). The difficulty with this view in philosophy is that it is impossible
to provide an accurate and complete translation of objective reality strictly in
terms of perceptions, a problem with a practical counterpart in OB which we
examine below.[28]

Advocates of the cognitive approach described above might well argue that
their interest is simply to predict behavior, not to describe the external environment, and perceptions of that environment may serve quite well as
instruments of prediction.[29] The ultimate point behind such research, however, is to identify and establish relationships between individual responses
and the environment. Therefore, the problem with using perceptions is that it
makes it difficult to interpret what those relationships mean because we cannot be sure what the environment to which they refer is really like. The
problem can be illustrated by comparing research designed to *identify* cognitive outcomes, which does not suffer from this problem, to that using
perceptions and other cognitive outcomes as causal factors, which does suffer
from it.

In cases of research designed to explain the outcome of cognitive processes
(e.g., Staw, 1975; Caldwell et al., 1983), the objective environment enters as
an independent variable; variations in that environment across individuals
(e.g., some receive rewards while others do not) explain the variation across
individuals in cognitive responses such as job satisfaction. It is only because
we know what the objective environment is for individuals that we can conclude that their different responses are influenced by cognition. If we only
have the cognitive response—perceptions of the environment without information on the objective environment—we cannot tell whether differences in
those responses are due to different information, different dispositions, or
differences in the way information was processed (cognition). In other words,
it is not clear what the perceptual variable means because it is not clear what it
really measures.[30]

And this leads to philosophers' concerns about translating the external
world through perceptions. Unless we know the relationship between the
objective environment and perceptions of that environment, then the causal
chain dead-ends with the individual: We may know that perceptions differ, but

we do not know why. Indeed, we cannot even be certain that the root cause of the variance in responses lies within the individuals. We cannot even argue that "some people are different" as the cause because, for example, we cannot rule out that the variance is due to differences in information that the individuals possess. There is no explanatory relevance or reasoning behind the result. This is what the social psychology critics of the cognitive approach (e.g., Cartwright, 1979; Sampson, 1981) imply when they argue that the use of perceptions is a "black box" approach which sheds no light on how the cognitive conclusion is achieved.

The inability to know what factors beyond the individual shape perceptions means that information on perceptions alone is as a practical matter all but useless. As Schnieder (1985) notes, organizations are interested in variables over which they have control. Such variables concern context—the environment internal to the organization (such as culture and personnel policies) and the relationship between the organization and its external environment. And cognitive responses can only be influenced through variables external to the minds of the participants; even persuasion is external. To illustrate the problem, knowing how employees' perceptions of job characteristics shape job satisfaction is of little help to an organization unless it also knows how to shape those perceptions through changes in actual job characteristics. The organization cannot use information about the relationship between perceptions and satisfaction unless it also understands the link between perceptions and reality. And while perceptions could be used to predict satisfaction, it is no more difficult to get right to the point and simply measure satisfaction directly. Perceptions as prediction devices are only useful where they indicate something about the objective environment.

The behavioral intentions literature represents the most advanced development in the above position. It uses cognitive independent variables, which are themselves cognitive outcomes based presumably on perceptions (such as intentions to quit), in order to explain other cognitive outcomes. It is even less obvious how a statement about intentions relates to the external world than it is for perceptions: If we ask about perceptions of the availability of alternative jobs, for example, at least we know by definition that the perceptions refer to the labor market, but if we ask about intentions to quit, there is no way of knowing even the type of information that any individual might use to determine their intentions. Further, because cognition is implicitly involved in perceptions, in processing those perceptions into intentions, and then in making the response, it is impossible to sort out the respective role of each of these cognitive processes with a single response measure of intentions. The relationship is underdetermined because there are more variables than degrees of freedom.

The obvious way around the methodological problem raised by cognition is to examine the objective external environment and the cognitive perceptions of that environment. Then, as Gibbs (1979) argues, it is possible to begin examining the relationships between the environment, cognition, and individual responses. The recent trend in OB toward examining context only indirectly, through individual perceptions, has the advantage of making OB research more consistent with the underlying paradigm in psychology, but at the price of a reduction in explanatory power and increased difficulty in relating individual responses to relevant causal variables. And there is another, potentially more important price being paid by the absence of context in research: it makes it impossible to integrate OB and macro organizational theories into a common science of organizations.

The Need for a Bridge to Macro Research:

One of the justification demands for normal science is that paradigms contain theories that are at the very least not contradictory and preferably are reconcilable. A requirement for reconcilable theories is that they be commensurate, that is, refer to similar concepts and variables. And, ideally, some argue that a normal science should strive toward unified theory in the sense that all its theories are logically linked and can be reduced to a common set of explanations. We can illustrate the difficulties associated with incommensurate theories by describing what happened to industrial sociology, a field that had much in common with OB.

From the 1940s through at least the 1960s, there was substantial literature in industrial sociology that paralleled most of the topics central to the concerns of OB, such as absenteeism, turnover, and morale (attitudes), using research methods that were rigorous and sophisticated for the time and that produced many useful insights. This stream of research has had little, if any, influence on OB research even when the same topics are examined. One reason why industrial sociology had little influence on OB is that the methods of industrial sociology relied largely on factors external to the individual, although internal to organizations, for explanations (see Miller & Form, 1964 for a survey of this research). These include, for example, the structure of authority relations (e.g., Gouldner, 1954) and other external arguments that are inconsistent with the internal explanations of the psychological model. More importantly, industrial sociology appears to be dead as a field within sociology. This is despite the fact that it was certainly among the dominant fields in sociology and was the forerunner of organizational sociology which, in turn, is the discipline behind much of organizational theory. (Some observers suggest that Buraway (1979) is the last U.S. work in the industrial sociology tradition.)

Halaby (1986) argues that the dominant approach even in sociology to questions such as worker attachment is now a psychological model based on satisfaction and commitment (e.g., Lincoln & Kalleberg, 1986) and that there has for some time been an absence of uniquely sociological approaches to such questions.

Hirsch (1975) suggests the cause of industrial sociology's downfall was that it became inconsistent with the rest of sociology, in particular, with the study of the sociology of organizations. Hirsch argues that industrial sociology incorporated a "closed systems" approach where the environment of the organization was assumed away. Some industrial sociologists soon found, however, that there was considerable variance across industrial organizations that could not be explained without appealing to variations in the environments of those organizations (e.g., Woodward, 1965). This led to an "open systems" approach which studied "the dependence of the system in question upon the supersystem of which it is a part" (Katz & Kahn 1966, p. 58) and required "an emphasis on *external* variables as primary agents of social change" (Hirsch, 1975 p. 4, his emphasis). In other words, there was no link between the industrial sociologists' explanations of individual behavior within the organization and the organizational sociologists' understanding of how the environment shapes the organization. As Meyer (1978, pp. 4–5) notes, sociology then moved "away from studies of individual people and the effects of contextual or social structural variables on individuals and toward studies of interrelations among structural variables. . . ." The inability to make this link between micro and macro behavior is an equivalent problem for OB as we will see below.[31]

It is debatable whether there are contradictory theories in OB,[32] but there is no doubt that at present, macro and micro organization theories are not reconcilable at least in part because they are not commensurate. The expansion of organizational studies to include theories about organizations (e.g., Pfeffer & Salancik, 1978; Aldrich, 1979) came about not only because there was a demand from external constituencies for information about how to understand (and ultimately design) organizations but also because these new theories did not conflict with the existing micro paradigm which had little to say about organizations. These organizational theories saw the external environment as a powerful factor in explaining organizational phenomena (e.g., see the studies in Meyer, 1978). They share neither variables nor in most cases explanations with the micro-level theories. There is no way to relate macro theories, with their focus on the environment, to micro behavior, or vis a versa. At present, therefore, it is not possible to speak of micro and macro organization research as being in the same paradigm.

This is not a problem unique to OB. In physics, what many regard as the most highly developed of the sciences, the reigning micro theory (quantum mechanics) and the reigning macro theory (general relativity) are not commensurate. The search for the so-called "unified field theory," which would identify a hypothesized common force behind both general relativity and quantum mechanics is driven in part by the problems that an incommensurate micro and macro theory have for the notion of a common physics paradigm. Similarly in economics, macro and micro theory had been until recently largely incommensurate (e.g., assumptions such as market failures and various irrationalities in macro were not shared by micro) until economics dealt with this problem by abandoning the established macro explanations, perhaps the best example of the power of the consistency condition (see, e.g., Rosenberg, 1976).[33] Staats (1983) argues that one of psychology's most important goals should be to develop a unified theory in order to overcome its incommensurate paradigm and that even abandoning many currently accepted theories (i.e., nonbehavioral theories) would be a worthwhile price for achieving that goal.

Most efforts to develop links between micro and macro theories fortunately do not require abandoning existing paradigms but instead rely on "bridge statement" which develop theoretical relationships between existing macro and micro laws. The most transparent bridge statements may occur in economics when they are created by assumption: a firm's interests are simply the interests of its stockholders or, where individual interests are heterogeneous, as in unions, the organization's behavior is determined as if by ballots of its members ("median voter" models). True bridge statements, however, are not assumptions but are empirical claims, such as Boltzmann's expression of the entropy of gases in terms of the properties of molecules, and are derived from rich analysis of the micro and macro phenomena.

The entire field of organizational studies may be thought of as a bridge area between psychology and sociology. Coleman (1986) notes that arguments from macro explanans (e.g., Protestant value systems) to macro explanada (e.g., capitalism) are the characteristic problems for sociology while micro to micro arguments are the characteristic psychology problems (Sewell, 1988). The unique focus for organizational studies should therefore be the links between micro and macro phenomena: organizational behavior, with its micro emphasis, should focus on the relationship between macro causes and micro effects while organizational theory's focus should be on the relationship between micro causes and macro effects.[34] With the development of bridge statements in these areas, it would then be possible to think of organizational behavior and organizational theory as part of the same paradigm. More important, organizational studies would then become the important crossing ground for all behavioral sciences and might eventually make a unified behavioral science possible—from psychology to sociology. It would also make links to other fields possible. Industrial relations, for example, which focuses on the relationship between the external environment and the structures governing employment, could more easily be linked to OB once these bridge statements were developed.

THE MEZOSCOPIC LEVEL AS A BRIDGE

Organizational studies has given surprisingly little attention to the need to bridge micro and macro concerns, although Rousseau (1985) provides an important exception. She argues that "cross-level" studies (between macro and micro variables) are necessary if organizational research is to establish a unique identity. How context and related macro variables affect micro behavior represents bridge statements for OB and are our concern here. These bridge statements can be developed in two ways. First, as we have suggested throughout, the environment can have a direct affect on individual behavior because individuals have at least some potential relationship with the outside labor market independent of the relationship with their organization. With an explicit consideration of the environment in both macro and micro theories, we have come much closer to correspondence between them.[35]

The second approach, which is more consistent with the traditional notion of a bridge statement, is to identify a middle step in the macro-micro relationship: the environment shapes organizational characteristics and phenomena which in turn shape individual behavior and attitudes. The first part of that notion, that the environment shapes organizations, is the basis for a good deal of organizational theory (see Meyer, 1978; Scott, 1981 for surveys). The gap is with the second part, the link between organizational phenomena and individual behavior and attitudes. Yet there is already a substantial body of evidence that such phenomena do play an important role in organizational behavior. Herman and Hulin (1972) summarize the early research showing relationships between structure and attitudes and behavior, and Rousseau (1978) points to previous research which suggests that organizational characteristics may be better predictors of certain attitudes than are individual characteristics, the traditional focus of OB research; Berger and Cummings (1979) review the few studies of organizational structure, updating a similar review by Porter and Lawler (1965), and are somewhat less impressed than Rousseau but nevertheless find considerable support for a relationship between structure and attitudes and behavior; Pfeffer's (1983) review of the demography literature concludes that the compositional characteristics of organizations have an important effect on individual behavior as well as the performance of organizations; Hulin and Roznowski's (1985, p. 64) review of research on technology also finds several relationships with individual behavior and attitudes.

This kind of bridging research is not without its problems, however. Rousseau's (1985) general observation that cross-level research suffers from a lack of theory is supported by the above reviews. Hulin and Roznowski (1985, p. 53) note, for example, that most of the results found so far between organizational structure and individual responses have been trivial because we do not understand the intervening factors. Berger and Cummings (1979) echo Porter and Lawler's (1965) concern about methodological problems with this line of research, especially that fact that many studies lack conceptual analysis for linking macro and micro variables. As Rousseau (1978) notes, evidence continues to mount that organizational context is an important factor in organizational behavior, but the underlying reasons are not understood. But the fact that these studies found important relationships even without any theory to guide them suggests that the underlying relationships must be significant.

Internal Labor Markets

The conceptual problem of establishing a bridge between organizational context and individual responses is really a problem of finding mechanisms through which context can affect the individual. Earlier in the paper, we suggested that individual behaviors and attitudes were affected directly by the external labor market. Because individual employees have contact with the outside labor market independent of their organizational affiliation, the mechanism in these cases is clear.

But the effects of the external environment are not always desirable for employers or their employees, and both parties may have interests in reducing such effects by insulating employment from the external environment. They do so by creating institutions and employment arrangements that "buffer" employment, protecting it from the uncertainty of the external environment. The arguments below suggest that the characteristics of these institutions moderate and, in effect, redefine the external environment for employees, helping in turn to shape their attitudes and behaviors. These employment institutions provide the "mesoscopic" link between organizational and individual-level analyses.

To better understand the need for these employment institutions, consider what things are like in their absence, if employment was organized around the model of an auction or "spot" market where workers have little attachment to any employer. Employers would see workers as interchangeable and rely on the external market to meet their needs. The market for casual labor as in agriculture or the temporary help industry fits this pattern as do some segments of highly-skilled occupational markets such as nursing or computer operators/programmers in tight regional markets like Silicon Valley. With contractions in external demand, employees are laid off; with expansions, many employees quit as alternatives elsewhere improve. The uncertainty associated with employment makes like very difficult for both employees and their employers, and planning becomes very difficult to do.

More importantly for the concerns of OB, the attitudes and behaviors of employees in this unbuffered world are now almost entirely driven by external concerns over which the organization has no influence. Because workers spend little time with any given employer and see their careers moving in and out of the market, comparisons are externally-based as are expectations and attitudes. Developments in the outside labor market and in the society as a whole—including not only changes in market wages and working conditions but also political developments such as rising class consciousness—have an exaggerated effect on attitudes and behavior. Especially where employees are not perfect substitutes, organizations have an interest in reducing the uncertainty associated with the auction-type labor market and increasing the control they can exercise over attitudes and behaviors. The employee relations practices of Japanese firms in the United States and of new greenfield plants provide excellent examples of attempts to insulate their employees from attitudes and expectations prevailing in the external community toward work.

Thompson (1967) argues that organizations create institutional buffers to protect their central or "core" technologies from the uncertainty associated with the external environment and substitute influences internal to the organization. Human resources can certainly qualify as components of a "core" technology (well-connected sales people, e.g. or key doctors in a hospital) that must also be protected, and internal labor markets do that by definition by reducing the influence and uncertainty exerted by the external market over employment decisions. Historical accounts of the rise of employment institutions and the personnel bureaucracies for running them (Kochan & Cappelli, 1984; Jacoby, 1985; Baron et al., 1987) suggest that uncertainty concerning the external environment—high rates of turnover, problems in acquiring skills, challenges from unions, legal challenges from the government—played the major role in their development.

An internal labor market can be defined as arrangements which reduce the influence of the external market over employment decisions such as promotions, skill acquisition, compensation, and job design. Within this general definition are a bewildering set of specific definitions of ILMs that vary depending on which aspects of employment one wishes to emphasize. Most researchers agree, however, that ILMs have the following characteristics: "job ladders" with hiring at one or a limited number of entry-level jobs and higher-level positions filled through promotion, job security, seniority as an important rule governing employment decisions, wages attached to jobs rather than workers and protected from market variations, and firm-specific training.[36]

Each of these aspects of ILMs buffers some aspect of the external environment, structuring alternatives, shaping referents, etc., and, in the process, producing effects on employee behavior and attitudes. Because these effects operate by countering the effects of the external labor market, they are most powerful for those behaviors and attitudes where the external environment exerted the largest role—turnover for job behaviors and commitment for attitudes. Consider the following relationships between ILMs and employee reactions:

- Job security. Low job security encourages employees to search for jobs outside the organization and therefore makes it more likely that they will find a better job and leave, independent of their satisfaction with their current job. Explicit job security not only reduces search and turnover directly but also makes it easier for employees to envision careers within the organization and to make the investment that will tie them more closely to their employer.
- Specific skills. More organization-specific skills tie the worker more closely to the organization, making it difficult to leave by reducing the fit between the worker's skills and the demands of jobs elsewhere. These skills are an example of the "side bets" which increase behavioral commitment. They also increase commitment in the sense described by Salancik (1977) by reducing opportunities to leave. Osterman (1984) argues that the combination of ILMs and specific skills creates incentives for both organizations and workers to develop idiosyncratic mixes of skills unique to the organization, mixes that typically lead to much broader jobs. The extent to which jobs provide a variety of tasks and demand a broader range of skills is an important job characteristic that may have significant effects on job attitudes (Hackman & Oldham, 1976).
- Seniority. Basing employment decisions on seniority explicitly reduces turnover and increases behavioral commitment by increasing the rewards associated with long service. Further, the use of objective decision rules like seniority may reduce the perceived inequity that many workers report about such decisions by reducing the subjective component of decisionmaking.
- Contracts. Economists argue that employers may reach implicit agreements with employees which involve a kind of contract; the organization

will protect their jobs and wages from business downturns and other external shocks to the organization, and in return, the employees will stick with the organization in expansions and will manifest greater loyalty and commitment. Such arguments are at the heart of paternalistic employment policies and represent an application of exchange theory. All decision rules governing employment such as contracts have the ability to shape referents as Goodman (1974) discovers and, in turn, shape expectations and attitudes.

- Promotion from within. Internal promotions are one of the rewards that encourage staying with the organization and have been found to reduce quit rates (Peterson & Spilerman, 1990). Promotion as a reward can also be used to reinforce a range of desired behavior such as improved job performance. It also makes it possible for individuals to envision an entire career within the same organization where they can take on a series of roles over time (Super & Hall, 1978), making the organization more attractive for recruiting, reducing turnover for career reasons, and increasing satisfaction as influenced by the match between individual needs and job demands. The other side of good internal promotion prospects is that they may make external offers unattractive and unrealistic options, increasing commitment by limiting options, as noted above. The possibility of promotion may also help shape workers' referents, causing them to identify with the interests of those further up the organizational ladder and to reduce their identification with coworkers in similar jobs. Among nonsupervisory workers, this pattern of identification can be thought of as reducing class consciousness and interest in unions. Identifying one's interests with those of higher-level officials, as opposed to the immediate concerns associated with one's current position, is what many implicitly mean by commitment.
- Compensation. The structure of compensation can be used to increase the attachment to the firm through, for example, seniority-based pay (Lazear, 1979) or through the structure of pensions which play a major role in reducing quits. Compensation can also reinforce desired job behaviors such as reducing absenteeism by rewarding attendance.
- Socialization. The longer employees are with an organization and the longer they expect to be, the more effective the organization can be in socializing those employees toward the values of the organization. One important goal of such socialization is to shape the referents of employees—toward those, for example, that will make them feel equitably treated. For example, management tries to shape the referents of lower-paid, 'B' tier workers toward similar workers in other firms and away from more senior, higher paid workers in the same firm in order to

reduce their perceived inequity (Cappelli & Sherer, 1990). Halaby (1978) finds that workers who have been in an organization longer have different views on how important different criteria should be in employment decisions such as promotions.

This list of relationships is illustrative rather than exhaustive as there are obviously many other characteristics of ILMs that could affect employee responses. Organizations with few or none of these characteristics correspond to the "secondary" labor markets described by Doeringer and Piore (1971). They argue that employees in such labor markets have high rates of turnover and absenteeism, little if any attachment to the employer, and often poor attitudes toward their jobs. At the other extreme, organizations with many of these characteristics fit Walton's (1985) definition of "high commitment" employers where workers have strong attachments—attitudinal as well as behavioral—and very positive work attitudes. Hulin and Rosnowski (1985) note that such relationships may also differ within organizations, that the responses of workers in lower-level jobs are governed more by job and organizational characteristics than are many upper-level jobs where the external environment is more important. Presumably this is because upper-level jobs such as the professions make greater use of the external labor market.

The topic of ILMs provides an especially good bridge area between micro and macro research because there is already a developing macro literature seeking to identify characteristics of ILMs with aspects of the external environment (e.g., Pfeffer & Cohen, 1984; Baron, Davis-Blake, & Bielby, 1986). But there are other bridge areas as well.

Unions and Other External Influences

The arguments about internal labor markets above suggest how organizations adjust to the external environment by creating employment structures that in turn affect individual responses. But the external environment itself may create such structures directly. For example, arguably the most common structural characteristic of employment in the United States is the distinction between exempt and nonexempt jobs, sometimes referred to as white and blue collar, because it creates different treatment in matters of pay and work schedules, different comparisons and expectations, and as a result often a sharp division between the two groups. Yet as Cappelli and Sherer (1989) observe, that distinction is created by labor law—the Fair Labor Standards Act—which is certainly part of the environment external to the organization. Similarly, occupational labor markets (separate markets for craft skills, e.g.) and external certification of skills and competencies (certified public accountants, e.g.) help shape how jobs are defined within organizations, prospects for mobility within and across firms, etc., and also are part of the external environment. The examination of how external forces shape the way employment is structured is the central theme of industrial relations where there is a long literature illustrating how the social and legal environment, technology, and market forces in particular shape employment (see Dunlop, 1957 for the seminal taxonomy).

Perhaps the most powerful external force shaping the structure of employment within organizations is organized labor. In a twist on Thompson's (1967) argument, workers (as a core technology) organize to create their own buffers from the external environment. Not surprisingly, the external environment which creates the need for internal labor markets also shapes the growth of unions and their structure: The seminal econometric model of union growth by Ashenfelter and Pencavel (1969) shows, for example, that higher unemployment in the previous recession is positively related to union growth as is inflation—workers organize to seek protection from both unemployment and inflation.[37] Farber and Saks (1980) find evidence that workers voting for unions do so because they want protection from the uncertainty associated with arbitrary management decisions. Characteristics of product markets have been shown to determine the shape of unions as organizations, expanding, for example, to cover all workers among competing firms as those product markets change (e.g., Ulman, 1958).

Through collective bargaining, unions help create many of the characteristics of internal labor markets that shape individual responses. And there is evidence that unionization effects the employment-related responses of its members. For example, quit rates tend to be significantly lower in unionized organizations even after controlling for better wages and conditions (e.g., Blau & Kahn, 1983). Further, quit rates fall for a given worker when they join a union but rise once they leave the union (Mincer, 1983). Unions also affect employee attitudes such as job satisfaction. Sherer's (1989) survey of the literature indicates that most studies find lower job satisfaction among union members even after controlling for employee characteristics. Part of this effect might be due to the job characteristics that are associated with union shops: Pfeffer and Davis-Blake (1986) provide controls for jobs and then find a positive relationship between unions and satisfaction. There is, for example, evidence that jobs are narrower, faster-paced, and less pleasant in union settings (Duncan & Stafford, 1980; Kochan & Helfman, 1981), suggesting that unions are working with jobs that are intrinsically less satisfying to begin with.

Other evidence suggests, however, that unions can play a direct role in shaping employee responses. Cappelli and Sherer (1988) find, for example, that the extent to which workers received their information about employment issues from the union was inversely related to satisfaction. As Mills (1948) argues, unions exist to channel discontent and use it (along with the threat of strikes driven by it) in order to secure changes from management. They can manage dissatisfaction not only by pointing out existing problems but, more importantly, by shaping comparisons and expectations. To illustrate, consider the conflicting tasks facing the union in shaping the attitudes of its members during collective bargaining. First, it must generate dissatisfaction with current conditions in order to persuade members to strike (but not to the point where member expectations will be difficult to meet) and then convince its members that conditions are good enough to end the strike, ratify the new contract, and go back to work. The new contracts are rarely different enough to explain the rather dramatic reversals in worker attitudes and behaviors— from striking to ratification—without the role played by unions in managing expectations and behaviors—from striking to ratification—without the role played by unions in managing expectations and attitudes.[38] Cappelli and Sterling (1988) find, for example, that union members vote down collective bargaining contracts, other things being equal, when unions have poor institutional relations with management.

This still leaves the following puzzle: If union members are generally less satisfied (for whatever reason), why are their quit rates lower? The mainstream OB approach to turnover, which relies on dissatisfaction, has a very difficult time explaining this. It is less difficult to understand with the focus on context developed above. First, unions introduce changes in the employment relationship that reduce the opportunities to move. They do this in part by establishing "side bets" in the form of benefits that tie workers to the firm, such as pensions and seniority-based terms and conditions (e.g., higher wages, better job choice, etc.). More generally, the fact that wages and benefits are higher in union firms may make it difficult to find alternatives that workers can afford to take without cuts in their standard of living. Second, unions also create institutions that provide alternatives to quitting as a way of dealing with dissatisfaction. These "voice" mechanisms include not only collective bargaining, but also arrangements for addressing the concerns of individual workers such as grievance procedures (Freeman and Medoff, 1984). And there is evidence that these mechanisms do reduce turnover (e.g., Kraft, 1986).

The institutions governing employment—external structures such as legislation, union negotiated practices, and organization-created ILMs—have important effects on employee responses through their ability to structure referents and expectations, opportunities and alternatives, rewards, and other employment events. These institutions provide an important bridge between the external environment and individual responses and between macro and micro research more generally because they are both shaped by the external environment (a macro relationship) and affect individual behavior (a micro relationship).

CONCLUSION

The arguments above suggest that research in OB has systematically abandoned contextual arguments in order to remain consistent with theoretical developments in the field of psychology. The abandonment of context comes despite substantial and wide-spread evidence of important relationships between contextual factors and the behavior of individual employees in organizations. The rise of cognitive approaches in OB research which systematically exclude considerations of the external environment leave the field with some interesting choices. If it continues on its current cognitive path, the field of OB is likely to miss the chance to establish any independent identity. What is unique about behavior in organizations is presumably that being in the organization—the context of the organization—somehow shapes behavior, and it is impossible to explore that uniqueness without an explicit consideration of context. Further, this direction will cut OB off not only from the rest of organizational studies but indeed the rest of the social sciences and the natural sciences as well, where research focuses on understanding the objective environment, and makes it much more difficult to establish links with those sciences. The alternative path of an explicit consideration of contextual issues involves a relatively minor departure from consistency with the psychological paradigm but offers better predictions, new sets of theories, and the opportunity to develop a unique role for OB as a bridge area between the behavioral disciplines of psychology and sociology.

ACKNOWLEDGMENTS

The authors are listed in order of their contribution to the manuscript. Thanks to Bob House, Christopher Kulp, Charles O'Reilly, Karlene Robert, George Strauss, and the editors for helpful comments. The first author received support from the Institute of Industrial Relations at the University of California at Berkeley for this research.

NOTES

1.   We use OB to refer to micro organizational behavior, organizational theory to refer to macro research, and organizational studies to refer to the combined micro-macro field.

2.   Some smaller fraction of OB research examines relationships between organizational characteristics and individual behavior, and for this research, context is just the environment external to the organization.

3.   While we recognize the range of additional topics in OB research, these employment issues are thought by many to be central to the field (e.g., Staw 1984).

4.   One individual characteristic, growth needs strength, is allowed to vary in the Hackman and Oldham model (1976) which makes it relatively unique in attempting to measure some aspects of the match from both sides (albeit as experienced by the individual). Matching tends to be much more of a concern to selection studies (e.g., Schneider, 1978, 1987) than satisfaction.

5.   Individuals may exert influence that helps shape their jobs, but the jobs and their characteristics are still external to those individuals.

6.   Important exceptions include Patchen (1961) and Goodman (1974), although most of these studies are limited to issues of pay.

7.   One problem with this study is that the measure for absenteeism is limited to days workers claimed to be absent due to illness, controlling for industry differences in sickness and accident rates. Other reported reasons for absence, such as personal days, might be a better predictor of truly voluntary absence.

8.   The cost associated with a fixed probability of job loss is higher when alternatives are less available, however, and that may create incentives to behave at work in ways that reduce the likelihood of being dismissed for cause such as reducing absenteeism. But presumably this explanation should only hold for those workers with absentee levels high enough to risk dismissal.

9.   As noted below, however, not all quits appear to be equally motivated by the attractions of alternative jobs. For such quits, we might expect the factors explaining them to be similar to those explaining absenteeism.

10.   Economists generally use the turnover to refer to involuntary layoffs and use quits for voluntary withdrawal. They focus more on layoffs—the firm's decision—while OB focuses more on quits—the worker's decision.

11.   There is a caveat to this argument, however. Stoikov and Raimon (1968) point out that high unemployment rates within one's own industry and firm may be directly associated with the quit rate because they signal to employees that the future for these organizations is bleak. This is likely to be the case where skills are not industry-specific so that opportunities are not limited to one's industry and associated with its current health.

12.   Because unemployment insurance characteristics vary by state, we should expect such effects to operate only on state-level variables.

13.   Assuming that the organizations are also "searching," trying out workers and dismissing those who do not fit, the matching process becomes quite complicated and takes on elements of what is sometimes referred to in the decision science literature as "the two-armed bandit problem": The information used by both job candidates and employers depends on each other's search.

14.   Pensions in these jobs tend to accommodate earlier retirement, and this can be seen as a compensating differential for less desirable jobs, a point we take up below.

15.   Mobley et al. (1979) consider intentions to search as part of the decision process and Price (1977) comes closest, considering the expected utility from search. But no behavioral studies that we know of examine search per se.

16.   Such situations are much more common in OB than in some of the natural sciences. For example, there are only a handful of situations where the theory of relativity in physics can be tested.

17.   The extreme version, advanced by Karl Popper (1968), suggests that falsification is the

most important consideration. Other characteristics of a theory (e.g., whether it appears to make "sense" intuitively) are much less relevant in judging its worth. Friedman (1966) is often thought to have made a similar argument for economics by relying on empirical tests as the basis for judging the truth of theories. Friedman in fact argued that the quality of assumptions—whether they corresponded to reality—used in empirical tests could be ignored along with a priori judgments about the quality of the underlying theory because the empirical test was all that mattered. The problem with this argument, however, is that if the assumptions do not accurately represent empirical reality, then it is no longer clear what the tests are actually measuring. The fact that a large proportion of current research in economics consists simply of models of hypotheses without any empirical tests suggests that the most important justification rule now in economics is internal consistency.

18.   These examples also illustrate the justification criterion known as conventionalism: more complicated theories should be abandoned in favor of simpler ones, in this case, relativity and Copernican theories, respectively. See Feyerabend (1988, p. 49) for a discussion.

19.   That may not always be a sufficient condition, however. For example, Newtonian mechanics generated relatively few comparatively small anomalies and yet was overthrown; the Copernican view of the solar system was not obviously better than the Ptolemaic approach when it was introduced. Other factors may also play a role as we will see.

20.   Specifically, the lack of empirical support for hypothesized links between job attitudes and behaviors combined with new arguments about the need to incorporate the effects of cognition to produce this approach. See Zen and Fishbind (1977).

21.   This condition should not be confused with truth-correspondence or falsification requirements which suggest that theories should correspond to empirical reality. The two are not in conflict, although they clearly compete for relative importance. Again, see Hempel (1964).

22.   More formally, if new theory B implies results that conflict with existing theory A in some areas, the consistency condition implies rejecting theory B, and the rejection presumably is based on theory A's results in other areas which may not yet have been examined. (See Feyerabend, 1988 p. 25.)

23.   Many of the best examples of these studies come from the Harvard Business School and would include, for example, the Western Electric studies (e.g., Roethlisberger, 1939).

24.   Economics, which had examined some of these issues, temporarily withdrew into a set of employment topics associated with unions (this tradition became separated from economics when a group of labor scholars split from the American Economic Association to form the Industrial Relations Research Association in 1947).

25.   Steiner (1986, p. 279) suggests that the borrowing in social psychology has been so thorough that "social psychology is hard to recognize" or distinguish from these other areas. Stagner (1981) notes that many of the famous figures in I/O psychology did their initial theses and work in other areas of psychology.

26.   Campbell (1958) presents an interesting attempt to sort out on something like empirical grounds whether groups exist separately as entities from individuals. He concludes that they do not, but the test he applies from the physical sciences is more restrictive than most philosophers would demand.

27.   The problem of the nature of objects when they are not being perceived is called fragmentariness. Berkeley dealt with this problem by arguing that God caused the objective world to continue to exist when we were not perceiving it.

28.   One can get a sense of the difficulty by trying to describe a material object so that it cannot be mistaken for any other object without using terms associated with the object itself, e.g., describe a book without saying "booklike" or "pages," but relying strictly on perceptions. Because perceptions may differ by location, time, environmental conditions, etc., there may be

an almost infinite number of separate perceptions that would be needed to accurately describe any given object. There are other problems as well (see Hirst, 1959 for a survey).

29. The essays in Royce and Rozenboom (1972) provide an interesting interchange between the ideas of philosophers and psychologists in the area of perception.

30. Economics faced a similar cognitive problem concerning the expectations of individuals which a priori could vary across individuals and differ from those determined rationally given objective data. The problem was assumed away with the device of "rational expectations" where all expectations approximate what should rationally be expected to occur.

31. It is interesting to note that industrial relations suffered from a related problem. The established paradigm relied on forces external to the organization for its explanations and were unable to explain recent events. The creation of a role for organization-level effects in industrial relations came as a result but also to help make the field more consistent with developing literatures in fields such as strategy (see Kochan, McKersie, & Cappelli, 1984). Coleman (1986) offers an additional argument for the decline of approaches like industrial sociology, that there has been a general shift in sociology in the unit of analysis toward individuals and a move away from social and community-based explanations toward psychological and demographic ones driven in part by statistical tools which are based on samples of individuals and generalizations about populations; there has been no equivalent development of tools for analyzing interacting systems of interdependence.

32. For example, theories of rationalization and rational individual decisionmaking do suggest contradictory hypotheses, but the question is whether the initial conditions can accurately differentiate which hypothesis should govern in individual cases.

33. There are other factors in these developments as well, perhaps the most important being an explicit reductionist assumption that "group" phenomena can be explained by theories of individual behavior—for physical compounds and social behavior as well. See Cappelli (1985).

34. Behling (1978) makes a similar argument that what sets OB apart from sociology or psychology is the study of relationships across different levels.

35. Rousseau (1985) points out several fallacies associated with efforts of this kind, most of which turn on the failure to recognize differences between group and individual behavior. (For example, "ecological fallacies" where individual behavior is assumed to be the same as for the group as a whole and "cross-level fallacies" where groups are treated as if they were individuals. The latter is better known as "the fallacy of composition.") The problem most relevant to our efforts here is what she calls the "fallacy of the wrong level" where the true nature of hypothesized effects changes at different levels. Roberts, Hulin, and Rousseau (1978, p. 87) argue that different specifications for relationships are needed at different levels of analyses and refer to rules specifying these different relationships as compositional theories.

36. Most of these concepts were assembled first by Doeringer and Piore (1971), and subsequent authors have emphasized some subset of characteristics; Williamson (1975) with specific skills, Piore (1975) with job security, Osterman (1984) with wages attached to jobs, Cappelli and Cascio (1989) with wages protected from market variations, etc. Althauser and Kelleberg (1981) review much of this literature.

37. Anderson, O'Reilly, and Busman (1980) use a similar model to explain union decline through decertification elections. Other external factors, such as changes in the legal and political environment, have also been found to play a role in union organizing (see Addison & Burton, 1985 Ch. 3).

38. When generating support for strikes, unions will emphasize external comparisons such as the conditions at other companies. When generating support for ratification, they often switch to internal comparisons such as the previous contract, management's ability to pay, etc.

REFERENCES

Abowd, J. M. & O. Ashenfelter. (1981). Anticipated unemployment, temporary layoffs, and compensating wage differentials. In S. Rosen (Ed.), *Studies in Labor Markets,* Chicago: University of Chicago Press, :141–170.

Adams, J. S. (1963). Toward an understanding of inequity. *Journal of Abnormal and Social Psychology, 67* :422–436.

Akerlof, G. A., A. K. Rose, & J. L. Yellen. (1988). Job switching and job satisfaction in the U.S. labor market. *Brookings Papers on Economic Activity, 2* :495–582.

Aldrich, H. (1979). *Organizations and Environments.* Englewood Cliffs, NJ: Prentice-Hall.

Allen, S. G. (1981). An empirical model of worker attendance. *Review of Economics and Statistics, 63* :77–87.

Allport, G. W. (1968). The historical background of modern social psychology. In G. Lindzey and E. Aronson (Eds.), *Handbook of Social Psychology, Reading, MA: Addison-Wesley, 1* (2nd ed.), :1–80.

Althauser, R. P. & A. L. Kallenberg. (1981). Firms, occupations, and the structure of labor markets: A conceptual analysis. In I. Berg (Ed.), *Sociological Perspectives on Labor Markets,* New York: Academic Press, :119–149.

Anderson, J. C., C. A. O'Reilly III, & Gloria B. Busman. (1980). Union decertification in the U.S.: 1974–1977. *Industrial Relations, 19* (Winter) :100–107.

Antel, J. J. (1988). Inter-related quits: An empirical analysis of the utility maximizing mobility hypothesis. *Review of Economics and Statistics,* (February) 1 :17–22.

Ashenfelter, O. & J. H. Pencavel. (1969). American trade union growth: 1900–1960. *Quarterly Journal of Economics, 83* (3) :434–448.

Austin, W., N. McGinn, & C. Susmilch. (1980). Internal standards revisited: Effects of social comparisons and expectancies of fairness and satisfaction. *Journal of Experimental and Social Psychology, 16* :426–441.

Ayer, A. J. (1958). *The Foundations of Empirical Knowledge,* (New York: St. Martin's Press.

Baron, J. N., F. R. Dobbins, and P. D. Jennings. (1986). War and peace: The evolution of modern personnel administration in U.S. industry. *American Journal of Sociology, 92* :350–383.

————, A. Davis-Blake, & W. T. Bielby. (1986). The structure of opportunity: how promotion ladders vary within and across organizations," *Administrative Science Quarterly, 31* :248–262.

Bartel, A. P. (1981). Race differences in satisfaction: A reappraisal. *Journal of Human Resources, 16* :422–436.

Becker, H. S. (1960). Notes on the concept of commitment. *American Journal of Sociology, 66* :32–42.

Behling, O. (1978). Some problems in the philosophy of science of organizations. *Academy of Management Review, 3* :193–201.

Berger, C. J. & L. L. Cummings. (1979). Organizational structure, attitudes, and behaviors. In B. M. Staw (Ed.), *Research in Organizational Behavior,* Greenwich, CT: JAI Press, *1* :169–208.

Berkowitz, L. C. Fraser, P. F. Treasure, & S. Cochran. (1987). Pay, equity, job gratifications, and comparisons in pay satisfaction. *Journal of Applied Psychology, 72* (4) :544–551.

Blau, D. M. (1983). Self-Employment and self-selection in developing country labor markets. *Southern Journal Of Economics, 52* (2) :351–363.

Blau, F. D. & L. M. Kahn. (1983). Unionism, seniority, and turnover. *Industrial Relations, 22* (3) :362–373.

Blood, M. R. & C. L. Hulin. (1967). Alientation, environmental characteristics, and worker responses. *Journal of Applied Psychology, 51* :284–290.

Brett, J. M. & A. H. Reilly. (1988). On the road again: Predicting the job transfer decisions. *Journal of Applied Psychology, 73* (4) :614–620.

Brickman, P. (1975). Adaptation level determinants of satisfaction with equal and unequal outcomes in skill and chance situations. *Journal of Personality and Social Psychology, 32* (2) :191–198.

Bull, C., O. Ornati, & P. Tedeschi. (1987). Search, hiring strategies, and labor market intermediaries. *Journal of Labor Economics, 5* :s1–s35.

Buraway, M. (1979). *Manufacturing Consent: Changes in the Labor Process Under Capitalism.* Chicago: University of Chicago Press.

Burton, J. F., Jr. & J. E. Parker. (1969). Inter-industry variations in voluntary labor mobility. *Industrial and Labor Relations Review, 22* :199–216.

Caldwell, D. F., C. A. O'Reilly III, & J. H. Morris. (1983). Responses to an organizational reward: A field test of the sufficiency of justification hypothesis. *Journal of Personality and Social Psychology, 44* :506–514.

Campbell, D. T. (1958). Common fate, similarity, and other indices of the states of aggregates of persons as social entities. *Behavioral Science, 3* :14–25.

Cappelli, P. (1985). Theory construction in industrial relations: Some implications for research. *Industrial Relations, 24* :90–112.

——— & P. D. Sherer. (1988). Satisfaction, market wages, and labor relations: An airline study. *Industrial Relations, 27* (1) :56–74.

———. (1989). Spanning the union/nonunion boundary. *Industrial Relations, 28* (2) :206–226.

———. (1990). Assessing worker attitudes under a two-tier wage plan. *Industrial and Labor Relations Review.*

——— & K. Chauvin. (forthcoming). An inter-plant test of the efficiency wage hypothesis. *Quarterly Journal of Economics.*

———. (forthcoming). An efficiency model of the grievance process. *Industrial and Labor Relations Review.*

——— & W. F. Cascio. (1989). Internal labor markets and wages: Tests of skill, tournament, and power models. OB/IR Working Paper, U.C.: Berkeley.

Carsten, J. M. & P. E. Spector. (1987). Unemployment, job satisfaction, and employee turnover: A meta-analytic test of the Muchinsky model. *Journal of Applied Psychology, 72* :374–381.

Cartwright, D. (1979). Contemporary social psychology in historical perspective. *Social Psychology Quarterly, 42* :83–93.

Clegg, C. W. Psychology of employee lateness, absence, and turnover: A methodological critique and an empirical study. *Journal of Applied Psychology, 68* (1) :88–101.

Chadwick-Jones, et. al. (1982). *The Social Psychology of Absenteeism.* New York: Praeger.

Coleman, J. S. (1986). Social theory, social research, and a theory of action. *American Journal of Sociology, 91* (6) :1309–1335.

Coser, R. A. & D. R. Dalton. (1983). Equity theory and time: A reformulation. *Academy of Management Review, 8* :311–319.

Cummings, L. L. (1981). Organizational behavior in the 1980s. *Decision Sciences, 12* :365–377.

———. (1982). Organizational behavior. *Annual Review of Psychology, 33* :541–579.

Dalton, A. & J. G. Marcus. (1987). Gender differences in job satisfaction among young adults. *Journal of Behavioral Economics, 16* (1) :21–32.

Dalton, D. R. & J. L. Perry. (1981). Absenteeism and the collective bargaining agreement: An empirical test. *Academy of Management Journal, 24* (2) :425–431.

Danforth, J. P. (1979). On the role of consumption and decreasing absolute risk aversion in the theory of job search. In S. A. Lippman and J. J. McCall (Eds.), *Studies in the Economics of Search,* New York: North Holland :109–131.

Defina, R. H. (1983). Unions, relative wages, and economic efficiency. *Journal of Labor Economics, 1* (4) :408–429.

Doeringer, P. & M. Piore. (1971). *Internal Labor Markets and Manpower Analysis,* Lexington, MA: Heath, Dore.

Dornstein, M. (1988). Wage reference groups and their determinants: A study of blue collar and white collar employees in Israel. *Journal of Occupational Psychology, 61* (3) :221–235.

Drory, A. & B. Shamir (1988). Effects of organization and life variables on job satisfaction and burnout. *Group and Organizational Studies, 13* (4) :444–455.

Duncan, G. J. & F. T. Stafford. (1980). "Do union members receive compensating wage differentials?" *American Economic Review, 70* (3) :353–371.

Dunham, R. B. & F. J. Smith. (1979). *Organizational Surveys: An Internal Assessment of Organizational Health,* Glenview, IL: Scott, Foresman.

Duhem, P. M. M. (1962). *The Aim and Structure of Physical Theory.* New York: Atheneum.

Dunlop, J. T. (1957). *Industrial Relations Systems,* New York: Holt.

———. (1957). The task of contemporary wage theory. In G. W. Taylor and F. C. Pierson (Eds.), *New Concepts in Wage Determination.* New York: McGraw-Hill.

Easterlin, R. A. (1980). *Birth and Fortune: The Impact of Numbers on Personal Welfare,* New York: Basic Books.

Elstrom, R. B., N. E. Freeberg, & D. A. Rock. (1987). The effects of youth employment program participation on later employment. *Evaluation Review, 11* (1) :84–101.

Farber, H. S. & D. H. Saks. (1980). Why employees want unions: The role of relative wages and job characteristics. *Journal of Political Economy, 88* :349–369.

Feyerabend, P. (1988). *Against Method.* London: Verso.

Fichman, M. (1984). A theoretical approach to understanding employee absence. In P. Goodman, R. S. Atkin, and Associates (Eds.), *Turnover.* San Francisco: Jossey-Bass.

Filer, R. K. (1986). The role of personality and tastes in determining occupational structure. *Industrial and Labor Relations Review, 39* (3) :412–424.

——— & P. A. Petri. (1988). A job charcteristics theory of retirement. *Review of Economics and Statistics, 70* :123–129.

Flanagan, R. J., G. Strauss, & L. Ulman. (1974). Worker discontent and work place behavior. *Industrial Relations, 13* :101–123.

Freeman, R. B. (1978). Job satisfaction as an economic variable. *American Economic Review, 68* :135–141.

——— & J. L. Medoff. (1984). *What Do Unions Do?* New York: Basic Books.

Friedman, M. (1979). The Methodology of Positive Economics. In F. Hahn and M. Hollis (Eds.), *Philosophy and Economic Theory,* Oxford: Oxford University Press.

Ford, J. P. (1981). Departmental context and formal structure as constraints on leadership behavior. *Academy of Management Journal, 24* :274–288.

Forrest, C. R., L. L. Cummings, & A. C. Johnson. (1977). Organizational participation: A critique and model. *Academy of Management Review* :586–601.

Gafni, A. & D. Peled. (1984). The effect of labelling on illness related absenteeism: An economic explanation for the case of hypertension. *Journal of Health Economics, 3* :173–178.

Gergen, K. J. (1973). Social psychology as history. *Journal of Personality and Social Psychology, 26* :309–320.

Garrison, K. R. & P. M. Michinsky. (1977). Evaluating the concept of absentee-proneness with two measures of absence. *Personnel Psychology, 30*:389–393.

Gibbs, J. C. (1979). The meaning of ecologically-oriented inquiry in contemporary psychology. *American Psychologist, 34* :127–140.

Gibson, R. O. (1966). Toward a conceptualization of absence behavior of personnel in organizations. *Administrative Science Quarterly, 11* :107–133.

Goodman, P. S. (1974). An examination of referents used in the evaluation of pay. *Organizational Behavior and Human Performance, 12* :170–195.

Gouldner, A. W. (1954). *Patterns of Industrial Bureaucracy.* New York: The Free Press.

Granovetter, M. S. (1974). *Getting a Job: A Study of Contracts and Careers.* Cambridge, MA: Harvard University Press.

Granrose, C. S. & J. D. Portwood. (1987). Matching individual career plans and organization career management. *Academy of Management Journal, 30* (4) :699–720.

Green, S. G., W. Blank, & R. Liden. (1983). Market and organizational influences on bank employee's work attitudes and behaviors. *Journal of Applied psychology, 68* :298–306.

Greenberg, J. & R. L. Cohen (Ed.). (1982). *Equity and Justice in Social Behavior.* (New York: Academic Press, 1982).

Griffin, R. W. (1983). Objective and social sources of information in task design: A field experiment. *Administrative Science Quarterly, 28* :184–200.

Gronau, R. (1971). Information and frictional unemployment. *American Economic Review, 61* :290–301.

Hackman, J. R. & E. E. Lawler, III. (1981). Employee reactions to job characteristics. *Journal of Applied Psychology, 55* :259–286.

———— & G. R. Oldham. (1975). The development of the job diagnostic survey. *Journal of Applied Psychology, 60* :151–170.

Halaby, C. N. (1978). Bureaucratic promotion criteria. *Administrative Science Quarterly, 23* :466–484.

————. (1986). Worker attachment and workplace authority. *American Sociological Review, 51* (5) :634–649.

Hamermesh, D. S. (1977). Economic aspects of job satisfaction. In O. Ashenfelter and W. E. Oates (Eds.), *Essays in Labor Market Analysis.* New York: Wiley :53–72.

————. (1984). Life-cycle effects on consumption and retirement. *Journal of Labor Economics, 2* :388–411.

Heckman, J. J. & G. Sedlacek. (1985). Heterogeneity, aggregation, and market wage functions: An empirical model of self-selection in the labor market. *Journal of Political Economy, 89* (6) :1077–1125.

Hempel, C. G. (1964). *Aspects of Scientific Explanation and other Essays in the Philosophy of Science,* New York: Free Press.

Herman, J. B. & C. L. Hulin. (1972). Studying organizational attitudes from individual and organizational frames of reference. *Organizational Behavior and Human Performance, 8* :84–108.

Hirsch, B. T. & J. T. Addison. (1985). *The Economic Analysis of Unions: New Approaches and Evidence.* Boston: Allen and Unwin.

Hirsch, P. M. (1975). Organizational analysis and industrial sociology: An instance of cultural lag. *The American Sociologist, 10* :3–12.

Hirschleifer, J. (1973). Where are we in the theory of information? *American Economic Review, 87* :31–39.

Hirst, R. J. (1959). *The Problems of Perception,* London: Allen and Unwin.

Homans, G. C. (1950). *The Human Group,* New York: Harcourt, Brace.

Hoppock, R. (1935). *Job Satisfaction,* New York: Harper and Row.

House, J. S. (1977). The three faces of social psychology. *Sociometry, 40* :161–177.

Howson, C. (ed.). (1976). *Method and Appraisal in the Physical Sciences: The Critical Background to Modern Science,* Cambridge: Cambridge University Press.

Hulin, C. L. (1969). Sources of variation in job and life satisfaction: The role of community and job-related variables. *Journal of Applied Psychology, 53* (4) :279–291.

———— & M. R. Blood. (1968). Job enlargement, individual differences, and worker responses. *Psychological Bulletin, 69* :41–55.

———— & M. Roznowski. (1985). Organizational technologies: Effects on organization's characteristics and individual's responses. In L. L. Cummings and B. M. Staw (Eds.), *Research in Organizational Behavior,* Greenwich, CT: JAI Press, *7* :39–85.

———— M. Roznowski, & D. Hachiya. (1985). Alternative opportunities and withdrawal decisions: Empirical and theoretical discrepancies and an integration. *Psychology Bulletin, 93* :233–250.

Ilgen, D. R. & J. R. Hollenback. (1977). The role of job satisfaction in absence behavior. *Organizational Behavior and Human Performance, 19* :148–161.

———— & H. J. Klein. (1988). Organizational behavior. *Annual Review of Psychology* NY: Annual Reviews. *40* :327–351.

Ippolito, R. A. (1987). Why federal workers don't quit. *Journal of Human Resources, 22* :281–299.

Jackofsky, E. F. & L. H. Peters. (1983). Job turnover versus company turnover: Reassessment of the March and Simon Participation Hypothesis. *Journal of Applied Psychology, 68* :490–495.

Jackson, P. R., E. M. Stafford, M. H. Banks, & P. B. Warr. (1983). Unemployment and psychological distress in young people: The moderating role of employment commitment. *Journal of Applied Psychology, 68* :525–535.

Jacobson, S. L. (1989). The effects of pay incentives on teacher absenteeism. *Journal of Human Resources, 24* (2) :280–286.

Jacoby, S. M. (1985). *Employing Bureaucracy: Managers, Unions, and the Transformation of Work in American Industry, 1900–1945,* New York: Columbia University Press.

————. (1987). Employee attitude surveys in historical perspective. *Industrial Relations, 27* :74–93.

Jones, D. R. & R. L. Martin. (1986). Voluntary and involuntary turnover in the labor force. *Scottish Journal of Political Economy, 33* (2) :124–144.

Johns, G. & N. Nicholson. (1982). The meanings of absence: New strategies for theory and research. In B. M. Staw and L. L. Cummings (Eds.), *Research in Organizational Behavior,* Greenwich, CT: JAI Press, *4.*

Johnson, W. (1979). A theory of job shaping. *Quarterly Journal of Economics.*

Kanter, R. M. (1977). *Work and Family in the U.S.: A Critical Review and Agenda for Research and Policy,* New York: Russell Sage.

Katz, D. & R. L. Kahn. (1966). *The Social Psychology of Organizations,* New York: John Wiley.

King, A. G. (1974). Occupational choice, risk aversion, and wealth. *Industrial and Labor Relations Review, 27* :586–596.

Kochan, T. A. & D. E. Helfman. (1981). The effects of collective bargaining on economic and behavioral outcomes. In R. Ehrenberg (Ed.), *Research in Labor Economics,* Greenwich, CT: JAI Press, *4* :321–365.

———— & P. Cappelli. (1984). The transformation of the industrial relations/personnel function. In P. Osterman (Ed.), *Internal Labor Markets,* Cambridge, MA: MIT Press.

————, R. B. McKersie, & P. Cappelli. (1984). Strategic choice and industrial relations theory. *Industrial Relations, 23* :16–39.

Konecni, V. J. (1977). The role of aversive events in the development of intergroup conflict: In W. Austin and S. Worchel (Eds.), *Social Psychology of Intergroup Relations*, Monterey, CA: Brooks/Cole.

Kraft, K. (1986). Exit and voice in the labor market: An empirical study of quits. *Journal of Institutional and Theoretical Economics*, :697–715.

Krueger, A. (1988). The determinants of queues for federal jobs. *Industrial and Labor Relations Review, 41* :567–581.

————— & L. Summers. (1986). Reflections on the inter-industry wage structure. In K. Lang and J. Leonard (Eds.), *Unemployment and the Structure of Labor Markets*, Oxford: Basil Blackwell.

Kuhn, T. S. (1970). *The Structure of Scientific Revolutions*, Chicago: University of Chicago Press.

Lakatos, I. (1976). History of science and its rational reconstructions. In C. Howson (Ed.), *Method and Appraisal in the Physical Sciences: The Critical Background to Modern Science*, Cambridge: Cambridge University Press.

Landman, J. & M. Manis. (1983). Social cognition: Some historical and theoretical perspectives. In L. Berkowitz (Ed.). *Advances in Experimental and Social Psychology*, Orlando: Academic Press, *16* :49–123.

Lazear, E. P. (1986). Retirement from the labor force. In O. Ashelfelter and R. Layard (Eds.), *Handbook of Labor Economics*, Amsterdam: Elsevier Science Publishers BV, *1* :305–356.

Lekhani, H. (1988). The effect of pay and retention bonuses on quit rates in the U.S. army. *Industrial and Labor Relations Review, 41* :430–438.

Leigh, J. P. (1985). The effects of unemployment and the business cycle on absenteeism. *Journal of Economics and Business, 37* :159–170.

Lewin, G. W. (Ed.) (1954). *Resolving Social Conflicts: Selected Papers on Group Dynamics by Kurt Lewin*, New York: Harper and Brothers.

Lincoln, J. R. & A. Kalleberg. (1986). Work organization and workforce commitment: A study of plants in the United States and Japan. *American Sociological Review, 50* :738–760.

————— & K. McBride. (1987). Japanese industrial organization in comparative perspective. *Annual Review of Sociology, 13* :289–312.

Locke, E. A. (1976). The nature and causes of job satisfaction. In M. Dunnette (Ed.), *Handbook of Industrial and Organizational Psychology*, Chicago, IL: Rand McNally, :1297–1350.

March, J. G. & H. A. Simon. (1958). *Organizations*. New York: Wiley.

Markus, H. & R. Zajonc. (1985). The cognitive perspective in social psychology. In G. Lindzey and E. Aronso (Eds.), *Handbook of Social Psychology*, New York: Random House, *1* 2nd.

Martin, J. (1981). Relative deprivation: A theory of distributive justice for an era of shrinking resources. In L. L. Cummings and B. M. Staw (Eds.), *Research in Organizational Behavior*, Greenwich, CT: JAI Press, *3* 53–107.

Martinson, O. & E. A. Wilening. (1984). Rural–urban differences in job satisfaction. *Academy of Management Journal, 27* :199–206.

Mattila, J. R. (1974). Job quitting and frictional unemployment. *American Economic Review, 64* :235–240.

McGuire, W. J. (1969). The yin and yang of progress in social psychology: Seven koan. *Journal of Personality and Social Psychology, 26* (3) :446–456.

Miller, D. C. & W. H. Form. (1964). *Industrial Sociology*, New York: Harper and Row, 2nd ed.

Miller, P. W. & P. A. Volker. (1984). The screening hypothesis: An application of the Wiles Test. *Economic Inquiry, 22* 121.

Mills, C. W. (1948). *The New Men of Power,* New York: Harcourt, Brace.

Mincer, J. (1983). Union effects: Wages, turnover, and job training. In J. D. Reid, Jr. (Ed.), *New Approaches to Trade Unions,* Greenwich, CT: JAI Press :217–252.

―――― and Jovanovic, B. (1979). Labor mobility and wages. In S. Rosen (Ed.), *Studies in Labor Markets,* Chicago: University of Chicago Press.

Mitchell, O. S. & G. S. Fields. (1984). The economics of retirement behavior. *Journal of Labor Economics, 2* :84–105.

Mobley, W. H. (1982). *Employee Turnover: Causes, Consequences, and Control.* Reading, MA: Addison-Wesley.

――――, R. W. Griffith, H. H. Hand, & B. M. Meglino. (1979). Review and conceptual analysis of the employee turnover process. *Psychological Bulletin, 86* :493–522.

Morgan, L. G. & J. B. Herman. (1976). Perceived consequences of absenteeism. *Journal of Applied Psychology, 61* :738–742.

Mortensen, D. T. (1988). Matching: Finding a partner for life or otherwise. *American Journal of Sociology, 94* ::S215–s240.

Mowday, R. T., L. W. Porter, & R. M. Steers. (1982). *Employee-Organizational Linkages,* New York: Academic Press.

Muchinsky, P. M. & P. C. Morrow. (1980). A multidisciplinary model of voluntary employee turnover. *Journal of Vocational Behavior, 17* :263–290.

Near, J. P., R. W. Rice, & R. G. Hunt. (1980). The relationship between work and nonwork domains: A review of empirical research. *Academy of Management Review, 5* :415–429.

Nicholson, N. (1977). Absence behavior and attendance motivation: A conceptual synthesis. *Journal of Management Studies, 14* :239–252.

O'Reilly, C. A. III. (1977). Person-job fit: Implications for individual attitudes and performance. *Organizational Behavior and Human Performance, 18* :36–46.

―――― & D. Caldwell. (1979). Informational influence as a determinant of perceived task characteristics and job satisfaction. *Journal of Applied Psychology, 64* :157–165.

Osterman, P. (1987). Choice of employment systems in internal labor markets. *Industrial Relations, 26* :46–67.

Patchen, M. (1961). *The Choice of Wage Comparisons,* Englewood Cliffs, N.J.: Prentice-Hall.

Parsons, D. O. (1986). The employment relationship: Job attachment, work effort, and the nature of contracts. In O. Ashelfelter and R. Layard (Eds.), *Handbook of Labor Economics,* Amsterdam: Elsevier Science Publishers BV, II :789–847.

Pervin, L. (1968). Performance and satisfaction as a function of individual-environment fit. *Psychological Bulletin, 69* :56–68.

Peterson, T. & S. Spilerman. (1990). Job quits from an internal labor market. In K. Ulrich Meyer and N. B. Tuna (Eds.), *Applications of Event History Analysis in Life Course Research,* Madison, WI: University of Wisconsin Press.

Pfeffer, J. (1983). Organizational demography. In L. L. Cummings and B. M. Staw (Eds.), *Research in Organizational Behavior,* Greenwich, CT: JAI Press, 5 :399–357.

――――Y. & Cohen. (1984). Determinants of internal labor markets in organizations. *Administrative Science Quarterly, 29* :550–572.

―――― & A. Davis-Blake. (1986): Unionization and the relationship between job attributes and job attitudes. Unpublished manuscript, School of Business, Stanford University.

―――― & J. Lawler. (1980). Effects of job alternatives, extrinsic rewards, and behavioral commitment on attitudes toward the organization: A field test of the insufficient justification paradigm. *Administrative Science Quarterly, 25* :38–56.

―――― & G. Salancik. (1978). *The External Control of Organizations: A Resource Dependence Perspective,* New York: Harper and Row.

Phelps, E. S. et al. (1970). *Microeconomic Foundations of Employment and Inflation Theory*, New York: Norton.

Piore, M. J. (1975). Notes for a theory of labor market stratification. In R. S. Edwards, M. Reich, and D. Gordon (Eds.), *Labor Market Segmentation*, Lexington, MA: D. C. Heath.

Popper, Sir R. (1986). *The Logic of Scientific Discovery*, New York: Harper and Row.

Porter, L. W. & E. E. Lawler III. (1965). Properties of organization structure in relation to job attitudes and job behavior. *Psychological Bulletin, 64* :23–51.

Price, J. L. (1977). *The Study of Turnover*. Ames, IO: The Iowa State University Press.

Poulton, R. G. & S. Hung Ng. (1988). Relationships between protestant work ethic and work effort in a field setting. *Applied Psychology: An International Review, 37* (3) :227–233.

Raff, D. M. G. & L. H. Summers. (1987). Did Henry Ford pay efficiency wages? *Journal of Labor Economics, 5* (Part 2) :s57.

Roberts, K. H. & W. Glick. (1981). The job characteristics approach to task design: A critical review. *Journal of Applied Psychology, 66* :193–217.

————, C. L. Hulin, & D. Rousseau. (1978). *Developing an Interdisciplinary Science of Organization*, San Francisco: Jossey-Bass.

Roethlisberger, F. J. et. al. (1939). *Management and the Worker: An Account of a Research Program Conducted by the Western Electric Company, Hawthorne Works, Chicago*, Cambridge, MA: Harvard University Press.

Rosen, S. (1986). The theory of equalizing differences. In O. Ashenfelter and R. Layard (Eds.), *Handbook of Labor Economics*. Amsterdam: Elsevier Science Publishers BV, *1* :641–692.

Rosenberg, A. (1976). On the inter-animation of micro and macro economics. *Philosophy of Social Sciences, 6* :35–53.

Ross, A. (1948). *Trade Union Wage Policy*, Berkeley, CA: University of California Press.

Ross, L. (1977). The intuitive psychologist and his shortcomings: Distortions in the attribution process. In L. Berkowitz (Ed.), *Advances in Experimental and Social Psychology*, New York: Academic Press, *10*.

Rousseau, D. M. (1978). Characteristics of departments, positions, and individuals: Contexts for attitudes and behavior. *Administrative Science Quarterly 23* :521–539.

————. (1985). Issues of level in organizational research: Multi-level and cross-level perspectives. In L. L. Cummings and B. M. Staw (Eds.), *Research in Organizational Behavior*, Greenwich, CT: JAI Press, *7* :1–38.

Royce, J. R. & W. W. Rozeboom (Eds.). (1972). *Psychology of Knowing*, New York: Gordon and Breach.

Rusbult, C. E. & D. Farrell. (1983). A longitudinal test of the investment model: The impact on job satisfaction, job commitment, and turnover of variations in rewards, costs, alternatives, and investments. *Journal of Applied Psychology, 68* :429–438.

Salancik, G. R. (1977). Commitment and the control of organizational behavior and belief. In B. M. Staw and G. R. Salancik (Eds.), *New Directions in Organizational Behavior*. Chicago: St. Clair Press, :1–54.

———— & J. Pfeffer. (1978). A social information processing approach to job attitudes and task design. *Administrative Science Quarterly 23* :427–456.

Sampson, E. E. (1977). Psychology and the American ideal. *Journal of Personality and Social Psychology, 35* :767–782.

————. (1981). Cognitive psychology as ideology. *American Psychologist, 36* :730–743.

Schneider, B. (1973). The perception of organizational climate: The customer's view. *Journal of Applied Psychology, 57* :248–256.

————. (1985). Organizational behavior. *Annual Review of Psychology, 36* :573–611.

————. (1987). The people make the place. *Personnel psychology, 40* :437–453.

Schneider, L. & C. Bonjean (eds.). (1983). *The Idea of Culture in the Social Sciences,* Cambridge: Cambridge University Press.

Schwab, D. P. & L. L. Cummings. (1970). Theories of performance and satisfaction: A review. *Industrial Relations, 9* :408–430.

Sewell, W. H., Jr. (1987). The theory of action, dialectic, and history: Comment on Coleman. *American Journal of Sociology, 93* :166–171.

Sherer, P. D. (1987). The workplace dissatisfaction model of unionism: What are its implications for organizing blacks and women? In *Proceedings of the 40th Annual Meeting of the Industrial Relations Research Association,* Madison, WI: IRRA, :135–141.

Smith, A. (1776). *The Wealth of Nations* (New York: Penguin Books, 1982, first published 1776).

Smith, C. A., D. W. Organ, & J. P. Near. (1983). Organization citizenship behavior: Its nature and antecedents. *Journal of Applied Psychology, 68* :653–663.

Spence, M. A. (1976). *Market Signaling: Informational Transfer in Hiring and Related Screening Devices,* Cambridge, MA: Harvard University Press.

Sprague, J. (1972). Is there a micro theory consistent with contextual analysis? In E. Ostrom (Ed.), *Strategies of Political Inquiry,* Beverly Hills: Sage, 99.

Staats, A. W. (1983). Paradigmatic behaviorism: Unified theory for social-personality psychology. In L. Berkowitz (Ed.), *Advances in Experimental and Social Psychology,* (Orlando: Academic Press, *16* :125–173).

Stagner, R. (1981). Training and experiences of some distinguished industrial psychologists. *American Psychologist, 36* :497–505.

Staines, G. L. & D. Pagnucco. (1977). Work and nonwork. In R. P. Quinn (Ed.), *Effectiveness in Work Roles: Employee Responses to Work Environments,* Ann Arbor: University of Michigan.

Starbuck, William H. (1976). Organizations and their environments. In M. D. Dunnette (Ed.), *Handbook of Industrial and Organizational Psychology,* Chicago: Rand-McNally, :1069–1123.

Staw, B. M. (1974). Attitudinal and behavioral consequences of changing a major organizational reward: A natural field experiment. *Journal of Personality and Social Psychology, 6* :742–751.

———. (1984). Organizational behavior: A review and reformulation of the field's outcome variables. *Annual Review of Psychology, 35* :627–666.

——— & G. R. Oldham. (1978). Reconsidering our dependent variables: A critique and empirical study. *Academy of Management Journal, 21* :539–559.

———, N. Bell, & J. Clausen. (1986). The dispositional approach to job attitudes: A lifetime longitudinal test. *Administrative Science Quarterly, 13* :56–77.

Steers, R. M. & R. T. Mowday. (1981). Employee turnover and post-decision accomodation processes. In B. M. Staw and L. L. Cummings (Eds.), *Research in Organizational Behavior,* Greenwich, CT: JAI Press, *3* :235–282.

Steers, R. M. & S. R. Rhodes. (1978). Major influences on employee attendance: A process model. *Journal of Applied Psychology, 63* :391–407.

Steiner, I. D. (1986). Paradigms and groups. In L. Berkowitz (Ed.), *Advances in Experimental and Social Psychology,* Orlando: Academic Press, *19* :251–286.

Stigler, G. (1962). Information in the labor market. *Journal of Political Economy, 70* :94–104.

Stoikov, V. & R. L. Raimon. (1968). Determinants of differences in the quit rate among industries. *American Economic Review, 58* :1283–1298.

Super, D. E. & D. T. Hall. (1978). Career development: Exploration and planning. *Annual Review of Psychology, 29* :257–293.

Sutton, R. I. & D. M. Rousseau. (1979). Structure, technology and dependence on a parent organization: Organizational and environmental correlates of individual responses. *Journal of Applied Psychology, 64* :675–687.

Taira, K. (1970): *Economic Development and the Labor Market in Japan,* New York: Columbia University Press.

Taylor, D. E. (1979). Absent workers and lost hours. *Monthly Labor Review, 102* (8) :49–53.

Telly, C. W. L. French, & W. G. Scott. (1971). The relationship of inequity to turnover among hourly workers. *Administrative Science Quarterly, 16* :164–172.

Thompson, J. D. (1967). *Organizations in Action,* New York: McGraw Hill.

Tobin, J. (1972). Inflation and unemployment. *American Economic Review, 62* :1–18.

Tomes, N. (1989). The effects of religion and denomination on earnings and the return to human capital. *Journal of Human Resources, 19* :472–488.

Turner, A. N. & P. R. Lawrence. (1965). *Industrial Jobs and the Worker: An Investigation of Response to Task Attributes,* Boston: Harvard University Graduate School of Business Administration.

Ulman, L. (1958). *The Rise of the National Trade Union,* Cambridge, MA: Harvard University Press.

Viscusi, W. K. (1980). *Employment Hazards,* Cambridge, MA: Harvard University Press.

Walster, E. G. W. Walster, & E. Berscheid. (1978). *Equity: Theory and Research,* Boston: Allen and Bacon.

Walton, R. E. (1985). From control to commitment in the workplace. *Harvard Business Review, 64* :76–84.

Wanous, J. P. (1976). Organizational entry: From naive expectations to realistic beliefs. *Journal of Applied Psychology, 61* :22–29.

Weick, K. E. (1979). Cognitive processes in organizations. In B. M. Staw (Ed.), *Research in Organizational Behavior,* Greenwich, CT: JAI Press, *1* :41–74.

Weiss, A. (1984). Determinants of quit behavior. *Journal of Labor Economics, 2* :371–387.

Weiss, Y. (1986). The determination of life cycle earnings: A survey. In O. Ashelfelter and R. Layard (Eds.), *Handbook of Labor Economics,* Elsevier Science Publishers BV, *II,* :525–600.

Williamson, O. E. (1985). *The Economic Institutions of Capitalism,* New York: The Free Press.

Willis, R. J. (1986). Wage determinants: A survey and reinterpretation of human capital earnings functions. In O. Ashelfelter and R. Layard (Eds.), *Handbook of Labor Economics,* Elsevier Science Publishers BV, *II.*

Winkler, D. (1980). The effects of sick-leave policy on teacher absenteeism. *Industrial and Labor Relations Review, 33* :232–240.

Woodward, J. (1965). *Industrial Organization: Theory and Practice,* Oxford: Oxford University Press.

Work in America (1973). Washington, D.C.: Department of Health, Education, and Welfare.

Youngblood, S. A., W. H. Mobley, & B. M. Meglino (1983). A longitudinal analysis of the turnover process. *Journal of Applied Psychology, 68* :507–516.

THE ROLE OF SITUATIONAL AND DISPOSITIONAL FACTORS IN THE ENHANCEMENT OF PERSONAL CONTROL IN ORGANIZATIONS

David B. Greenberger and Stephen Strasser

ABSTRACT

A cognitive adaptation model of personal control in organizations is presented. There are three themes focal to this model. First, it is posited that people have a general desire for control which propels them to enhance their perceptions of covariation between their actions and desired outcomes, and they are predicted to be particularly likely to act on this desire after they have experienced a reduction in control. Second, people are likely to rely on a variety of responses in order to maintain or enhance their personal control. Third, situational and dispositional factors are predicted to influence whether people react to changes in their control, and nature of their reactions. Despite organizational impediments, employees are expected to persist in their attempts to enhance personal control, sometimes in organizationally undesirable ways, and often in areas unrelated to the source of the loss of control. The implications of this model for

Research in Organizational Behavior, Volume 13, pages 111–145.
ISBN: 1-55938-198-1

management—emphasizing the importance of individualized interventions designed to provide employees with increased options—are discussed.

An enduring issue in management has concerned the extent to which the behavior of individuals should or should not be controlled by the organization. Too often, the discussion of this issue has relied on a general model of environmental determinism. This model—perhaps as a consequence of the strong behaviorist influences in organizational behavior—suggests that individuals are malleable and that properly implemented management programs can cause all employees to respond in a specified, desired manner. Thus, for example, traditional management education in this country generally has sought to teach managers how to place limits on the actions of employees, but has not given sufficient consideration to potentially negative side effects from the consequent loss of control experienced by individual employees. A dramatic example of the counter-productive way in which people in organizations may respond to blocked freedom of action occurred in the late 1960s. Some of the young employees at what was then the new, prototypical General Motors assembly plant at Lordstown, Ohio severely sabotaged the cars they were producing, in part because they believed that they should have been more involved in decisionmaking. Although, over the years, there has been some nondeterministic discussion which points to the importance of individual needs (Argyris, 1954: Alderfer, 1972; Hackman & Oldham, 1972; Maslow, 1943), prevailing management thought continues to pay too little attention to individual variation in disposition and in the processing of information. Only recently have a few authors in the organizational area described approaches which emphasize these individual variations (Bell & Staw, 1989; Kanter, 1983; Staw, 1986).

The model of personal control presented here focuses on the individualized nature of employees' reactions to loss of control. The persistence and magnitude of individual characteristics in determining behavior within organizations is fundamental to our conceptualization: when people perceive their organizations as blocking or decreasing opportunities for control, they respond by attempting to increase it, each in his or her unique fashion. Our work describes the active role taken by individuals in an attempt to perceive some link between their actions and outcomes—despite organizational impediments to control. Our work also points to the existence of *generalized* responses to control loss (Greenberger & Strasser, 1986; Rothbaum, Weisz, & Snyder, 1982); by generalized we mean that the individual has access to a wide repertoire of responses to enhance control and is not limited only to responses which *directly* restore the lost control. Thus, individuals in organizations are hypothesized to be acting regularly to restore losses in control, even in areas seemingly unrelated to the original source of the blocked freedom.

It is well established that people possess a generalized desire to enhance control, unless they are in a state of helplessness (cf. Baum & Singer, 1980). The question now confronting researchers concerns the *specific* factors which influence when and how people attempt to enhance control. The theory and research on personal control up to this point has not addressed these issues. So, for example, conventional management theory cannot assist our understanding of the following situation. Suppose employees are told by their supervisor that the organization is concerned with accountability, and insists that they leave a detailed "paper trail" of all of their actions so that someone in an external position can monitor them. Although the employees understand the reason for the new requirements, they quickly discover that the time and energy required to fulfill them undermines their ability to accomplish their tasks. When confronted by demands similar to these, why does one employee work harder to accomplish all of her tasks, while another engages in petty sabotage, and a third starts to interfere in the actions of coworkers? Put more generally, why do people respond to control loss in different ways within organizational settings?

In order to answer this question, we do the following three things in this chapter. First, we define and discuss the nature of personal control. Literature on the role of personal control in organizations is summarized. Second, we reformulate our compensatory model of personal control to focus on the consequences of personal control loss. Specifically, we look at those factors which trigger a reaction to perceived loss of control, and which also may explain the different types of responses to control loss. We hypothesize that there exist at least two distinct and identifiable sets of moderating factors; (a) dispositional factors and (b) specific situational cues within the environment. These two sets of factors may act independently or may interact to predispose each individual to respond to control loss in unique but potentially predictable ways. Finally, the implications for management are presented.

THE NATURE OF PERSONAL CONTROL

Based upon a considerable body of literature, we have viewed personal control as reflecting "an individual's beliefs at a given point in time, in his or her ability to effect a change in a desired direction" (Greenberger & Strasser, 1986; p. 165). Personal control has been similarly conceptualized as the individual's perception of covariation between his or her actions (as the casual agent) and outcomes (Alloy & Tabachnik, 1984).

Our conceptualization of personal control is distinct from the more commonly studied constructs of power and influence. Work on power and influence supposes that many behaviors are designed to influence others. However, our work in personal control recognizes that people frequently initiate actions for other reasons: to influence their own self-perceptions, to resolve inconsistent self-perceptions, and to relay prior behaviors so as to assess or re-evaluate the potential efficacy of those behaviors. These kinds of behaviors are not aimed at achieving power or influence and are not externally motivated; rather they are internally motivated and are related to self-perceptions of control. For example, although we might have thought our actions affected an outcome, only by engaging in that action again can we obtain the information we need to make this attribution with certainty.

We have operationalized the construct of personal control (Greenberger, 1982) as being based upon the level of influence people have over all aspects of their lives, including their work, their work space, and other people. We have hypothesized that the degree of personal control possessed by an individual is represented by the aggregate of various specific perceptions of influence. This operationalization has as its focus the fundamental characteristic of perceived covariance between action and desired outcome. That is, the magnitude of control perceptions is seen as related to the number of actions which will generate desired outcomes. The greater the number of desired outcomes which are viewed as resulting from intentional actions, the greater the perceived and anticipated control.

Our conceptualization of personal control—by recognizing and by aggregating all of the individual's specific perceptions of control—is broader than that of many other authors. Some of these authors have developed typologies of control which focus on particular characteristics of limited number of kinds of control. Averill (1973), for example, distinguishes among behavioral control, cognitive control, and decisional control. Rothbaum, Weisz and Snyder (1982) assert that there are four different types of control: predictive control, illusory control, vicarious control, and interpretive control. Staw (Staw, 1986; Bell & Staw, 1989) suggests that there are three general categories of control: control over outcomes, control over behavior, and the ability to predict outcomes and behavior. These typologies suggest that control perceptions are based upon different sources of information, yet the sources of information subsumed within these typologies is not an exhaustive list. Thus, while all of these typologies are useful for theoretical and conceptual purposes, they may unwittingly mask critical components of the personal control construct because they represent only general categories of an infinite variety of types of control.

Regardless of the typology employed, research on personal control typically suggests that people generally are motivated to seek control (White, 1959) and that control is necessary for the individual's well being. A variety of studies which have examined the impact of control reduction support this. This is considerable evidence that loss of control has a variety of negative consequences, including increased depression (Alloy & Abramson, 1980; Seligman, 1975), heightened stress (Averill, 1973; Glass & Singer, 1965), decreased performance and job satisfaction (Greenberger, Strasser, Cummings, & Dunham, 1989), lowered alertness, and even increased mortality (Langer & Rodin, 1976), to list just a few. The critical role played by control in cognitions and behavior is evident in attribution theory. In this theory of attribution, Kelley (1971) stated that individuals make attributions so as to gain and maintain control; "the purpose of casual analysis . . . is effective control" (p. 22). Researchers have found that when control is decreased by presenting subjects with unexpected information and negative outcomes, increased attributional analysis results (Steele, 1988).

Although it is critical for attribution and other theories, personal control has significance in its own right. Without a belief in covariation between action and outcome, people perceive events as occurring at random. It has been suggested that if we were unable to control and predict our actions and those of others, we would be unable to function (Fiske & Taylor, 1984). Moreover, the world would be a frightening place if we lacked the ability to anticipate the consequences of our actions. It is noteworthy that attempts at exercising control begin very early. Infants in the first weeks of life learn to manipulate their own bodies, their environment, and the people in their environment. As they mature, they learn that they are separate from their mothers and from other components of the external world. One of the ways in which they learn to differentiate themselves from the external world is by seeing that their actions have some impact upon the world. For example, a child repeatedly hits the rattle hanging from his crib and cries whenever the rattle falls so that his or her father will pick it up. By these actions, the child comes, over time, to understand the relationship between action and outcome, and learns to act as to achieve a desired outcome.

In sum, the concept of personal control measures the degree to which an individual perceives covariation between his or her actions and an intended outcome. The desire for control is persistent in most people, and motivationally based. Control is important because (1) it helps us to understand human cognition and behavior in organizations, (2) it underlies many motivations, and (3) when absent it can negatively influence our well-being.

A COMPENSATORY MODEL OF PERSONAL CONTROL

We (Greenberger & Strasser, 1986) have previously proposed a model of reaction to personal control loss which extends the earlier work of Wortman and Brehm (1975) to the organizational context. We suggested that individuals are confronted by a variety of situations in which control is perceived to be weakened, and that based upon the salience of these situations the individual will be more or less likely to react to control loss. Although there has been little attention to personal control in the organizational literature, our model is generally consistent with the extent literature (e.g., Bazerman, 1982; Bell & Staw, 1989; Jackson, 1983; Staw, 1977; 1987).

The model which we have presented differs from the previous literature in one important respect. Most of the earlier work pointed to the significance of restoring control directly (i.e., restoring control by removing the blockage or addressing the source of the loss). In contrast, we believe in a compensatory model of control and see people as opportunistic in their efforts to enhance control. Thus, for example, when a person's sales territory is cut, she may choose to enhance control in a way unrelated to the loss of control, such as by modifying a computer spreadsheet to keep track of her sales more accurately. Situational and dispositional factors affect whether control enhancement occurs in direct or indirect ways, at work or outside of the work setting. For instance, a person denied a promotion—after working diligently on a difficult project for a year—may compensate for the loss of personal control by deciding to redecorate a room at home. This response may be uniquely control-enhancing for this person. For a different individual, however, such a response would never be considered, or would not be effective in enhancing control even if attempted. Instead, this second individual responds to self-perceptions of lowered control by throwing himself into his 11 year old daughter's figure skating career.

Our compensatory model of control is shown in Figure 1. As control is reduced below expected levels, we hypothesize that people utilize specific, individualized modes of control-enhancing responses. If one control-enhancing method is anticipated to fail, or if it is unsuccessfully attempted, other methods are likely to be substituted, given the person's persistent desire for control. This substitution of methods is consistent with research by Taylor (1983), who suggests that when the original plan is thwarted an alternative plan with the same goal or the same value is substituted. The greater the blockage and the less the likelihood of success from reactance, the greater the likelihood of substitution.

In the following sections, the various components of our model of control

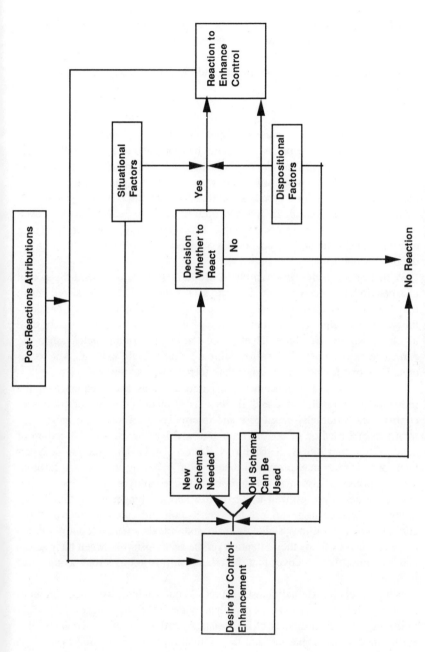

Figure 1. Model of Control Enhancement in Organizations

are discussed. Specifically, we describe the sources of change in control, the factors that affect whether an individual attends to the change, the nature of the reactions aimed at enhancing control, the dispositional and situational factors which moderate the reactions, and the post-reaction attributions.

Sources of Change in Control Perceptions

The desire to enhance control propels the individual through the model. Without this desire, the person would not be motivated to act or would be in a state of helplessness (Martinko & Gardner, 1982; Seligman, 1975). Although the desire for control has many sources, four general types of sources can be identified. The first two types, generalized desire for control and the self-reinforcement of control, motivate people to enhance personal control even when there has been no control loss. The second two types, internal and external control reduction, encompass sources which directly relate to a reduction in control.

With respect to the first two types, we already have discussed the notion that people have a generalized desire to seek control. This generalized desire may stem from such diverse needs as those for self-esteem, mastery, predictability, and reduction of uncertainty, each of which may have been established in childhood or may have developed later in life. Additionally, since the enhancement of control is self-reinforcing, individuals may attempt to increase control for no reason other than to repeat these rewards.

Efforts at control enhancement also may arise as a consequence of the reduction of control. Fiske and Taylor (1984) identify two general kinds of control loss: externally-based loss and internally-based loss. The most common external method of control reduction involves the denial of freedom of action (Brehm, 1966; S. S. Brehm & Brehm, 1981). For example, a supervisor or coworker may prevent someone from behaving in a desired fashion. The environment also may create constraints. Employees may find that resources which were utilized to perform a task no longer exist. Finally, although no change in covariance between action and outcome ostensibly occurs, a salient event may suddenly make individuals attend to control. When these employees focus their attention on the relationship between their action and outcome, they discover that the relationship is not as strong as they had believed.

With respect to externally-based sources of control loss, we (Greenberger & Strasser, 1986) have proposed a discrepancy model of personal control similar to the psychological models of inconsistency (Abelson, et al., 1968). In this earlier model, we suggested that the motivation to react is a function of the comparison of two aspects of personal control: the amount of control a person possesses as compared to the amount of control that person desires. We hypothesized that the greater the discrepancy between these two measures, the more likely people are to react to gain control. A recent article by Higgins (1989) proposes a social comparison model which may contribute another perspective. Higgins suggests that individuals compare the amount of control they possess with the amount of control they perceive someone like themselves as having. A negative comparison (i.e., they perceive themselves as possessing less control than someone like themselves) is expected to enhance the likelihood that people will seek control. Moreover, the greater the difference between the images of the other and themselves, the greater the likelihood that people are motivated to enhance their control. For example, suppose a high school "blue chip" basketball prospect is in his senior year. Like the other seniors, he never questioned where he was going to high school or who coached the team. It was clear to him that high school student athletes simply did not question these things. During his first season at college, the "blue chipper" hears many discussions about how important he is to the success of the team and also about the success of other "star" players in dictating how they are utilized. On the basis of these comparisons, he starts to question his coach's judgment and even his own selection of a school. Although he had never really asked about his freedom of action, based upon these comparisons he now perceives himself as one who should have greater input into a variety of issues that affect him. As a result, he goes to the coach and tells him that he has decided to sit out a year and transfer to another school. Hence the perception of control loss and the need to enhance it may not occur until people scan their environments for social comparison information.

In contrast to external sources of control reduction are internal sources. These exist when individuals themselves induce a loss in perceptions of control. First, by not concentrating on their tasks, people may find that they have lost control. Langer (Chanowitz & Langer, 1981; Langer 1975), for instance, suggests that when people overlearn a task, they tend to perform it automatically (i.e., without attending to it). This state, which she terms "mindlessness," is characterized as one in which people give up conscious control over a task. As long as the task remains constant, people will perform well despite their mindlessness, but problems can arise when the task is altered. In new conditions, relinquished conscious control may result in decreased performance. Second, self-induced loss of control may occur because of the errors people have made in assessing relevant information about covariation. For instance, instead of doing a thorough search to determine whether their control is in fact diminished, people rely on small samples of information (Tversky & Kahneman, 1973) and overgeneralize. So, despite actually having control, a few disconfirming instances may lead them to think that they really have lost control. Third, while both of these types of internally-based control reductions can be viewed as nondeliberate, persons also may be more active in reducing control. The abundant research suggests that self-serving attributional biases of externalizing failure occur frequently in order for people to avoid harming their self-esteem (Snyder, Stephan & Rosenfield, 1978). Those who chronically attribute their failures to external factors may reduce their ability to establish control; by habitually externalizing the causes of events they fail to see themselves as casual agents even when they are. In contrast, people sometimes deliberately take responsibility for an event; even when they are not actually the cause (Weiner, Frieze, Kukla, Reed, Rest, & Rosenbaum, 1972), in order to experience obtaining control in the future. For example, although it would have been easy to externalize the failure to solve all the problems in a new computer software product, I may take responsibility for all the "bugs" in a new, terribly complex software product. By making this initial attribution of failure, I work harder, and increase the likelihood that I will succeed in accomplishing this task in the future.

It is clear, then, that personal control can be reduced in a number of ways. First, the environment can constrain control; the historical reliance on traditional "control" mechanisms is the best example of this. Second, persons may be architects of their own reduced control. This can occur through deliberate as well as more automatically triggered cognitions.

Process of Response: New versus Old Schemata

Previously, we (Greenberger & Strasser, 1986) sought to explain why people attend to control. Clearly individuals do not focus all of their attention on control all of the time; instead, it is reasonable to believe that only a small part of their attention is directed to control. In our earlier work, we demonstrated that the amount of attention directed to control varies with the degree of novelty associated with the event which engenders the change in perceived control. In this section, we relate the novelty of the event to the *process* by which persons respond to changes in personal control.

The response to changes in perceptions of control varies depending upon the individual's answer to the following question: Can existing schemata effectively respond to the change in events that I perceive? When people are exposed to an event, they go through a two stage process (Pyszcznski & Greenberg, 1987). In the first stage, individuals first try to rely upon "preexisting casual theories," (i.e., old schemata) to determine whether events are consistent with their expectations. If they are, existing schemata are used to enhance control, or there is no reaction at all. In contrast, when the events to which they have been exposed are novel or unexpected, people move to the second state; they utilize "active hypothesis testing." Movement to this stage may necessarily involve an assessment of control. When people find that they do not have a schema readily available to respond, they experience a further loss of control and generate new schemata in order to respond. The process thus is similar to that described by Taylor and Fiske (1978) who, in writing about the role of salience in the processing of information, asserted that people are likely to attend to actions which are novel and unexpected; actions or events which are as expected are more likely to be processed automatically.

For the organization, the development of new schemata may have different implications. It may be advantageous to the organization if employees have the time to generate new schemata and if the new schemata which are developed channel the employees' efforts toward organizationally desirable outcomes. However, the consequent increased attention to control has the potential for diverting attention from task performance. Consider the example of the Eastern Airlines plane which crashed in the Florida Everglades some years ago. As they were beginning their descent into Miami, the pilots noticed that an indicator light suggested a problem with the landing gear. As the plane continued to descend, the pilots devoted all of their attention to trying to control this unexpected and novel (but not at all life threatening) situation and they literally forgot about flying the plane. Their attention to accomplishing the new task involving the landing gear so completely consumed the pilots that they failed to notice the altimeter—which they normally would have been monitoring in a landing approach—until the plane was just above the ground. Even when they finally noticed the altimeter—eight seconds before they crashed—they were so involved in the task involving the light, that they failed to take corrective action. Although most employees rarely face such dramatic consequences, this problem of focusing exclusively on developing solutions or schemata for a novel task, at the expense of other tasks, has more widespread implications.

Reactions to Control Loss

The previous section considered the *process* by which people respond to a loss of control. In this section, we discuss the *form* that the reaction may take. Critical to our model is the belief that people react in indirect as well as in direct ways. In part, this is because direct restoration of diminished control is not always possible. For example, when a supervisor does not permit a desired behavior, there is frequently nothing which can be done to restore the freedom and thereby enhance control perceptions. Yet, we do not typically find entire organizations composed of helpless people because people opt to enhance their control in ways seemingly unrelated to the initial source of lowered control, and perhaps even in ways outside of the work setting. We now will consider general categories of responses—both direct and indirect—that people may have to losses of control.

First, people may react directly (Brehm, 1966; Wortman & Brehm, 1975). According to Brehm, the greater the individual's expectation of freedom of action or the greater the importance of the event to the individual, the greater the reactance. The most studied manifestation of reactance is behavior aimed at directly restoring lost freedom (other manifestations include feelings of anger and changes in the perception of the outcome).

Second, people may respond to a loss of control with physiological reactance. Evidence suggests that when an aversive event occurs, individuals are more likely to suffer from stress-related problems if they have no control over the events. These problems include performance deficits and physiological responses such as heart pounding, sweating, jitters (Averill, 1972; Thompson, 1977). In one of our studies (Dansky, Greenberger, & Strasser, 1989), we found a significant inverse relationship between control perceptions and stress, and between control perceptions and burnout.

Third, reactions to the loss of control may take the form of cognitive adjustments. Individuals in organizations may utilize self-serving biases when confronted with lost control. Abundant research indicates that people generate theories that view their "own attributes as more predictive of desirable outcomes and are reluctant to believe in theories that imply that their own attributes might be related to undesirable events" (Kunda, 1987, p. 646). In other words, they may not accept an interpretation that their actions were unsuccessful or that they were the cause of a failure. So long as the individual does not do so chronically (discussed above as leading to diminished control) externalizing failure may enhance perceptions of control. Additionally, people may cognitively (or behaviorally) take credit for positive consequences in which they actually had no involvement. We all know of instances in organizations when coworkers and supervisors who initially opposed some course of action, later tried to take credit for all the good which resulted. Most persons like to be around those who are succeeding and avoid being associated with those who fail. The self-serving bias research (e.g., Miller & Ross, 1975) suggests that the value of this lies not only in affecting the beliefs of others, but also in changing one's own self-perceptions of control.

Fourth, persons may react to a reduction in control by seeking more information. The interrelationship of attribution theory and personal control illustrates this (Kelley, 1967). When individuals' beliefs are undermined, their sense of control is reduced and they begin an attributional search to understand the cause. For example, when employees are given new tasks to perform and find that their performance is subpar, it is not uncommon to find that they question their own abilities. In order to determine the cause of their performance deficit, they try to accumulate information on such subjects as the task, other employees, and their skills. It should be noted, though, that while the search to enhance control may be a well-organized search for information, it also may be random and indiscriminate (Fiske & Taylor, 1984).

Of course, the real issue is probably not the amount of data obtained, but the ability of the individual to accumulate and process these data into meaningful information. Data of the wrong type or quantity, or discrepant information may have an adverse impact upon control perceptions. Too much information which cannot be processed and summarized can lead the individual to a heightened feeling of loss of control. This is a problem which corporate MIS and marketing research departments confront on a daily basis. It is not uncommon to find an employee complaining that he is overwhelmed with a problem which has been dumped on his desk and that before he comments on the problem, he "needs to get a handle" on the issue by sorting through the available data. As the data are sorted, the employee develops a heightened sense of control. It is important to note that errors in the processing of information may create inaccuracies—though the person typically is unaware of this.

Fifth, people may respond proactively to an anticipated loss of control by avoiding the event that is perceived to threaten to cause a loss. In one study, we (Dansky, Greenberger, Strasser, and Dansky, 1990) examined the importance of personal control in physician's decisions to treat AIDS patients. Physicians expect that their ministering will have an observable consequence, and even when treating an incurable illness, generally anticipate that their treatment will result in a reduction of pain and extension of life. However, some physicians feel that there is little they can do to help AIDS patients. For these physicians, then, it would be predicted that the anticipated treatment of AIDs patients would result in a lowering of perceived control. Specifically, it was predicted that the lower the perceived control over the outcome, the less likely physicians would be to treat AIDS' patients. Results of the study confirmed these expectations.

Sixth, people may respond to repeated or dramatic losses in control by entering a state of helplessness. This is likely to occur when environmental cues demonstrate the futility of responding, such as happens when the environment cannot be altered or when efforts to restore control go unrewarded. According to Abramson, Seligman & Teasdale (1978), the greater danger of helplessness comes not from learning that one cannot control a particular component of the environment, but rather from the generalization of helplessness to a variety of related, but different situations. For example, employees may find that their inputs to their supervisor are ignored, despite the correctness of their assertions. They begin to stop making suggestions because they conclude, correctly, that their comments are treated as inconsequential. However, the reaction is not confined to reduced suggestion-making; instead, management finds that overall productivity starts to fall because feelings of helplessness have now generalized to the wider work setting. One of the enduring issues related to control concerns the generalizability of self-perceptions and, more specifically, the generalizability of low control perceptions. When people perceive a loss of control in a specific situation, they may carry this loss over to other situations at work and elsewhere.

Some authors have suggested that responses to control loss may be hierarchical. This really is the basis of Wortman and Brehm's (1975) model. When confronted by a loss of freedom of action, they hypothesized that people will engage in a type of reactance and that only when reactance is repeatedly unsuccessful will they end up feeling helpless. Staw (1989) goes further and hypothesizes that among these different general types of responses to lost control, there is a hierarchy in desirability that is uniform for all people. So, for example, to Staw outcome control is the most desirable; persons will attempt to influence pay, promotions, benefits, and the like. When control over outcomes is not feasible, employees attempt to control behaviors (e.g., control over methods, pace). Finally, when neither of these is possible, people attempt to reduce ambiguity by predicting behavior and outcomes.

We agree with Staw in one important respect: a hierarchy of responses most likely exists and is critical for the understanding of personal control in organizations. However, in contrast to Staw, we believe that a hierarchy exists *within* the individual and is not necessarily common for all people. We hypothesize that individuals in organizations develop their own characteristic ways of viewing and responding to personal control loss. Situational and dispositional factors interact in the following ways: (1) they influence cognitions about when control has been lost; (2) they affect the decision whether to react; and, (3) if a decision is made to react, they determine the nature of the reaction. In the next sections, we discuss these factors in more detail. We believe that the examination of these factors will help us to predict the nature of responses to loss of personal control.

Factors Moderating Reactions to Control Loss

We believe that there are two sets of factors—dispositional and situational—which moderate reactions to control loss and determine the behavioral ways in which individuals will respond. Our model thus is consistent with the work of Alloy and Tabachnik (1984) who propose that perceptions of covariation between action and outcome are a consequence of both dispositional and situational factors. According to Dweck and Leggett (1987), dispositions are individual difference variables that determine the a priori probability that an individual will adopt a particular behavior pattern; situational factors are seen by them as potentially altering these probabilities. Where the situation offers no cues, the predispositions should determine how people behave. When the situation is salient or has particular information, the situation can override the predispositions. The weaker the predisposition, the more likely it is to be overridden by external cues. In this section, we first examine the dispositional factors and then consider situational ones.

Dispositional Factors. In general, examination of dispositional factors in relation to personal control has been too limited; it has concentrated either on a few personality differences, such as self-monitoring (Bell & Staw, 1989) or locus of control (Davis & Phares, 1969), or on individuals' cognitive generalizations, such as attributional styles (Peterson & Seligman, 1984). We review and go beyond our earlier work and that of other authors, and discuss additional dispositional factors which are expected to influence strongly the individuals decision to react to control loss and the form of the reaction.

1. Information monitoring and blunting. Miller, Brody and Summerton (1988) suggest that when people are threatened with an aversive event—such as one that reduces control—their information processing differs along two dimensions. First, individuals differ in the extent to which they seek out and *monitor* information about the threat. Second, they differ in the extent to which they cognitively distract themselves from and thus psychologically *blunt* the impact of threat-relevant information.

These individual differences have relevance for the processing of all control loss information. While all persons monitor and blunt information to some degree, individual differences in the extent to which persons monitor and blunt clearly may exist. We all know of people working together in organizations who process information differently. One person will carefully pick up on every threat to his or her freedom; another person is oblivious to most everything. That is, some people simply do not seem to process information about threats to their control, and if they do monitor the information, they may be more likely psychologically to blunt this information. Such a person is less likely to react to control loss. In addition, because a vast amount of information is ignored or blunted by some persons, some opportunities for control enhancement may not be noticed by them. In contrast, those who monitor more and blunt less, are more likely to search for and identify opportunities for control enhancement.

2. Styles of control enhancement.   In a recent study, we (Porter, Greenberger, Miceli, & Strasser, 1990) proposed that individuals characteristically employ one of a number of broad classes of actions to enhance control. Moreover, we suggested that people are predisposed to a particular type of control-enhancing action for two reasons. First, individuals learn over time that particular styles work for them and have the potential for providing information about covariation. Second, individuals are psychologically comfortable with particular styles; these styles fit their perceptions about themselves. A factor analysis of different responses to control loss (Porter, et. al., 1990) suggested that there are six characteristic ways in which people may be predisposed to enhance personal control.

First, some people appear to increase their control by interfering in the actions of others. We describe this as interference because these individuals seemingly having no organizational need to interact as they do. These people apparently see control mostly in terms on interpersonal relations: they want to affect the actions of other people. By concentrating primarily within the interpersonal realm, they quickly exhaust designated organizational relationships and turn to become involved with persons with whom they apparently have little legitimate purpose. Actions could include setting up rules or procedures for others over whom they have no reason or authority to exercise power or striving to prevent others from exercising freedom of choice in areas in which they have no reason to be involved. They engage in these interfering actions even as they ignore non-interactive tasks over which they do have some legitimate authority. An employer who recognizes these tendencies in an employee may be able to channel them in a productive non-obstructionist direction. For example, the employer may suggest the employee organize an annual toy drive for needy children, thus giving the employee opportunities to perceive control over a peripheral, but beneficial activity.

Second, some people may attempt to develop or intensify conflict. Instigating conflict has two positive effects for the individual attempting to enhance control. Conflict can provide people with information which suggests that they can alter normal patterns of interaction. Prior to their actions there was peace and stability at work; as a consequence of their actions, people are now fighting with one another. At the same time, conflict can create a chaotic reference. A person's activities might not have appeared to lead to outcomes in comparison to a stable and productive work environment, but in comparison to an environment characterized by disorder and distractions, even a few successes can be judged by the person as meaningful.

Third, some individuals enhance their control through the initiation of a business or other venture. A number of authors in the entrepreneurship area have pointed to the importance of dispositional factors to explain why certain individuals begin their own businesses (see Brockhaus, 1982). We agree with Brockhaus that much of the emphasis on such personality variables as locus of control, achievement motivation, and risk taking are overstated; research simply does not allow us to make the desired discrimination. In an earlier article, Greenberger and Sexton (1988) pointed to the importance of personal control in precipitating the decision to begin a new venture. Clearly, changes in perceptions of control (i.e., losses of control) act as a situational influence, but in addition, it is now our belief that some people also may have a particular predisposition to enhance their control by starting their own business.

Fourth, as we mentioned earlier, our preliminary data suggest that some people equate control with the possession of information. Moreover, it is reasonable to expect that the withholding of information from others also can enhance the individual's self-perception of control. The effectiveness of withholding information is derived not only from possessing the information, but also through the comparison with those who do not possess the information.

Fifth, some individuals attempt to enhance their control by increasing their immersion in their work. This can be manifest in two common forms. First, some people become "workaholics." No doubt this is related to the Type A personality, described by Friedman and Rosenman (1974), which points to the desire of some persons to do more and more things in less time. Workaholics may be understood as continually struggling, like the mythical Sisyphus, to establish covariation between their actions and outcomes; they need to do more all the time because having once accomplished an outcome, the sense of covariation has no lasting power. They thus are driven to establish new action—outcome relationships. Second, people who are perfectionists tend to immerse themselves in their work. These people may see covariation as occurring only when the outcomes are perfect. Whether the individual is labeled as a workaholic or a perfectionist, people who chronically attempt to enhance their control in these ways are directed internally. Rather than focusing on the activities of others, they enhance their covariation perceptions through their attention to their own work. They appear to believe that the most important source of action—outcome information comes from the information they derive from work they perform.

Sixth, certain individuals in organizations may try to be good bureaucratic citizens. This type of person appears to derive control through the predictability of an organization. As the trend in organizations moves away from traditional bureaucratic designs, individuals who have predisposition for this style should feel increasingly insecure and less in control.

As we continue to research these different styles of control enhancement, we can only speculate on their origins. These styles may be learned or they may be innately based. For example, individuals may have learned that specific kinds of action at work have a high probability of success. If they compare this type of action to ones with a much smaller probability of success, then the former action should be more salient and more likely to be learned. Alternatively, fundamental differences in personality—such as Dweck and Leggett's (1988) goal orientations of concern for learning versus concern for performance—may underlie these different responses.

The individual's unique style of control enhancement is expected to have an impact on both the decision to react as well as on the precise nature of the reaction. First, the style may predispose someone to identify a control loss situation and to respond to it. For example, a person whose style is to turn to interpersonal interference may feel particularly threatened by interfering in the activities of others, and be quick to commit herself to control enhancement when so threatened. Second, once people are committed to the enhancement of personal control, they may rely on existing styles with which they are comfortable. People will continue to behave in ways consistent with their style in new or altered situations, even when opportunities to enhance control are available.

3. Sampling.   Research points to individual differences in biases related to the sampling of information. As Kahneman and Tversky (1974) note, people tend to be poor samplers of information; they primarily attend to information which supports existing beliefs, even when contradictory evidence is available. Different people are more or less predisposed to these biases, and this difference has implications for the decision to react. For example, some people may tend to rely on extremely small samples when they seek information. Furthermore, they may tend to seek information only from friends or others whose opinions they are likely to share. This process will lead to confirmation of their initial belief that may bias them to react when it is objectively unnecessary; conversely, it may lead them not to react when they should. In addition, since their sampling is inadequate, they are likely not to perceive information which points to a larger number of control enhancing options—thus, minimizing their potential repertoire of control-enhancing behaviors.

4. Perceived ability.   The degree to which people perceive themselves as capable of accomplishing a task is expected to affect the level of attention to control, and also the way in which they react to enhance control. Wicklund and Braun (1987) suggested that interest in increasing control rises when people are inexperienced in a task or when they perceive themselves as not competent. These researchers proposed that the source of these perceptions about competence may be internal—such as by having a low self esteem—or external—such as cues associated with certain types of uniforms, or the requirement that a task be performed in an unfamiliar manner. Those who have reason to doubt their abilities were found to attend to their own traits so as to be more competent in the future. Thus, in our model, it is expected that when people have some reason to question their competence or detect some cue in the environment which draws their attention to their competence, they are more likely to try to enhance control generally, by any method. In particular, they should be expected to be attracted to tasks with which they know they are competent, including ones involving few challenges. Success on these tasks should raise their self-esteem and overall control and reduce anxiety. If they were to continue on a task for which they were not competent, they would be likely to experience failure; further failures could lead to feelings of helplessness.

5. Personality differences. Many different personality constructs have been identified, and each of these may interact with the decision to enhance control and with the method employed to accomplish the enhancement. Some of the more well known constructs, including locus of control, self-monitoring, and risk-taking, are discussed here.

Locus of control (Rotter, 1966) may lead different people to use different control enhancement interventions. Fiske and Taylor (1984) suggest that those high on the internal end of the locus of control scale benefit more from interventions which involve the self. Because they see themselves as the casual agents, these people would be expected to work harder and to move themselves to situations where they have a higher probability of detecting covariation between action and outcome. In contrast, persons high on the external end of the scale are more likely than internals to perceive external threats to their control. Externals also are expected to be more likely to seek out information on covariance—rather than to make the changes themselves—because they see the environment and not themselves as the basis of covariation information. As a result, externals probably see fewer possible opportunities available to themselves to alter their control and are more likely to end up feeling helpless.

Both we (Greenberger & Strasser, 1986) and Bell and Staw (1989) have hypothesized that self-monitoring may affect perceptions of personal control. People who are low self-monitors—that is, people whose internal cues dictate their social behavior—have a high correspondence between their dispositional characteristics and their behaviors (Snyder & Ickes, 1985). High self-monitors, in contrast, respond far more to external cues and are more likely to adapt their behavior accordingly. In the latter case, there will be a low correspondence between dispositional characteristics—other than degree of self-monitoring—and observed behavior. In addition, Bell and Staw (1989) argue that low self-monitors are, because of their focus on internal states, more likely to seek control. However, because of the focus on internal cues, we believe that low self-monitors may be less likely than high self-monitors to respond to control loss contingencies in the environment. That is, they simply may not perceive as many control loss situations as the high self-monitoring person and thus, are less likely to respond to externally-based control loss. In addition, because of their internal focus, low self-monitors are likely to rely on internally-based characteristics for control enhancement. This could include greater attention directed to the performance of personal work goals. High self-monitors, because of their external focus, may be more likely to try to enhance control by altering such situational factors as interpersonal relations.

Finally, the topic of risk taking has been discussed both within the context of need for achievement (McClelland, 1985) and as a personality factor thought to predispose people toward entrepreneurial activities (Brockhaus, 1982). We believe that the desire to take risks is associated with perceptions of loss of control and with the attractiveness of other events which may enhance control. People who have high needs for risk are expected to attend more to high risk situations and to perceive them as potentially control enhancing, and are expected to be more likely to attempt to enhance control in risky ways. These risky ways could include participating in novel situations, including opportunities—such as certain entrepreneurial activities provide—which are labelled as "high risk" by others. People with low needs for risk-taking may be more inclined to attend to their own failures in high risk situations because they do not expect to succeed. Further, low risk-takers are expected to avoid situations which they evaluate as risky, including those which are novel.

6. *Attributional styles.* Seligman and others have suggested that attributional style affects how people react to uncontrollable contingencies. Alloy, Peterson, Abramson, and Seligman (1984) found that performance deficits generalize from an unsolvable situation to a new, dissimilar task only among subjects who attribute bad events to global causes. Seligman and Peterson (1984) have proposed a model of personality which emphasizes the explanatory style. Based upon the reformulation of the learned helplessness model (Abramson, Seligman, & Teasdale, 1978), they suggest that people to a greater or lesser extent explain bad events in ways which emphasize stability, global nature, and internality of the events. Specifically, some people have styles which they term "vulnerable," meaning that they are more likely to blame themselves and expect failures to occur in the future. This style also makes them more likely than those with less vulnerable styles to suffer negative changes in self-esteem, and less likely to respond to control deficits. Seligman and Schulman (1986) found that this explanatory style was associ-

ated with poor productivity. Hence, when people make global attributions of their failures, they are much less likely to attempt to enhance their control or even to search for the cause of the their control loss (and are in a state of helplessness). They are more likely to accept the situation as typical and overlook the possibility of their increasing their control.

Situational Factors. Increasingly, research in psychology has examined the situational factors which affect individual cognitions. In this section, we discuss the impact of a number of these situational factors upon control perceptions. Situational factors, like dispositional ones, have an impact upon two areas: the decision to enhance control and, in turn, the specific ways in which people attempt to increase control.

1. Contrast. In one series of studies, Newman and Benassi (1989) examined the influence of context upon judgments of control. One of the older and more interesting of these context factors is the "contrast effect." According to Newman and Benassi, when subjects first experience a heavy stimulus, they judge a less heavy stimulus to be lighter than did a control group of subjects who had no initial experience. In their experiment, Newman and Benassi found that context also influences perceptions of response-outcome covariation. Specifically, they found that when people initially judged a situation to involve high levels of control, their subsequent judgments of a medium control stimulus were lower than those of individuals who initially were exposed to a low control stimulus. In explaining their results, Newman and Benassi conclude that "judgments of control are often made within a priori contrast" (p. 888); that is, the context may interact with the length of exposure to different contingent factors in affecting control perceptions.

The implications of Newman's and Benassi's findings for the present model are clear. First, and central to the model, a reduction in control should increase the likelihood that people will initiate effort to enhance control. Second, as a consequence of the contrast effect, even a relatively minor decrease in control is likely to be experienced as a substantial reduction. This could be a particular problem in organizations undergoing restructuring, since an individual whose perception of lost control is exaggerated is likely to over-react to regain control.

It is possible, as an extension of Newman's and Benassi's research, that the contrast effect is heightened when the context has been stable for a long period of time. Thus, when life at work has followed a familiar routine—with a constant level of control—any change may take on heightened importance. If employees in a stable work environment are accustomed to lunch at a particular hour, for example, altering the time of lunch may be perceived as a substantial intrusion—with concomitant feelings of lost control—even though the change would be considered minimal by any objective evaluation. If, on the other hand, events have been unsettled—particularly so far as covariation perceptions are concerned—even a more significant loss of control might go unnoticed. In organizations where restructuring has become common, then, a reduction in covariation may not trigger reactions aimed at enhancing control.

2. *Consistency.* It is well established that information which is consistent with an individual's expectations is more likely to be processed than is information which is inconsistent. Moreover, Lord, Lepper & Ross (1979) have shown that information which is disconfirmatory is more likely to be subject to greater scrutiny. This is similar to the work of Newtson (1976) who found that unexpected or novel information is more likely to be subject to finer grain analysis than is expected information. With respect to our model, the work of these researchers suggests that information about successful control-enhancement strategies is more likely to be accepted, encoded, and remembered—thus making those strategies available for repetition. In addition, however, people may continue to employ control-enhancing responses which are *not* effective in a given context because negative information about the efficacy of these responses is ignored.

3. *Modeling.* An important contextual feature concerns the observed actions of other people. Vicarious learning, discussed by Bandura (1977), is relevant because of its potential for increasing personal control. Rather than being dependent solely upon the consequences of their own behaviors, individuals can learn about action—outcome relationships by observing the actions of others. According to Bandura, the learning may take one of three forms (similar to those discussed by Manz and Sims, 1981). First, persons may re-evaluate the degree of control they possess when they observe others engaging in activities similar to their own; they observe that for others like themselves, actions and outcomes in a given context are in fact related or unrelated. Second, persons may learn new repertoires of responses. Rather than conceptualizing covariation between action and outcomes in traditional ways, for example, employees may see that there are a tremendous variety of ways to increase desired outcomes. Third, observations of others' behaviors may serve to remove people's inhibitions. The observer may have thought about engaging in an action which could demonstrate covariation, but may have believed that it would be inappropriate to do so. Noting that others engage in the behavior, the observer becomes more likely to try it as well.

Manz and Sims (1981) discuss a number of characteristics which affect the probability that a model will influence an observer. Models are more likely to be imitated if they have high status, are successful, are attractive, and are similar to the observer. Additionally, when the relevant behaviors of the model are very detailed—so that they can more easily be imitated—there is an increased likelihood that they will influence the observer.

Finally, while the above discussion may emphasize vicarious learning in the context of increasing control, individuals also may learn vicariously that actions and outcomes are independent. So, for example, when employees who believe that their actions have an impact upon outcomes observe others performing similar actions, they may come to realize that their own actions actually were inconsequential. This may be a particular problem with participation programs like quality circles. One of the more universal, positive effects of quality circles is the sense of involvement and excitement which comes from being a part of these programs. This initially can lead participants to believe that their actions are influential in altering outcomes within the organization. Because of their involvement in their own cohesive group, they cognitively enhance their perceptions of their group and its activities. At some later point, however, when they observe the behavior of other similar groups —that is, those with which they are not directly involved—they may see the other group less positively and reevaluate their own group as actually having little impact. The lack of involvement in these other groups can provide a detached and less biased view of what the groups really do or do not accomplish. If participation groups are not perceived to be accomplishing desired outcomes, then people should be less inclined to view them as control-enhancing mechanisms.

4. Structure of the situation. In the social cognition literature, a wide variety of studies have examined the importance of environmental structuring. There are many different levels of structure, including the structure of the organization as a whole, the overall structure of each employee's job, and the structure of the particular tasks.

We believe that individuals detect the cues concerning the structure of the environment and that their assessment of and responses to control loss are consistent with these cues. In general, the less structured the environment, the more likely people are to employ creative and unorthodox strategies for control enhancement. The more highly structured the situation, the more likely it is that the individual will utilize routine, already learned, schemata. Moreover, if the environment is highly structured, the person will be less likely to be concerned with control loss—so long as change does not occur and the structure does not cause the person to feel controlled.

5. Priming. Research on priming (Wyer & Srull, 1980) suggests that information which has been activated recently or frequently has a greater probability of coming to mind than information which has not been activated. This has two principle applications for personal control enhancement. First, if an employee recently has been shown an action which can enhance control, he or she is more likely to engage in that activity in the future. Second, if a person has recently utilized a particular control-enhancing schema, then there is an increased likelihood that it will be employed again. Wyer and Srull explain this effect by suggesting that, in a sense, a schema which has been recently activated, has displaced other schema.

In order to be a useful prime, it is essential that the prime come before the stimulus. That is, a particular behavior is a prime if the covariation between the action and outcome is spelled out prior to the action occurring. In contrast, if an event occurs, and then the relationship between action and outcome is discovered, the event has less of a priming effect. In organizations, then, people are more likely to repeat a behavior when they initially perform it with the expectation that it will be rewarded, than if they first perform the action and only afterward are told of the reward.

The negative impact of layoffs on the survivors remaining in the organization (Brockner, 1988; Stassen, 1989) may be analyzed in the context of priming. Increasingly large numbers of organizations are finding that single restructurings are insufficient to reduce their work forces to levels consistent with their business. Even hitherto "secure" companies, like A.T. & T. and I.B.M., have found it necessary to reduce their work forces on a number of occasions. As both Brockner (1988) and Armstrong-Stassen (1989) suggest, there may be dramatic consequences (e.g., increases in stress) associated with these repeated layoffs. We believe that layoffs act to prime the survivor to expect a lack of relationship between their actions and the outcome (in this case, termination). The effect on control perceptions may be worsened when the organization—in an attempt to be compassionate and fair—makes the cuts through attrition and by encouraging senior employees to accept contract buyouts, rather than on the basis of performance. When the organization repeats these reductions in work force—regardless of perceptions of justice or injustice—they become permanent 'primes' and employees come to expect that there is little covariation between action and outcome.

6. Group norms. Research on group norms (Feldman, 1984) suggests that norms are quite functional to the group. Norms, for instance, allow people to know which actions are acceptable and which ones are not. The setting of behavioral standards also acts to reduce the flow of extraneous information because group members do not need to attend to all the activities of each individual in the group—their behaviors are predictable. Hence, group members can attend to group performance goals. Norms, then, can be expected to affect control in a number of ways. First, when control is perceived as lost and employees attempt to enhance their personal control, group norms are expected to affect the selection of strategies. Different groups are expected to formally or informally sanction particular behaviors which can increase control. This explains why we see different groups chronically engaging in different types of control-enhancing actions—some of which may be organizationally undesirable. Second, some groups may possess norms which encourage members to enhance their individual control. This can be seen in the empowerment of employees in autonomous work groups. When the group processes are properly developed, norms are established which link legitimate individual control enhancement with group and organizational performance. The fact that groups may establish norms which are inconsistent with or demonstrate a lack of concern for individual control enhancement in part may explain the mixed results found in participation programs. Group members, for example, may decide that the only way they can accomplish their goals is to work together on all projects. By so doing, they lessen the likelihood that individual members will perceive a relationship between their actions and specific outcomes. Third, as suggested above, when norms are present people are less likely to be distracted by other group members—whose behaviors are predictable—and so they can attend to their own enhancement of control.

As suggested, group norms can be counter-productive. Particularly when organizations deny opportunities to exercise control, groups may turn to dysfunctional means of control-enhancement—even to the point of industrial sabotage. Again, this demonstrates the persistence with which people respond to control loss. The high probability of success inherent in destruction (demonstrated so clearly when we were children breaking block towers) easily shows individuals the covariance between action and outcome. Further, because of its novelty and unexpectedness, the destruction of objects has the effect of making personal control salient (Allen & Greenberger, 1979). Thus, while group norms can be an obstacle to destruction, norms which permit sabotage may develop when the organization blocks productive means of exercising control.

7. Goal clarity. With the increase in research on goal setting (see, Locke, Shaw, Saari, & Latham, 1981), we have seen a rise in the application of some of the basic principles of goal setting to organizations. The relationship between goal clarity and control-enhancing interventions, however, is a complex one. One should find that people are attracted to situations of goal clarity for the enhancement of their control. As Locke, et al. discuss, the clearer the goals, the more likely people are to obtain specific feedback on their outcomes and, as discussed elsewhere in this paper, people typically desire feedback. Of course, the increased information related to covariance may enhance or diminish perceived control because goal clarity has the potential for increasing the salience of failures as well as successes. Since, as is frequently argued, goal clarity tends to increase performance on tasks, the net result for an organization with clear goals should be increased perceptions of control. To the extent that it operates to enhance control, goal clarity can help the organization diminish the individual's use of nonproductive means of control enhancement. Moreover, since research (Zadny & Gerard, 1974) suggests that people remember information that is consistent with success on tasks better than information which is consistent with failure, people are more likely to remember and repeat successes connected with clear goals. Thus, tasks with clear goals should be effective in enhancing control. While clarity of goals is important, however, so is variety. Consequently, organizations should seek out situations where the goals are clear, but also should provide alternative goals and other paths to achieve those goals. If only a small number of goals exist, then the employee's personal control may be diminished. This is discussed in more detail in the next section.

Post-Reaction Attributions

Throughout this paper, it has been suggested that the perception of covariation between action and outcome normally will lead to enhancement of perceived control. As we have just indicated, however, after people detect an action—outcome linkage, they may, in some cases, perceive themselves as having *less* control. That is, the perception of a relationship between action and outcome generally contributes positively to feelings of control, but it also has the potential to reduce feelings of control.

We believe that after reacting to a loss of control, people evaluate their response in order to determine (1) whether the reaction had the intended outcome, and (2) whether they can accurately perceive themselves as having freely chosen to react as they did. People do this in order to judge their efficacy and to make certain that they—rather than the organization—are the true source of the outcome. When people view the organization or some other individual as forcing them to behave in a specified manner in order to accomplish a particular task, they may discount their own contribution to the action—outcome relationship and instead attribute it to control by management. Rosenfield, Folger, and Adelman (1980) found just such an effect. Contingent rewards can enhance motivation if the reward is interpreted by the recipient as cuing competence, but if the reward is interpreted as an effort by management to control behavior— that is, if it is seen as undermining freedom of action—then motivation can be reduced. Attributions of being controlled, thus, could undermine the effectiveness of processes like MBOs or goal-setting more generally.

Thus, it is critical that employees perceive that they have a variety of opportunities to achieve action—outcome covariation. When management suggests that the range of acceptable outcomes and means of accomplishing them are too narrow, the subordinate attributions may be that management is trying to manipulate them. Implementation, then, of a program of greater participation in decisionmaking, without other choices for the employees, may be construed as simply an attempt by management to "control" them.

In addition to the possibility that people may experience diminished feelings of control after achieving an action—outcome success, it also is possible that people may experience enhanced feelings of control after a failure. This may occur when a person engages in a particular action with a specific goal in mind. Despite failing to accomplish the goal, the individual may experience powerful feelings of control solely as a consequence of having performed the action. For example, a person may attend a city council meeting with the intention of speaking out and dissuading council members from adopting a street lighting policy which the individual regards as dangerous. The individual speaks out but the council nevertheless adopts the policy. This individual, secure in the knowledge that she did "the right thing," may derive from her efforts an enhanced sense of control, despite her lack of success. The process by which post-reaction control perceptions are enhanced in such a case may include the individual redefining the intended outcome as the performance of the action by itself, without regard to consequence.

Finally, it must be noted that how each individual assesses his or her reaction depends to a large extent on the same dispositional and situational variables discussed in the preceding sections. Accordingly, considerable individual variation in post-reaction perceptions of control should be expected.

MANAGERIAL IMPLICATIONS

Our model traces the role of personal control in the organizational setting. It suggests that because individuals are unique in the ways in which they respond to control loss and seek control-enhancement, management cannot simply rely on general programs—discussed in the literature or proposed by consultants— to increase employee perceptions of personal control. Rather, careful and continual monitoring of situational and dispositional factors is required in order for organizations to develop and implement successful interventions. The care with which organizations employ market research before introducing a new product, also must be exercised when a change in the organization is contemplated. Analogous to asking members of a focus group what they think about a new advertising campaign, management should develop focus groups of employees to respond to proposed changes and to evaluate the effect of changes upon perceptions of control. Recognizing that people differ in their responses to control loss, the organization, and individual managers must shape changes in the context of these personal differences—even if this means altering the focus for each employee.

An important implication of this model is that because of the failure to consider individual differences regarding personal control, opportunities viewed by management as potentially control-enhancing actually may be experienced by employees in just the opposite way. Management typically has concentrated its efforts to increase employee control in two areas: technology and behavioral interventions. With regard to the first area, enhancement of control has been seen as a benefit associated with the increasing introduction of technologically sophisticated equipment (e.g., robotics) into the workplace. Such equipment has the potential for increasing the amount of information available to the employee, and may eliminate from the job many of the tasks which do not contribute to control. Instead of enhancing control, however, individuals may find that the technology denies them a feeling of being instrumental in bringing about a desired outcome. For example, airplanes are becoming increasingly automated; the newest planes are designed almost to fly and land themselves. Airlines and the airplane manufacturers no doubt expect that this automation will increase predictability and, hence, control. However, pilots may perceive their control as reduced because they no longer personally affect each aspect of the plane's flight. In addition, technology may make them less attentive to the plane and this "mindlessness" may further reduce their perceived control, leading to more of the types of errors in distraction which were discussed earlier.

The second major way in which organizations have attempted to increase employee perceptions of control is through empowerment in the organization process (e.g., Kanter, 1986). And indeed, increasing empowerment does have the potential for enhancing control. This is because an individual who can choose from a wide range of actions is more likely than a person with limited options to be able to select an action which will have a successful outcome— and thus the former individual is more likely to experience control-enhancement. Moreover, while our model does not directly address this possibility, it is likely that the availability of many options—in and of itself—imparts an enhanced sense of control. In other words, even if an employee chooses not to take advantage of the many options available (i.e., chooses not to act), the employee may feel enhanced control merely as a consequence of knowing that these options exist. This is not unlike the sense of security Americans derive from knowledge of their constitutional rights to due process—this, despite the fact that we are law-abiding citizens, and expect never to need to invoke these rights.

Thus, providing persons with more choices about how to accomplish their work can provide opportunities for control enhancement. However, the prevailing emphasis on generally-applicable methods of empowerment and worker participation, as contrasted with a more individualized program of control enhancement, may be misdirected. As we discussed in an earlier paper (Greenberger & Strasser, 1986), techniques of increasing employee involvement— such as empowerment and participation in decision making—should result in heightened expectations of control because control is made salient and because employees perceive that others are experiencing increases in control. However, for any of a variety of reasons, employees may not end up feeling as though their own control is increased. As discussed elsewhere in this paper, in these circumstances employees may perceive themselves as actually having lost control. For this reason, we expect that many of the employee ownership plans, like ESOPs, may not have dramatic effects on performance and satisfaction. Implementation of an ESOP should result in an initial increase in satisfaction and performance as expectations rise, but if there are constraints on the action— outcome relationship (such as those caused by the assumption of greater debt) and these constraints become salient, levels of satisfaction and performance may drop.

There are two principle reasons why empowerment may not be successful in increasing control perceptions. First, because of dispositional or situational factors, opportunities for control enhancement may go unrecognized. The employee may not see that she can accomplish the outcomes set out by management. Second, the increased opportunities for freedom of action may not actually enable the employee to accomplish his or her goals. Even though an employee may, for example, choose when to do his tasks, the employee still may not be able to accomplish them. Thus, presentation of different strategies for accomplishing goals is important for the enhancement of control, but it is not sufficient.

Clearly, organizations must somehow provide opportunities for employees to accomplish their tasks. This, of course, is essential in order for the organization to survive, but it also is important because it can provide employees with the opportunity to see some link between action and outcome. Unfortunately, many managers realize that while their employees make a valuable contribution to the organization by in fact achieving desired outcomes, the employees themselves often are unaware of their contributions. In such situations, the inadequacy of feedback on outcomes may cause low-control perceptions that are inaccurate and destructive. In our earlier article (Greenberger & Strasser, 1986) we suggested that personal control may underlie the desire of persons to receive feedback (Ashford & Cummings, 1983). In order to enhance control perceptions, management clearly needs to increase the amount of information available to employees about the effect of their actions, and to increase the salience of this information. There are a variety of ways that management can do this. With respect to employees who work in groups, management can provide specific feedback regarding each individual's contribution, rather than emphasizing how the activities of the group contribute as a whole to the performance of the organization. Individuals can receive reports from MIS groups on their own activities more frequently than yearly or even quarterly—perhaps on a weekly basis. In addition, information about outcomes can be derived directly and indirectly from contingent extrinsic rewards.

Organizations also can encourage the development of desirable group norms. These norms could include employees assisting each other to accomplish individual tasks, or developing new procedures to increase productivity. Organizations also should discourage the kind of group norms—such as those that occur in a group sports, like rowing—which deliberately minimize information about individual performance. While these norms may enhance group identity and cohesiveness (e.g., by team building), they diminish opportunities for individual performance within the group to be recognized and rewarded.

It should be noted that while management often equates responsibility for decisionmaking with control, employees do not always want responsibility in areas suggested, or demanded, by management. When unwanted responsibility is imposed, employees may experienced diminished perceptions of control. This may explain Bazerman's (1982) results which suggest that what he termed "overcontrol" can lower performance. We had a relevant experience in a service sector company in which we suggested that it might be best for the organization to restructure into autonomous work groups. We found that interest in autonomous work groups was low because employees simply did not want to make decisions. Repeatedly, they indicated that they had enough to do and did not want to have to worry about the correctness of decisions. Instead, they wanted more information about how they fit into the organization and wanted to control the physical space within their work unit. Although at the time we were unimpressed by their suggestions, in the context of the present model we now view their suggestions as appropriate for the situation and the people involved.

Finally, the importance of the physical environment in altering personal control should not be overlooked. In a note in the *Wall Street Journal* (1988), it was stated that "personal control by workers of their open-office environment continues to be a design issue for Herman Miller, Inc." (p. B1). The article reported that the company developed a heating tile which could be controlled by an individual at a workstation. In contrast, the movement in organizations toward greater standardization of the working unit perhaps has contributed to the overall aesthetics but may have reduced individual control. For example, when a major law firm moved to new surroundings, associate offices were refurnished with desks and bookcases secured to the wall. In addition, the desks were placed in such a way as to force the associates to sit with their backs to the doors which meant that they could not see when someone came by. When the firm moved, some of the associates were so upset with the loss of freedom that they vandalized the new offices. Limiting freedom to change surroundings reduces control and constrains one's repertoire of control enhancing behaviors. This, too, may have adverse consequences for the organization.

CONCLUSION

In sum, we have discussed a model of personal control which has important implications for organizations. The model suggests that people have a general desire for control, and that they will utilize a variety of different techniques to compensate for losses in control. Because people are opportunitistic in their approaches to control-enhancement, when other alternatives are inadequate, they may turn to organizationally undesirable methods of enhancing control, including, for example, industrial sabotage. Thus, the model suggests that organizations need to be proactive in developing productive strategies for increasing employee perceptions of control. In order for these strategies to succeed, organizations must adapt a micro focus. Generally-applicable programs to encourage empowerment and participation in decisionmaking, while well intentioned, may not be sufficient to alter perceptions of control if they fail to take into account the wide range of dispositional and situational factors which influence the unique way in which each individual responds both to losses in control and to opportunities for control-enhancement. We are advocating an approach in which managers are concerned with changes in individual employees' perceptions of the linkages between their actions and outcomes, and not simply with altering in uniform fashion the opportunities for all employees. Increased research on these topics, as well as in areas of organizational change and training and development, needs to be conducted.

ACKNOWLEDGMENTS

The authors are very grateful to Larry Cummings and Barry Staw for their insightful comments on earlier drafts of the manuscript.

REFERENCES

Abelson, R. P., Aronson, E., McGuire, W. J., Newcomb, T. M., Rosenberg, M. J., & Tannenbaum, P. H. (Eds.) (1968). *Theories of cognitive consistency: A sourcebook.* Chicago: Rand McNally.

Abramson, L. Y., Seligman, M. E. P., & Teasdale, J. D. (1978). Learned helplessness in humans: Critique and reformulation. *Journal of Abnormal Psychology, 87,* 49–74.

Alderfer, C. P. (1972). *Existence, relatedness and growth: Human needs and organizational settings,* New York: Free Press.

Allen, V. L. & Greenberger, D. B. (1980). Destruction and perceived control. In A. Baum and J. E. Singer (Eds.) *Advances in environmental psychology* (Vol. 2). Hillsdale, NJ: Erlbaum.

Alloy, L. B., Peterson, C., Abramson, L. Y., & Seligman, M. E. P. (1984). Attributional style and generality of learned helplessness. *Journal of Personality and Social Psychology, 46,* 681–687.

Alloy, L. B. & Tabachnik, N. (1984). Assessment of covariation by humans and animals: The joint influence of prior expectations and current situational information. *Psychological Review, 91,* 112–149.

Alloy, L. B., Peterson, C., Abramson, L. Y., & Seligman, M. E. P. (1984). Attributional style and generality of learned helplessness. *Journal of Personality and Social Psychology, 87,* 681–687.

Argyris, C. (1964). *Integrating the individual and the organization.* New York: Wiley.

Armstrong-Stassen, M. A. (1989). *The impact of work-force reduction on retained employees: How well do job survivors survive?* Unpublished doctoral dissertation. The Ohio State University, Columbus.

Ashford, S. J. & Cummunigs, L. L. (1983). Feedback as an individual resource: Personal strategies of creating information. *Organizational Behavior and Human Performance, 32,* 370–398.

Averill, J. R. (1973). Personal control over aversive stimuli and its relationship to stress. *Psychological Bulletin, 80,* 286–303.

Bandura, A. (1977). Self-efficacy: Toward a unifying theory of behavioral change. *Psychological Review, 89,* 191–215.

Bazerman, M. H. (1982). Impact of personal control on performance: Is added control always beneficial? *Journal of Applied Psychology, 67,* 472–479.

Bell, N. E. & Staw, B. M. (1989). People as sculptors versus sculpture: The roles of personality and personal control in organizations. In M. B. Arthur, D. T. Hall, and B. S. Lawrence (Eds.) *Handbook of career theory,* 232–250. New York: Cambridge University Press.

Brehm, J. W. (1966). *Response to loss of freedom: A theory of psychological reactance.* New York: Academic Press.

Brehm, S. S. & Brehm, J. W. (1981). *Psychological reactance: A theory of freedom and control.* New York: Academic Press.

Brockhaus, R. H. (1982). The psychology of the entrepreneur. In C. Kent, D. Sexton & K. Vesper (Eds.) *Encyclopedia of Entrepreneurship.* Englewood Cliffs, NJ: Prentice Hall, 39–56.

Brockner, J. (1988). The effects of work layoff on survivors: Research, theory, and practice. In B. M. Staw and L. L. Cummings (Eds.) *Research in Organizational Behavior,* Vol. 10. Greenwich, CT: JAI Press, 213–256.

Chanowitz, B. & Langer, E. J. (1981). Premature cognitive commitment. *Journal of Personality and Social Psychology, 41,* 1051–1063.

Dansky, K. H., Greenberger, D. B., & Strasser, S. (1989). *Personal control as an antecedent of burnout in health care settings.* Paper presented at the Annual Meeting of the Academy of Management. Washington.

Dansky, K. H., Greenberger, D. B., Strasser, S., & Dansky, L. S. (1990). *Analysis of physician attitudes toward persons with AIDS.* Unpublished manuscript.

Deci, E. L. (1972). The effects of contingent and noncontingent rewards and control on intrinsic motivation. *Organizational Behavior and Human Performance, 8,* 217–229.

Dweck, C. S. & Leggett, E. L. (1988). A social-cognitive approach to motivation and personality. *Psychological Review, 95,* 256–273.

Fiske, S. T. & Taylor, S. E. (1984). *Social cognition.* New York: Random House.

Feldman, D. C. (1984). The development and enforcement of group norms. *Academy of Management Review, 9,* 47–53.

Friedman, M. & Rosenman, R. H. (1974). *Type A Behavior and Your Heart.* Greenwich, CT: Fawcett.

Glass, D. C. & Singer, J. E. (1972). *Urban stress: Experiments on noise and social stressors.* New York: Academic Press.

Greenberger, D. B. & Sexton, D. L. (1988). An interactive model of new venture initiation. *Journal of Small Business Management, 26,* 1–7.

Greenberger, D. B. & Strasser, S. (1986). The development and application of a model of personal control in organizations. *Academy of Management Review, 11,* 164–177.

Greenberger, D. B., Strasser, S. Cummings, L. L. & Dunham, R. B. (1989). The impact of personal control on performance and satisfaction. *Organizational Behavior and Human Decision Processes, 43,* 29–51.

Greenberger, D. B., Strasser, S., & Lee, S. (1988). Personal control as a mediator between perceptions of supervisory behaviors and employee reactions, *Academy of Management Journal, 31,* 405–417.

Hackman, J. R. & Oldham, G. R. (1976). Motivation through the design of work: Test of a theory. *Organizational Behavior and Human Performance, 16,* 250–279.

Higgins, E. T. (1989). Self-discrepancy theory: What patterns of self-beliefs cause people to suffer? In L. Berkowitz (Eds.). *Advances in experimental social psychology,* (Vol. 22). New York: Academic Press, 93–131.

Jackson, S. C. (1983). Participation in decision making as a strategy for reducing job related tension. *Journal of Applied Psychology, 68,* 3–19.

Kahneman, D. & Tversky, A. (1973). On the psychology of prediction, *Psychological Review, 80,* 237–251.

Kanter, R. M. (1983). *The changemasters.* New York: Basic Books.

Kunda, Z. (1987). Motivated inference: Self-serving generation and evaluation of casual theories. *Journal of Personality and Social Psychology, 53,* 636–647.

Langer, E. J. (1982). *The psychology of control.* Beverly Hills, CA: Sage.

Langer, E. J. & Rodin, J. (1976). The effects of choice and enhanced personal responsibility: A field experiment in an institutional setting. *Journal of Personality and Social Psychology, 34,* 191–198.

Langer, E. J. (1989). Minding matters: The consequences of mindlessness-mindfulness. In L. Berkowitz (Ed.) *Advances in experimental social psychology* (Vol. 22). New York: Academic Press, 137–174.

Locke, E. A., Shaw, K. M., Saari, L. M., & Latham, G. P. (1981). Goal setting and task performance: 1969–1980. *Psychological Bulletin, 90,* 125–52.

Lord, C. G., Ross, L., & Lepper, M. R. (1979). Biased assimilation and attitude polarization:

The effects of prior theories on subsequently considered evidence. *Journal of Personality and Social Psychology, 37,* 2098–2109.

McClelland, D. C. (1985). *Human motivation.* Chicago: Scott Foresman.

Making open offices a little less open. (1988, November 8). *The Wall Street Journal.* p. B1.

Manz, C. C. & Sims, H. P. (1981). Vicarious learning: The influence of modeling on organizational behavior. *Academy of Management Review, 6,* 105–113.

Martinko, M. J. & Gardner, W. L. (1982). Learned helplessness: An alternative explanation for performance deficits. *Academy of Management Review, 7,* 195–204.

Maslow, A. H. (1943). A theory of human motivation. *Psychological Bulletin, 50,* 370–396.

Miller, D. T. & Ross, M. (1975). Self-serving biases in attribution of causality: Fact of fiction? *Psychological Bulletin, 82,* 213–225.

Miller, S. M., Brody, D. S., & Summerton, J. (1988). Styles of coping with threat: Implications for health. *Journal of Personality and Social Psychology, 54,* 142–148.

Newman, S. E. & Benassi, V. A. (1989). Putting judgments of control into context: Contrast effects. *Journal of Personality and Social Psychology, 56,* 876–889.

Newtson, D. (1976). Foundations of attribution: The perception of ongoing behavior. In J. Harvey, W. J. Ickes, & R. F. Kidd (Eds.), *New directions in attribution research* (Vol. 1). Hillsdale, NJ: Erlbaum.

Peterson, C. & Seligman, M. E. P. (1984). Casual explanations as a risk factor for depression: Theory and evidence. *Psychological Review, 91,* 347–374.

Porter, G., Greenberger, D. B., Miceli, M. P., & Strasser, S. (1990). Dispositional factors and enhancement of personal control: A preliminary investigation. Unpublished manuscript. The Ohio State University.

Pyszczynski, T. & Greenberg, J. (1987). Toward an integration of cognitive and motivational perspectives on social inference: A biased hypothesis testing model. In L. Berkowitz (Ed.) *Advances in experimental social psychology,* (Vol. 20). New York: Academic Press.

Rosenfield, D., Folger, R., & Adelman, H. F. (1980). When rewards reflect competence: A qualification of the overjustification effect. *Journal of Personality and Social Psychology, 39,* 368–376.

Rothbaum, F. M., Weisz, J. R., & Snyder, S. S. (1982). Changing the world and changing the self: A two process model of perceived control. *Journal of Personality and Social Psychology, 42,* 5–37.

Rotter, J. B. (1966). Generalized expectancies for internal versus external control of reinforcement. *Psychological Monographs, 80 (whole No. 609).*

Seligman, M. E. P. (1975). *Helplessness: On depression, development and death.* San Francisco: Freeman.

Seligman, M. E. P. & Schulman, P. (1986). Explanatory style as a predictor of productivity and quitting among life insurance agents. *Journal of Personality and Social Psychology, 50,* 832–838.

Snyder, M. & Ickes, W. J. (1985). Personality and social behavior. In G. Lindzey and E. Aronson (Eds.), *The handbook of social psychology* (Vol. II) (3rd Ed.), New York: Random House, 883–948.

Snyder, M., Stephan, W. G., & Rosenfield, D. (1978). Attributional egotism. In J. H. Harvey, W. J. Ickes, & R. F. Kidd (Eds.), *New directions in attribution research* (Vol. 2). Hillsdale, NJ: Erlbaum.

Staw, B. M. (1977). Motivation in organizations: Synthesis and redirection. In B. M. Staw and G. R. Salancik (Eds.) *New directions in organizational behavior.* Chicago: St: Clair.

Staw, B. M. (1986). Beyond the control graph: Steps toward a model of perceived control in organizations. In R. N. Stern and S. McCarthy (Eds.), *The organizational practice of democracy.* Chicester, UK: Wiley Ltd.

Taylor, S. E. & Fiske, S. T. (1978). Salience, attention, and attribution: Top of the head phenomena. In L. Berkowitz (Eds.), *Advances in experimental social psychology,* (Vol. 11). New York: Academic Press.

Tversky, A. & Kahneman, D. (1973). Availability: A heuristic for judging frequency and probability. *Cognitive Psychology, 5,* 207–232.

Weiner, B., Frieze, I., Kukla, A., Reed, L., Rest, S., & Rosenbaum, R. M. (1972). Perceiving the causes of success and failure. In E. E. Jones, D. E. Kanouse, H. H. Kelley, R. E. Nisbett, S. Valins, & B. Weiner, *Attribution: Perceiving the causes of behavior.* Morristown, NJ: General Learning Press.

Wicklund, R. A. & Braun, O. L. (1987). Incompetence and the concern with human categories. *Journal of Personality and Social Psychology, 53,* 373–382.

White, R. W. (1959). Motivation reconsidered: The concept of competence. *Psychological Review, 66,* 297–333.

Wortman, C. & Brehm, J. C. (1975). Responses to uncontrollable outcomes: An integration of reactance theory and the learned helplessness model. In L. Berkowitz (Ed.) *Advances in experimental social psychology,* vol. 8: 278–336. New York: Academic Press.

Wyer, R. S. Jr. & Srull, T. K. (1981). Category accessibility: Some theorietical and empirical issues concerning the processing of social stimulus information. In E. T. Higgins, C. P. Herman, & M. P. Zanna (Eds.) *Social cognition: The Ontario Symposium* (Vol. 1). Hillsdale, NJ: Erlbaum.

Zadny, J. & Gerard, H. B. Attributed intentions and information selectivity. (1974). *Journal of Experimental Social Psychology, 10,* 34–52.

BEHAVIORAL NEGOTIATION THEORY:

A FRAMEWORK FOR CONCEPTUALIZING DYADIC BARGAINING

Margaret A. Neale and Gregory B. Northcraft

ABSTRACT

This chapter summarizes a series of research perspectives that contribute to our understanding of dyadic bargaining, and develops a framework for future research in this area. In describing the state of dyadic negotiation research, two major research streams are considered: research about the *context* of negotiation settings and research about the *negotiators* themselves. From this review, we propose two major levels of factors which influence the dyadic negotiation process. This duality leads through contextual factors to the *claiming* of value and through negotiators' reconceptualization of their task to the *creating* of value in dyadic negotiation. Implications of this framework for future research directions are discussed.

Research in Organizational Behavior, Volume 13, pages 147–190.
Copyright © 1991 by JAI Press Inc.
All rights of reproduction in any form reserved.
ISBN: 1-55938-198-1

147

Negotiation has a large and diverse research tradition. It has been defined as "the process by which two or more interdependent parties who do not have identical preferences across decision alternatives make joint decisions" (Bazerman & Carroll, 1987:1). Further, negotiations occur "whenever the allocation of gains among participants to an agreement is subject to their own choice rather than predetermined by their circumstances" (Cross, 1969:1). It is our view that negotiation is a particular type of decisionmaking—decisionmaking in the larger sense of a social, psychological, and economic process. It is a joint interdependent process that entails coordinated action of parties with non-identical preference structures. The key elements of these definitions are *multiple, interdependent parties* with *non-identical preferences* making decisions that result in the *allocation of resources*. The focus of this paper is dyadic (two-person) bargaining and negotiation.

A number of scholars from a variety of disciplines have attempted to understand and conceptualize two-party bargaining behavior. Unfortunately, these same scholars, for the most part, each have been bound by a particular discipline or research tradition. In this chapter, we summarize a series of research perspectives to identify what is known about the nature of two-party bargaining or negotiation and develop a framework for future research in the area. To accomplish this, we propose a *behavioral negotiation theory* which specifically incorporates the theory and empirical results of a number of different research traditions. Incorporating the application and responsiveness of economic models of negotiation with psychological, cognitive, and communication research effectively integrates and extends the applicability of negotiation research to a wide variety of audiences.

A number of reviews of the negotiation literature have categorized previous research and variables of interest in a number of ways (Hamner, 1980; Lewicki, Weiss, & Lewin, 1989; Rubin & Brown, 1975). In formulating a behavioral theory of negotiation, this chapter is structured around two major research streams, portions of which have surfaced in previous reviews:

1. research concerning *contextual characteristics* of the negotiation setting; specifically, structural features of the negotiation and prominent other people; and
2. research concerning the *negotiators;* specifically, their cognitions and interaction processes.

The categorization of research within this behavioral negotiation theory framework is meant to be treated as suggestive rather than definitive and there is a certain allocation fluidity of research to categories. Many pieces of research could be placed in multiple categories and the categories themselves are not always conceptually distinct. This simply represents both the evolving nature of this framework and the ubiquitous nature of the phenomenon.

After summarizing these two research streams and providing examples of representative research in each, we will propose an integration in the form of the behavioral negotiation theory framework. Finally, the paper concludes with some directions for future research suggested by the framework.

CONTEXTUAL INFLUENCES

The context of a dyadic negotiation is the situation in which negotiators find themselves, and which the negotiators must treat as relatively fixed. In this section we review two classes of contextual influences on dyadic negotiation: (1) several *structural variables* incorporated in game theory models (power, deadlines, and integrative potential) whose influence has been subjected to empirical validation; and (2) another class of contextual features—*other people*—that also substantially influence dyadic negotiation processes and outcomes.

Structural Variables

Game theory provides an important theoretical backdrop for understanding and conceptualizing dyadic bargaining behavior. Rapoport (1959) has defined the "elementary game situation" as one:

> . . . in which two individuals whose interests are not coincident are in control of different sets of choices and endeavor to make their respective choices in such a manner as to emerge with an advantage (1959: 51).

There are obvious parallels between this definition of games and the definitions offered in the introduction to this paper for negotiation. Both involve multiple parties with non-identical preferences making interdependent decisions that allocate valued resources.

Rapoport notes that the elementary game situation is operationalized as (1) a range of choices (alternatives) for each player and (2) a range of consequences associated with the choices. The classic "game" is the Prisoner's Dilemma (Rapoport & Chammah, 1965), an example of which is provided in Figure 1. The dilemma here is that if both players select the lower price (intending to "corner the market") they will simply end up splitting the market at a lower price. Higher pricing offers greater possible *joint* benefit, but at the risk of personal loss to one player if the other prices are low.

A second game—the elementary negotiation situation—has been described

Retailer A

	price = $.90	price = $1.00
price = $.90	A = $45 B = $45	A = $0 B = $90
price = $1.00	A = $90 B = $0	A = $50 B = $50

Retailer B (row label at left)

Figure 1.

by Siegel and Fouraker (1960). In one example (Pruitt & Drews, 1969), a buyer and seller negotiate the selling price of an object whose value a priori falls somewhere between $2.50 and $15. Several researchers have offered mathematical analyses of bidding and concession rate strategies for this elementary negotiation problem (e.g., additional demands will be made in a dyadic negotiation as long as the expected benefit to be realized from those demands remains positive [Zeuthen, 1930; Cross, 1969:24]).

What is the relevance of game theory to understanding dyadic bargaining and negotiation? Formally, game theory has little to do with *observed* choice behaviors. Game theorists instead focus on the *logic* of (mythical) players' choices, and attempt to deduce the appropriate choices based upon mathematical calculations. These calculations assume: "super rationality" on the part of the players, complete information, and a simplified utility structure focused on exclusive self-interest. The province of game theory is to develop theorems about appropriate competitive choice over different classes of game (Roth, in press).

Game theory has been described as "unfit" as a descriptive model of the negotiation process because it is based upon such extreme assumptions (Rapoport, 1959). Recent updates of game theory have attempted to explore the ramifications of more relaxed assumptions, such as socially-moral utility functions (e.g., Camerer, 1989) or incomplete information (e.g., Myerson, 1986).

Another appealing criticism of game theory as a model of negotiation is that its emphasis on "mathematicizing" social interaction ignores the dynamic flavor of the negotiation interaction (Rapoport, 1959). Game theory concerns itself with the context in which dyadic negotiation occurs (e.g., equal vs. unequal power, incentive conditions) and how outcomes can be deduced from contextual features alone. Game theory ignores the role of behaviors and cognitions in *producing* negotiated outcomes. This is hardly accidental. Taken at its most extreme, the position of game theory is that the context of games (in this case, dyadic negotiations) determines outcomes. The behaviors and cognitions of negotiators simply represent the *unfolding* or "playing out" of the context's influence on outcomes.

Game theory has made two critical contributions to our understanding of dyadic bargaining. First, the mathematical modelling of game theory has provided bargaining researchers a "science of outcomes" against which bargaining behaviors can be measured. This "science of outcomes" includes such elements as *pareto optimality* and Nash equilibria (1953).

Second, game theory has spawned an impressive amount of derivative *empirical* research aimed at demonstrating and validating the tenets of game-theoretic mathematical modelling of choice behaviors. It is this tradition of game theory derivative research which provides much of our understanding of the actual influences of structural characteristics on dyadic negotiation. By 1977, for instance, more than 1000 studies had examined the choice behaviors of actual decisionmakers facing the Prisoner's Dilemma. (For a review of this work, see Rapoport & Chammah, 1965; Pruitt & Kimmell, 1977.)

The experimental results suggest that traditional game-theoretic models are "terrible predictors" of actual negotiator behavior (Roth, in press:2). However, classical game theory has catalyzed empirical researchers in their tests of the potential influence of structural variables on dyadic negotiation. Three structural variables are examined here: negotiator power, deadlines, and integrative potential. While the initial research in these areas might be described as direct tests of game theoretic assumptions, these traditions of research have grown well beyond their original roots.

Negotiator Power. Past research on the impact of power on the behavior of dyadic negotiators typically has examined the importance of equal power between negotiators within a simplified game theory paradigm such as a Prisoner's Dilemma. Power in these studies has been manipulated in two ways—through the status of the players and through the payoff matrices or experiment's reward structure (Rubin & Brown, 1975). In research using the status manipulation of power, Rekosh and Fiegenbaum (1966), Faley and Tedeschi (1971), and Baranowski and Summers (1972) all found that subjects made more cooperative choices when playing against an individual of *equal* status in contrast to playing against an opponent of higher status. When reward structure rather than status of the opponent was manipulated, studies conducted by McClintock, Messick, Kuhlman, and Campos (1973), Sheposh and Gallo (1973), Solomon (1960) and Swingle (1970) found that negotiators with equal power were more likely to behave cooperatively than those with unequal power. These findings have been replicated using other bargaining research paradigms. In a recent study, McAlister, Bazerman, and Fader (1986) found that dyadic negotiations in a competitive market are more likely to reach maximum joint benefit when the parties are of equal (rather than unequal) power.

Some research using the Prisoner's Dilemma paradigm has shown that dyads with *unequal* power make more cooperative choices than those with equal power (Komorita, Sheposh, & Braver, 1968; Tedeschi, Bonoma, & Novinson, 1970). An unpublished study by Roloff, Tutzauer, and Dailey (1987) also supports the contention that in dyadic negotiations, dyads with unequal power are more likely to reach agreements of higher joint benefit than those dyads with equal power. However, there has been little attempt to integrate these findings with the more commonly-held belief that equal power leads to more cooperative behavior.

The issue of power in dyadic negotiations also has been explored by examining the effects of BATNAs on dyadic negotiations. BATNA stands for Best Alternative To a Negotiated Agreement, and BATNA represents the options available to negotiating parties if no resolution is reached. BATNAs constitute a form of power for negotiators since a good BATNA reduces a negotiator's urgency to reach agreement and therefore decreases the likelihood that the negotiator will make concessions or search for settlement alternatives. A study by Pinkley, Neale, and Beggs (1989) used an eight-issue negotiation (adapted from Thompson & Hastie, in press). Each member of each negotiating dyad was in one of three conditions: high BATNA (very good alternative), low BATNA (very poor alternative), or no explicitly assigned BATNA. The results of this study demonstrated that dyads which had *equal* BATNAs, whether high or low, achieved superior outcomes when compared to those dyads with unequal power.

This result confirms previous research findings suggesting that within the dyad, unequal power affects the behavior of both the high-power and low-power party. However, the competitive disadvantage of unequal power dyads found by Pinkley, et al., (1989) may provide indirect support of previous research that suggests that the high-power party will act exploitatively and the low-power party will act submissively (Johnson & Ewens, 1971; Stevens, 1970; Swingle, 1970; Thibaut & Gruder, 1969). In focusing attention on exploitative or submissive behavior, the members of these unequal power dyads may ignore the opportunities available to them by maximizing the available joint outcomes. Thus, the quality of a particular negotiator's BAT-NA significantly influenced the amount of resources that particular negotiator received in the final negotiated settlement.

In trying to reconcile these mixed findings, one possible explanatory contender may have little to do with the cognitive activity of the negotiators. Rather, differences in the negotiation *tasks* may account for these inconsistent results. For example, in McAlister, et al., (1986) and Pinkley, et al., (1989), the issues to be negotiated included both integrative and distributive ones. The Roloff, et al. study (1987) and the Prisoner's Dilemma games each utilized only one *type* of issue: either distributive issues *or* integrative issues. When only one type of issue is available for allocation, the structure of the game may push the disputants to the pareto efficient frontier[1]—a pressure not experienced when *both* distributive and integrative issues are present.

Deadlines. There has been a great deal of anecdotal information about the frequency of eleventh hour agreements in naturally-occurring negotiations. In addition, game theorists have proposed deadline effects (Roth, in press) as well as providing empirical, laboratory support for these effects (Roth, Murnighan, & Schoumaker, 1988).

Stevens' (1963) work on collective bargaining suggests that the approach of deadlines brings pressure to bear on negotiators which manifests itself in changing the "least favorable terms upon which each party is willing to settle." (p. 100). Pruitt and Drews (1969), in an empirical test of the impact of deadlines, argues that deadlines (or time pressure) were effective because they (1) increased the perceived importance of reaching an agreement, (2) narrowed the number of options available to the negotiator for reaching an agreement, and (3) provided the negotiator with a rationale (other than weakness) for making concessions. The results of their study suggests that time pressure does indeed reduce levels of demands, aspirations and bluffing. However, they did not find any difference in size of concessions offered as a function of time pressure. Subsequent research (Benton, Kelley, & Liebling, 1972; Komorita & Barnes, 1969; Pruitt & Johnson, 1970) has found that heightened time pressure produces larger (or more frequent) concessions.

Not surprisingly, these deadline effects also manifest themselves in the final agreements reached by negotiators. Yukl, Malone, Hayslip, and Pamin (1976) found that negotiators under time pressure reached agreements sooner, but they also reached agreements of lower joint benefit. In fact, under low time pressure, 65 percent of the dyads reported disclosing their true interests; only 35 percent of the dyads disclosed under high time pressure.

In a related study, Carnevale and Lawler (1986) found the effect of time pressure on negotiation is dependent on the orientation of the participants. For individualistically-oriented negotiators (i.e., those focusing only on personal gain), high time pressure impeded their ability to reach an agreement as well as their ability to reach an agreement with high joint outcome. For negotiators with a cooperative orientation (i.e., those focusing on *both* own and others gains), time pressure had no effect either on their ability to reach an agreement or the quality of that agreement. According to the authors, these results suggest that while time pressures may foster greater cooperation by lowering aspirations (Pruitt, 1981), they also reduce information exchange and reduce the use of trial-and-error strategies (Carnevale & Lawler, 1986).

Integrative Potential.   An important structural feature of any negotiation is the range of possible agreements (settlements) and the capacity of any possible settlement to integrate the needs or demands of both parties. Explicit consideration of "integrative bargaining" can be traced to the work of Walton and McKersie (1965) which was derived from Follett's (1940) perspectives on integration. Generally, a negotiated settlement is said to be *integrative* to the extent that it reconciles (rather than compromises) the parties' interests and provides high joint benefit (Pruitt, 1981).

Integrative agreements are possible when negotiators differentially value elements of a dispute. The "Ugli Orange" case (Lewicki, Bowen, Hall, & Hall, 1988) provides a classic example of integrative potential in a negotiation. Two negotiators both have claims on and must agree to the disposition of a single shipment of oranges. Both desperately want the entire shipment; neither reasonably could expect more than half the shipment--a fair split between the two. However, one party really needs only the peels of the oranges, while the other party needs only the juice. The discovery of this differential valuing of these two elements of the settlement (peel and juice) results in a settlement of high joint benefit. One party receives a full shipment of orange peels and one party receives a full shipment of orange juice, all from a single shipment of oranges. This settlement *integrates* the needs of *both* parties. In contrast, a distributive agreement is one which simply divides available resources between parties without attempting to integrate their differential needs or values (e.g., half of the shipment of oranges to each party). Distributive agreements often seem unavoidable when negotiating parties equally value all elements of a settlement (for instance, if both parties wanted only the peels of the oranges).

Pruitt (1983) provides support for two antecedents to integrative bargaining: high aspirations and a problem-solving orientation. High aspirations refer to a negotiator's desire to fulfill completely his or her needs, and therefore an unwillingness to settle for a simple split (distribution) of available resources. A problem-solving orientation is a negotiator's predisposition to look beyond simple resource splits and identify or discover differential needs that make integrative trade-offs possible. Of course, these antecedents refer to factors which encourage the parties to implement strategies that increase the probability that *if* integrative potential exists, it will be realized. To the extent that there are multiple issues (or settlement elements) and negotiators have different preferences for these issues, then the negotiation has integrative potential.

Past research on dyadic bargaining has focused almost exclusively on joint benefit or joint utility as the primary indicator of outcome quality (cf., Pruitt, 1981; Bazerman, Magliozzi, & Neale, 1985; McAlister, Bazerman, & Fader, 1986; Neale, Huber, & Northcraft, 1987). In negotiations with logrolling potential (i.e., trading off differentially-valued elements of the settlement), joint utility is the sum of the *subjective* value to each party of the final negotiated agreement. Typically, researchers have assumed that higher joint benefit means higher quality, more integrative outcomes. The joint-maximum settlement usually represents a single settlement which maximizes the value of available resource distribution.

Recent work by Tripp (1989) argues that focusing on the joint utility of a settlement ignores a second fundamental aspect of settlement quality—efficiency. A settlement is efficient to the extent that it can be improved for either party *only* at the expense of the other party (i.e., it has not wasted any available resources). Figure 2 provides the joint utility curve for a negotiation with integrative potential. If Negotiator 1 takes home everything up for grabs in the negotiation (Settlement A), Negotiator 1 would realize $8000 worth of benefit, and the total joint benefit of the agreement would be $8000. This would be a completely efficient settlement—either negotiator could do better only at the expense of the other. Notice that Settlement B would provide equal joint benefit ($8000) but would not be equally efficient, since either party could do better (Settlements C or D) without any loss by the other party. Because the two parties in this case differentially value different elements of the settlement, logrolling their complementary needs could yield an agreement like Settlement E, which is as efficient as Settlement A but of higher joint benefit ($12,000).

Mumpower (1989) argues that a third aspect of dyadic negotiation settlement quality is *equity*. He suggests that agreements may differ in terms of efficiency, joint utility, and the absolute differences in utility "scores" between the negotiators. He notes that while typically there will be a large

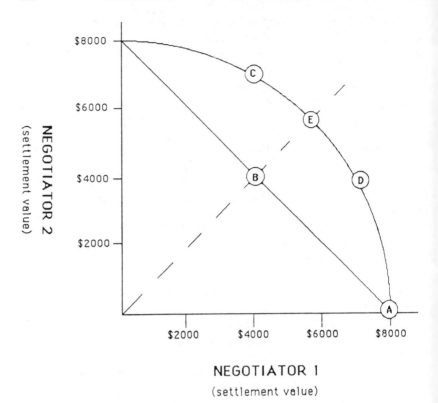

Figure 2.

number of possible equitable agreements to a negotiation (depicted by the dotted line in Figure 2), many of these points (such as Settlement B) would not be efficient.

Interestingly, the recent work of Mumpower (1989) and to a lesser extent Roth (in press), among others, highlights the importance of fairness and equity in the negotiated outcome, which in turn emphasizes the importance of the negotiating other. Thus, it is not sufficient for negotiation researchers to know the structure or form of the task or game. Critical to the understanding and prediction of outcomes is the negotiator and his or her opponent. It is with the addition of these human variables that the study of negotiation moves from a clean set of assumptions and axioms to the infinitely "messier" context of social interaction.

PEOPLE AS CONTEXT

Other people represent an important contextual influence on dyadic negotiator behavior. Two examples of people contextual influences are constituencies and third-parties.

Just as game theory provides a theoretical backdrop for understanding structural influences, *agency theory* (e.g., Jensen & Meckling, 1976) may provide some theoretical underpinnings for people as contextual influences on dyadic bargaining. Agency theory is focused on the distinction in business between those who own capital (called "principals"—for instance, the owners of a firm) and those who act as "agents" of the owners (for instance, the firm's managers). Agency theory is concerned with the differences between the perspectives of these two parties and the likely impact of these differences on principals' and agents' behaviors. In a dyadic negotiation, for instance, a party negotiating for himself or herself (a principal) is likely to experience different incentives than if negotiating (as an agent) for a constituency.

These principal/agent distinctions are consequential in dyadic bargaining. If an agent is able to view a dispute more objectively than either principal, that objective detachment also may translate into less motivation to search for high quality integrative agreements, rather than simply accepting compromises or not making concessions (Rubin & Sander, 1988). A common example of agent-mediated dyadic bargaining occurs in the residential real estate market in the United States. Real estate agents, acting as agents of the seller (although one usually nominally represents the buyer) facilitate the negotiation between sellers and potential buyers.

A laboratory simulation of the real estate negotiation compared the process and outcome when there were agents in the negotiation and when the negotiations occurred directly between the two principals. There were significantly more impasses when agents were involved in the negotiation than when they were not. In addition, the real estate sold for significantly higher prices when the negotiation included agents as compared to the direct negotiation condition (Bazerman, Neale, Valley, Zajac, & Kim, 1990). Thus, the introduction of agents into this type of negotiation fundamentally altered the outcome, and had (at least for buyers) a negative effect.

Constituencies

An important component of the situation in which the negotiator finds him or herself is whether or not the negotiator represents a constituency. Audiences that are to any extent dependent on a bargainer for representation of their interests are constituencies. While not cast within this framework, research on constituencies has indirectly explored many of the issues raised by agency theory. Research on constituencies suggests that the physical or mere psychological presence of a constituency or audience motivates the negotiator to seek positive, and avoid negative, evaluation (Brown, 1968; 1970; Brown & Garland, 1971). Findings have demonstrated that audience members need not be known to the negotiator nor have any control over rewards to exert considerable influence over a negotiator's behavior (Rubin & Brown, 1975).

The negotiator's need for positive evaluation may be a function of the accountability of the negotiator to the constituency and the commitment and loyalty a negotiator expresses towards this constituency (Rubin & Brown, 1975). In a study of contract negotiations between International Harvester and the United Autoworkers, McKersie, Perry, and Walton (1965) found that labor and management constituencies (and dependent audiences in general) have the power to apply sanctions to those negotiators who do not perform adequately. In such situations, sanctions might include the removal of the negotiator from his or her role, reduced constituency support, and damage to the negotiator's reputations (Rubin & Brown, 1975).

The pressure generated by constituencies towards loyalty, commitment, and advocacy of a particular position may not be in the best interest of either the constituency or the negotiator. Empirical evidence (Blake & Mouton, 1961; Roby, 1960; Lamm & Kogan, 1970) suggests that as the negotiator's commitment to the positions espoused by a salient, dependent audience increases, his or her ability to evaluate alternative proposals (especially those initiated by an opponent) and to act (either by reciprocal concession or acceptance) is significantly decreased. Thus, the presence of a constituency may decrease the probability that a negotiator will demonstrate the problem-solving orientation noted by Pruitt (1983) to be a critical antecedent to high-quality settlements.

These impression management concerns in response to the existence of a constituency pose a serious dilemma for the negotiator when it comes to concessionary behavior. To reach a resolution, each side must make concessions. However, the very act of compromising is likely to be viewed by a constituency as a sign of weakness. Thus, concessions must be minimized to maintain the illusion of strength for the constituency. One way in which a negotiator may mitigate this dilemma is through the introduction of a third party. While research suggests that parties to a dispute typically view a third party's intervention as disruptive (Pruitt & Johnson, 1972; Rubin, 1980), there are some benefits from the involvement of a third party. Rubin (1980) reports that negotiators were less apprehensive about making concessions at the request of a third party than they were when no third party was present. Such concessions can be attributed (for instance, when explaining them to a constituency) to the influence of the third party and may provide additional pressure for reciprocal concessions from an opponent. Thus, concessions can be made without the loss of face which may occur in a typical negotiation. However, constituency-oriented behavior is not the only way in which third parties influence negotiator behavior. As described in the following section, third parties are another major factor in predicting negotiator behavior in dyadic encounters.

Third Parties

Much of the research on third parties in dyadic negotiation has focused on the changes brought about by the existence of a third party charged with resolving the dispute if the parties fail to do so. Typically the research in this area has been limited to examinations of institutional third parties such as mediators or arbitrators. In addition to emphasizing this form of third party intervention, research has shown that negotiators alter their behavior based upon the knowledge of third-party impasse procedures that would be used in the event of an impasse. For example, Neale (1984) found that when the potential costs of third party intervention (e.g., arbitration) were made salient to the negotiators, both concession and settlement rates increased.

Arbitration. Arbitration is a process whereby the third party has control over the outcome of the intervention. The two most typical types of arbitration are conventional arbitration and final offer arbitration. In conventional arbitration, the arbitrator is not limited by the positions of the parties in determining the final award (Elkouri & Elkouri, 1981). Farber, Neale, and Bazerman (in press) examined the importance of the costs of conventional arbitration in the context of two-person union management contract negotiations of wage rates. Direct costs were manipulated by rewarding subjects monetarily for their attained agreements minus a penalty if arbitration were invoked. To the extent that subjects incurred direct costs, they were more likely to obtain a settlement, even in cases where there was no theoretical overlap of positions or interests between the negotiators.

Under final offer arbitration, the arbitrator determines the award by selecting one or the other of the last positions of the parties. Laboratory (Grigsby & Bigoness, 1981; Notz & Starke, 1978, Starke & Notz, 1981; Neale & Bazerman, 1983; Farber, Neale, & Bazerman, 1989) and field research (Kochan, Mironi, Ehrenberg, Baderschneider, & Jick, 1979; Feuille, 1979; Delaney & Feuille, 1984) provide evidence that resolution rates are higher when negotiators are threatened with final offer arbitration than when they are threatened with conventional arbitration. In addition, negotiators are more willing to make concessions under final offer arbitration than under conventional arbitration (Stevens, 1966; Neale & Bazerman, 1983).

The two previous sections have focused on third parties that are, for the most part, impartial. Recent research has begun to examine other types of third parties such as those who are partial (i.e., agents who have a vested interest in the outcome) as well as those (for instance, managers) whose intervention behaviors are not constrained by regulation, practice, or institutions (Neale, Pinkley, Brittain, & Northcraft, 1989).

Despite its apparent relevance, however, agency theory has only recently been explored as a theoretical backdrop for dyadic negotiation research (Bazerman, Neale, Valley, Zajac, & Kim, 1990). While research on negotiator constituencies is actually a form of agency theory research, even these obvious connections have not been made. Agency theory might provide a useful and refreshing framework for thinking about the behavior of third parties. For instance, it seems that there are two contributions that researchers can make through the study of principals and agents in negotiations. First, they could investigate exactly who third-parties in negotiations view as their principals—the individual, the institution (e.g., the union or management of a company, the shareholders of an organization,) or society. Second, researchers could identify the goals of third parties—for instance, do those goals include the creating of effective, efficient, or fair agreements?

NEGOTIATOR INFLUENCES

Negotiation has been defined as "the deliberate interaction of two or more complex social units which are attempting to define or redefine the terms of their interdependence" (Walton & McKersie, 1965:35). Featured in this definition is the idea that *the behavioral processes of interaction between parties* are important components of dyadic negotiation. Several authors (e.g., Kochan, 1980; Kipnis & Schmidt, 1983) have noted that negotiation research typically focuses on the connection between bargaining episode contexts (specifically, structural and situational features) and negotiated outcomes. The thoughts and plans of negotiators and their actual bargaining behaviors—what is said by whom and with what effect—are treated as something of a "black box." The next section of this chapter examines two of the contents of this "black box" of negotiation: *negotiator interaction processes,* including influence tactics and communication behaviors; and *negotiator cognitions,* including planning, information processing, and affect.

Interaction Processes

Influence Tactics. While social scientists have been interested for some time in generating a simple taxonomy of interpersonal influence tactics, the results to date remain unconvincing. Several deductive schemes have been proposed, including French and Raven's (1959) five bases of power (rewards, coercion, expertise, legitimacy, and charisma), and Kelman's (1958) three strategies for opinion change (compliance, identification, and internalization). Most deductive taxonomies have resisted attempts at empirical validation. Kipnis and Schmidt (1983) suggest that deductive schemes of influence tactics may resist validation because they tend to confuse resources which are the basis for influence tactics and the influence tactics themselves.

Classification schemes also have been derived empirically in several different settings. Goodchild, Quadrado, and Raven (1975) asked students to write brief essays on the topic, "How I get my way." Kipnis, Schmidt, and Wilkinson (1980) used a similar recall-of-critical-incidents methodology to evaluate the influence tactics used by managers when trying to negotiate with subordinates, peers, and superiors. Empirically-derived classification schemes of these sort typically find three primary *dimensions* of interpersonal influence along which persuasive tactics vary: assertion, rational argument, and manipulation (Kipnis & Schmidt, 1983).

Researchers also have attempted to identify contextual factors that determine which persuasion tactics might be used and when. As noted in Figure 3, some strategies are preferred when dealing with superiors, others when dealing with subordinates. In general, more assertive tactics are preferred when dealing with someone of apparently lower power or status (e.g., Wilkinson & Kipnis, 1978). Choice of persuasion tactics also may be predicated on the intended objective. Legitimate organizational objectives will be pursued with assertion (to subordinates) or rational argument (to superiors): the pursuit of personal objectives is likely to favor "softer" (manipulative) tactics, like ingratiation. Tactics employed also may vary according to the perceived probability that a request will be favored. More coercive tactics are likely to be employed when compliance to a request appears unlikely.

Figure 3.   Most to Least Popular Strategies Used in All Countries

	When Managers Influenced Superiors*	When Managers Influenced Subordinates
Most popular	Reason Coalition Ingratiation Bargaining	Reason Assertiveness Ingratiation Coalition
Least Popular	Assertiveness Higher Authority	Bargaining Higher Authority Sanctions

*The strategy of sanctions is omitted in the scale that measures upward influence (from Kipnis & Schmidt, 1983).

It seems odd that persuasion tactics in bargaining have received so little attention, since tactical action is at the very heart of the negotiation enterprise (Bacharach & Lawler, 1981) and can be consequential. In a study reported in Roloff, et al., (1987) negotiators' choices of persuasion tactics were significantly related to the likelihood of impasse. Thus, these variables are potent determinants of negotiated outcomes, but heretofore remain relatively unexplored.

Communication.   Communication has been defined as "the production, transmission, and interpretation of symbols" (Roloff, 1987:485). Several researchers have commented on the importance of communication to negotiation, noting (for instance) that communication is "at the heart of the negotiating process . . . is the central instrumental process" in the negotiation enterprise (Lewicki & Litterer, 1985:157).

Research on communication tactics has followed two paths: (1) studies which focus on the effects of communication on outcomes, and (2) studies which focus on determinants of communication tactical choices. Within this first category, research has examined the effects of both communication content and form.

Communication content and settlements.   Theye and Seller (1979) have argued that what is important in communication research is what the parties communicate to each other. In examining both verbal and non-verbal behavior, these researchers found that negotiations characterized by more friendly interaction were more likely to reach a settlement. Those negotiations which were characterized by a negative tone were more likely to end in impasse.

Other researchers (e.g., Lewis & Fry, 1977) also have found that integrative agreements are more likely to occur if negotiators avoid using insults and threats.

Roloff, Tutzauer, and Dailey (1987) found that in distributive bargaining contexts, arguing about responsibility was more likely to lead to impasse, while increasing the negotiator's authority was less likely to lead to impasse. When both negotiators had low authority, each was more likely to respond to the opponent with arguments rather than with concessions or offers. This greater use of argumentation among low-authority negotiators may occur because they have fewer options available.

In recent years, research into the phenomenon of organizational justice has been redirected to include a social component. In the past, research in this area has been focused almost exclusively on the "narrowly psychological" and individual issues of the *perception* of justice and has failed to acknowledge that "an injustice [could] create a 'social' predicament for the harm-doer," and that "people want to know the reasons for an allocation decision, as a means of determining the fairness of such an action" (Bies, 1987: 293). Bringing in the notion of a social interaction clears the way to include interactional justice and the concepts of accounts in the content of communications between negotiators.

As an illustration of the importance of accounts as communication content in dyadic negotiations, Bies, Shapiro, and Cummings (1988) asked MBA students to recount a request or proposal they had recently made of their current employer—a request that was rejected. The purpose of this study was to determine the impact of the accounts given with the rejection on the individual's subsequent judgments of fairness. Accounts included claims of mitigating circumstances, the perceived adequacy of the reasoning supporting the claim, and the perceived sincerity of the employer. Interestingly, there were no differences in the fairness judgments regardless of whether or not mitigating circumstances were claimed. In contrast, claims that were perceived to be based upon adequate reasoning or when the employer was perceived to be sincere were negatively related to feelings of anger, procedural *in*justice, and disapproval of the employer by the employee. Other research (Bies, 1987, Bies & Shapiro, 1988; Brockner, Grover, Greenberg, in press; Folger & Martin, 1986) has supported the notion that causal accounts with adequate reasoning and sincerity are able to reduce employees' negative feelings to a rejection or, in some cases, an unfair decision.

Communication form and settlements. A set of studies by Donohue (1981a; 1981b) takes the perspective that communication rules have a direct effect on the outcome of negotiation. This work suggests that winners and losers in a negotiation situation use communication rules differently. More successful negotiators made more offers and stuck to them, rejected losers' offers more often, and made fewer concessions. In contrast, less successful negotiators made more concessions and were less firm in their positions than successful negotiators. Similar findings also were reported by Harnett and Cummings (1980). Lewis and Fry (1977) found more integrative agreements when their negotiators suggested many proposals and solicited reactions to their proposals.

From a different tact, Greenberg (in press) provides support for the premise that the *appearance* of fairness in dyadic negotiation is at least as important as *being* fair. In fact, he argues that justice is an important consideration in social exchanges for impression management reasons (Schlenker, 1980; Giacalone & Rosenfeld, in press). As a form of impression management, the appearance of justice may be used as the conduit for attaining other goals. While it may be difficult to determine the specific motivations of a particular behavior, Greenberg (1978) found that equitable divisions of reward were made by persons claiming to be trying to maximize their own gain or the gain of others. In an unpublished piece by McClintock, he found that as soon as children were able to understand the differences between equity and equality norms, they chose to apply the particular norm that maximized their return. Thus, this suggests that individuals may select a particular norm ostensibly as a "fair" means of allocation, while the particular norm chosen actually is the one which maximizes their share of the resource (Leventhal, 1976; Greenberg & Cohen, 1982).

Communication as outcome.   Apparently communication tactics play an important role in the unfolding of a dyadic negotiation. Some research has looked at the other side of this issue—that is, the factors that predict which communication tactics will be used. For instance, Putnam and Jones (1982) found that labor negotiators were more likely to use threats and rejections; managers were more likely to use commitments and self-supporting arguments. Carnevale and Isen (1986) found that recently-amused negotiators use less contentious tactics. Donohue, Weider-Hatfield, Hamilton, and Diez (1985) found that when conflict was high and when negotiators were required to use a decisionmaking procedure to settle the conflict, they used less immediate and more formal language. Finally, Donohue, Diez, and Hamilton (1984) demonstrated that organizational role also may influence communication tactics choices. Using union-management negotiations as the setting for their study, they found that union negotiators tended to use more attacking tactics.

Negotiator Cognitions

Negotiator cognitions are what goes on in the heads of negotiators. We will consider three broad classes of negotiator cognitions: planning, information processing, and affect. Finally, individual differences (i.e., personality variables) will be explored as stable sources of information processing and affect influences. The distinction between information processing and affect is meant to parallel the distinction between "cold" and "hot" cognitive processing prevalent in psychology in the 1970s. Information processing refers to a negotiator's intake and compilation of environmental inputs in order to make sense of the negotiation context. Affect is the expression of emotions and needs in cognitions. Both information processing and affect are of interest particularly as they influence the planning and execution of bargaining strategy and tactics.

Negotiation Planning. Planning for the negotiation is one of the primary ways in which an individual can identify systematic mechanisms for developing and implementing bargaining strategies. In support of the importance of planning to develop strategies and tactics, Lewicki and Litterer have suggested that "planning and preparation are the most important parts of negotiation" (1985:47). Work by Bass (1966), Carroll, Bazerman, and Maury (1988), Donohue, Weider-Hatfield, Hamilton, and Diez (1985), and Druckman (1968) have all suggested that features of the planning process significantly and systematically influence bargaining outcomes. Until recently, however, little empirical research has been conducted which focuses on the planning process specifically. This seems unfortunate because the plans of negotiators can provide considerable insight into the behavioral intentions, maneuvers, and strategic mistakes made by each party (Chmielewski, 1982; Wall, 1985).

Roloff and Jordon (1989) have initiated a series of studies to clarify the relationship among negotiator plans, interactions, and outcomes. In the first study, they examined three components of negotiator plans: strategic elements of the plan (argumentation, relationship-building, logrolling, concession-making, and coercion); the interactive nature of the plans (extent to which the negotiator takes into consideration the strategic alternatives of the other); and the nature of revisions to the plans (what alternative strategies and tactics are considered if the original ones prove ineffective). This first study considered the impact of three sets of independent variables on negotiator plans: level of aspiration (high or low); integrative potential (high or low); and role (buyer or seller). The results suggested that negotiators with high aspirations in games with integrative potential are likely to logroll; 81 percent of the subjects in this condition suggested this "trade-off" strategy, compared with 38 percent of subjects with low aspirations. Negotiators generally proved unwilling or unable to switch strategies during the session; in their revised or back-up plans, negotiators typically became more coercive and were less willing to consider concession-making or relationship-building as viable strategies. Finally, there was a significant relationship between general bargaining experience and the extent to which individuals were likely to consider logrolling in their plans.

Information Processing

Recent research in the cognitive tradition has identified a variety of ways in which information processing strategies—in particular, cognitive heuristics or "rules of thumb"—have influenced negotiator performance. For a recent review of negotiation research from this perspective, see Bazerman and Carroll (1987). The appropriate use of these "rules" results in more efficient cognitive processing. However, when used inappropriately these cognitive heuristics systematically bias negotiator performance. Negotiation researchers have identified five information processing strategies that produce biases in negotiators' performance: framing, anchoring-and-adjustment, availability, overconfidence, and reactive devaluation.

Framing. The impact of framing on negotiators arises in changes in the negotiator's risk attitude when confronting potential gains versus confronting potential losses. Decisionmakers are risk-averse when evaluating potential gains and risk-seeking when evaluating potential losses. (See Tversky & Kahneman, 1981, for a detailed discussion.) In negotiation, the risk-averse course of action is to accept an offered settlement; the risk-seeking course of action is to hold out for future, potential concessions. In a number of studies researchers have found that positively framed negotiators complete more transactions and, thus, outperform negatively framed negotiators in a competitive market. However, negatively framed negotiators are able to complete individual transactions of greater average value (Bazerman, Magliozzi, & Neale, 1985; Neale & Bazerman, 1985b; Neale & Northcraft, 1986; Neale, Huber & Northcraft, 1987).

Anchoring and Adjustment. Slovic and Lichtenstein (1971) found that an arbitrarily chosen reference point will significantly influence value estimates, and that those estimates will be insufficiently adjusted away from this reference point when estimating the true value of an object.

Use of the anchoring-and-adjustment heuristic can bias the negotiation process in a number of ways. First, it can provide at least a partial explanation for the importance of initial offers in bargaining. Rubin and Brown (1975) note that early moves are critical in determining the psychological context in which negotiation occurs. Research has shown that final agreements are more strongly influenced by initial offers than by subsequent concessionary behavior (Liebert, Smith, Hill & Keiffer, 1968). Since issues in a negotiation often are of uncertain or ambiguous value, an initial offer can "anchor" subsequent estimates by both sides of the value of that issue. Thus, tough-to-soft and door-in-the-face strategies are both more successful than their counterparts (soft-to-tough and foot-in-the-door, respectively) because they take advantage of the anchoring effects of high initial offers (Chertkoff & Conley, 1967; Coker, Neale, & Northcraft, 1987).

Anchoring and adjustment also provides an explanation for the effectiveness of goal setting (Huber & Neale, 1986) and limit-setting (Neale & Bazerman, 1985a) on negotiation settlements. Just as initial offers may act as a cognitive anchor, adjusting the negotiator's perception of what is possible, goals or limits may drive a negotiator's perception of what is attainable or even acceptable. In fact, setting goals in a negotiation may serve as a strategic countervailing force to the opponent's use of an initial offer to anchor the negotiation.

Availability. Not all of a negotiator's past experiences are equally likely to be coded in memory nor are all of his or her related experiences equally likely to be recalled. Consequently, the availability of past and present information plays an important role in the negotiator's evaluation of alternatives (Tversky & Kahneman, 1973).

Colorful, dynamic, concrete, and otherwise vivid or distinctive information disproportionately garners attention and thereby is likely to be overused when negotiators make decisions (Taylor & Thompson, 1982). Northcraft and Neale (1986), for instance, found that because opportunity costs are much less concrete than out-of-pocket costs, they are much less likely to be included in financial decisionmaking. Similarly, in a laboratory study of bargaining, Neale (1984) found that manipulating the availability of personal and organizational costs produced systematic changes in negotiator behavior. When personal costs of settlement were made particularly salient or vivid, negotiators were less likely to settle. When third-party intervention costs were made salient, negotiators were more likely to settle. Particularly vivid past experiences are also likely to disproportionately influence negotiators simply because these experiences can so easily be recalled from memory.

Overconfidence. There is clear evidence that decisionmakers in general and negotiators specifically have unwarranted levels of confidence in their judgment abilities (Einhorn, 1978), particularly in novel or unusual situations (Einhorn & Hogarth, 1978). In fact, research has demonstrated that the probability estimates assigned to uncertain events are unjustifiably high [and reported confidence intervals of 98 percent cover as little as 60 percent of the actual events (Alpert & Raiffa, 1982)].

Bazerman and Neale (1982), for instance, found that negotiators who were subject to final offer arbitration estimated that there was, on average, a 67.8 percent probability that their offer would be accepted. While any one offer submitted under final offer arbitration might have a 67 percent probability of acceptance, the opposing offer could necessarily have only a 33 percent probability of acceptance. This overconfidence was found to reduce the amount of concessionary behavior and increase the number of negotiations that ended in impasse.

Reactive Devaluation.   Reactive devaluation is the tendency for disputants to devalue each other's concessions simply because they were conceded by the other side (Stillinger, Epelbaum, Keltner, & Ross, in press). Therefore, terms that appear mutually beneficial when advanced by one's own side may seem disadvantageous when proposed by the other party, even if the terms of the proposal are identical.

A number of explanations have been offered as the basis for reactive devaluation. For instance, the willingness of an adversary to offer concessions may convey information about the value the adversary attaches to what would be given up. In fact, one might assume that an adversary places less value on what is being given up than what, potentially, could be gained in an exchange of concessions. A second explanation for reactive devaluation is that concessions readjust the other's expectations of what can be attained. Finally, it may be that concessions are discounted because they were offered by a negative source—the opponent. In fact, any interpretations about the basis for the concession, omissions, or ambiguities are likely to be the most malevolent possible (Stillinger, et al., in press).

These five heuristics—framing, anchoring-and-adjustment, availability, overconfidence, and reactive devaluation—hardly provide an exhaustive list of the information processing strategies to which negotiators may fall prey, and that bias the processes and outcomes of negotiation. These heuristics do illustrate some ways in which negotiators' information processing can alter their behaviors and negotiation outcomes.

Beyond heuristics.   There is a more global sense in which negotiator's information processing strategies influence the processes and outcomes of negotiation. Negotiator cognition is the lens through which negotiation occurs. The use of the word "lens" here is important. Negotiators do more than just process (perhaps incorrectly) information about the context in which negotiations occur. Negotiators also *perceive* that context, and react to their perceptions in ways that validate or enact (Weick, 1979) those perceptions. Thus, it is negotiators' cognitions which *contextualize* negotiations.

An example of cognitive contextualization by negotiators was provided in the BATNA study conducted by Pinkley, Neale, and Beggs (1989). When subjects were asked to estimate the BATNA of the other party in the negotiation, the results showed that subjects tended to project their own BATNA onto their perceptions of their opponent. If they had a high BATNA, they assumed that their fellow-negotiator also had a high BATNA. Given the effects (noted earlier) that power can have on dyadic bargaining, this perceptual distortion of the actual power dynamics could be expected to be quite consequential.

The cognitive contextualization of situations by negotiators becomes particularly important in view of the role of scripts in social interaction processes. Schank and Abelson (1977) define a script as:

> . . . a structure that describes appropriate sequences of events in a particular context. A script is made up of slots and requirements about what can fill those slots—a predetermined stereotyped sequence of actions. . . (1977: 41).

Thus, particular interpretations of situations will elicit particular scripts. These scripts in turn dictate which behaviors are either encouraged or prohibited, and even which aspects of a situation are relevant or irrelevant. A particular interpretation of a situation thus creates a whole set of actions and expectations. For instance, research suggests that initial offers in dyadic negotiations are not sensitive to the unique structure of the negotiation but are often at the extreme ends of the bargaining zone (Bazerman, et al., 1989). This may occur because negotiators invoke an "extreme first offer" script. However, research on scripts in dyadic bargaining is woefully underdeveloped.

"Fixed Pie" Assumption. An important example of cognitive contextualization by negotiators is the "fixed pie" assumption. The distributive perspective views the bargaining process as a procedure for the division of a fixed pie of resources. Thus, one side gains at the necessary expense of the other. In contrast, an integrative perspective on negotiation focuses on the tradeoffs that can be made to the mutual benefit of the parties. Walton and McKersie (1965) suggest that negotiators tend to view bargaining with a distributive, rather than integrative, cognitive filter.

However, most disputes have more than one issue at stake and the parties often have different relative preferences for each of these issues, so that most negotiations do have the potential for integrative joint gains. In one of the few pieces of research to measure negotiator's assumptions directly, Thompson and Hastie (in press) found that two-thirds of their student negotiators assumed that their opponents had interests that directly conflicted with their own.

The notion of cognitive contextualization by negotiators highlights the importance of research which assesses the interpretative assumptions (and biases) that negotiators bring to the situation-interpretation task. For instance, Pinkley (in press), has identified three dimensions necessary to describe disputants' cognitive representations of conflict situations: Relationship/task, Emotional/intellectual, and Compromise/win. In a test of the importance of these dimensions on negotiated outcome, Pinkley and Northcraft (1989) found that negotiators' interpretations of a dispute significantly influenced the content of agreements. For instance, when negotiators perceived a dispute in emotional terms, they tended to include apologies or statements about how the negative feelings generated by the dispute were to be handled.

Affect

One of the least studied areas of dyadic negotiation is the impact of affect on negotiation processes and outcome. In other contexts, positive affect has been shown to influence generosity and helpfulness (Isen, 1970; Isen & Levine, 1972), enhance liking of others and improve conceptions of human nature (Gouaux, 1971; Veitch & Griffitt, 1976), and to lessen aggressiveness and hostility (Baron, 1984). Specifically, work by Isen and her colleagues (Isen, 1983; Isen & Daubman, 1984; Isen, Johnson, Mertz, & Robinson, 1985) suggest that those who are made to "feel good" will tend to be able to solve problems creatively.

In one of the few studies to assess the impact of affect on negotiator performance, Carnevale and Isen (1986) found that "good humor" (the receipt of a small gift) facilitates creative problem solving and integrative agreements. Other research has shown that the display of positive emotions can bring about a variety of desirable outcomes. Tidd and Lockard (1978) examined the influence of smiling by a cocktail waitress over the tips she received from 96 customers. The 48 patrons who received broad smiles offered larger tips ($23.20 total) as compared to those who were offered weak or minimal smiles ($9.40 total). Positive emotions around an event have been shown to be associated with making that event more available from memory (Isen & Shalker, 1982; Teasdale & Fogarty, 1979). A recent review piece on the influence of emotion in organizational life calls for more research, both quantitative and qualitative, in this area (Rafaeli & Sutton, 1989).

Need-Based Illusions. Need-based illusions represent another way that affect influences dyadic bargaining. Need-based illusions are similar in some respects to the cognitive biases described previously. However, need-based illusions are motivated not by hard-wired tendencies of cognitive biases; rather, they are motivated by an individual's need to reinterpret reality to make it more palatable. In a study by Janis (1962) examining reactions to warnings, he suggests that individuals may underestimate the danger or potential risk of a threatening situation to reduce their felt needs for vigilance and reassurance.

Taylor and Brown (1988) have described three of these need-based illusions: the illusion of superiority, the illusion of optimism, and the illusion of control. The illusion of superiority is based upon an unrealistically positive view of the self, both in absolute and relative terms. This is exemplified in the individual's emphasis on his or her positive aspects and discounting of the negative aspects. In relative terms, the illusion of superiority leads individuals to believe that they are more honest, capable, intelligent, courteous, insightful, and fair than others. In line with the notion of the fundamental attribution error, individuals give themselves more responsibility for their successes and take less responsibility for their failures while holding others both responsible for their own failures and not responsible for their own successes (Schlenker & Miller, 1977; Taylor & Koivumaki, 1976).

The second illusion is one of optimism. Individuals are unrealistically optimistic about their future relative to others and also relative to some normative base-rate. Individuals underestimate the likelihood that they will experience "bad" future events and overestimate the likelihood that they will experience "good" future events relative to others who might experience this event.

A final need-based illusion—and one at least as pervasive as superiority and optimism—is the illusion of control. People have been found to believe that they exert some control even over obviously random events such as throwing dice (Langer, 1975; Langer & Roth, 1975) as well as to overestimate their control in heavily chance-determined events (Crocker, 1982). Many of the findings in research on the impact of "voice" on people's perception of the fairness of a situation can be at least partially explained by this illusion. Research by Tyler and others suggests that even when a decision already has been made, individuals perceive the process to be more fair if they were allowed to express their concerns, reservations, and opinions (Lind & Tyler, 1988).

Dual Concern Model. A final issue in the realm of affect in negotiations concerns the emotional tone of a negotiator's orientation toward the other negotiator in a dyad. Most of the empirical work done in this area has focused on tests of the *dual concern model* (e.g., Pruitt & Rubin, 1986). The dual concern model (DCM) hypothesizes that there are two dimensions of concerns that individuals in conflict have: concern about own outcomes and concern about others' outcomes. Pruitt suggests that these two dimensions of concerns result in four strategies: yielding, inaction, problem solving, and contending. Research into DCM typically emphasizes factors which lead individuals to select the problem solving strategy. In fact, each of the studies used to support this model (described in Pruitt & Rubin, 1986) have consistently shown problem solving to be the best strategy for maximizing own and others outcomes.

Lowenstein, Thompson, and Bazerman (1989) have suggested that inter-personal orientation in dyadic negotiations can be studied through the use of social utility functions. Social utility functions specify levels of satisfaction as a function of outcome to self and other (Messick & Senis, 1985). In this series of studies, relationship (positive, negative, neutral) between disputants and dispute context (business or social) or dispute issue (vacant lot/invention) were manipulated. Concern for self, advantageous inequity (a positive dif-ference between own and other outcome), and disadvantageous equity (a negative difference between own and other outcome) were the dependent variables of interest.

Their results suggest that individual utility or value for disputed outcomes depends on the magnitude of own outcomes and the difference between own and other outcomes. In general, disputants preferred equal payoffs over either advantageous or disadvantageous inequity. When outcome equality could not be maintained, disputants preferred advantageous inequity to disadvantageous inequity. Further, when the disputant relationship shifted from positive to negative, there also was a shift towards selfishness (i.e., subjects became more concerned with own payoffs and were more accepting of advantageous inequity).

Individual Differences

While there has been a great deal of research on the impact of personality variables on negotiator behavior, we will consider two characteristics—Machiavellianism and perspective taking ability (PTA)—as examples of the way in which individual differences influence dyadic negotiator performance. Machiavellianism is an example of an individual difference variable that af-fects the emotional tone of a dyadic negotiation; PTA represents an individual difference variable which affects negotiators' information processing.

Machiavellianism. Consistent differences have been found in the behav-iors of individuals who are low and high scorers on a Machiavellianism scale.

Those reporting high MACH scores tend to have a cynical view of people. They are much more candid about their feelings of hostility and distrust. They are much less likely to think or act in ways that others deem socially desirable. In addition, they tend not to fit easily into conventional standards of morality, honesty, and reliability. Moreover, they do not typically behave altruistically, are selfish and unsympathetic towards others, and are unwilling to change their opinions under social pressure (Christie & Geis, 1970).

Research which specifically has examined Machiavellianism in game situations has found high MACHs to be much more proactive in their strategies, often testing the limits of the rules. They tend to control the initiation of bids, make more offers, and are highly valued as coalition partners. High MACHs are more successful to the extent that their power base is ambiguous and not publicly known to others. In contrast, low MACHs are seldom members of winning coalitions and often lose the game or are shut out of the winning coalition (Christie & Geis, 1970). As such, this research suggests that high MACHs have an interest in and a gift for manipulating others that is facilitated by their responsiveness to interpersonal cues. Unlike low MACHs, high MACHs are quite capable of adapting to changes in both situations and opponents' behaviors.

Perspective Taking Ability. Several researchers have pointed out the importance of considering the other party's cognitions in dyadic negotiation. Samuelson and Bazerman (1985) found that negotiators in situations with asymmetric information do not include the diagnostic information available about an opponent's behavior. Ignoring the cognitions of the competitive other can lead to what these and other researchers have termed the "winner's curse." Bazerman and Carroll (1987) have argued that this bias occurs because "individuals in competitive situations make simplifying assumptions that deviate from normative logic about the decisions of opponents in order to make the task cognitively more manageable" (1987, p. 260).

A familiar example which illustrates this problem is the dollar auction (Shubik, 1971; Teger, 1979). In this situation, a dollar is auctioned off to the highest bidder. In addition, in this game, the second highest bidder must pay but does not receive anything in return. The bidding begins with multiple parties offering bids until the amount approaches or equals $1. Then, there are typically two bidders who find themselves offering multiple bids over a dollar in hopes that the other party will simply "give up." Each participant views his or her bid choice as selecting between losing "X" amount of money for certain or by making another bid to lose "X + bid − $1. " The participants, in entering this auction, are either unable or unwilling to consider the cognitions and likely behaviors of the other participants as they contemplate entering the game. As a result, the common pattern is that individuals bid far in excess of the value of the dollar.

Perspective taking ability is a personality variable which captures a negotiator's capacity to understand another party's point of view during a negotiation and thereby to predict that other party's strategies and tactics, including goals, aspiration levels, and negotiation resistance points (Neale & Bazerman, 1983). PTA may also be valuable if it allows a disputant to sense when a fellow disputant is going to adhere to or defect from a reciprocity norm in the interaction. The strategic value of PTA was raised by Walton and McKersie (1965) in their comments about the strategic importance of being able to identify the other's resistance point without divulging one's own.

Experimental results concerning the effects of PTA on bargaining behavior have been mixed. Neale and Bazerman (1983) found PTA to be a significant predictor of the number of issues resolved in a dyadic collective bargaining task and the dollar value of the final contract. On the other hand, Bazerman and Neale (1982) found evidence that high PTA negotiators may be particularly susceptible to overconfidence. As a group, high PTA negotiators rated the probability that their offers would be accepted by an arbitrator under final offer arbitration as significantly higher than those with low PTA.

Other researchers (e.g., Greenhalgh & Neslin, 1983; Mannix, 1989) have found that PTA has no effect on negotiator behavior. One interpretation for these inconsistent findings is that PTA, unlike Machiavellianism, can be substantially influenced by the structural demands of the negotiating situation. Thus, the information processing advantages of individuals with native PTA for improving negotiator performance are probably salient only in selective situations.

By way of concluding this discussion about the role of personality variables in dyadic negotiation, it should be noted that the literature concerning the effects of individual difference variables on negotiation processes and outcomes is inconclusive. While some studies repeatedly have demonstrated that individual characteristics affect the exchange process (cf., Hermann & Kogan, 1977; Lewicki & Litterer, 1985; Rubin & Brown, 1975), other research has been characterized by non-significant findings and little predictive power (Druckman, 1977; Hamner, 1980; Hermann & Kogan, 1977). Specifically, the results of a study conducted by Hermann and Kogan (1977) found that not one of eight personality factors was consistently responsible for the process or outcome of a bargaining situation. Thus, Terhune's (1970) conclusion that personality effects have been sufficiently elusive to render the overall results of this area of negotiation research equivocal still finds support almost a decade later. In a recent review of the role the negotiator's personality plays in bargaining, Lewicki and Litterer (1985) were unable to identify a single dispositional variable that is directly linked to negotiator behavior. Given the discrepant findings on the impact of personality characteristics on bargaining, negotiation researchers have reduced their reliance on individual differences as an explanatory variable in negotiation research (White, 1978; Lewicki & Litterer, 1985).

Interestingly, a recent review of the literature concerning dispositional influences on job attitudes among organizational researchers paints a considerably more optimistic picture of the explanatory power of individual differences (Staw, Bell, & Clausen, 1986). Weiss and Adler (1984) report that the poor predictive power of dispositional variables may be an artifact of research design preferences. They suggest that the theoretical rigor of many research studies is directed towards understanding situational or structural influences on behaviors; dispositional effects are, at best, an afterthought. Consistent with these more optimistic views of the predictive power of dispositional variables, Lewicki and Litterer (1985) posit that in negotiation research, the lack of clear relationships between dispositional variables and bargaining behavior may result from: (1) the selection of inappropriate dispositional variables for study which do not encompass the complex nature of the interaction between personality and negotiation behavior; (2) the use of what appear to be "convenient" rather than theoretically relevant dispositional variables; and (3) over-reliance on student samples and unrealistic negotiating simulations which bear little resemblance to real-life, consequence-bearing interactions. Conclusions about the effects of dispositional variables are also suspect when the success of the negotiation is determined by an investigator or experimenter rather than the participants.

Though previous research findings tend to discount the contributions of a dispositional approach, it may not be the case that such variables are too subtle or elusive to provide insight into the interaction between negotiators. Hermann and Kogan (1977) argue that the strength of the relationship between personality and negotiator behavior may depend on the constraints imposed upon the negotiator. Monson, Hesley, and Chernick (1982) have shown that personality is more predictive of behavior in *ambiguous* situations than in settings where there are strong prescriptions for behavior. In situations in which participants have little information about a negotiating opponent or the correct response schema, they may rely on their predispositions to define their responses. Once parties are involved in an interaction or the interaction is a familiar one, then structural features or scripts may direct the individual's responses. Thus, if one were to pick a situation in which the dispositional influences of the parties were most likely to have the greatest impact on negotiator behavior, it would likely occur early in the negotiation interaction between relative strangers.

A BEHAVIORAL NEGOTIATION THEORY FRAMEWORK

Figure 4 provides a proposed integration of the broad variety of research which this paper has reviewed concerning dyadic negotiation. This framework is not meant to represent a strictly causal model; rather the arrows in the framework reflect important sources of influence that must be taken into account to appreciate the unfolding of a dyadic negotiation.

As has the paper to this point, the framework suggests two broad categories of research on dyadic negotiation: context effects and negotiator effects. Within context effects are both structural effects (e.g., power) and the influences of other people (e.g., constituency effects). As noted in the figure, the empirical research for both of these contextual influences is grounded in a strong formal theory: game theory for structural effects, and agency theory for the influences of other people (though agency theory has been less formally explored as the backdrop for negotiation research and theorizing).

Within negotiator effects are both negotiator cognitions and interaction processes. Much of the research on negotiator cognition effects in negotiation (e.g., work on framing and overconfidence) is theoretically grounded in behavioral decision theory (BDT). However, BDT seems most appropriate for understanding negotiator cognitions as the processing mechanism for contextual effects. The larger role of negotiator cognitions explored in this paper (including cognitive influences on the subjective experiencing of contextual characteristics, i.e., "recontextualization") might more accurately be described as grounded in theories of social perception or ethnomethodology. Research on interaction processes in dyadic negotiation (influence and communication tactics) to date seem less grounded in formal background theory.

The arrangement of research proposed in this framework highlights two important aspects of the dyadic negotiation enterprise. First, the figure emphasizes *two levels* of influences on the dyadic negotiation enterprise. These two levels might usefully be compared to the two levels at which a sporting event (such as a football game) occurs. On one level are the rules for the game, the setting, the crowd, even the coaches' instructions. These are all the *contextual* effects which provide the background against which the game is played. On a different level are the players playing the game, their thoughts, and their interactions with each other. The players, their thoughts, and their interactions are the vehicle through which the contextual effects have their influence.

The translation of contextual effects into behaviors is hardly direct, however. Players can misperceive or forget the coach's instructions, and their interaction on the field can unfold in a way seemingly independent of or in

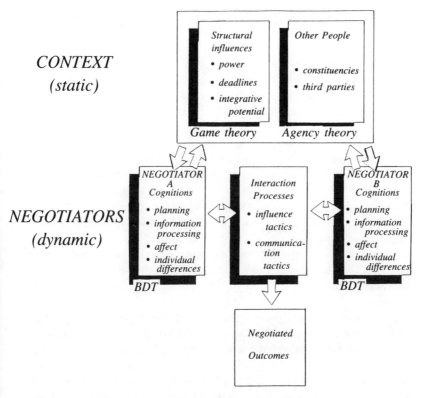

Figure 4.

addition to that suggested by the contextual influences (such as when fights ·
erupt or "game-within-a-game" rivalries develop as the game progresses).
These possibilities all speak to the *dynamic* potential of negotiator variables.

   The dynamic potential of negotiator communication and persuasion tactics
has been raised by Tutzauer (1989). Tutzauer identified four primary functions
served by communication in negotiations: (1) communication is a vehicle for
transmitting and accepting offers; (2) communication is a means for conveying information; (3) communication is a mechanism for shaping the relationship between the bargainers via argumentation; and (4) communication is
a lens for uncovering outcomes. The first of these two functions again suggests that the behavioral processes of negotiation are a means of playing out
(perhaps imperfectly) the intended effects of contextual factors. However, the
third and fourth functions identified by Tutzauer suggest that communication
tactics also play a dynamic role in dyadic negotiations. Shaping the relationship between negotiators and influencing what each side perceives as the

focus of the negotiation go substantially beyond simply implementing contextual influences.

The dynamic potential of negotiator cognitions was raised earlier in this chapter. In a review of the anthropology of disputes and negotiation, Barley (in press) argues that negotiators' interpretations of the situations they occupy are critical to the actions they choose to take, and that these interpretations themselves often are negotiated (Anderson & Helm, 1979). Barley's point is a methodological one with far-ranging implications—that the controlled environments of the laboratory assure researchers of a reasonably direct translation of intended context into experienced context. In the stimulus-rich, messy, and uncertain real world, this translation is hardly assured. In particular, some contexts are formally defined and "set aside" as negotiation episodes (e.g., the annual salary negotiation). Other situations are perceived by some (but not all) as bargaining opportunities. This suggests that negotiation contexts in practice may be quite fluid—from the viewpoint of the negotiators, that is—and that context effects will be only as consequential as negotiator perceptions are likely to reflect them. It also suggests that controlled laboratory research may dramatically *underestimate* the importance of dynamic effects in dyadic negotiation.

The identification of dynamic potential in dyadic negotiation seems particularly important because of the distinction offered by Lax and Sebenius (1986) between the two fundamental tasks of negotiation: *claiming* and *creating* value. Claiming value seems a more static process, and therefore one whose effects are tied to context variables. To borrow a phrase from the psychology of perception, context variables are the "ground" against which dyadic negotiation occurs; negotiator variables are the "figure." And like this "figure/ground" distinction, context variables (the "ground") will have their effects, but the "figure" is where the action is—where the effects of variables do or do not unfold.

The creation of value in negotiation is dynamic and ultimately must trace its roots to the unfolding of dyadic negotiation through negotiator variables. By way of demonstrating this distinction, Greenhalgh (1987) has noted the importance of personal relationships in negotiations. Relationships act as superordinate goals and provide negotiators access to high quality agreements through trust and information sharing. Communication tactics choices may determine whether a negotiator will be able to draw upon a relationship effectively during a negotiation. However, communication tactics choice also may *create* relationships where none existed before, thereby not only improving the possibility of discovering high quality agreements but additionally adding new issues to the negotiation agenda (such as the preservation of a newly-formed relationship). Similarly, the use of certain tactics (in particular, coercive ones) can prove detrimental to the long-term relationships among negotiators. (See Deutsch's discussion concerning destructive and productive conflicts, 1969.) Fisher and Ury (1979), for instance, note that "Egos tend to become involved in substantive positions" (1979: 20). Once egos are involved, the substance of the negotiation is fundamentally altered. Thus inappropriate influence tactics (in particular, contentious ones) may alter a negotiation from a simple division of resources to *whose* proposal is the "better" one, or which negotiator is going to be the "winner." The point here is that tactics of persuasion are more than just a way for the natural effects of contextual characteristics on negotiations to unfold. Tactical choices indeed may alter the course of negotiation episodes by bringing new issues (e.g., ego) into a negotiation.

It is important to note that this static-claiming/dynamic-creating dualism does *not* necessarily map directly onto the more familiar distributive/integrative dichotomy. As noted in Figure 4, integrative potential—specifically, complementary needs within a negotiating dyad—is a property of the context for negotiators to discover (perceive) and exploit. The dynamic aspects of cognitions may influence how much of this potential negotiators discover. However, dynamic negotiator effects also may bring into play variables (for instance, negotiator relationships) *not contained* in the initial context of the negotiation. While these dynamic additions could either increase or decrease the probability of effective dispute resolution (for instance, by adding or subtracting integrative potential), they *will* fundamentally alter the nature of a dispute by taking it beyond the parameters initially defined by the context. In this sense, dyadic negotiations are like good conversations: they must begin somewhere, and where they begin probably affects where they go. But they also can take on a life of their own that makes people forget where they ever began.

Figure 4 emphasizes the point that any formal behavioral theory of negotiation cannot be a monolithic theory. This seems especially apparent in view of the distinction between claiming and creating value in negotiations, and the idea that different variables might control these two different functions of dyadic negotiations. Understanding dyadic negotiation means understanding both claiming and creating processes, and therefore implies an understanding of game theory, agency theory, behavioral decision theory, and something about social interaction. *Each* of these theoretical backdrops figures prominently in our understanding of dyadic bargaining.

Future Research

The behavioral negotiation framework presented in this paper, as well as the review of the related literature of dyadic negotiation, presents some clear avenues for future research. To close this paper, we will consider three.

First, virtually all negotiation research seems focused on predicting how negotiators will behave once they are locked into a negotiation. As noted by Barley (in press), however, this makes a huge assumption about the distinctiveness of bargaining episodes from the on-going stream of daily social life. This paper has argued instead that the opportunity to negotiate is in the eye (really, the cognitions) of the beholder—a matter of what sort of context the perceiver chooses to construct. But what determines these constructions?

One possibility that has been ignored in the dyadic negotiation literature is the selection of a negotiating opponent. It seems likely that the perception of a negotiation opportunity will be intimately tied to perceptions of the available options of negotiating opponents. For instance, there may be specific and predictable limits to the selection of negotiation opponents. Power differences influence negotiated settlements in formal bargaining settings, but might power differences also make negotiation less likely to be perceived as an option? In determining dyadic interaction partners, the importance of the demographic characteristics of individuals could also play a major role. While early social psychological research has suggested that interpersonal attraction is a function of perceived similarity (Heider, 1958), recent work by Pfeffer (1985)and others (Stewman & Konda, 1983; Wagner, Pfeffer, & O'Reilly, 1984) suggests that cohort identity is important in the selection of interaction partners. All things being equal, for example, new employees are likely to interact more with other new employees. Similarity in time of entry and in other dimensions such as age and education leads to increased communication frequency. Communication frequency tends to increase perceived similarity in values; similarity in values and attitudes produce greater integration and cohesion among cohort members. Thus, it may be important to consider demographic characteristics in predicting interactional patterns among negotiating dyads.

The decision to negotiate also may be predicated on individual predisposition. The propensity to negotiate (PTN) is important because one must, on some level, see a potential exchange as an opportunity to negotiate before one engages in negotiating behavior. Just how intentional the decision is to negotiate may be as much a learned behavior as it is a carefully constructed perception. There may be no calculation of the relative expected benefit of negotiating versus transacting. Instead, people may find themselves in situations where they are faced with unexpected, potentially incompatible goals and may resort to habitual, dispositionally-based responses.

The results of an unpublished study by Neale and Northcraft (1988) found that individuals who scored high on a "Propensity to Negotiate" scale were significantly more likely to report that they would negotiate than those who scored low on the PTN scale when (1) power was equal between the dispu-

tants, (2) there was no on-going relationship, (3) when the issue was important, and (4) when there was no previous contract covering the dispute (marginally significant). In addition, PTN was correlated with gender and income;
males and individuals with higher incomes reported themselves to be more
likely to negotiate than did females or those with lower incomes.

A second ripe avenue for research in dyadic bargaining concerns the extent
to which dyadic negotiation research has been method-bound. An inheritance
from the game theory perspective, much research in negotiation minimizes the
opportunity for participants to differentially perceive and, thereby, cognitively
recontextualize the activity. When simple games (such as the Prisoner's Dilemma) are used as the backdrop for dyadic bargaining exchanges, negotiators
may find it difficult, if not impossible, to re-interpret through the cognitive
lens what they confront in the dyadic interaction. There is a need here to turn
the original research question of the impact of context on negotiator performance back on itself. Researchers need to consider what effects negotiators
have on contextual influences. For example, what impact does a manager's
involvement have on his or her subordinates' willingness to resolve a dispute?
Such a study would need to consider not only the context of the dispute but
also the impact of the manager's involvement on the disputants' reconceptualization of the dispute.

This concern argues for additional research paradigms that are richer—
perhaps "messier" in some real world sense—in what they present to subjects. This may mean research designs in which negotiation is not an obvious
option and certainly not a demand. It could also mean spending time talking
with that small portion of subjects who choose to "unvolunteer" when they
find out a study is formally about bargaining.

Finally, the most important implication of this perspective is a call for better
understanding of the *dynamic nature* of negotiator effects. Dynamic negotiator effects appear to be essential to the creation of value in dyadic bargaining. There are a couple of facets to this call. As noted by Barley (in press),
dyadic bargaining research typically has focused on contexts and the outcomes they (may) produce. Relatively ignored has been the unfolding of
bargaining exchanges. It is telling in Figure 4 to note that while contextual
(and particularly structural) influences on bargaining are grounded in formal
theory (e.g., game theory), our formal understanding of negotiator interaction
processes is not nearly so systematic. Further, the unfolding of negotiator
interactions cannot be completely described as an economic, cognitive, and
social endeavor. While economics seems well-represented in dyadic bargaining research and our understanding of cognition in this enterprise is clearly on
the rise (e.g., Bazerman & Carroll, 1987; Neale & Northcraft, 1989), the
social side of dyadic negotiation remains (with some noteworthy exceptions;

see Pruitt, 1981) largely ignored. In this vein, an expanded role for agency theory in bargaining research is overdue.

CONCLUSIONS

Kurt Lewin once noted that "there is nothing so practical as a good theory." And in the arena of negotiation, Raiffa (1982) has argued that a good theory about bargaining must be grounded in a solid understanding of how people actually behave. The behavioral negotiation theory framework proposed in this paper represents an attempt to tackle that formidable task. Behavioral negotiation theory is about negotiator behaviors, their economic, cognitive, and social origins, and how they (both the behaviors and their origins) fit together. It is a framework for distinguishing between the roles of negotiators and contexts in producing negotiated outcomes. As such, it can provide a way-station to catalyze further research, and to integrate and extend our knowledge of the factors which influence dyadic negotiation.

ACKNOWLEDGMENTS

The order of authorship is alphabetical as both authors contributed equally to the development of this manuscript. The authors wish to thank the participants of the Dispute Resolution Research Center for their helpful comments on previous drafts of this manuscript as well as acknowledging the support provided by Borg-Warner to the first author.

NOTE

1.   The pareto efficient frontier represents a series of possible solutions which can be improved only at the expense of one of the two parties. In Figure 2, the curve on which points C, D, and E lie is the pareto efficient frontier.

REFERENCES

Alpert, M., & Raiffa, H. (1982). A progress report on the training of probability assessors. In D. Kahneman, P. Slovic, & A. Tversky (Eds.), *Judgment under uncertainty: Heuristics and biases*. Cambridge: Cambridge University Press, 294–305.
Anderson, W. T., & Helm, D. T. (1979). The physician-patient encounter: A process of reality negotiation. In E. G. Fago (Ed.), *Patients, physicians, and illnesses*. New York: Free Press, 259–271.
Bacharach, S. B., & Lawler, E. J. (1981). *Power and politics in organizations*. San Francisco: Jossey-Bass.

Bass, B. R. (1966). Effects on subsequent performance of negotiators studying issues or planning strategies alone or in groups. *Psychological Monographs: General and Applied, 80,* 1–31.

Baranowski, T. A., & Summers, D. A. (1972). Perceptions of response alternatives in a prisoner's dilemma game. *Journal of Personality and Social Psychology, 21,* 35–40.

Barley, S. R. (in press). Contextualizing conflict: Notes on the anthropology of dispute and negotiation. In M. Bazerman, R. Lewicki, & B. Sheppard (Eds.), *Handbook of research in negotiation,* Vol. 3, Greenwich, CT: JAI Press.

Baron, R. A. (1984). Reducing organizational conflict: An incompatible response approach. *Journal of Applied Psychology, 69,* 272–279.

Bazerman, M. H. & Carroll, J. S. (1987). Negotiator cognition. In B. Staw & L. Cummings (Eds.), *Research in organizational behavior, 9,* 247–288.

Bazerman, M. H., Magliozzi, T., & Neale, M. A. (1985). The acquisition of an integrative response in a competitive market. *Organizational Behavior and Human Decision Processes, 35,* 294–313.

Bazerman, M. H., & Neale, M. A. (1982). Improving negotiator effectiveness: The role of selection and training. *Journal of Applied Psychology, 67,* 543–548.

Bazerman, M. H., Neale, M. A., Valley, K. L., Zajac, E., & Kim, Y. M. (1990). *The effects of agents and mediators on negotiation outcomes.* Working paper, Northwestern University, Evanston, IL.

Benton, A. A., Kelley, H. H., & Liebling, B. (1972). Effects of extremity of offers and concession rate on the outcomes of bargaining. *Journal of Personality and Social Psychology, 24,* 73–83.

Bies, R. J (1987). The predicament of injustice: The management of moral outrage. In L. L. Cummings & B. M. Staw (Eds.), *Research in organization behavior,* Vol. 9, Greenwich, CT: JAI Press, 289–319.

Bies, R. J., Shapiro, D. L., & Cummings, L. L. (1988). Causal accounts and managing organizational conflict. *Communication Research, 15,* 381–399.

Bies R. J., & Shapiro, D. L. (1987). Interactional fairness judgments: The influence of causal accounts. *Social Justice Research, 1,* 199–218.

Blake, R. R., & Mouton, J. S. (1961). Loyalty of representatives to ingroup positions during intergroup competition. *Sociometry, 24,* 177–183.

Brockner, J., Grover, S., & Greenberg, J. (in press). The impact of layoffs on survivors: An organizational justice perspective. In J. Carroll (Ed.), *Advances in applied social psychology: Business settings.* Hillsdale, NJ: Lawrence Erlbaum Associates.

Brown, B. R. (1968). The effects of need to maintain face on interpersonal bargaining. *Journal of Experimental Social Psychology, 4,* 107–122.

Brown, B. R. (1970). Face-saving following experimentally induced embarrassment. *Journal of Experimental Social Psychology, 6,* 255–271.

Brown, B. R. & Garland, H. (1971). The effects of incompetency, audience acquaintanceship, and anticipated evaluative feedback on face-saving behavior. *Journal of Experimental Social Psychology, 7,* 490–502.

Camerer, C. (1987). *Behavioral game theory.* Paper presented at the Insights Conference, University of Chicago, Chicago, IL, April.

Carnevale, P. J., & Isen, A. M. (1986). The influence of positive affect and visual access on the discovery of integrative solutions in bilateral negotiations. *Organizational Behavior and Human Decision Processes, 37,* 1–13.

Carnevale, P. J., & Lawler, E. J. (1986). Time pressure and the development of integrative agreements in bilateral negotiations. *Journal of Conflict Resolutions, 30,* 636–659.

Carroll, J. S., Bazerman, M. H., & Maury, R. (1988). Negotiator cognitions: A descriptive approach to negotiators' understanding of their opponents. *Organizational Behavior and Human Decision Processes, 41,* 352–370.

Chertkoff, J. M., & Conley, M. (1967). Opening offer and frequency of concession as bargaining strategies. *Journal of Personality and Social Psychology, 7,* 298–303.

Chmielewski, T. L. (1982). A test of a model for predicting strategy choice. *Central States Speech Journal, 33,* 505–518.

Christie, R., & Geis, F. L. (Eds.) (1970). *Studies in Machiavellianism.* New York: Academic Press.

Coker, D. N., Neale, M. A., & Northcraft, G. B. (1987). *Structural and individual influences on the process and outcome of negotiation.* Working paper, University of Arizona, Tucson.

Crocker, J. (1982). Biased questions in judgment of covariation studies. *Personality and Social Psychology Bulletin, 8,* 214–220.

Cross, J. (1969). *The economics of bargaining.* New York: Basic Books.

Delaney, J., & Feuille, P. J. (1984). Police interest arbitration: Awards and issues. *Arbitration Journal, 39,* 14–24.

Deutsch, M. (1969). Conflicts: Productive and destructive. *Journal of Social Issues, 25,* 7–41.

Donohue, W. A. (1981a). Development of a model of rule use in negotiation interaction. *Communication Monographs, 45,* 247–257.

Donohue, W. A. (1981b). Analyzing negotiation tactics: Development of a negotiation interact system. *Human Communication Research, 7,* 273–287.

Donohue, W. A., Diez, M. E., & Hamilton, M. (1984). Coding naturalistic negotiation interactions. *Human Communication Research, 10,* 403–425.

Donohue, W. A., Weider-Hatfield, D., Hamilton, M., & Diez, M. E. (1985). Relational distance in managing conflict. *Human Communication Research, 3,* 387–405.

Druckman, D. (1968). Prenegotiation experience and dyadic conflict resolution in a bargaining situation. *Journal of Experimental Social Psychology, 4,* 367–383.

Druckman, D. (Ed.) (1977). *Negotiations.* Beverly Hills, CA: Sage Publications.

Einhorn, H. J. (1978). Decision errors and fallible judgment: Implications for social policy. In K. R. Hammond (Ed.), *Judgment and decision in public policy formation.* Denver, CO: Westview Press.

Einhorn, H. J., & Hogarth, R. M. (1978). Confidence in judgment: Persistence illusion of validity. *Psychological Review, 85,* 395–416.

Elkouri, F., & Elkouri, E. (1985). *How arbitration works.* Washington: Bureau of National Affairs.

Faley, T. & Tedeschi, J. T. (1971). Status and reactions to threats. *Journal of Personality and Social Psychology, 17,* 192–199.

Farber, H. S., Neale, M. A., & Bazerman, M. H. (in press). The impact of risk aversion and arbitration costs on disputed outcomes. *Industrial Relations.*

Feuille, P. J. (1975). Final offer arbitration and negotiating incentives. *Arbitration Journal, 32,* 203–220.

Fisher, R., & Ury, W. (1981). *Getting to yes.* New York: Houghton-Mifflin.

Folger, R., & Martin, C. (1986). Relative deprivation and referent cognitions: Distributive and procedural justice effects. *Journal of Experimental Social Psychology, 22,* 531–546.

Follett, M. (1940). Constructive conflict. In H. Metcalf & L. Urwick (Eds.), *Dynamic administration.* New York: Harper & Row.

French, J. R. P., & Raven, B. (1959). The bases of social power. In D. Cartwright (Ed.), *Studies in social power.* Ann Arbor: Institute for Social Research, University of Michigan.

Giacalone, R. A., & Rosenfeld, P. (in press). *Impression management in the organization.* Hillsdale, NJ: Lawrence Erlbaum Associates.

Goodchild, J. D., Quadrado, C., & Raven, B. H. (1974). *Getting one's way.* Paper presented at the meeting of the Western Psychological Association, Sacramento.

Gouaux, C. (1971). Induced affective states and interpersonal attraction. *Journal of Personality and Social Psychology, 20,* 37–43.

Greenberg, J. (1978). Effects of reward value and retaliative power on allocation decisions: Justice, generosity, or greed? *Journal of Personality and Social Psychology, 38,* 579–585.

Greenberg, J. (1990). Looking for fair versus being fair: Managing impressions of organizational justice. In B. M. Staw & L. L. Cummings (Eds.), *Research in organizational behavior,* Vol. 12, Greenwich, CT: JAI Press, 111–157.

Greenberg, J., & Cohen, R. L. (1982). Why justice? Normative and instrumental interpretations. In J. Greenberg & R. L. Cohen, (Eds.), *Equity and justice in social behavior,* New York: Academic Press, 437–469.

Greenhalgh, L. (1987). Relationships in negotiation. *Negotiation Journal, 3* (3), 235–243.

Greenhalgh, L., & Neslin, S. (1983). Determining outcomes of negotiation: An empirical assessment. In M. H. Bazerman & R. J. Lewicki (Eds.), *Negotiating in Organizations* (pp. 114–134). Beverly Hills, CA: Sage.

Grigsby, D. W., & Bigoness, W. J. (1982). Effects of mediation and alternative forms of arbitration on bargaining behavior—a laboratory study. *Journal of Applied Psychology, 67,* 549–554.

Hamner, W. C. (1980). The influence of structural, individual, and strategic differences. In D. L. Harnett & L. L. Cummings (Eds.), *Bargaining Behavior* (pp. 21–80). Houston, TX: Dame Publishing.

Harnett, D. L., & Cummings, L. L. (1980). *Bargaining Behavior* (pp. 21–80). Houston, TX: Dame Publishing.

Heider, F. (1958). *The psychology of interpersonal relations.* New York: Wiley.

Hermann, M. G., & Kogan, N. (1977). Effects of negotiators' personalities on negotiating behavior. In D. Druckman's (Ed.), *Negotiation: Social psychological perspectives.* Beverly Hills, CA: Sage.

Huber, V. L., & Neale, M. A. (1986). Effects of cognitive heuristics and goals on negotiator performance and subsequent goal setting. *Organizational Behavior and Human Decision Processes, 38,* 342–365.

Isen, A. M. (1970). Success, failure, attention, and reactions to others: The warm glow of success. *Journal of Personality and Social Psychology, 15,* 294–301.

Isen, A. M. (1983). *The influence of positive affect on cognitive organization.* Paper presented at the Stanford Conference on Aptitude, Learning and Instruction: Affective and Cognitive Processes.

Isen, A. M., & Daubman, K. A. (1984). The influence of affect on categorization. *Journal of Personality and Social Psychology, 47,* 1206–1217.

Isen, A. M., & Levine, P. F. (1972). Effect of feeling good on helping: Cookies and kindness. *Journal of Personality and Social Psychology, 21,* 384–388.

Isen, A. M., & Shalker, T. E. (1982). The effect of feeling state on evaluation of positive, neutral, and negative stimuli: when you "accentuate the positive" do you "eliminate the negative"? *Social Psychology Quarterly, 45,* 58–63.

Isen, A. M., Johnson, M. M., Mertz, E., & Robinson, G. F. (1985). The influence of positive affect on the unusualness of work associations. *Journal of Personality and Social Psychology, 48,* 1413–1426.

Janis, I. (1962). Psychological effects of warnings. In G. W. Baker & D. W. Chapman, (Eds.), *Man and society in disaster.* New York: Basic.

Jensen, M. C., & Meckling, W. H. (1976). Agency theory. *Journal of Financial Economics,* 1976, *3,* 305–360.

Johnson, D. W., & Ewens, W. (1971). Power relations and affective style as determinants of confidence in impression formation in a game situation. *Journal of Experimental Social Psychology, 7,* 98–110.

Kelman, H. C. (1958). Compliance, identification, and internalization: Three processes of opinion change. *Journal of Conflict Resolution, 2,* 51–60.

Kipnis, D., & Schmidt, S. M. (1983). An influence perspective on bargaining within organizations. In M. Bazerman & R., Lewicki (Eds.), *Research on negotiation in organizations, 1,* 303–319.

Kipnis, D., Schmidt, S. M., & Wilkinson, I. (1980). Intra-organizational influence tactics: Explorations in getting one's way. *Journal of Applied Psychology, 65,* 440–452.

Kochan, T. A. (1980). *Collective bargaining and industrial relations.* Homewood, IL: Irwin.

Kochan, T., Mironi, M., Ehrenberg, R., Baderschneider, J., & Jick, T. (1979). *Dispute resolution under factfinding and arbitration: An empirical analysis.* New York: American Arbitration Association.

Komorita, S. S., & Barnes, M. (1969). Effects of pressures to reach agreement in bargaining. *Journal of Personality and Social Psychology, 13,* 245–252.

Komorita, S. S., Sheposh, J. P., Braver, S. L. (1968). Power, the use of power and cooperative choice in a two-person game. *Journal of Personality and Social Psychology, 8,* 134–142.

Lamm, H., & Kogan, N. (1970). Risk taking in the context of intergroup negotiations. *Journal of Experimental Social Psychology, 6,* 351–363.

Langer, E. (1975). The illusion of control. *Journal of Personality and Social Psychology, 32,* 311–328.

Langer, E. & Roth, J. (1975). Heads I win, tails it's chance: The illusion of control as a function of the sequence of outcomes in a purely chance task. *Journal of Personality and Social Psychology, 32,* 951–955.

Lax, D. A., & Sebenius, J. K. (1986). *The manager as negotiators.* New York: Free Press.

Leventhal, G. S. (1976). The distribution of rewards and resources in groups and organizations. In L. Berkowitz & E. Walster (Eds.), *Advances in experimental social psychology,* Vol. 9, New York: Academic Press, 91–131.

Lewicki, R. J., Bowen, D. D., Hall, D. T., & Hall, F. S. (1988). *Experiences in management and organizational behavior.* New York: John Wiley.

Lewicki, R. J., & Litterer, J. A. (1985). *Negotiation.* Homewood, IL: R. D. Irwin.

Lewis, S. A., & Fry, W. R. (1976). Effects of visual access and orientation on the performance of integrative bargaining alternatives. *Organizational Behavior and Human Performance, 20,* 75–92.

Liebert, R. M., Smith, W. P., Hill, J. H., & Keiffer, M. (1968). The effects of information and magnitude of initial offer on interpersonal negotiation. *Journal of Experimental Social Psychology, 4,* 431–441.

Lind, E. A., & Tyler, T. R. (1988). *The social psychology of procedural justice.* New York: Plenum.

Lowenstein, G., Thompson, L., & Bazerman, M. H. (1989). Social utility and decision making in interpersonal contexts. *Journal of Personality and Social Psychology.*

Mannix, E. A., (1989). *Coalitions in the organizational context: A social dilemma perspective.* Unpublished doctoral dissertation, University of Chicago.

McAlister, L., Bazerman, M. H., & Fader, P. (1986). Power and goal setting in channel negotiations. *Journal of Marketing Research, 23,* 228–236.

McClintock, C. G., Messick, D. M., Kuhlman, D. M., & Campos, F. T. (1973). Motivational bases of choice in three-choice decomposed games. *Journal of Experimental Social Psychology, 9,* 572–590.

McKersie, R. B., Perry, C. R., & Walton, R. E. (1965). Intraorganizational bargaining in labor negotiations. *Journal of Conflict Management, 9,* 463–481.

Monson, T. C., Hesley, J. W., & Chernick, L. (1982). Specifying when personality traits can and cannot predict behavior: An alternative to the abandoning the attempt to predict single act criteria. *Journal of Personality and Social Psychology, 43,* 385–399.

Mumpower, J. L. (1989). *The cognitive characteristics of negotiators and the structure of negotiations.* Working paper, Center for Policy Research, State University of New York-Albany.

Myerson, R. (1986). *Analysis of incentives in dispute resolution.* Working paper, Dispute Resolution Research Center, Kellogg Graduate School of Management.

Nash, J. (1953). Two-person cooperative games. *Econometrica, 21,* 129–140.

Neale, M. A. (1984). The effect of negotiation and arbitration cost salience on bargainer behavior: The role of arbitrator and constituency in negotiator judgment. *Organizational Behavior and Human Performance, 34,* 97–111.

Neale, M. A., & Bazerman, M. H. (1983). The role of perspective-taking ability in negotiating under different forms of arbitration. *Industrial and Labor Relations Review, 36,* 378–388.

Neale, M. A., & Bazerman, M. A. (1985a). When will externally set aspiration levels improve negotiator performance? A look at integrative behavior in competitive markets. *Journal of Occupational Behavior, 6,* 19–32.

Neale, M. A., & Bazerman, M. H. (1985b). The effects of framing and negotiator overconfidence on bargainer behavior. *Academy of Management Journal, 28,* 34–49.

Neale, M. A., & Northcraft, G. B. (1986). Experts, amateurs, and refrigerators: Comparing expert and amateur decision making on a novel task. *Organizational Behavior and Human Decision Processes, 38,* 305–317.

Neale, M. A., & Northcraft, G. B. (1988). Predicting the decision to negotiate: The development of the propensity to negotiate scale. Working paper, University of Arizona, Tucson, AZ.

Neale, M. A., Huber, V. L., & Northcraft, G. B. (1987). The framing of negotiations: Context versus task frames. *Organizational Behavior and Human Decision Processes, 39,* 228–241.

Neale, M. A., Pinkley, R. L., Brittain, J. W., & Northcraft, G. B. (1989). *Managers as third party intervenors: A research proposal.* Grant funded by the Fund for Research in Dispute Resolution, Washington, DC.

Northcraft, G. B., & Neale, M. A. (1986). Opportunity costs and the framing of resource allocation decisions. *Organizational Behavior and Human Decision Processes, 37,* 348–356.

Northcraft, G. B., & Neale, M. A. (in press). Dyadic negotiation. In M. Bazerman, R. Lewicki, & B. Sheppard (Eds.), *Handbook of negotiation research.* Greenwich, CT: JAI Press.

Notz, W. W., & Starke, F. M. (1978). The impact of final offer arbitration versus conventional arbitration on the aspirations and behaviors of bargainers. *Administrative Science Quarterly, 23,* 189–203.

Pfeffer, J. (1985). Organizational demography: Implications for management. *California Management Review, 28,* 67–81.

Pinkley, R. L. (1990). Dimensions of conflict frame: Disputant interpretations of conflict. *Journal of Applied Psychology, 75,* 117–126.

Pinkley, R. L., Neale, M. A., & Beggs, R. *The impact of alternatives to negotiation on the process and outcome of negotiation.* Working paper, Northwestern University, Evanston, IL.

Pinkley, R. L., & Northcraft, G. B. (1989). *Cognitive interpretations of conflict: Implications for disputant motives and behavior.* Working paper, Southern Methodist University, Dallas, TX.

Puritt, D. G. (1981). *Negotiation Behavior.* New York: Academic Press.

Pruitt, D. G. (1983). Achieving integrative agreements. In M. H. Bazerman & R. J. Lewicki (Eds.), *Negotiation in organizations.* Beverly Hills, CA: Sage.

Pruitt, D. G., & Drews, J. L. (1969). The effect of time pressure, time elapsed, and the opponent's concession rate on behavior in negotiation. *Journal of Experimental Social Psychology, 5,* 43–60.

Pruitt, D. G., & Johnson, D. F. (1970). Mediation as an aid to face saving in negotiation. *Journal of Personality and Social Psychology, 14,* 239–246.

Pruitt, D. G., & Kimmell, M. J. (1977). Twenty years of experimental gaming: Critique, synthesis, and suggestions for the future. *Annual Review of Psychology, 28,* 363–392.

Pruitt, D. G., & Rubin, J. Z. (1986). *Social Conflict,* New York: Random House.

Putnam, L. L., & Jones, T. S. (1982). The role of communication in bargaining. *Human Communication Research, 8,* 262–280.

Rafaeli, A., & Sutton, R. I. (1989). The expression of emotion in organizational life. In. L. L. Cummings & B. M. Staw (Eds.), *Research in Organizational Behavior* (pp. 1–42), Volume 11, Greenwich, CT: JAI Press.

Raiffa, H. (1982). *The art and science of negotiation.* Cambridge, MA: Belknap.

Rapoport, A. Critiques of game theory. (1959). *Behavioral Science, 4,* 49–66.

Rapoport, A., & Chammah, A. (1965). *Prisoner's dilemma: A study in conflict and cooperation.* Ann Arbor: University of Michigan Press.

Rekosh, ·J. H., & Feigenbaum, K. D. (1966). The necessity of mutual trust for cooperative behavior in a two-person game. *Journal of Social Psychology, 69,* 149–154.

Roby, T. (1960). Commitment. *Behavioral Science, 5,* 253–264.

Roloff, M. E. (1987). Communication and conflict. In C. R. Berger & S. H. Chaffee (Eds.), *Handbook of communication science* (pp. 483–534), Newbury Park: Sage.

Roloff, M. E., & Jordan, J. (1989). *Strategic communication within bargaining plans: Forms, antecedents, and effects.* Paper presented to the second biannual Conference of the International Association for Conflict Management, Athens, GA.

Roloff, M., Tutzauer, F., & Dailey, W. O. (1987). *The role of argumentation in distributive and integrative bargaining contexts: Seeking relative advantage but at what cost?* Paper presented at the First International Conference of the Conflict Management Group, Fairfax, VA.

Roth, A. E., Murnighan, K. J., & Schoumaker, F. (1988). The deadline effect in bargaining: Some experimental evidence. *American Economic Review, 78,* 806–823.

Roth, A. E. (in press). An economic approach to the study of bargaining. In M. Bazerman, R. Lewicki, & B. Shephard (Eds.), *Research on negotiation in organizations,* Greenwich, CT: JAI Press.

Rubin, J. Z. (1980). Experimental research on third party intervention: Towards some generalizations. *Psychological Bulletin, 87,* 379–391.

Rubin, J. Z., & Brown, B. R. (1975). *The social psychology of bargaining and negotiation.* New York: Academic Press.

Rubin, J. Z., & Sander, F. E. A. (1988). When should we use agents? Direct vs. representative negotiation. *Negotiation Journal, 4,* 395–401.

Samuelson, W. F., & Bazerman, M. H. (1985). The winner's curse in bilateral negotiations. In V. Smith (Ed.), *Research in Experimental Economics, 3,* 105–137, Greenwich, CT: JAI Press.

Schlenker, B. R. (1980). *Impression management: The self-concept, social identity, and interpersonal relations.* Belmont, CA: Brooks/Cole.

Schlenker, B. R., & Miller, R. S. (1977). Egocentrism in groups: Self-serving biases or logical information processing? *Journal of Personality and Social Psychology, 35,* 755–764.

Seigel, S., & Fouraker, L. (1960). *Bargaining and group decision making: Experiments in bilateral monopoly.* New York: McGraw-Hill.

Schank, R. C., & Abelson, R. P. (1977). *Scripts, plans, goals, and understanding: An inquiry into human knowledge structures.* Hillsdale, NJ: L. Erlbaum Associates.

Sheposh, J. P., & Gallo, P. S., Jr. (1973). Asymmetry of payoff structure and cooperative behavior in the prisoner's dilemma game. *Journal of Conflict Resolution, 17,* 312–333.

Shubik, M. (1971). The dollar auction game: A paradox in non-cooperative behavior and escalation. *Journal of Conflict Resolution, 15,* 109–111.

Slovic, P., & Lichtenstein, S. (1971). Comparison of Bayseian and regression approaches to the study of information processing in judgment. *Organizational Behavior and Human Performance, 6,* 649–744.

Solomon, L. (1960). The influence of some types of power relationships and game strategies upon the development of interpersonal trust. *Journal of Abnormal and Social Psychology, 61,* 223–230.

Starke, F. M., & Notz, W. W. (1981). Pre- and post-intervention effects on conventional versus final offer arbitration. *Academy of Management Journal, 24,* 832–850.

Staw, B. M., Bell, N. E., & Clausen, J. A. (1986). The dispositional approach to job attitudes: A lifetime longitudinal test. *Administrative Science Quarterly, 31,* 56–77.

Stevens, C. M. (1963). *Strategy and collective bargaining negotiation.* New York: McGraw-Hill.

Stevens, C. M. (1966). Is compulsory arbitration compatible with bargaining? *Industrial Relations, 5,* 38–50.

Stevens, O. J. (1970). Behavior patterns in power-nonsymmetric simulated conflict models: An experimental investigation. *Dissertation Abstracts, 30,* 5527–A.

Stewman, S., & Konda, S. L. (1983). Careers and organizational labor markets: Demographic models of organizational behavior. *American Journal of Sociology, 88,* 637–685.

Stillinger, C., Epelbaum, M., Keltner, D., & Ross, L. (in press). The 'reactive devaluation' barrier to conflict resolution. *Journal of Personality and Social Psychology.*

Swingle, P. G. (1970). Exploitative behavior in non-zero-sum games. *Journal of Personality and Social Psychology, 16,* 121–132.

Taylor, S. E., & Brown, J. D. (1988). Illusion and well-being: A social psychological perspective. *Psychological Bulletin, 103,* 193–210.

Taylor, S. E., & Koivumaki, J. H. (1976). The perception of self and others: Acquaintanceship, affect, and actor-observer differences. *Journal of Personality and Social Psychology, 33,* 403–408.

Taylor, S. E., & Thompson, S. (1982). Stalking the elusive "vividness" effect. *Psychological Review, 89,* 155–181.

Teasdale, J. D., & Fogarty, S. J. (1979). Differential effects of induced mood on retrieval of pleasant and unpleasant events from episodic memory. *Journal of Abnormal Psychology, 88,* 248–257.

Tedeschi, J. T., Bonoma, T., & Novinson, N. (1970b). Behavior of a threatener. Retaliation vs. fixed opportunity costs. *Journal of Conflict Resolution, 14,* 69–76.

Teger, A. I. (1979). *Too much invested to quit.* New York: Pergamon.

Terhune, K. (1970). The effects of personality in cooperation and conflict. In P. Swingle (Ed.), *The structure of conflict* (pp. 193–234). Beverly Hills, CA: Sage.

Theye, L. D., & Seller, W. J. (1979). Interaction analysis in collective bargaining: An alternative approach to the prediction of negotiated outcomes. In D. Nimmo (Ed.). *Communication Yearbook, 3,* (pp. 375–392). New Brunswick, NJ: Transaction Press.

Thibaut, J., & Gruder, C. L. (1969). Formation of contractual agreements between parties of unequal power. *Journal of Personality and Social Psychology, 11,* 59–65.

Thompson, L., & Hastie, R. M. (in press). Social perception in negotiation. *Organizational Behavior and Human Decision Processes.*

Tidd, K. L., & Lockard, J. S. (1978). Monetary significance of the affiliative smile: A case for reciprocal altruism. *Bulletin of the Psychonomic Society, 11,* 344–346.

Tripp, T. (1989). *Pareto-efficiency versus joint gain variables in bargaining: Which is better and when does it matter?* Working paper, Northwestern University, Evanston, IL.

Tutzaur, F. (1989). Bargaining outcome, bargaining process, and the role of communication. I. B. Dervin (Ed.), *Progress in communication science,* ABLEX Communication and Information Science Series.

Tversky, A., & Kahneman, D. (1981). The framing of decisions and the psychology of choice. *Science, 40,* 453–463.

Tversky, A., & Kahneman, D. (1974). Judgment under uncertainty: Heuristics and biases. *Science, 185,* 1124–1131.

Tversky, A., & Kahneman, D. (1973). Availability: A heuristic for judging frequency and probability. *Cognitive Psychology, 4,* 207–232.

Tyler, T., & Hastie, R. (in press). The social consequences of cognitive illusions. In M. H. Bazerman, R. J. Lewicki, & B. Sheppard (Eds.), *Handbook of Negotiation Research: Research on Negotiation in Organizations,* Vol. 3, Greenwich, CT: JAI Press.

Veitch, R., & Griffitt, W. (1976). Good news-bad news: Affective and interpersonal effects. *Journal of Applied Social Psychology, 6,* 69–75.

Wagner, W. G., Pfeffer, J., & O'Reilly, C. A. (1984). Organizational demographics and turnover in top-management groups. *Administrative Science Quarterly, 29,* 74–92.

Wall, Jr., J. A. (1985). *Negotiation: Theory and practice.* Glenview, IL: Scott, Foresman.

Walton, R. E., & McKersie, R. B. (1965). *A behavioral theory of labor negotiation.* New York: McGraw Hill.

Weiss, H. M., & Adler, S. (1984). Personality in organizational behavior. In B. M. Staw & L. L. Cummings (Eds.), *Research in organizational behavior.* Greenwich, CT: JAI Press, 1–50.

Weick, K. E. (1979). *The social psychology of organizing.* Reading, MA: Addison Wesley, 2nd Edition.

White, J. K. (1978). Individual differences and the job quality-worker response relationship: Review, integration, and comments. *Academy of Management Review, 3,* 267–280.

Wilkinson, I., & Kipnis, D. (1978). Interfirm use of power. *Journal of Applied Psychology, 63,* 315–320.

Yukl, G. A., Malone, M. P., Hayslip, B., & Pamin, T. A. (1976). The effects of time pressure and issue settlement order on integrative bargaining. *Sociometry, 39,* 276–281.

Zeuthan, F. (1930). *Problems of monopoly and economic warfare.* London: Routledge.

INTERGROUP RELATIONS AND ORGANIZATIONAL DILEMMAS:
THE ROLE OF CATEGORIZATION PROCESSES

Roderick M. Kramer

ABSTRACT

The competitive nature of intergroup relations has been acknowledged in many contemporary views of organizations. However, there is much about the determinants of such competition that remain unclear. The primary purpose of the present chapter is to present an analysis of intergroup competition that is derived from recent social psychological research on social categorization processes and interdependent decision making in resource dilemmas. Based on this research, a general model of intergroup relations in organizations is presented. According to the model, intergroup relations are shaped by organizational factors that affect the interdependence between groups with respect to critical resources and psychological factors that affect how that interdependence is construed. The chapter draws out implications of the model with respect to such issues as the resolution of intergroup conflict, the development of intergroup cooperation, and the social nature of decisionmaking in organizations.

Research in Organizational Behavior, Volume 13, pages 191–228.
Copyright © 1991 by JAI Press Inc.
All rights of reproduction in any form reserved.
ISBN: 1-55938-198-1

*"Groups in transaction with one another over time rarely remain neutral to-
ward one another. Between them and their individual members, there develop
reciprocal states of friendship or hatred, trust or mistrust, aggressive intent or
willingness to give a helping hand. This is the undeniable fact of social life."*

—Sherif, *In Common Predicament*

*"Interdependence is the reason why nothing works out quite the way one wants
it to."*

—Pfeffer & Salancik, *The External Control of Organizations*

Contemporary views of organizations have frequently drawn attention to the
competitive and conflictual nature of intergroup relations (e.g., Baldridge,
1971; Blake, Shepard, & Mouton, 1964; Cyert & March, 1963; March &
Simon 1958). Research suggests that intergroup competition is not only ubiquitous in organizations, but that it can develop from even the most minimal
intergroup interactions (Blake & Mouton, 1984; Blake, Shepard, & Mouton,
1964; Sherif, 1966). As a result, many organizational researchers have regarded intergroup competition as an almost inevitable consequence of intergroup contact. Perhaps the most forceful expression of this view was provided by Blake and Mouton (1989) who noted that, "The striking conclusion
from research is that when groups are aware of one another's psychological
presence, *it is natural for them to feel competition . . . . These findings
suggest a very basic incipient hostility* is operating at the point of contact
between primary groups" (p. 93, emphasis added).

Although the prevalence of intergroup competition in organizations is well
documented empirically, the origins of this competition are less clear. In
trying to explain such competition, organizational theorists seem to have
converged on at least one point, however: namely, that interdependence between groups with respect to critical resources plays a central role in the
development of competition. Pfeffer and Salancik (1977), for example, characterized organizations as consisting of multiple coalitions engaged in a contest for the acquisition and control of organizational resources. Similarly,
Baldridge (1971) described organizations as pluralistic systems in which conflict arises from competition among various groups or subunits for limited
resources. And Pondy (1967) identified the "discrepancy between aggregated
demands of the competing parties and the available resources" (p. 299) as a
primary source of conflict in organizations.

While organizational theorists have consistently drawn attention to the importance of resource interdependence in shaping intergroup relations, how-

ever, the links between interdependence and the development of competition have not been explicated in any systematic fashion. For example, although many macro-level treatments (e.g., Miles, 1980; Swingle, 1976) have cited "common pool dependencies" as a source of competition in organizations, the causal links between mutual dependence on organizational resources and the development of intergroup competition have not been articulated. Similarly, while several studies have demonstrated a relationship between resource scarcity and conflict in organizations (e.g., Hills & Mahoney, 1978; Pfeffer & Moore, 1980; Salancik & Pfeffer, 1974), we do not have very detailed models to explain this relationship. Thus, although both theoretical perspectives and empirical research on organizations indict interdependence as a primary source of intergroup competition, there is much about the conceptual underpinnings of the relationship between interdependence and competition that remains unclear.

Accordingly, one of the primary aims of the present chapter is to examine the relationship between resource interdependence and the emergence of intergroup competition. The central question this chapter addresses is, "What are the organizational and psychological determinants of intergroup competition?" In addressing this question, the conceptual framework that will be developed will draw heavily on a perspective on intergroup relations that is emerging from recent experimental research on behavior in situations known as *common dilemmas* (see Brewer & Schneider, 1989; Kramer & Brewer, 1986; Kramer, 1989a for overviews). It will be argued here that organizations share many features with such dilemmas. The analogy between organizational dilemmas and commons dilemmas suggests that intergroup relations in organizations can be viewed as the product of decisional dilemmas which are *inherent* in complex organizations. These dilemmas are inevitable because of the diverse and often incompatible claims groups make on an organization's limited resources.

While drawing attention to the central role that resource interdependence plays in intergroup relations, however, the chapter also argues that such relations cannot be explained simply or solely in terms of the objective features of that interdependence. Instead, it is necessary to take into account how individuals in groups perceive or *construe* their interdependence. In developing this argument, I will present evidence suggesting that perceptions of interdependence, in turn, are shaped largely by the nature of the organizational categories that are salient to individuals during decisionmaking and social interaction.

The present chapter was motivated by several observations. First, despite its relevance, research on the commons dilemma has had little impact on organizational theory. The many theoretical perspectives and conceptual insights which are emerging from dilemmas research (see, e.g., Dawes, 1980; Edney, 1980; Edney & Harper, 1978; Messick & Brewer, 1983 for reviews) have seldom been utilized by organizational researchers (the work by Fort & Baden, 1981; Mannix 1989a, 1989b are exceptions). This neglect is unfortunate, since research on the commons dilemma has identified many factors that affect how individuals respond to situations involving resource interdependence—and behavior in such situations remains a central concern of organizational theory.

Along similar lines, although there is a substantial literature on the effects of social categorization on interpersonal and intergroup behavior (see Brewer & Kramer, 1985; Messick & Mackie, 1989; Rothbart & John, 1985; Tajfel, 1982a, 1982b; Wilder, 1981, 1986 for overviews), the importance of categorization processes in organizations has been largely overlooked by organizational behavior researchers (see, however, Baron & Pfeffer, 1989, Strang & Baron, 1989; Lansberg, 1989).

One reason that organizational scholars may have given little attention to these issues may be simply that the relevance of this research has not been made evident. A second objective of the present chapter, therefore, is to discuss how these important strands of social psychological research contribute to our understanding of intergroup relations in organizations. My hope is that, in doing so, organizational researchers will be stimulated to explore further the application of research on resource dilemmas and categorization processes to the study of intergroup relations. At the same time, my hope is that this chapter will suggest to social dilemmas researchers that organizational settings are interesting and important arenas in which such dilemmas arise and can be studied.

INTENT AND SCOPE OF THE PRESENT CHAPTER

It may be useful to make a few preliminary remarks at the outset regarding the scope and intent of the present chapter, as well as indicate how it differs from previous work on this topic. The conceptual framework presented in this chapter departs from other research on intergroup relations in organizations in at least one important respect. Other recent work has focused attention primarily on structural or macro-level determinants of intergroup behavior. Two notable aspects of such macro-level studies are, first, that they have treated the group as the unit of analysis and, second, that they have minimized, or at least afforded minimal attention to, psychological assumptions and processes.

In contrast with such research, the present chapter adopts a *social psychological* perspective in explaining intergroup competition. According to this perspective, it is the individual in the organization that provides a focal point for understanding intergroup behavior. In justifying why the individual is a particularly appropriate level of analysis for understanding intergroup relations, Stephan (1985) pointed out that it is "the individual's perception of social reality and the processing of this information that influences individual behavior [and] the individual's interpretations of social reality that are crucial rather than the 'real' nature of the situation" (p. 599).

Thus, in the present framework, the relevant unit of analysis will be the individual organizational actor. Importantly, however, this individual is conceptualized not as an independent or socially isolated decisionmaker, but rather as a *social* actor embedded in a complex network of intra- and intergroup relationships. When individuals assume membership in organizations, they acquire multiple levels of identity associated with the various organizational categories into which they are placed. This process of categorization, I will argue, affects individuals' motives, expectations, and perceptions in ways that enhance the emergence of competitive orientations towards members of other categories or groups.

The present chapter is not intended as a review of the extensive literature on intergroup relations in organizations. Excellent treatments of this topic are available elsewhere (e.g., Alderfer, 1977; Alderfer & Smith, 1982; Blake, Shepard, & Mouton, 1964). Nor does it attempt to demonstrate all of the relevant applications of research on commons dilemmas and categorization processes to understanding organizational behavior. This would be a large undertaking, given the breadth of work in social psychology on each of these topics. Rather, the intent of the present chapter is to highlight an important subset of issues and theoretical insights that have been largely overlooked by organizational researchers interested in intergroup relations.

To accomplish these goals, the chapter is organized as follows. First, the general notion of a commons dilemma is introduced. Next, the parallels between life on the commons and intergroup relations in organizations are suggested. A general model of interdependent decisionmaking is then presented. The chapter examines how categorization processes affect individuals' responses to such interdependence. These elements are then incorporated in a general model of intergroup relations in organizations. The chapter concludes by stating some of the implications and contributions of the model and suggesting directions for future research.

"THE TRAGEDY OF THE COMMONS"—A TALE WITH ORGANIZATIONAL RELEVANCE

In an article that came to exert an enormous influence on social scientists across many disciplines, the biologist Garrett Hardin (1968) described a form

of resource interdependence which he called the "tragedy of the commons."
The commons were community pastures which existed during the nineteenth
century. Herders were free to graze their private stocks on these public lands.
Because access to the commons was free, it was to the advantage of each
individual herder to increase his or her personal wealth by adding as many
animals as possible to it. Yet, if all of the herders pursued their individual self-
interests in this fashion, the commons was overgrazed and eventually de-
stroyed. Hence, the tragedy.

The decisional conflict embodied in the commons dilemma has been regarded as prototypic of many contemporary resource allocation problems.
Such problems include the conservation of natural resources such as clean air,
fresh water, and forests, as well as manufactured resources such as electricity
and gasoline (Hardin & Baden, 1977). In each of these situations, individuals
are interdependent with each other with respect to valuable but potentially
scarce resources. In response to such interdependence, individuals can choose
either a *competitive* course of action that furthers their own interests at the
expense of others, or a *cooperative* response that furthers their joint interests.
The two defining properties of a commons dilemma are (1) all of the decisionmakers are better off if all decide to cooperate than if all compete, but (2) each
decisionmaker receives a larger "payoff" for the competitive choice than for
the cooperative choice (Dawes, 1980).

Commons dilemma situations thus confront individuals with a choice between two alternatives, each of which is problematic. On the one hand,
because resources are finite, each individual should exercise some degree of
restraint (cooperate) in order to conserve resources for future use. On the other
hand, individuals realize that their own efforts to conserve resources will have
little impact if others do not do the same. Thus, in the absence of assurances
that others will reciprocate, individuals have little incentive to cooperate
themselves.

The dilemma which haunted Hardin's herders, and which plague more
contemporary social communities sharing scarce resource pools, are strikingly
similar to problems which plague groups in complex organizations. In the
next section, this analogy between socially and organizationally based dilemmas is explored further.

THE ORGANIZATION AS A COMMONS

To more readily see the parallels between social and organizational dilemmas,
it is useful to conceptualize organizations abstractly as large "pools" of valuable but finite resources which must be allocated among multiple groups
within them. In large universities, for example, faculty members from differ-

ent departments compete for valuable resources such as research funds, offices with scenic views, and talented graduate students. An important feature of such resources is that, although they are replenishable over time, they are in limited supply at any given point in time.

As these examples suggest, organizational resources assume many forms. They can be very concrete and tangible, such as physical space, staff, information, and fiscal resources. Other organizational resources, such as status and recognition by organizational elites, are more symbolic. Although less tangible, these resources may be no less important to the groups seeking to acquire them. Moreover, to the extent that they are perceived to be limited, competition for them may be quite acute.

Perhaps one of the most prevalent types of commons dilemma that is found in organizations involves the dependence of two or more groups on a central resource pool. An example of this type of dilemma is the familiar *budget dilemma* where groups are mutually dependent on a centralized allocator for their fiscal resources. Each group knows that the organization as a whole would be better off if it (as well as other groups) only consumes those fiscal resources it actually needs. However, it also knows that future allocations may be based on its current level of consumption. The more resources the group uses now, the more it is likely to be allocated in the future. Thus, there are strategic incentives to consume resources in excess of actual needs. Since each group reasons similarly, the result may be a serious drain on the organization's resources. Thus, decisions which are rational from the standpoint of furthering the short-term interests of each group in the organization lead to a collective outcome that is undesirable. The long-term consequences of such behavior, of course, can be as tragic for the organization as they were for commons users of earlier times: Resources which might have been used to achieve important organizational goals, or provide slack resources to help the organization weather unexpected environmental shocks are used in an inefficient and wasteful manner.

Figure 1 depicts a simple and rather stylized version of a prototypical organizational resource dilemma. Two otherwise independent groups are mutually dependent on a common resource pool in the organization. This mutual dependence constitutes the structural basis of their interdependence. The abundance or scarcity of resources in the pool at any given point in time, for example, determines whether the interdependence between the groups is objectively high or low. In addition to this objective interdependence structure, however, there are important social and psychological dimensions to resource interdependence. As I discuss in more detail below, these subjective construals of interdependence influence the development of social relations between groups.

Conceptualizing the organization as a commons draws attention to the

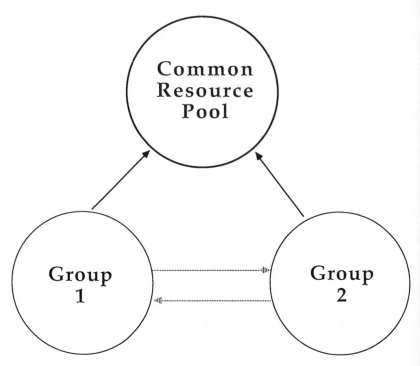

Figure 1. Prototypic Features of "Common Pool" Dilemmas in Organizations.

mixed-motive nature of intergroup relations in organizations.[1] In their dealings with members of other groups, individuals have incentives to both cooperate with each other and compete against each other. This raises the question, "What factors influence how group members respond to such interdependence?" To answer this question, it is useful to first introduce a general model of interdependent decisionmaking.

A BASIC MODEL OF INTERDEPENDENT DECISION MAKING

Social psychological research (Kelley & Thibaut, 1978; Thibaut & Kelley, 1959) has shown that interdependent decisionmaking is affected by both objective or structural features of social situations *and* the way in which those situations are construed by decisionmakers. In resource dilemmas, for example, behavior has been shown to reflect both the structure of the dilemma (or, in game theoretic terminology, the payoff matrix that is associated with it) as well as the way in which that structure is perceived by decisionmakers (Liebrand, 1984; Kramer, McClintock, & Messick, 1986; McClintock & Liebrand, 1989). The relationship between the structural basis of interdependence among individuals and their subjective representations of it has been described in terms of the notion of psychological *transformations*.

Kelley (1979, 1983, 1985) has provided the most systematic treatment of the role transformations play in interdependent relationships. According to his model, when individuals encounter situations involving interdependence with others, they do not act directly in response to the objective or *given* payoff matrix associated with the situation. Instead, they transform this given matrix into what he characterizes as an *effective* payoff matrix.[2] This transformation of the objective matrix into a subjective representation reflects the fact that individuals tend to be attentive and responsive to only selected features of interdependence situations. For example, individuals who are interested in developing cooperative relationships with others may be selectively responsive to those features of the given interdependence structure that afford an opportunity to signal their cooperative intentions.

In discussing the role of transformations, Kelley (1983) primarily emphasized their positive functions. "Better given outcomes," he argued, "can be assured and/or inefficient conflict processes can be avoided if, through reconceptualization, the persons transform the pattern of their interdependence" (p. 12). The importance of transformations in shaping intergroup relationships is illustrated by examining how a given psychological transformation might affect behavior. Kelley suggests that transformations function in social rela-

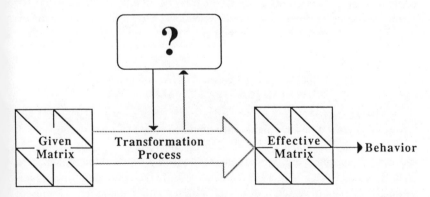

Figure 2.   A Basic Model of Interdependent Decision Making (adapted from Kelley, 1979).

tionships much like decision "rules" that individuals use to govern interdependent behavior. As an example of such a rule, Kelley described how individuals can use reciprocity-based strategies such as "turn-taking" to foster the development of cooperative relationships.

In the case of common pool problems in organizations, groups can agree to "take turns" with respect to using scarce resources. In an academic department where faculty fellowships are scarce, for example, they may agree to rotate award of the fellowships across groups. Thus, one year an economics professor may receive the award, while a finance professor may receive it in the following year. By reconceptualizing their interdependence as a repeated game, competition and conflict are avoided. Through the use of such cooperative transformations, Kelley argues, interdependent actors can alter what might have been perceived as a zero-sum situation into a positive-sum one, whereby each has an opportunity to obtain resources on a regular and, importantly, equal basis.

Although Kelley attached special significance to cooperative transformations, there are also noncooperative or competitive transformations that individuals can make in such situations. For example, if individuals in one group construe the goal of their behavior as maximizing the difference between how well their group is doing compared to another, then strategies such as turn-taking will obviously have little appeal. Instead, they may prefer more distributive tactics, such as pre-empting the other group by taking its resources.

To summarize, the discussion thus far has identified two general classes of transformations (competitive and cooperative) that interdependent actors can make in resource dilemmas. Nothing has been said, however, about which type of transformation is likely in a given situation. Figure 2 is uninformative about this—it indicates only a "?" where this critical link should be specified. In the following sections, I will review evidence suggesting that categorization may play a particularly important role in the transformation process.

CATEGORIZATION PROCESSES IN ORGANIZATIONS

Complex organizations are highly differentiated social systems (Scott, 1987). Structural and functional differentiation are necessary in organizations because many specialized groups are needed to get the work of the organization done (Lawrence & Lorsch, 1967; Miles, 1980). In recognition of this, organizational theorists have often discussed differentiation primarily in terms of how it furthers the accomplishment of organizational goals. For example, it has been noted that the degree of segmentation or categorization of organizational members can be driven by technical and administrative imperatives within the organization (Baron & Bielby, 1986) as well as a variety of other organizational needs such as task requirements (Miles, 1980). The level of differentiation is reflected in the multiplicity of organizational categories which exist in most organizations, including departmental divisions, ranks, job titles, specialized roles, etc.

Although such categories may exist primarily to fulfill organizational needs, they have both social and psychological consequences. As a result of assignment to organizational categories, individuals in the organization find themselves sorted and classified into distinctive categories or groups which act to differentiate them (and other within-category members) from other individuals in the organization. This process of categorization can have pervasive effects on the nature of the relationships that develop between individuals who occupy those different categories or groups. One of the significant consequences of the functional categorization of organizational members, then, is that it activates *social* categorization processes whose consequences may be quite dysfunctional.

The social and psychological ramifications of categorization processes in organizations are only just now beginning to receive attention from organizational researchers. Their importance in this regard has been described by Baron and Pfeffer (1989), who noted that, "Organizations are certainly very much in the business of creating categories . . . [thus] it is quite likely that these categories, organizationally defined and institutionalized, *order the social world, determine the contours of social comparison and interaction, and shape the pattern of reward allocations observed*" (p. 14, emphasis added).

Although the importance of categorization processes has been acknowledged by organizational theorists, however, there are still few detailed discussions or systematic frameworks for thinking about how categorization processes affect interpersonal and intergroup behavior in organizations. The framework which is introduced below attempts to address at least part of the gap in this literature by examining how categorization affects competitive transformations among interdependent individuals. In discussing this topic, it will be necessary first to make some general remarks about the relationship between categorization processes and psychological transformations in general.

Categorization Processes and Psychological Transformations

How can categorization affect individuals' perceptions of their interdependence with others? According to the categorization perspective, "psychological group membership has primarily a perceptual or cognitive basis . . . it considers that individuals structure their perception of themselves and others by means of abstract social categories [and] that they internalize these categories as aspects of their self concepts. . . . The first question determining group-belongingness is not, 'Do I like these other individuals?' but 'Who am I?' *What matters is how we perceive and define ourselves* and not how we feel about others" (Turner, 1982, p. 16, emphasis added).

There are at least two important psychological functions served by categorization processes. First, they help individuals define themselves, a process called *self-categorization* (Turner, 1987). Second, the level of categorization helps individuals define their social relations with other members of the organization. In this sense, these categories serve as frames of reference that locate the individual in the complex network of intra- and intergroup relationships within the organization. The process of categorization thus influences not only an individual's personal identity and self-perception, but also his or her *social identification* as well.

Categorization and Level of Social Identification

It is assumed here that the level of social identification between an individual and other members of an organization is determined largely by the organizational categories into which they are sorted and which are salient during intergroup interactions. The present framework thus posits that when members of an organization interact with each other, they interact not as individuals *qua* individuals, but in terms of the organizational categories and groups with which they identify.[2] Sherif (1966) suggested that this, in fact, was the essential feature of intergroup behavior which distinguishes it from interpersonal behavior. "Whenever individuals belonging to one group interact, collectively or individually, with another group or its members *in terms of their group identifications,*" he argued, "we have an instance of intergroup behavior" (p. 5, emphasis in the original).

In organizations, there are typically a number of different levels of categorization that are possible. These, in turn, imply different levels of identification. Research on categorization and identification processes (Brewer, 1989; Brewer & Schneider, 1989; Hogg & Abrams, 1988; Kramer & Brewer, 1986; Turner, 1987) has generally focused on three distinct and particularly important levels. These can be characterized as (1) a personal or individual-level identity that leads individuals to define their interdependence at the *interpersonal* level, (2) a group-level identity that leads individuals to define their interdependence at the *intergroup* level, and (3) a superordinate-level identity that causes individuals to define their interdependence at the organizational or collective level.

The personal level of identity reflects an individual's conception of him-or her-self that is defined primarily in terms of those unique individual attributes that differentiate the self from others. Being a marathon runner, liking film noir, and eating only green pasta may be traits that help differentiate a faculty member from other members of an academic institution. Group level identity, in contrast, is defined at the level of the primary organizational group in which an individual holds membership (e.g., the major work group, subunit or department he or she belongs to). The attributes of the individual that are associated with this level of identity include all of those attributes that individuals share with other members of that category and which distinguish them from members of other categories in the organization. Finally, organizational-level identity is defined at the level of the organization as a whole (i.e., in terms of common membership in the organization itself). The constellation of attributes that is salient at this level of identification includes those characteristics that are generally common to all of the members of the organization. One source of such common characteristics, of course, is the organization's culture (e.g., being at a school where faculty always wear coats when teaching, work with their doors closed, etc.).

One consequence of categorization is that it defines the level of social identification which is salient to an individual. When a personal or individualistic level identity is salient, the organizational community is cleaved by the self into 'me' and the 'rest of you.' Social and psychological distance between the self and others is increased. When an intergroup level identity is salient, in contrast, the organization is perceived to be divided into an *ingroup* containing the self and other members of one's own group, and a set of *outgroups* containing all of the other members of the organization. Social and psychological distance is reduced with respect to ingroup members, but increased with respect to other members of the organization. Finally, when an organizational-level identity is salient, social and psychological distance between the self and all of the other members of the organization is reduced.

An important implication of the categorization perspective, then, is that an individuals' identity in the organization is not fixed. Instead, it can vary over time and across situations. In fact, an individual's identity can change dramatically, even within the course of a single day. In the morning, for example, a faculty member in a business school may find herself to be the only economist in a meeting involving accountants. In this situation, disciplinary orientation may become highly salient or "loom large" during her interactions with other members of the seminar. She is likely to categorize herself as well as *be* categorized by others largely in terms of this single salient dimension. Later, in a meeting with other economists in her department concerning who to hire as a new assistant professor, the fact that she is a microeconomist may influence her identification with others in the meeting. Finally, in a meeting between economists from her business school and economics department, she may be particularly aware of her status as an economist housed in a business school.

The situational or contextual plasticity of an individual's level of identification with others is suggested in Figure 3. The figure illustrates the impact of different levels of salient organizational categorization on an individual's level of identification with others. In applying for a research grant available to faculty members in a department, for example, an individual may perceive her identity primarily at the interpersonal level (Figure 3a). At this level of identification, interpersonal dimensions along which she might compare herself (S) with other members of the organization (O) with whom she is competing for these resources may assume prominence or become salient (e.g., the number of publications, previous success in obtaining funding, etc.).

In the case of competition between the economics group and the organizational behavior group for a pool of research funds, in contrast, her identity may be defined primarily in terms of ingroup-outgroup membership (Figure 3b). Attributes which differentiate herself (and her group) from members of the organizational behavior group may become salient, and her identity defined at the group level. Finally, in a situation involving an external threat to the organization (e.g., publication of a business magazine poll suggesting that her business school is no longer ranked as highly as another), she may define her interdependence now in terms of organizational-level identity (Figure 3c). In this context, her relationship with other members of the organization is construed in terms of a single category "us" (faculty of her business school) versus "them" (the other schools that were ranked). Under these circumstances, interpersonal distinctions and group boundaries within the organization may be regarded as irrelevant and their impact markedly attenuated.

In summary, it is argued that the level of categorization that is salient to individuals influences how they perceive their interdependence with other organizational members. The level of categorization is assumed to affect the specific interpersonal dimensions along which individuals define their social relationships. It is in this sense that categorization shapes the transformation process.

Primacy of Intergroup-level Categorization

Although the level of salient categorization is assumed to vary across situations, it is postulated here that organizational identification is defined, all else being equal, at the level of the individual's primary group in the organization. By primary group is meant simply the group with which an individual

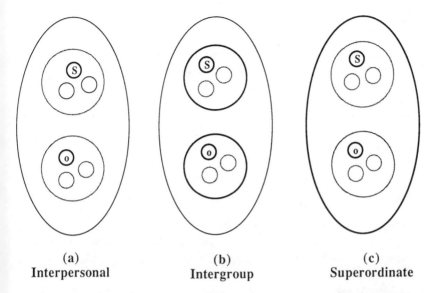

Figure 3. Effects of Level of Categorization on Perceptions of Interdependence and Identification.

most frequently interacts and in terms of which other members of the organization interacts with him or her. The importance of this level of categorization is suggested by the degree to which it dominates all of the intraorganizational transactions in which the individual is involved. For example, the extent to which it affects who in the organization contacts her, how she is referenced in organizational communications such as memos, the nature of the task assignments she is given, and so forth. The primary status of this level of categorization is revealed both in terms of how it affects an individual's self-categorization and also how others categorize the individual.

There are several reasons why this level of categorization may be so dominant in shaping social identification and interdependent behavior in the organization. First, as Ashforth and Mael (1989) have observed, task interdependence, interpersonal proximity, and similarity are all greater with respect to the individual's primary group. To the extent that occupants of organizational categories share other social attributes such as race, gender, or age (Alderfer & Thomas, 1988; Strang & Baron, 1989), the level of perceived similarity within a group relative to between groups may be even greater than consideration of the organizational category itself would suggest.

There may be psychological reasons why this level of categorization is particularly salient to individuals. As Brewer (1989; Brewer & Schneider,

1989) has recently proposed, individuals seem to have a preference for identification with relatively small, distinctive groups. This level of group categorization permits differentiation between the self and others, therefore reaffirming the self's uniqueness or distinctiveness, while simultaneously satisfying the individual's desire for affiliation and social support. Moreover, there may be nontrivial "economies" involved in social interaction at this level—the individual gains all of the psychological benefits of affiliation, but at relatively low costs (once the initial setup costs of forming a close relationships with other ingroup members have been paid). In contrast, trying to maintain the same level of intimacy and interaction with larger groups or whole organizations may be cognitively and emotionally taxing—especially in situations where membership in the larger group may continually change due to turnover, rotation, etc.

Preference for interaction with small proximate groups may be reinforced in organizational settings by what Stephan and Stephan (1985) have termed "intergroup anxiety." They define such anxiety in terms of the discomfort associated with the ambiguities and uncertainties associated with interacting with members of different groups. Because of intergroup anxiety, individuals may avoid members of other groups, thus affirming even further the psychological status and salience of the primary group to them.

The important implication of this assumption that categorization in organizations is most often associated with the individual's primary group is that it implies interdependence is likely to be defined in terms of *intergroup-level categories* that differentiate or draw sharp demarcations between groups. For example, all else being equal, organizational policies and practices regarding resource allocations will be interpreted in terms of how they affect the individual's group compared to other groups.

Having described in general terms how the level of salient categorization affects an individual's level of social identification and perceptions of interdependence within an organization, we are now in a position to identify some of the factors that promote the development of competitive transformations. As will be seen in the next section, the psychological preference or tendency for individuals to define interdependence at the intergroup level contributes to the emergence of competitive orientations between groups.

COMPETITIVE TRANSFORMATIONS IN INTERGROUP-LEVEL INTERACTIONS

Empirical evidence linking intergroup-level categorization with the emergence of competitive behavior between groups is quite substantial. Many studies, using a variety of paradigms, have demonstrated that categorizing individuals into distinctive groups is sufficient to produce intergroup competition (See, e.g., Brewer, 1979; Insko, Pinkley, Harring, Holton, Hong, Krams, Hoyle, & Thibaut, 1986; Insko & Shopler, 1987; Rabbie & Horwitz, 1969). Of particular relevance to the present analysis are studies that have shown that increasing the salience of intergroup-level categories in commons dilemma situations increases the level of competition for resources (e.g., Brewer & Kramer, 1985, 1986; Brewer & Schneider, 1989; Kramer, 1989d; Kramer & Brewer, 1984; Komorita & Lapworth, 1982). Taken together, these studies suggest that intergroup-level categorization produces several distinctive cognitive and motivational transformations of interdependence relations. In the following sections, I discuss these transformations in more detail.

Categorization and Motivational Transformations

Individuals desire to maintain high levels of self-esteem and positive identity in organizational settings, just as they do in other social settings (Brockner, 1988). Empirical studies suggest that individuals are generally motivated to maintain a positive personal identity (see e.g., Taylor, 1989; Taylor & Brown, 1988). To the extent that membership in social and organizational categories constitutes an integral part of an individuals' identity, it seems reasonable to argue, then, that individuals will be motivated to maintain positive *social* identities as well. Indeed, social identity theorists such as Tajfel and Turner (1986; Turner, 1975) have proposed that the need for positive social identity leads individuals to seek to maximize intergroup distinctiveness along dimensions which have positive implications for their self-esteem. As a consequence of the need for a positive self-identity, a kind of *social competition* is created "in which individuals are motivated to define the situation—and the characteristics of other participants—in terms that are associated with positive ingroup status and to avoid comparisons on characteristics that are unfavorable or irrelevant to ingroup identity" (Brewer & Miller, 1984, p. 282).

Social competition between groups may be especially acute in organizations because comparative outcomes are often of greater significance to groups than absolute outcomes in such settings. For example, the *proportion* of available resources which are allocated to a group may be much more important than the absolute amount of resources it receives. Thus, to the extent that individuals define the success or failure of their group in relative terms, social competition may lead them to adopt competitive orientations towards resources, since doing well means surpassing other groups by as large a margin as possible.

The notion of social competition draws attention to the psychological significance of competitive behavior in organizations. Intergroup competition for resources is motivated not simply by the instrumental value associated with acquiring those resources (i.e., their utility with respect to accomplishing work goals), but on the basis of the psychic benefits derived from the fact that one's own group possesses more than others. This is one important way in which a social psychological perspective on resource interdependence differs from other perspectives, especially those which emphasize the political and strategic value of resources (e.g., Pfeffer, 1981b).

The process of social competition implies a fundamental transformation in the motivation underlying individuals' behavior in situations involving resource interdependence. Instead of acting only to maximize their personal gain, individuals in intergroup contexts become motivated to maximize the relative gains of their group relative to other outgroups. Thus, the salient reference point for evaluating success and failure are no longer individual level outcomes, but group level ones.

Although social competition suggests one reason why the level of intergroup competition may increase when intergroup-level categories are salient, it is important to note that it is not necessary to assume that this is the only reason why individuals behave competitively in such situations. Another reason pertains to individuals' perceptions of *ingroup entitlement*.

Categorization and Perceptions of Ingroup Entitlement

In many cases, individuals' decisions about how much they should take from a common resource pool in an organization may reflect their perceptions of how much they are entitled to take (i.e., what constitutes their fair share of resources). Social comparison theory suggests that such judgments are likely to be defined comparatively, especially when objective standards or criteria are not readily available. Evidence of the importance of comparative processes in judgments about entitlement is provided, for example, by research on relative deprivation and perceived equity in organizations (Martin, 1981). When applied to intergroup-level comparisons, these relative deprivation and equity models posit that individuals' perceptions of entitlement are likely to be affected by comparisons involving such things as the ratio of inputs to outputs of their own group relative to those of other groups (Taylor & Moghaddam, 1987). To varying degrees, these models assume that individuals act much like "rational accountants" maintaining intergroup balance sheets that are more or less veridical.

Research suggests that such judgments are often far from veridical, however (Brewer, 1979; Brewer, 1986). Instead, they appear to be contaminated by a variety of systematic distortions that are associated with the ingroup-outgroup status of the actors. In illustrating how intergroup categorization can affect individuals' perceptions of entitlement, I will focus here on the role of one particular cognitive bias—the availability bias. The availability bias reflects a tendency for individuals to use the ease with which they can recall events to estimate their relative frequency (Tversky & Kahneman, 1974). For example, in trying to estimate the number of rainy versus clear days that occurred last year, an individual might try to recall as many of each day that he can. Since there are a variety of factors that can affect the availability of information in memory but which are uncorrelated with the actual frequency of the event (e.g., the intensity or recency of a particularly severe series of storms), reliance on availability as a heuristic for estimating relative frequencies can lead to systematic errors in the estimation process.

The availability bias can produce a similarly distorted pattern of results with respect to estimates of ingroup versus outgroup entitlement to organizational resources. When judging the relative deservedness of one's own group and other groups, individuals may try to recall relevant evidence, such as how hard members of their group worked compared to members of other groups. Since individuals have extensive interaction and contact with members of their own groups, they will typically be able to recall many instances of such behavior. For the same reason, they will be able to recall comparatively fewer instances of such behavior by outgroup members (see Leary & Forsyth, 1987 for a more extended discussion of group-serving biases in social judgment).

The tendency to overestimate the positive behaviors of one's own group and underestimate those of other groups has two important consequences with regard to the development of competitive orientations. First, because it leads individuals to have inflated perceptions of the entitlement of their group to organizational resources, their perception of what constitutes their fair share of organizational resources may be at odds with other groups' perceptions. Second, and relatedly, they may perceive other groups as receiving *more* than *they* are entitled to. Thus one's own group is perceived to be underbenefitted and underrewarded, whereas other groups are perceived to be overrewarded. As a result of such perceptions, groups may find themselves engaged in a competition for resources that is driven by strongly held but mutually inconsistent convictions regarding their entitlement to organizational resources.

Categorization and Expectations

Even in situations where members of different groups might prefer to cooperate with each other, they may be reluctant to initiate such cooperation themselves. In the absence of guarantees that members of another group can be trusted to reciprocate, individuals may act competitively in order to avoid or defend against being exploited. Because of this possibility of exploitation, a number of researchers have emphasized the importance of trust in the development of intergroup cooperation in resource dilemmas (Brewer, 1979; Kramer & Brewer, 1984).

Why should intergroup-level categorization affect individuals' perceptions of the trustworthiness of outgroup members? One reason concerns the cognitive consequences of categorization (Tajfel, 1969). Research by Brewer and her students (Brewer, 1979; Brewer & Silver, 1978) has shown that categorization into groups, even when based on arbitrary and transient criteria can lead ingroup members to perceive outgroup members as less trustworthy, less honest, and less cooperative than members of their own group. The low levels of trust associated with intergroup categorization can lead individuals to underestimate reciprocity from outgroup members. As a result, they may foreclose prematurely on the possibility of establishing more cooperative relationships, leading to defensively motivated noncooperation (Kramer, 1989d).

To summarize, evidence from many studies has shown that intergroup-level categorization enhances competitive responding among resource interdependent individuals. This relationship can be attributed to a number of distinctive psychological transformations in individuals' motives, perceptions, and expectations. The convergent effects and cumulative impact of such transformations help explain the high levels of incipient hostility and competition that have been widely noted by previous organizational researchers.

Although the discussion up to this point has focused only on the effects of intergroup-level categorization, a more general theory about the role of resource interdependence and categorization processes in intergroup relations in organizations is implicit in much of what has been said. This model will be described in the next section.

A GENERAL MODEL OF INTERGROUP RELATIONS

The general model of intergroup relations that is depicted in Figure 4 incorporates all of the essential features of the basic model of interdependent decisionmaking that was introduced earlier (Figure 1), but it also fills in several gaps in that original model. In particular, it specifies the important role that categorization processes play in the transformation of interdependence in organizations. In addition, the model identifies environmental and organizational factors that affect interdependent behavior. The model proposes that individuals' decisions to behave cooperatively or competitively with other individuals with whom they are interdependent in an organization are directly linked to how they perceive that interdependence. These perceptions, in turn, are influenced by (1) the actual interdependence which exists between them and (2) the transformed psychological representation of that interdependence. The specific transformations that are made of the actual interdependence matrix, as argued earlier, are determined primarily by the level of organizational categorization that is salient to individuals during decisionmaking.

Actual Resource Interdependence. The structural interdependence that exists between two or more groups can be quite complex, as Schmidt and Kochan (1972) and Thompson (1967) illustrated. For example, intergroup interdependence with respect to resources can be pooled, reciprocal, or sequential. For the purposes of the present discussion, resource interdependence will be operationalized primarily in terms of the availability of resources to groups (i.e., their abundance or scarcity). As suggested in the figure, the availability of resources is affected by both environmental factors external to the organization, as well as internal organizational factors.

Environmental Factors. March and Simon (1958) were among the first organizational researchers to articulate how external factors shape internal organizational events. In particular, they proposed that the "munifience" of an organization's environment with respect to resources affected the development of conflict between groups within it. External events such as unexpected economic downturns. for example, can produce sudden decreases in the flow

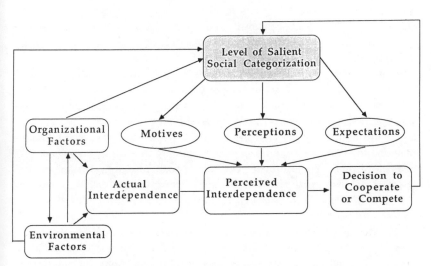

Figure 4. A General Model of Intergroup Relations in Organizations.

of resources into an organization, leading to increased competition for those dwindling resources (Hills & Mahoney, 1978; Salancik & Pfeffer, 1974).

Another external factor that may shape intergroup relations within an organization is information concerning how comparable groups in other organizations are doing with respect to acquiring organizational resources. Social comparisons occur not only within but also *across* organizational boundaries. For example, the salary expectations of workers at one airline may be affected by what workers at rival airlines, who are performing similar tasks or who have similar job titles, are receiving. On the basis of such information, individuals may recalibrate their expectations or aspirations. As a consequence, they may feel deprived or discontented with their current resource endowments even in situations where they are objectively doing better than other groups within the organization.

Organization-Environment Interactions. As the figure indicates, the availability of resources is also affected by organization-environment interactions. In particular, the extent to which the organization is successful at strategically manipulating its environment in order to obtain necessary resources determines to a large extent how much is available for distribution within the organization (Pfeffer & Salancik, 1978).

Internal Organizational Factors. Internal organizational factors can also affect the availability of resources to different groups. For example, the amount of resources that a group receives is likely to reflect various formal and informal allocation mechanisms in the organization. There are a variety of criteria by means of which such allocations may be made, including considerations of merit, equality, or need (Martin & Harder, 1988).

Political processes undoubtedly play an important role as well in influencing the distribution of resources among groups (Pfeffer, 1981b; Pfeffer & Salancik, 1977). Along such lines, the relative power and status of groups becomes an important consideration in determining how much they receive of an organization's resources (Baldridge, 1971; Brett & Rognes, 1986). Groups may employ cooptational strategies in attempting to neutralize less powerful competitors in the contest for scarce organizational resources (Pfeffer, 1981a). Political contests may give rise to emergent structures such as coalitions (Mannix, 1989a, 1989b; Murnighan, 1986; Pfeffer, 1981a).

Perceived Resource Interdependence. Although we would expect at least some correlation to exist between actual interdependence conditions in an organization and individuals' perceptions of those conditions, the spirit of the present analysis has been to draw attention to evidence that they are not perfectly correlated. The importance of perceptions of scarcity is illustrated by consideration of two other general psychological processes that can affect how individuals respond to resource interdependence problems. The first involves attributional processes.

Resources scarcities can result from many different causes, some of which are internal to the organization and in principle controllable, and others of which are external and less uncontrollable (although Pfeffer and Salancik's resource dependence theory illustrates the many ways in which organizations can attempt to exert control over external events). There is evidence that how individuals respond to resource scarcities is influenced by the attributions they make regarding the cause(s) of those scarcities. In particular, when resource scarcities are attributed to external factors over which group members have no control, they are more likely to cooperate. When scarcities are attributed to mismanagement by the organization or groups within it, in contrast, they may be more likely to compete. This general hypothesis is supported by both laboratory simulations of resource dilemmas (Messick, 1986; Rutte, Wilke, & Messick, 1987; Samuelson, 1988; Kramer, Goldman & Davis, 1989) and field research on resource consumption behavior (Talarowski & McClintock, 1978).

The importance of perceptions is suggested also by research on distributive justice and procedural fairness in organizations. Extrapolating from this research, we might hypothesize that the willingness of members of different groups to cooperate when sharing resources and/or their willingness to accept a given resource allocation is dependent not only on the actual distribution of resources (how much was afforded them), but also the perceived fairness of the procedures used to achieve that distribution (see Lind & Tyler, 1988 for a review of relevant literature).

CONTRIBUTIONS AND IMPLICATIONS OF THE PRESENT FRAMEWORK

This chapter began by noting that, although intergroup relations in organizations are often competitive in nature, there have been few systematic examinations of the underlying causes of such competition. By drawing out the implications of empirical studies and appropriating concepts from several strands of social psychological research, we have been able to provide the outline for a general model of intergroup relations in organizations. In leading up to this model, we have covered a fair bit of ground. It seems appropriate, therefore, to pause at this point and raise some questions about the value of the framework that has been presented. Two broad questions readily suggest themselves. First, is the categorization perspective useful to organizational theory? Should we pay more attention to categorization processes in organizations? Second, does the commons analogy contribute to our understanding of organizational behavior—and, if so, in what ways?

These are fair questions and they merit consideration. In trying to answer them, I would like to suggest a number of general implications of the present framework and some contributions it makes to our understanding of individual and group behavior in organizations. The first pertain to what the framework tells us about resolving intergroup competition for resources.

Reducing Intergroup Competition and Conflict

As adaptive systems, organizations generally attempt to keep competition and conflict between groups from going beyond acceptable bounds. In fact, one of the major ways in which intergroup relations in organizational settings differ from other social contexts is that organizations have at their disposal a variety of institutional mechanisms for regulating competition and conflict (March & Simon, 1958; Pondy, 1967). For example, organizations can use political processes to resolve conflicts involving resources (March & Simon, 1958; Pfeffer, 1981b); managers can intervene as third parties in order to mediate or arbitrate disputes over scarce resources (Notz, Starke, & Atwell, 1983); and groups may use negotiation in trying to resolve such conflicts themselves (Morley, Webb, & Stephenson, 1988).

Although each of these approaches is useful, the framework depicted in Figure 4 suggests at least two additional approaches that may be effective at reducing competition for resources. The first, and perhaps most obvious, approach consists of structural interventions or solutions (see Kramer, 1989c; & Messick & Brewer, 1983 for a more detailed discussion of structural solutions to resource dilemmas). Structural approaches consist of efforts to change the objective interdependence which exists between two or more groups. These include altering organizational interfaces so as to reduce interdependence (Brown, 1983), changing resource allocation procedures, and introduction of superordinate goals (Sherif, 1966; Sherif, et. al., 1988; Blake & Mouton, 1984).

In many instances, of course, implementing major structural changes or introducing superordinate goals may be costly, difficult, or even impossible. The categorization perspective implies another set of approaches to modifying the interdependence between groups in organizations: Instead of attempting to change the actual interdependence between them, it may be possible to change how that interdependence is perceived or construed.

Research on categorization suggests at least three distinctive ways of changing how intergroup interdependence is perceived by group members. All are predicated on manipulating the salience of group categories or boundaries. One approach entails increasing the salience of superordinate or collective-level group boundaries, so that the impact of intergroup-level categorization processes is weakened or attenuated. A number of experiments (Kramer, 1989d; Kramer & Brewer, 1984, 1986; Brewer & Kramer, 1984, 1986) have shown that this strategy can be quite effective in reducing intergroup competition for resources—at least in the context of laboratory simulations of resource dilemmas. Along related lines, Gaertner and his associates (Gaertner, Mann, Murrell, & Dovidio, 1989) have demonstrated that "decategorizing" groups by making salient superordinate boundaries can reduce the level of intergroup bias in perceptions.

A second approach to attenuating the deleterious impact of intergroup-level categorization may be to use criss-crossing or cross-cutting group memberships (Brewer, Ho, Lee, & Miller, 1987; Deschamps & Doise, 1978; Pruitt & Rubin, 1986). Nelson (1989) identified at least three reasons why cross-cutting group memberships might be effective. First, they may contribute to the development of more positive sentiment among group members. Second, they may reduce intergroup polarization because intergroup boundaries remain permeable. As a result, critical information can be exchanged between groups. Finally, they provide a channel for conflict resolution. In support of his general arguments, Nelson found that organizations in which there were relatively high numbers of strong intergroup ties had lower levels of intergroup conflict.

Along these lines, Baron has noted (Personal Communication) that one feature often observed in organizations that put a premium on cooperative problem solving, such as Japanese firms, is extensive job rotation. This practice is important not only in terms of the technical expertise and social ties that develop, but also the cognitive implications of exposing individuals to many positions in the organizations. To the extent that category incumbency shapes perceptions, extensive rotation may discourage individuals from taking any parochial category as particularly salient or dominant.

A third approach suggested by categorization research entails reducing the salience of intergroup-level categories by *individuating* members of outgroups (Gaertner et. al., 1989; Wilder, 1978). Individuation reduces category-based interactions. It thus provides a mechanism for overriding the tendency to view outgroup members in relatively homogeneous, stereotypical and negative terms.

A fourth approach to reducing intergroup competition and conflict is suggested by research on symbolic management in organizations (Bies, 1987; Pfeffer, 1981a; Sutton & Kramer, 1989). Broadly construed, the symbolic management perspective posits that an important function of top management in organizations is to legitimate and rationalize organizational actions and conditions to individuals and groups within the organization (as well as important constituencies external to the organization).

To see how this research might be relevant to understanding intergroup relations, it is important to note that previous research on the management of intergroup competition and conflict has focused almost entirely on how organizations try to resolve conflicts that have become manifest (Pondy, 1967). In other words, attention has been given primarily to how organizations react to conflicts that are already in progress. It may be possible, however, to manage conflicts before they become emergent by manipulating individuals' perceptions of organizational and environmental conditions. Management can attempt to strategically manipulate individuals' perceptions, motives, and expectations in order to control the specific transformations they make in response to a given set of organizational circumstances.

Research on symbolic management provides a conceptual framework for thinking about how organizations might try to do accomplish such strategic manipulations. One way that management might try to control perceptions of organizational resource allocations is to manipulate the attributions that group members make regarding such allocations. For example, they could encourage workers to attribute resource scarcities to external factors (unexpected economic downturns or the behavior of foreign organizations), so that attention is deflected away from groups within the organization. In this way management may divert blame from the organization or its management.

Organizations could also attempt to control group members' perceptions of entitlement by manipulating the information they receive about the behavior of their own group compared to other groups. For example, management could selectively provide information to create the impression that the efforts, contributions or worth of some groups are less than those of others. To reinforce such perceptions, organizations could even strategically create new categories that constrain social comparisons across groups. By creating new job titles or classifications, management might be able to legitimate reward discrepancies between groups, even though they are doing substantively the same work (Baron, 1988; Baron & Pfeffer, 1989).

Such symbolic actions by management operate by directing attention, controlling perceptions, suppressing reactions, and fostering acceptance of organizational conditions. They thus function to keep conflict below thresholds of awareness or perception (Bies, 1987; Martin, 1989; Sutton & Kramer, 1990). While the symbolic management approach has a decidedly Machiavellian—and to that extent unsavory—flavor, we should at least be cognizant of its potential scope and implications for understanding intergroup relations in organizations. There is no reason to think that management in some organizations might not at least attempt to manipulate or control the nature of the psychological transformations that individuals make of their interdependence. In this respect, it is clear that, although categorization is a "natural" process in organizations, it can be used as a strategic one as well.

Development of Intergroup Cooperation

In addition to shedding light on the origins of competition and conflict in organizations, the categorization perspective has a number of implications for understanding how cooperation around resources emerges as well. In large organizations, it is costly and difficult to continuously monitor intergroup relations or the resource consumption behaviors of individuals. Consequently, most organizations depend to some degree on voluntary cooperation among organizational members.

Research on the effects of categorization suggests several reasons why cooperation might emerge when collective-level categories are reinforced or made salient. The first concerns the process of *tacit cooperation* (Schelling, 1960). Tacit cooperation is achieved when two or more interdependent actors simultaneously and without communication converge on a solution to a dilemma that enables them to successfully coordinate their choices and thereby avoid conflict. Why might superordinate-level categorization increase tacit cooperation among organizational groups? It was noted earlier that individuals' willingness to voluntarily exercise self-restraint in resource dilemmas has been found to depend, at least in part, on their expectations or trust that others will do the same. Along these lines, Brewer (1981) has argued that, "Common membership in a salient social category can serve as a rule for defining the boundaries of low-risk interpersonal trust that bypasses the need for personal knowledge and the costs of negotiating reciprocity with individual others. As a consequence of shifting from the personal or group level to the collective group level of identity, the individual can adopt a sort of 'depersonalized trust' based on category membership alone" (p. 356). When collective or organizational-level categorization is salient, therefore, a generalized reciprocal trust may develop, leading individuals to voluntarily cooperate, because they are confident that others will do so as well.

A second reason that collective categorization may lead to the emergence of tacit cooperation is suggested by the notion of *self-reflexive restraint* (Kramer, 1989c). In a clever study, Quattrone and Tversky (1984, Experiment 2) explored what they termed the "voter's illusion." They proposed that there are situations where "an individual may regard his or her own decisions as diagnostic of the decisions likely to be made by other 'like-minded' persons.

If the individual recognizes that beneficial outcomes would ensue if very many like-minded persons select a particular alternative, then the individual may select that alternative, even if the choice is costly, not witnessed by others, and not likely by itself to affect the final outcome. *In these circumstances, the choice is made to 'induce' others who think and act like oneself to do the same"* (p. 244, emphasis added).

In the case of deciding whether or not to cooperate, an individual might reason that, if she or he cooperates, then *like-minded others* will be likely to do the same. On the other hand, if she or he fails to cooperate, then like-minded others will also not cooperate. Using this "logic," the individual concludes that he or she had better cooperate! Research on social categorization has shown that ingroup categorization leads to greater belief similarity among individuals (see e.g., Wilder, 1984). As a consequence of superordinate categorization, therefore, individuals may be more likely to expect that other individuals with whom they share category membership will interpret the situation and respond to it in the same way, leading to a "spontaneous" emergence of cooperation.[3]

Social Decision Making in Organizations

In recent years, there has been a great deal of interest in the nature of interdependent decisionmaking, with respect to both organizational and social dilemmas. There have been literally hundreds of studies in economics, sociology, and psychology on such decisionmaking. In most of these studies, individual decisionmakers have been characterized as self-interested, egocentric, and asocial actors. These conceptions of interdependent decisionmaking, especially those derived from game theoretic and economic models, have treated as axiomatic the proposition that individuals will act primarily to maximize their own outcomes when interacting with others. In his analysis of behavior in resource dilemmas, for example, Ostrom (1977) characterized decisionmakers as "self-interested, rational, and maximizing others" (p. 174). Although the assumption of individual self-interest has proven to be analytically useful and parsimonious, its power in predicting actual behavior has been disappointingly low (see, e.g., Orbell, van de Kragt, & Dawes, 1988; Organ, 1988).

In light of such empirical evidence, a number of researchers have suggested that the assumption that individual decision making in resource dilemmas is motivated primarily by egotistic motives or concern about self-interests alone needs to be reexamined (Edney, 1980, 1981; Kramer & Brewer, 1986; Lynn & Oldenquist, 1986). As Granovetter (1985) has observed, recent research on economic and social behavior has been dominated by an "atomistic, *under-*

socialized conception of human action. . . . Actors do not behave or decide as atoms outside a social context, [rather] their attempts at purposive action are embedded in concrete, ongoing systems of social relations" (p. 483, 487, emphasis added).

Along similar lines, Perrow (1986) has argued that we need a more complex notion of self-interest to explain organizational behavior. The behavior of individuals in organizations, he notes, is not only self-regarding, it is at times *other regarding* as well. Perrow argues that self-interest, therefore, should be regarded as a variable, not a constant.

The framework presented in this chapter suggests some of the conditions under which such other-regarding behavior may surface. Specifically, the categorization perspective implies that what constitutes an individual's self interests may depend on the nature of the social and organizational categories that are salient to him or her at the time of decisionmaking. Thus, the model presented in this chapter provides at least the beginnings of a theoretical framework that supports a more socialized conception of interdependent decisionmaking.

Usefulness of the Commons Analogy

In assessing the contribution of the present framework, I should also raise the question as to whether or not the commons analogy is useful for organizational theory. Does it add anything to our conception of organizations? There are at least two ways in which conceptualizing organizations as posing dilemmas for their members may be valuable. The first has to do with the usefulness of the dilemmas perspective for bridging previous work on intergroup relations in organizations. As suggested earlier in the chapter, previous research has generally adopted either one of two distinct level of analysis. Research at the macro-level has examined primarily structural determinants of intergroup relations, while research at the micro-level has focused on the psychological underpinnings of intergroup behavior.

Unfortunately, these two perspectives have remained fairly independent of each other. For example, while many macro-level theories have acknowledged the importance of interdependence, they have not drawn out any of the *psychological* implications of this interdependence. In particular, they have not specified in any detail the underlying processes which link a particular interdependence structure with the emergence of competitive or cooperative behavior. In these models, the organizational stage on which intergroup life is enacted is brightly illuminated, but the actors themselves remain inanimate black boxes. In contrast, psychological theories have opened up the black box, but they have ignored the setting within which behavior occurs. They have thus animated the actors, but left them without a stage on which to move. The commons perspective provides a framework for integrating these structural and psychological perspectives.

The second way in which the commons perspective may prove useful is purely heuristic. Our understanding of organizational phenomena has often been sharpened through the use of new metaphors and analogies. Such metaphors and analogies can evoke fresh perspectives on "old" phenemona and thereby stimulate new research. Cohen, March, and Olsen's (1972) characterization of organizational decisionmaking as a "garbage can" process is one prominent example. Through the use of this metaphor, Cohen et al. were able to draw our attention to sources of irrationality inherent in organizational decisions which might otherwise have escaped notice. In a similar way, conceptualizing organizations as mixed-motive environments that pose difficult dilemmas for their members may help us identify organizational and psychological factors that jointly shape intergroup relations. I hasten to add, however, that this is not to put the commons analogy on par with the garbage can model; nor it is to claim that the particular way in which the analogy has been sketched here is the most useful way of doing so. Rather, the point is simply to suggest that the general analogy of the commons dilemma is useful and should be exploited further.

DIRECTIONS FOR FURTHER RESEARCH

The evidence reviewed in this chapter implicates both organizational and psychological factors as determinants of intergroup competition and cooperation. Although the framework presented in Figure 4 does a reasonably good job of organizing much of this evidence, it also draws our attention to a number of important gaps in our knowledge about intergroup relations in organizations. First, although the model suggests that there are a variety of contextual factors that increase the salience of a particular level of categorization, we clearly need to learn more about the determinants of category salience. I have argued above that intergroup-level categorizations are particularly salient in organizations. However, it is also obvious that there are circumstances under which other levels of categorization become salient. Unfortunately, there has been relatively little research which identifies organizational and psychological variables affecting category salience in organizations. In the absence of such research, the model tentatively proposes that both environmental events and organizational variables affect the level of salient categorization.

There is research that provides at least hints as to some possible candidates for such variables. First, with respect to environmental factors, there is some evidence that crises or threats to an organizations' well-being, especially, when they are attributed to external factors beyond the organizations' control, may heighten a sense of collective identity (Janis, 1963; Kramer, Goldman, & Davis, 1989). This is also suggested, at least implicitly, by Staw, Sandelands, and Dutton's (1981) threat-rigidity model of organizational behavior. According to their model, when organizations are threatened and those threats are attributed to external factors, group cohesiveness increases. Conversely, when these threats are attributed to internal factors, group cohesiveness may decrease.

With respect to organizational-level factors, experimental findings suggest that the distinctiveness of a category in a given situation (e.g., whether it has "solo status") may affect its salience (Fiske & Taylor, 1984). Category salience may also be affected by group and organizational outcomes. For example, when organizations experience successful outcomes or positive events happen to them, individuals in the organization may be motivated to enhance their identification with the organization. As a result, organizational-level categorization may be more salient than intraorganizational-level categories. Introduction of a highly successful product may lead to feelings that, "*We* (the organization) did it." In contrast, when negative events happen to the organization, individuals may attempt to dissociate themselves from these outcomes, leading either individualistic or group-level categories to become salient, e.g., "*They* (top management) goofed up, but *we* (the group) did all we could to warn them." Lyndon Johnson provided an amusing illustration of this shift in salient categorization during the 1960 presidential elections. Upon hearing some of the incoming election returns, he called John F. Kennedy and commented, "I hear *you're* losing Ohio but *we're* doing fine in Pennsylvania" (Sorensen, 1965). Support for this general hypothesis is provided by two streams of social psychological research: (1) work on "basking in reflected glory" (Cialdini et al., 1976) and behavior in identity-enhancing and identity-threatening situations (Tedeschi, 1981).

The analysis presented here has defined intergroup interdependence only in terms of dependence on a shared resource pools. Obviously, there are other forms of interdependence characteristic of organizations in which resources would seem to play, at most, only a marginal or peripheral role. For example, Perrow (1986) emphasized the importance of conflict over goals in intergroup conflicts, and Brett and Rognes (1986) focused on power-dependence relations and interface issues that affect conflict between groups. This raises the question, "Is the commons perspective too narrow in emphasizing only resource-based conflicts?" I would argue that it is not. First, when we analyze other forms of organizational interdependence, resources eventually enter into the picture. Thus, conflicts over goals are often manifested in terms of disputes regarding the ends to which organizational resources (whether they be human or otherwise) are to be put. Similarly, when we talk about power-dependence relations between groups, it is often necessary to operationalize such relations in terms of the extent that different groups possess and/or control organizational resources. Second, the general model which is offered here could easily be modified to accommodate a more complete typology of interdependence situations (in fact, Kelley's 1983 taxonomy provides a first step in doing so).

Given the complexity of intergroup phenomena in organizations, any single perspective on intergroup relations is likely to raise as many questions as it answers. Certainly, the present chapter does not bring closure to the topic, nor was it intended to do so. However, it hopefully achieved the more modest goal of providing a general framework for conceptualizing some of the necessary, even if not sufficient, components that a more comprehensive theory of intergroup relations in organizations might include.

ACKNOWLEDGMENTS

The writing of this chapter benefitted greatly from discussions with Jeff Pfeffer, Marilynn Brewer, Joanne Martin, Blair Sheppard, and Bob Sutton. I am especially grateful to Jim Baron for his detailed and helpful comments. Barry Staw and Larry Cummings deserve many thanks for their cogent critiques of an earlier version of this chapter.

NOTES

1. There are many other situations in organizations that have this mixed-motive character: transfer pricing; sharing information; helping each other, etc.
2. Social identity is also based, of course, on membership in social and demographic groups (e.g., gender, age, educational level). Although the focus here will be on identities that are derived from organizationally-created categories, it is important to bear in mind that organizational and social identities are often intertwined and may interact (Alderfer, 1977; Alderfer & Thomas, 1988; Lansberg, 1989).
3. Although Baron (Personal Communication) raised the intriguing possibility that individuals might use this same logic to justify "free riding" in such situations. In other words, if I think that like-minded people are going to cooperate, then there is no need for me to do so afterall! I can count on others to do the same.

REFERENCES

Alderfer, C. P. (1977). Group and intergroup relations. In J. R. Hackman & J. L. Suttle (Eds.), *Improving life at work*. Santa Monica, CA: Goodyear.
Alderfer, C. P., & Smith, K. K. (1982). Studying intergroup relations embedded in organizations. *Administrative Science Quarterly, 27*, 33–65.

Alderfer, C. P., & Thomas, D. A. (1988). The significance of race and ethnicity for understanding organizational behavior. In C. L. Cooper & I. Robertson (Eds.), *International review of industrial and organizational psychology*. New York: John Wiley.

Ashforth, B. E., & Mael, F. (1989). Social identity theory and the organization. *Academy of Management Review, 14*, 20–39.

Baldridge, J. V. (1971). *Power and conflict in the university*. New York: John Wiley.

Baron J. N. (1988). The employment relation as a social relation. *Journal of the Japanese and international economies, 2*, 492–525.

Baron, J. N., & Bielby, W. T. (1986). The proliferation of job titles in organizations. *Administrative Science Quarterly, 31*, 561–586.

Baron, J. N., & Pfeffer, J. (1989). The social psychology of organizations and inequality. Unpublished manuscript. Stanford University.

Bies, R. J. (1987). The predicament of injustice: The management of moral outage. In L. L. Cummings & B. Staw (Eds.), *Research in Organizational Behavior*, Vol. 9. Greenwich, CT: JAI Press.

Blake, R., & Mouton, J. (1984). *Solving costly organizational conflicts*. San Francisco: Jossey-Bass.

Blake, R., & Mouton, J. (1989). Lateral conflict. In D. Tjosvold and D. Johnson (Eds.), *Productive conflict management*. Edina, MN: Interaction Book Co.

Blake, R., Shepard, & Mouton, J. (1964). *Managing intergroup conflict in organizations*. Houston, TX: Gulf Publishing Co.

Brett, J. M., & Rognes, J. K. (1986). Intergroup relations in organizations. In Paul Goodman, (Eds.), *Work group effectiveness*. San Francisco: Jossey-Bass.

Brewer, M. B. (1979). In-group bias in the minimal intergroup situation: A cognitive-motivational analysis. *Psychological Bulletin, 86*, 307–324.

Brewer, M. B. (1981). Ethnocentrism and its role in interpersonal trust. In M. B. Brewer & B. E. Collins (Eds.), *Scientific inquiry and the social sciences*. New York: Jossey-Bass.

Brewer, M. B. (1986). Ethnocentrism and its role in intergroup conflict. In S. Worchel & W. G. Austin (Eds.), *Psychology of intergroup relations*. Chicago: Nelson-Hall.

Brewer, M. B. (1989). Optimal distinctiveness. A theory of group identification. Unpublished manuscript. University of California, Los Angeles.

Brewer, M. B., Ho, H., Lee, J., & Miller, N. (1987). Social identity and social distance among Hong Kong school children. *Personality and Social Psychology Bulletin, 13*, 156–165.

Brewer, M. B., & Kramer, R. M. (1984). Subgroup identity as a factor in the conservation of resources. Paper presented at the American Psychological Association annual convention, Washington, D. C.

Brewer, M. B., & Kramer, R. M. (1985). The psychology of intergroup attitudes and behavior. *Annual Review of Psychology, 36*, 219–243.

Brewer, M. B., & Kramer, R. M. (1986). Choice behavior in social dilemmas: Effects of social identity, group size, and decision framing. *Journal of Personality and Social Psychology, 50*, 543–549.

Brewer, M. B., & Miller, N. (1984). Beyond the contact hypothesis: Theoretical perspectives on desegregation. In N. Miller & M. Brewer (Eds.), *Groups in contact: The psychology of desegregation*. New York: Academic Press.

Brewer, M. B., & Schneider, S. K. (1989). Social identity and social dilemmas: A double-edged sword. In D. Abrams & M. Hogg (Eds.), *Social identity theory. Constructive and critical advances*. NY: Harvester-Wheatsheaf.

Brewer, M. B. & Silver, M. (1978). Ingroup bias as a function of task characteristics. *European Journal of Social Psychology, 8*, 393–400.

Brockner, J. (1988). *Self-esteem at work: Research, theory, and practice.* Lexington, MA: D. C. Heath.

Brown, L. D. (1983). *Managing conflict at organizational interfaces.* Reading, MA: Addison-Wesley.

Cohen, M. D., March, J. G., & Olsen, J. P. (1972). A garbage can model of organizational choice. *Administrative Science, Quarterly, 17,* 1–25.

Cialdini, R. B., Borden, R. J., Thorne, A., Walkder, M. R., Freman, S., & Sloan, L. R. (1976). Basking in reflected glory: Three (football) field studies. *Journal of Personality and Social Psychology, 34,* 463–476.

Cyert, R. M. & March, J. G. (1963). *A behavioral theory of the firm.* Englewood Cliffs, NJ: Prentice-Hall.

Dawes, R. M. (1980). Social dilemmas. *Annual Review of Psychology, 31,* 169–193.

Deschamps, J. C., & Doise, W. (1978). Crossed-category membership in intergroup relations. In H. Tajfel (Ed.), *Differentiation between social groups.* London: Academic Press.

Edney, J J. (1980). The commons problem: Alternative perspectives. *American Psychologist, 35,* 131–150.

Edney, J. J., Harper, C. S. (1978). The commons dilemma: A review of contributions from psychology. *Environmental Management, 2,* 491–507.

Fiske, S., & Taylor, S. (1984). *Social cognition.* New York: Random House.

Fort, R. D., & Baden, J. (1981). The federal treasury as a common resource pool and the development of a predatory bureaucracy. In J. Baden & R. L. Stroup (Eds.), *Bureaucracy vs. environment: The environmental costs of bureaucratic governance.* Ann Arbor: University of Michigan Press.

Gaertner, S. L., Mann, J., Murrell, A., & Dovidio, J. F. (1989). Reducing intergroup bias: The benefits of recategorization. *Journal of Personality and Social Psychology, 57,* 239–249.

Grannovetter, M. (1985). Economic action and social structure: The problem of embeddedness. *American Journal of Sociology, 91,* 481–510.

Hardin, G. (1968). The tragedy of the commons. *Science, 162,* 1243–1248.

Hardin, B., & Baden, J. (1977). *Managing the commons.* San Francisco: W. H. Freeman.

Hills, F. S., & Mahoney, T. A. (1978). University budgets and organizational decision making. *Administrative Science Quarterly, 23,* 454–465.

Hogg, M. A., & Abrams, D. (1988). *Social identifications: A social psychology of intergroup relations and group processes.* London: Routledge.

Hoyle, R. H., Pinkley, R. L., & Insko, C. A. (1988). Perceptions of social behavior: Evidence of differing expectations for interpersonal and intergroup interaction. Unpublished manuscript.

Insko, C. A., Pinkley, R. L., Harring, K., Holton, B., Hong, G., Krams, D. S., Hoyle, R., & Thibaut, J. (1986). Beyond categorization to competition: Expectations of appropriate behavior. Unpublished paper.

Insko, C. A., & Shopler, J. (1987). Categorization, competition, and collectivity. In C. Hendrick (Ed.), *Group Processes.* Beverly Hills: Sage.

Janis, I. L. (1963). Group identification under conditions of external danger. *British Journal of Medical Psychology, 36,* 227–238.

Katz, D. (1964). Approaches to managing conflict. In R. L. Kahn & E. Boulding (Eds.), *Power and conflict in organizations.* New York: Basic Books.

Kelley, H. H. (1979). *Personal relationships.* Hillsdale, NJ: Erlbaum.

Kelley, H. H. (1983). The situation origins of human tendencies: A further reason for the formal analysis of structures. *Personality and Social Psychology Bulletin, 9,* 8–30.

Kelley, H. H. (1985). The theoretic description of interdependence by transition lists. *Journal of Personality and Social Psychology, 47,* 956–986.

Kelley, H. H., & Thibaut, J. W. (1978). *Interpersonal relations: A theory of interdependence.* New York: Wiley,

Komorita, S. S., & Lapworth, C. (1982). Cooperative choice among individuals versus groups in an n-person dilemma situation. *Journal of Personality and Social Psychology, 42,* 487–496.

Kramer, R. M. (1989a). Helping the group or helping yourself? Cognitive and motivational determinants of cooperation in resource conservation dilemmas. In David Schroeder (Ed.), *Social Dilemmas.* New York: Praeger.

Kramer, R. M. (1989b). The more the merrier? Social psychological aspects of multi-party negotiations in organizations. In R. Lewicki, M. H. Bazerman, & B. Sheppard (Eds.), *Research on Negotiations in Organizations.* Greenwich, CT: JAI Press.

Kramer, R. M. (1989c). When the going gets tough: The effects of resource scarcity on group conflict and cooperation. In E. Lawler & B. Markovsky (Eds.), *Advances in Group Process.*

Kramer, R. M. (1989d). Windows of vulnerability or cognitive illusions? Cognitive processes and the nuclear arms race. *Journal of Experimental Social Psychology, 25,* 79–100.

Kramer, R. M., & Brewer, M. B. (1984). Effects of group identity on resource use in a simulated commons dilemma. *Journal of Personality and Social Psychology, 46,* 1044–1057.

Kramer, R. M., & Brewer, M. B. (1986). Social group identity and the emergence of cooperation in resource conservation dilemmas. In H. Wilke, C. Rutte, & D. M. Messick (Eds.), *Experimental studies of social dilemmas.* Frankfurt, Germany: Peter Lang Publishing company.

Kramer, R. M., Goldman, L., & Davis, G. (1989). Social Identity, expectations of reciprocity, and cooperation in social dilemmas. Unpublished manuscript.

Kramer, R. M., McClintock, C. G., & Messick, D. M. (1986). Social values and cooperative response to a simulated resource conservation crisis. *Journal of Personality, 54,* 576–592.

Lansberg, I. (1989). Social categorization, entitlement, and justice in organizations: Contextual determinants and cognitive underpinnings. *Human Relations, 41,* 871–879.

Lawrence, P. R., & Lorsch, J. W. (1967). Differentiation and integration in complex organizations. *Administrative Science Quarterly, 12,* 1–47.

Leary, M. R., & Forsyth, D. R. (1987). Attributions of responsibility for collective endeavors. In C. Hendrick (Ed.), *Group Processes.* Beverly Hills, CA: Sage.

Levine, R. A., & Campbell, D. T. (1972). *Ethnocentrism: Theories of conflict, ethnic attitudes, and group behavior.* New York: John Wiley.

Liebrand, W. G. (1984). The effect of social motives, communication and group size on behavior in an n-person multi-stage mixed-motive game. *European Journal of Social Psychology, 14,* 239–264.

Lind, E. A., & Tyler, T. R. (1988). *The social psychology of procedural justice.* New York: Plenum.

Lynn, M., & Oldenquist, A. (1986). Egoistic and nonegoistic motives in social dilemmas. *American Psychologist, 41,* 529–541.

Mannix, E. A. (1989a). Coalitions in an organizational context: A social dilemmas perspective. Unpublished paper.

Mannix, E. A. (1989b). Organizations as resource dilemmas: The effects of power balance on group decision making. Unpublished paper.

March, J. G., & Simon, H. A. (1958). *Organizations.* New York: John Wiley.

Martin, J. (1981). Relative deprivation: A theory of distributive injustice for an era of shrinking resources. In L. L. Cummings & B. Staw (Eds.), *Research in Organizational Behavior, 3,* 53–107. Greenwich, CT: JAI Press.

Martin, J. (1989). Deconstructing organizational taboos: The suppression of gender conflict in organizations. *Organizational Science.*

Martin, J., & Harder, J. (1988). Bread and roses: Justice and the distribution of financial and socio-emotional rewards in organizations. Unpublished manuscript. Stanford University.

McClintock, C. G., & Liebrand, W. B. (1988). Role of interdependence structure, individual value orientations, and another's strategy in social decision making: A transformational analysis. *Journal of Personality and Social Psychology, 55*, 396–409.

McKinley, W., Cheng, J. L., & Schick, A. G. (1986). Perceptions of resource criticality in times of resource scarcity: The case of university departments. *Academy of Management Journal, 29*, 623–632.

Messick, D. M. (1986). Decision making in social dilemmas: Some attributional effects. In B. Brehmer, H. Jungermann, P. Lourens, & G. Sevon (Eds.), *New directions in research on decision making*. North-Holland: Elsevier.

Messick, D. M., & Brewer, M. B. (1983). Solving social dilemmas: A review. In L. Wheeler (Ed.), *Review of Personality and Social Psychology* Beverly Hills, CA: Sage Publications.

Messick, D. M., & Mackie, D. M. (1989). Intergroup relations. *Annual Review of Psychology, 40*, 45–81.

Messick, D. M., Wilke, H., Brewer, M. B., Kramer, R. M., Zemke, P., & Lui, L. (1983). Individual adaptations and structural change as solutions to social dilemmas. *Journal of Personality and Social Psychology, 44*, 294–309.

Miles, R. H. (1980). *Macro organizational behavior*. Santa Monica, CA: Goodyear Publishing Co.

Morley, I. E., Webb, J., & Stephenson, G. M. (1988). Bargaining and arbitration in the resolution of conflict. In W. Stroebe, A. Kruglanski, D. Bar-Tal, & M. Hewstone (Eds.), *The social psychology of intergroup conflict*. New York: Springer-Verlag.

Murnighan, K. (1986). Organizational coalitions: Structural contingencies and the formation process. In R. J. Lewicki, B. H. Sheppard, & M. H. Bazerman (Eds.), *Research on negotiation in organizations, Volume 1*. Greenwich, CT: JAI Press.

Nelson, R. E. (1989). The strength of strong ties: Social networks and intergroup conflict in organizations. *Academy of Management Journal, 32*, 377–401.

Notz, W. W., Starke, F. A., & Atwell, J. (1983). The manager as arbitrator: Conflicts over scarce resources. In M. H. Bazerman & R. J. Lewicki (Eds.), *Negotiating in organizations*. Beverly Hills, CA: Sage.

Orbell, J. M., van de Kragt, A., & Dawes, R. M. (1988). Explaining discussion-induced cooperation. *Journal of Personality and Social Psychology, 54*, 811–819.

Organ, D. W. (1988). Organizational citizenship behavior: The god soldier syndrome. Lexington, MA: D. C. Heath.

Ostrom, E. (1977). Collective action and the tragedy of the commons. In G. Hardin & J. Baden (Eds.), *Managing the commons*. San Francisco: W. H. Freeman & Co.

Perrow, C. (1986). *Complex organizations* (third edition). New York: Random House.

Pfeffer, J. (1981a). Management as symbolic action: The creation and maintenance of organizational paradigms. In L. L. Cummings & B. Staw (Eds.), *Research in Organizational Behavior*, Vol. 3. Greenwich, CT: JAI Press.

Pfeffer, J. (1981b). *Power in organizations*. Boston: Pitman.

Pfeffer, J., & Moore, W. L. (1980). Power in university budgeting: A replication and extension. *Administrative Science Quarterly*.

Pfeffer, J., & Salancik, G. R. (1977). Organization design: The case for a coalitional model of organizations. *Organizational Dynamics*, 15–29.

Pfeffer, J., & Salancik, G. R. (1978). *The external control of organizations*. New York: Harper & Row.

Pondy, L. R. (1967). Organizational conflict. *Administrative Science Quarterly, 12*, 296–320.

Pruitt, D. G., & Rubin, J. Z. (1986). *Social conflict: Escalation, stalemate, and settlement.* New York: Random House.

Quattrone, G. A., & Tversky, A. (1984). Causal versus diagnostic contingencies: On self-deception and the voter's illusion. *Journal of Personality and Social Psychology, 46,* 237–248.

Rabbie, J. M., & Horwitz, M. (1969). Arousal of ingroup bias by chance win or loss. *Journal of Personality and Social Psychology, 13,* 269–277.

Rothbart, M., & John, O. P. (1985). Social categorization and behavioral episodes: A cognitive analysis of the effects of intergroup contact. *Journal of Social Issues, 41,* 81–104.

Rutter, C. G., Wilke, H., & Messick, D. M. (1987). Scarcity or abundance caused by people or the environment as determinants of behavior in a resource dilemma. *Journal of Experimental Social Psychology, 23,* 208–214.

Salancik, G. R., & Pfeffer, J. (1974). The bases and use of power in organizational decision making: The case of a university. *Administrative Science Quarterly, 19,* 453–473.

Samuelson, C. D. (1988). Causal attributions for group performance: Effects on preferences for allocation rules in resource dilemmas. Unpublished manuscript.

Schelling, T. C. (1960). *The strategy of conflict.* New Haven, CT: Yale University Press.

Schmidt, S. M., & Kochan, T. A. (1972). Conflict: Toward conceptual clarity. *Administrative Science Quarterly, 17,* 359–370.

Scott, W. R. (1987). *Organizations: Rational, natural, and open systems* (second edition). Englewood Cliffs, NJ:Prentice-Hall.

Sherif, M. (1966). In common predicament: Social psychology of intergroup conflict and cooperation. New York: Houghton Mifflin.

Sherif, M., Harvey, O. J., White, B. J., Hood, W. R., & Sherif, C. W. (1988). *The robbers cave experiment: Intergroup conflict and cooperation.* Middletown, CT: Wesleyan.

Sorensen, T. C. (1965). *Kennedy.* New York: Harper & Row.

Staw, B. M., Sandelands, L. E., & Dutton, J. E. (1981). Threat-rigidity effects in organizational performance. *Administrative Science Quarterly, 28,* 582–600.

Stephan, W. G. (1985). Intergroup relations. In G. Lindsey & E. Aronson (Eds.), *The handbook of social psychology* (Third edition), Vol. 2. New York:Random House.

Stephan, W. G., & Stephan, C. W. (1985). Intergroup anxiety. *Journal of Social Issues, 41,* 157–175.

Strang, D. G., & Baron, J. N. (1989). Categorical imperatives: The structure of job titles in California state government agencies. Unpublished manuscript. Stanford University.

Sutton, R., & Kramer, R. M. (forthcoming) Transforming failure into success: Impression management, the Reagan administration, and the Iceland arms control talks. In R. Kahn, M. Zald, & R. Sutton (Eds.), *International conflict and cooperation: Organizational perspectives* (tentative title). San Francisco: Jossey-Bass.

Swingle, P. G. (1976). *The management of power.* Hillsdale, NJ: Erlbaum.

Tajfel, H. (1969). Cognitive aspects of prejudice. *Journal of Social Issues, 25,* 79–97.

Tajfel, H. (1982a). Social psychology of intergroup relations. *Annual Review of Psychology, 33,* 1–39.

Tajfel, H. (1982b). *Social identity and intergroup relations.* Cambridge: Cambridge University Press.

Tajfel, H., & Turner, J. C. (1986). The social identity theory of intergroup behavior. In S. Worchel & W. G. Austin (Eds.), *Psychology of intergroup relations.* Chicago: Nelson-Hall.

Talarowski, F., & McClintock, C. G. (1978). *The conservation of domestic water: A social psychological study. Final report to the Water Resources Center.* Davis, CA: University of California Davis.

Taylor, D. M., & Moghaddam, F. M. (1987). *Theories of intergroup relations: International social psychological perspectives*. New York: Praeger.

Taylor, S. E. (1989). *Positive illusions: Creative self-deception and the healthy mind*. New York: Basic Books.

Taylor, S. E., & Brown, J. D. (1988). Illusion and well-being: A social psychological perspective on mental health. *Psychological Bulletin, 103*, 193–210.

Tedeschi, J. T. (1981). *Impression management theory and social psychological research*. New York: Academic Press.

Thibaut, J. W., & Kelley, H. H. (1959). *The social psychology of groups*. New York: Wiley.

Thompson, J. D. (1967). *Organizations in action*. New York: McGraw-Hill.

Tjosvold, D., & Johnson, D. (1989). Conflict and authority hierarchies. In D. Tjosvold, D. & D. Johnson (Eds.), *Productive conflict management*. Minneapolis, MN: Interaction Book Company.

Turner, J. C. (1975). Social comparison and social identity. Some comparisons for intergroup behavior. *European Journal of Social Psychology, 5*, 5–34.

Turner, J. C. (1982). Toward a cognitive definition of the group. In H. Tajfel (Ed.), *Social identity and intergroup relations*. Cambridge, England: Cambridge University Press.

Turner, J. C. (1987). *Rediscovering the social group: A self-categorization theory*. Oxford: Basil Blackwell.

Tversky, A., & Kahneman, D. (1974). Judgment under uncertainty: Heuristics and biases. *Science, 185*, 1124–1135.

Walton, R. E., & Dutton, J. M. (1969). The management of interdepartmental conflict: A model and review. *Administrative Science Quarterly, 14*, 73–84.

Wilder, D. A. (1978). Perceiving persons as a group: Effects on attributions of causality and beliefs. *Social Psychology, 1*, 13–23.

Wilder, D. A. (1981). Perceiving persons as a group: Categorization and intergroup relations. In D. Hamilton (Ed.), *Cognitive processes in stereotyping and intergroup behavior*. Hillsdale, NJ: Erlbaum.

Wilder, D. A. (1986). Social categorization: Implications for creation and reduction of intergroup bias. In L. Berkowitz (Ed.), *Advances in experimental social psychology*. Orlando, FL: Academic Press.

THE POLITICAL PROCESS OF
INNOVATION

Peter J. Frost and Carolyn P. Egri

ABSTRACT

Innovation is, at its core, a political and social process of change. This chapter uses a framework of organizational power and politics to re-analyze several case studies of product and social innovation. This analysis of various political strategies and tactics (at both the observable surface and less observable deep structural levels of social integration) demonstrates that the interplay of power and politics at numerous levels—individual, intraorganizational, interorganizational and societal—is integral to determining the eventual success or failure of a proposed innovation. The role of innovators as the corporate heroes and champions of technological and social change is also explored. Drawing from these case study analyses and related empirical research, a number of propositions are developed for consideration.

We then examine a societal perspective that implicitly has assigned the role of villain to those who resist change. To do so, an organizational politics analysis of the deep structure of the prevailing technological paradigm of innovation (and scientific progress) is used to challenge the alleged technical and social neutrality of the process of innovation. In conclusion, we advocate an expanded and integrated agenda for organizational science research on innovation which

Research in Organizational Behavior, Volume 13, pages 229–295.

includes the immediate and longer term technical and social implications of innovation for organizations and society.

The invention of the typewriter in 1873 by Christopher Sholes represented a landmark achievement in communication technology. The typewriter made it possible for people other than typesetters to produce printed matter quickly and in a consistent form. Its easily decipherable product also overcame the problems and mistakes created by illegible handwriting. Later the typewriter keyboard became the initial man-machine interface for computer technology and the information explosion that it engendered.

But as anyone who has tried to master a typewriter or computer keyboard appreciates, it can be a frustrating and tedious learning process. Unknown to many is the fact that this particular configuration of keys was purposely anti-engineered to slow down typists in order to accommodate the limitations of a machine invented in 1873 and which is now obsolete. Furthermore, many are also unaware that a significantly improved configuration of keys which overcomes the difficulties of this cumbersome keyboard has been in existence since 1932! As the case of the Dvorak Simplified Keyboard (DSK) demonstrates, the reasons why a superior technological innovation has not gained acceptance or widespread implementation are often not grounded in rational scientific logic but rather in the political battles of a solitary inventor against vested interests with a stake in maintaining the status quo.

For over 30 years, Dr. August Dvorak fought a number of interest groups (typewriter manufacturers, sales outlets among others) through experimental rational means—he and his colleagues conducted time and motion studies to prove the technical superiority of the DSK at international typing contests and even arranged for trial tests in the federal government. However in response, Dvorak encountered political resistance to his invention, for example, the covering up of results showing the superiority of his machines, the ruthless sabotage of his machines at typing contests, etc. Much of this was orchestrated by the typewriter manufacturers who, for self-interested pecuniary reasons, worked to prevent the adoption of Dvorak's invention. Later in this paper we will recount the details of why and how this technological innovation has failed to bear fruit. Perhaps the most significant lesson to be gained from this and other accounts of innovation is that it is not safe to assume that the best or superior inventions/innovations will survive on their own merits. Given the prominence and desirability accorded innovation for the survival and growth of our organizations (Nayak & Ketteringham, 1986; Peters & Waterman, 1982; Pettigrew, 1985) and national economies (Hayes & Abernathy, 1980; Kanter, 1983; Peters, 1987), it is a lesson which challenges a complacent belief in the objective nature of the scientific process.

This stated desirability for innovation has provided the impetus for a wealth of academic research on the incidence and promotion of technological and social change. The proliferation of such studies has yielded substantial quantitative information on the phenomenon. However, many reviewers of the innovation literature have also called for a redirection of research towards innovation *as a process,* thereby necessitating an emphasis on the qualitative dynamics of innovation. In a critique of the prevailing rational myth of innovation as a goal-directed orderly enterprise, Schon (1967, p. 8) notes that: "In fact, bringing new technology into being is a complex process in which goals are discovered, determined and modified along the way." And indeed, some researchers have focussed on innovation as the social process of enacting and implementing a new idea or invention (Becker & Whisler, 1967; Carroll, 1967; Knight, 1967; Mansfield, 1971; Sayles, 1974; Thompson, 1965; Wilson, 1966). Furthermore, by describing, analyzing and questioning both the meaning and outcomes of innovation, we are focusing on the process of innovation as a socio-political reality.

In our description of power and politics, we propose that politics is often the inevitable consequence of self-interested contests between and among actors which are engendered by the inherent ambiguity of issues, ideas and things. In that innovation *at its core* is about ambiguity and is replete with disputes caused by the differences in perspectives among those touched by an innovation and the changes it engenders, we believe that innovation often becomes a very political process. Rather than viewing these struggles for ascendancy in a negative light, we propose that politics serves both a natural and necessary role in the course of human interaction. Judging political actions and outcomes as good or bad, right or wrong, is to a large extent a function of the perspective, the values and the interests of the evaluator. Our interest then is on examining the way organizational politics impacts on innovation.

To focus on the process of innovation, we use a framework of organizational power and politics that clarifies some typically unasked or unnoticed aspects of innovation. We examine, through analyses of a series of cases and a series of propositions developed from these analyses, what organizational science has to say about innovation. The implications of this perspective on innovation also accentuates what organizational science has often failed to recognize, namely, the power of existing and previous systems of influence.

However, we cannot talk about process without also talking about human agency and action. We access what this means first, on the surface level in terms of political tactics; second, in the deep structure as the socio-historical underpinnings of current orders of surface action—including politics. Third, on the surface, we attend to the role of human agents in the innovation process—through the roles and origins of champions in the innovation process. And finally, we return to the deep structure to examine the political roots of innovation itself.

Fundamentally, in using an organizational power and politics perspective to understand innovation as a contested process of change, we are focussing on the following questions:

- *why* are certain innovations adopted and not others?
- *why* do certain innovations succeed where others fail?
- *what* are the obstacles to the change inherent to innovation?
- *what* enhances or promotes innovation?
- *who* determines the course of innovation in organizations and in society? *who* sets the criteria? *who* makes the decisions?
- *what* are the real impacts of innovation? *why* are some of these impacts less often discussed, researched, or acted upon than others?

The political perspective also challenges the acknowledged pro-innovation bias found in much of the literature. We seek to uncouple the tight linkage of innovation and "progress," the unquestioned assumption of innovation as good, by delving into the dynamics of the change process at both the observable surface and less observable (but powerful) deep structural levels of a social system. The roots of this bias are shown to be not unique to the innovation literature but rather to be based in theories of scientific knowledge and societal change. We will use the contributions from organizational science in a call for a broader study of the organization's role in innovation in terms of intentions and consequences at multiple levels—technical, social, ethical, and ecological. The intent of this chapter is to provide one framework within which scholars might address a more complete picture of innovation and change than, we believe, is currently addressed in the organizational science literature. It is also intended to assist decisionmakers to make more balanced and informed decisions regarding innovation. By addressing these issues, we present a revised perspective to study and understand innovation as a system of technological and societal change and the role of organizations and individuals within that system. In this way, perhaps we *will* be able to spark reflection, debate and research which will lead to the practice of innovation that incorporates a balancing of the technical, political and ethical aspects of individual, organizational and societal action (Frost & Egri, 1990a).

In the sections which follow, we will deal briefly with the current literature on innovation and then discuss more fully the political perspective on innovation.

ACADEMIC LITERATURE ON INNOVATION

Derived from the Latin word *innovare,* innovation means *to renew.* Such a renewal can be through the introduction of something which is either objectively (in terms of time or place) or subjectively perceived to be new. Kanter (1983, p. 20) defines innovation as being "the generation, acceptance, and implementation of new ideas, processes, products, or services." Daft (1983) also points out that change or innovation can take place in the arenas of technology (new techniques for making products or services), product (modifications of existing products or development of new product lines), administration (changes in organizational structure, goals, information and other systems) or people (changes in leadership ability, communication, problem solving skills and so forth). Fundamental to the notion of innovation is the element of change which it initiates in the material and/or social world as part of a process of renewal which often involves the alteration of relationships and prior ways of doing things.

The record of research on innovation has been a prolific one. Rogers (1983) recounts that over 3000 studies of innovation had been conducted to that date and the recent resurgence of interest in the phenomenon has only enlarged this number. Within the organizational behavior domain, innovation research has been the subject of several noteworthy reviews by Daft (1982), Kanter (1988), Kimberly (1980), Roberts (1988), Utterback (1974), and others. Very briefly, thus far, much of the research focus has been on:

(a)   the diffusion of innovation throughout populations of organizations;[1]
(b)   the identification of stages of the innovation process—within the organizational context, it has been proposed that there are three stages: (1) initiation of an idea or proposal; (2) adoption; and (3) implementation (Pierce & Delbecq, 1977);[2]
(c)   the categorization of innovations on dimensions of product-process;[3] radical-incremental change;[4]
(d)   the identification of organizational structural (organic vs. mechanistic), processual (communication patterns and roles), and contextual (environmental change, product life cycles, etc.) characteristics which affect the adoption and implementation of various innovations;[5]
(e)   the identification of the causes of innovation success and failure;[6] and
(f)   the ascertainment of means by which innovation can be engendered and/or resistance to change (at the individual and group levels) can be overcome within organizations.[7]

Generally, the approach taken to date has been one which follows a traditional path of quantitative research with the identification of variables for the generation of numerous contingency models of innovation. However, there have been a number of conceptual and methodological issues raised regarding the utility of many of these research findings. For example, as identified by Downs and Mohr (1976), Kimberly (1980, 1987), and Rogers (1983), the relative overemphasis on the quantifiable aspects of innovation has led to a relative neglect of the *process* of innovation. The quest for aggregate scores of attributes of innovation and organizations has led to a proliferation of cross-sectional data (of often marginal correlational significance) which precludes hypotheses of causality. Whereas analysis of these tangible markers is of considerable merit, a more integrative understanding of innovation as a social dynamic requires a critical approach to not only what is invented but also why, for what purpose and under which conditions innovations are selected and implemented. Essentially, the process is more appropriately represented by a multiplicative model of social dynamics where innovation is a "function of an interaction among the motivation to innovate, the strength of obstacles against innovation, and the availability of resources for overcoming such obstacles" (Mohr, 1969, p. 111).

More longitudinal interactive models are needed to ferret out the important process dynamics of innovation rather than, as is more typically the case, having them viewed negatively as unknown influences to be relegated to a theoretical model's error terms. One current challenge of innovation research is to deconstruct these error terms (which at times can be quite substantial) into their constituent parts: variation due to social and political dynamics and unexplainable variation due to measurement and research artefacts.

Another implication of embarking on a political analysis of innovation is that the evaluation of innovation cannot be postponed as Van de Ven (1986) has proposed:

> Innovation is often viewed as a good thing because the new idea must be useful—profitable, constructive, or solve a problem. New ideas that are not perceived as useful are not normally called innovations; they are usually called mistakes. Objectively, of course, the usefulness of an idea can only be determined after the innovation process is completed and implemented (p. 592).

This statement is indicative of many of the tenets of the rational view of innovation which, with Schon (1967), we take issue. First of all, it defines utility in rational terms ("profitable, constructive, problem solving"). The political perspective would muddy the issue by first questioning profitability as a criterion and secondly, asking who is making the assessment of utility. Furthermore, the provision for delay of evaluation of an innovation until full implementation has been achieved can lead to an avoidance of the critical social goals of change. For as Marx (1987, p. 39) observes, this "belief in the sufficiency of scientific and technological innovation . . . makes instrumental values fundamental to social progress, and relegates what formerly were considered primary, end-states (justice, freedom, harmony, beauty, or self-fulfillment) to a secondary status."

Thus far, the rational approach to the study of innovation has resulted in a fragmented proliferation of models—each a frozen slice of time and replete with operational conflicts, contradictions and exceptions. These models of innovation depict an incomplete representation of reality which bears only tangential reference to the energy and forces of the human agents involved. A more complete agenda for the study of innovation would encompass both objective and subjective facets of the process and outcomes and the immediate and derivative impact of an innovation on individual, organizational, and societal levels. Given that the political approach emphasizes process and a complex, often subtle one at that, there is a need for studies that include the time dimension and use of qualitative methods. It is an interactive recursive model of innovation which does not lend itself to easy and sure answers but rather highlights ethical and social concerns for the present and for the future.

ORGANIZATIONAL POWER AND POLITICS

Free enquiry is *never* free . . . it is just not glaringly obvious who is manipulating it (Burke, 1989).

In order to examine the innovative process, it is instructive to clarify a perspective on organizational power and politics within which to discuss the topic. In this section, we lay out a framework for thinking about power and politics. In the following sections we apply this understanding to the innovation process.

The organizational politics perspective leads us to focus on contests among and between actors as the two fundamental activities of organizational life. First are the contests among interdependent actors operating from different perspectives/frames of reference and motivated by different self-interests and preferences as they strive to acquire, manage and control resources and to determine the means/ends of doing organizational work (Baldridge, 1971; Cyert & March, 1963). Second are the struggles for collaboration among actors in the performance of organizational work when the means/ends for getting it done are unclear and/or subject to dispute (Barnard, 1938, Pfeffer, 1981; Thompson, 1967; Wilkinson, 1983). Organizational innovation at *its* core is about ambiguity—it represents something new. Also it typically engages and arouses human actors who have different interests and perspectives and who stand to gain or lose in different ways as a result of a particular innovation. Contests and struggles for collaboration are often part and parcel of the innovation process. It is often played out through the exercise of power. Innovation is an interesting and rich organizational process through which to examine the contributions of power and politics to organizational functioning and thus to our development of organizational theory.

Within the organizational politics framework, power has traditionally been seen as the potential capacity to get others to do things they might otherwise not want to do and/or to resist others' efforts to get one to do what they want one to do (Dahl, 1957). Politics is viewed as enacted power, as power in action. It is goal-directed action that is self-interested and that would be resisted if detected by others with different self-interests (Frost, 1987; Porter, Allen, & Angle, 1981). In our discussion, we treat power as a more multi-faceted phenomenon than this rational approach would suggest (Astley & Sachdeva, 1984; Boulding, 1989; Lukes, 1974). We view power as operating at different levels of awareness (Lukes, 1974). Organizational politics is both power in action and in the power of conception, of creating the frame in which actions take place (Frost, 1987).

The most compelling aspect of this multi-facetedness is that one aspect of power and politics seems to take place on the *SURFACE* of organizational life, in the day-to-day contests and struggles for collaboration. Surface power politics typically deal with attempts by one or more parties to exploit (bend, resist, implement) the rules of the situation they are in to their own advantage.

The other aspect of power takes place in the *DEEP STRUCTURE* of organizations, influencing, usually in hard to detect ways, not only the way the rules of a situation are played but the very way the rules are framed in the first place. Such deep structure power has its origins in earlier struggles, movements and maneuvers in day-to-day situations that settle, for a time, the way things come to be perceived, valued and acted out. These social, political and historical roots of current organizational frames and actions are often forgotten or never recognized by most contemporary actors. If noted at all, they are seen as "the way things are," or as rationally derived prescriptions for behaving in organizations. [See Clegg (1981) and Frost (1988) for a more detailed discussion of these concepts.]

We argue for an *interactive* relationship between surface and deep structure power and political action. On the one hand, power in the deep structure shapes and influences (but does not directly *determine*) the actions on the surface of organizations. Surface, contemporary, day-to-day political action can alter the impact, direction and nature of power in the deep structural influences on tomorrow's surface politics. [See Giddens (1981) and Frost

(1987) for more extensive discussions of such relationships between deep and surface actions.]

While deep structure is embedded and implicit, there are actors in the system who have access to, can recognize and harness this power to their advantage. One aspect of this argument is that organizational politics involves opportunity to act (current and embedded), orientation (will and skill) and intention (goals). The role of human agents as surface actors and as intermediaries between the deep and surface structures impact the innovation process. These features of power and politics are developed and illustrated in our cases of innovation which are presented later.

The exercise of surface power and its attendant strategies and tactics are more readily accessible and have been the subject of much of the academic focus on this topic. With Crozier and Friedberg (1980), Mintzberg (1983) and Frost (1987), we find it useful to examine organizational politics in terms of the metaphor of games—as strategic, tactical maneuvers between and among actors where the rules of the games themselves can be revised for definition and redefinition as the game playing process is initiated and unfolds. Political games involve attempts at manipulation and influence for outcomes which actors intend to benefit themselves and/or to benefit other actors in the game. We are interested in the processes of innovation. Thus the political game metaphor provides a useful dynamic as well as a lever for understanding innovation. Political games can be played out at the surface and/or in the deep structure of organizations.

Surface Politics. Surface political games can be played out in at least three arenas: that of individuals, of intraorganizational groups, and between and among organizations. Individual games focus on gaining, maintaining and withholding the context or frame of reference in organizations which serve the player's self-interest (Culbert & McDonough, 1985). As identified in Table 1, some individual political games involve the acquisition or expansion of power within the organization while others are used to guard against any further encroachment of existing power bases. One example of the expansion of power is the familiar *empire building* of departments within organizations to increase the scope and domain of influence and authority over organizational decisions. In contrast, games such as *lording* and *rule citing* serve as defensive measures to protect current power bases against unwanted interlopers or power acquisitors (Kanter, 1983).

Individual influence strategies often focus on the manipulation of communication channels and/or information. A number of authors have noted that the *choice* of political strategies is often a function of an individual's self-confidence, experience, skills, objectives and the intended direction of influ-

Table 1.   Organization Power and Politics[1]

SURFACE	*Interests*	*Nature of Conflict*
	Unitary	Temporary—can be avoided or resolved
	Pluralist	Restricted Conflicts
	Radical–Critical	Repressed Conflict (Structural contradictions)
DEEP STRUCTURE		

[1]The authors wish to thank Mats Alveson for his insights for the development of this table which also reflects the contributions of Lukes (1974), Mintzberg (1979), Frost (1987).

Primary Control Emphasis	*Political Games*
Gaining/Maintaining/Withholding Context	Acquisition/expansion of power: - making it, mentoring, sponsorship, upward influence, empire building.
	Maintenance of existing power bases: - lording, rule citing, appeals to higher authority for support.
Controlling resources, outcomes/managing territories/managing, resisting change	Manipulative communication: - impression management, labelling, reasoning, assertiveness, manipulative persuasion, gatekeeping, covering up, networking.
	Controlling resources/outcomes: - Competitive Control: budgeting, expertise, line vs. staff, rival camps, making out. - Collaborative Control: negotiation, bargaining, coalition building, strategic candidates (developing champions), building consensus, framing perspectives.
	Managing/resisting change: - controlling decision premises & agendas, selective use of objective criteria.
Ideological Control for gaining/preserving sectional interests	Naturalization Neutralization Legitimation Socialization

ence (Frost, 1987; Kipnis, Schmidt & Wilkinson, 1980). Studies of upward influence tactics relate a decided preference for rational informational persuasion (overtly manipulative) over less rational and sanction based strategies (Ansari & Kapoor, 1987; Porter, Allen, & Angle, 1981; Schilit & Locke, 1982). In this context, rational action entails openness in terms of the detailed disclosure and explanation of the basis, intent and logical foundation of one's intended outcome (Kipnis et al., 1980). These findings can be interpreted either as a reflection of the relative limitations imposed on those lower in the organizational hierarchy (therefore not realistically having access to sanction based strategies) or as a reflection of the dominant influence of the organizational paradigm founded on the fundamental premise of "rationality" (as detailed by Brown, 1978) which limits the scope of envisioned action.

Intraorganizational games for control of strategic contingencies can be either competitive or collaborative between individuals and/or groups. Competitive intraorganizational games (which are most likely to emerge under conditions of resource scarcity, Roberts, 1986) emphasize the control of organizational resources and outcomes; the management of organizational territory; and/or the management of resistance to change of the status quo (Frost, 1987; Mintzberg, 1983; Morgan, 1988).

In contrast, collaborative intraorganizational games often focus on the identification and promotion of strategic candidates within the organization's dominant coalition to either promote or oppose projects or proposals to alter organizational activities (Mintzberg, 1983). Comparative research on intraorganizational competitive versus cooperative innovation implementation strategies indicates that expert persuasive and highly participative strategies are most successful (Nutt, 1986). The underlying thrust of the collaborative approach is considered to be preferred but one which incurs high process costs and creates logistical problems.

The political machinations of organizations or societal interest groups are very similar to those of groups within organizations in that the focus of interorganizational politics is also on the control of resources, the expansion and protection of territory, and the management of change. At this level, however, there are greater opportunities for actors to challenge the rules of the game and to create new rules that will serve some interests and not others and to present such actions in ways that seem rational rather than political to the unpracticed or uninformed eye. In addition to previously identified strategies, political action at this level can involve developing legislative policies and procedures, establishing legal contracts, and creating interlocking boards of directors.

Deep Structure Politics.   Interorganizational surface games often intersect the deep structure of organizations, particularly when the games involve changing the rules themselves. Within the *deep structure* of organizations, power covertly informs collective interpretive frames and individual cognitive maps of organizational members (Clegg, 1981). The power to set the frame is the focus of deep structure politics. Its aim is to effect "the systematic distortion of communication so as to maintain and enhance power relations that favor one social reality over other possible alternatives, that favor some interest groups at the expense of others" (Frost, 1988, p. 42). For these reasons, deep structure power is very difficult to identify without a careful tracing of the social, historical and political origins of these frames and the rules of the current organizational game (Conrad, 1983; Ranson, Hinings, & Greenwood, 1980).

Deetz (1985) identifies four ways in which human agents systematically distort reality for their own benefit. These are examples of deep structure games that seem to be particularly relevant to the study of innovation.

1. *Naturalization:* Existing forms and privileges are treated by an interest group (for their own benefit) as inviolate and therefore not subject to discussion, debate or change (Deetz, 1985; Pfeffer, 1981). For example, it is the "natural order" that managers manage and workers work.

2. *Neutralization:* The particular value base of a set of positions and activities that favors one interest group over another is denied. Such positions are treated as value free, or as the only ones that exist. They become a matter of fact, not of choice. (Deetz, 1985) For example, powerful groups in organizations often utilize the rhetoric of rationality to control the rules of relevance thereby controlling both the definition and content of a dominant organizational reality (Brown, 1978; Culbert & McDonough, 1985).

3. *Legitimation:* Higher order explanatory device such as sacrifice, loyalty, one's country, religion, etc., are invoked to justify and sustain the self-interests of an elite in the system. Allusions to such higher levels serve to maintain the compliance of lower power players while cloaking the real motivation and goals of the powerful. This particular game is evident in discussions and studies of intimidation rituals concerning whistleblowers (O'Day, 1974). As illustrated in the case of Morton Thiokol engineer Roger Boisjoly, whistleblower in the NASA Challenger Space Shuttle disaster (Boisjoly, Curtis, & Mellican, 1989), the whistleblower or reformer not only raises a moral challenge to the ethical nature of upper management decisions, but as a self-appointed change agent he/she also challenges the deep structure power relations of hierarchical authority. The organizational response to such action is often to focus on establishing the illegitimacy of the whistleblower as a party to the decisionmaking process.

4. *Socialization:* Actions, systems and processes that serve to direct and shape the behaviors, attitudes, values and interpretive schemes of some players to the benefit of others (Frost, 1987; Van Maanen & Schein, 1979). The process of socialization forms the basis of much work on how organizational cultures emerge, develop and function. As identified in this arena of organization theory, those in positions of power have access to a diverse array of normative, reward and structural mechanisms to guide the individual and organizational learning of what they deem to be appropriate (and inappropriate) values, beliefs and behaviors (Schein, 1985).

Individually, these political strategies are most often used as defensive measures to preserve the prevailing distribution of power. In concert, they operate to institutionalize existing power relations in a self-perpetuating manner (Burawoy, 1979; Pfeffer, 1981). However, as we noted earlier, deep structure power relationships are not static and can be used in a proactive way to facilitate change. In that current deep structure power is the derivation of past political activity, the outcomes of current political activity form the foundation of future deep structure power relations.

The interaction between the surface politics level and the deep structural level can take three forms. First, some surface political games can be used to fend off the deep structure through either passive resistance, secrecy or confrontation. This is found most often in games involving manipulative communication and the control of resources and outcomes. Second, other surface games work because they tap into the deep structure by gaining the support of powerful interest groups. The efficacy of these games which focus on the acquisition/expansion or maintenance of power bases is due in large part to their harmony with the values of the prevailing gatekeepers and other powerful resource holders. Thirdly, surface politics can influence and/or change the deep structure through the present day framing of perspectives by the selection of decision premises, agendas and criteria which in turn impact on the construction of the future deep structure.

THE POLITICAL NATURE OF INNOVATION

The innovator makes enemies of all those who prospered under the old order, and only lukewarm support is forthcoming from those who would prosper under the new . . . because men are generally incredulous, never really trusting new things unless they have tested them by experience (Niccolo Machiavelli in *The Prince*, as cited by Rogers & Shoemaker, 1971, p. 174).

As observed long ago by Machiavelli, the introduction of an innovation or change continues to induce and become the focus of political activity in modern society and its organizations (Kimberly, 1980, p. 93). It is in these disputes over the ambiguous means and ends of an envisioned change that the process of innovation becomes political. How then, does an innovation emerge and survive whatever conflict it engenders? Under what conditions and when does organizational politics flourish in the innovation process? Empirical research indicates that political gamesmanship is most likely to be positively correlated with the level of innovation originality (Pelz, 1983; Pelz & Munson, 1982) and perceived risk and complexity (Fidler & Johnson, 1984). Perhaps the most vulnerable time of the innovation process is during the implementation stage when the dysfunctional nature of organizational politics is most often highlighted. It is responsible for, among other things, unnecessary delays, excessive conflict, compromised outcomes, and some-times, ultimate failure (Corwin, 1972; Delbecq & Mills, 1985; Guth & Mac-millan, 1986; Nelkin, 1984; Pelz & Munson, 1982; Yin, 1977). Studies of innovative changes in the public arena concerning the passage and implemen-tation of legislation of social and technological innovations depict similar outcomes in the interorganizational domain (Bardach, 1977; Pressman & Wildavsky, 1973; Reppy, 1984).

The main theme throughout these studies is on the "problem" of the social and political dynamics engendered by innovation (Sapolsky, 1967; Van de Ven, 1986; Zaltman, Duncan, & Holbek, 1973). Consistent with the general pro-innovation bias found in society, these resistances to innovation are gener-ally regarded by managers as threats rather than opportunities. As Kimberly (1987, p. 238) observed in his review of technological innovation in informa-tion systems: "Thus, while managers responsible for innovation might yearn for greater rationality, it appears that where innovation is concerned decisions are messy, and the influence of politics and intuition is likely to be great." For those managers who are more entrenched in the organization (either by virtue of age, seniority or through the benefits accorded them by the status quo) the resultant disorder and 'muddling through' required can be particularly dis-tasteful thereby resulting in avoidance or resistance behaviors (Kasper, 1986; Sayles, 1974).

To understand the tangle and complexity of the innovation process, we have found it useful to examine several case studies which describe the process in some detail. Outside of such case study reports and those cited here, there do not appear to be as many studies of innovation which deal with the politics of innovation. Most common treatments of innovation either do not address process or gloss over or truncate its detail in the interest of limited space or because the authors are addressing other questions.

Case Studies of Innovation

Our preliminary review of documented cases of innovation yielded a number of prospects for inclusion in this section. It has not been an exhaustive or random sampling of the literature. The case studies summarized in this section serve primarily as illustrations of the political dynamics involved in innovation success and failure.[8] They are useful as a way to ground a description and subsequent discussion of the innovation process as a political phenomenon. These cases deal with innovations in the individual, intraorganizational and interorganizational arenas.

In the review of innovations to follow, a number of issues will be addressed. First, what are the various surface and deep structure political tactics used in successful and failed innovations? Are there variances in the type and number of political strategies employed in product versus administrative innovations? successes versus failures? Which political strategies are most often employed by proponents of innovations? Which are preferred by those opposing an innovation?

We present seven cases in all. The first three innovations (at "Chipco," Hewlett-Packard, and Data General) deal largely with surface politics enacted in largely supportive political underpinnings (deep structure). The fourth case (administrative innovation within ICI) brings us face to face with a less benign political context. The final three analyses (of the Dvorak keyboard; new practices in a mental health community; automatically controlled machine tools) deal squarely with the powerful countervailing forces in the deep structures of organizational systems.

Innovative Reminders in an Integrationist Organization. One unique feature about the "Chestnut Ridge" Production Project was that it was a social innovation with one objective being to stimulate other innovations. The company in which this innovation took place, "Chipco," had all the features of what Kanter (1983) describes as an integrative innovation-stimulating culture. Chipco had been at the forefront of developing grass roots employee involvement years before quality circles became a common term. It was also a model of an organization which provided its managers with the resources and support needed to innovate, and as a result, had reaped the benefits in terms of a 25 percent to 35 percent annual growth rate in sales and profits.

However, in 1977, the pressures of rapid growth, stiffer market and technological competition were leading Chipco's managers to consider several organizational changes in order to gain tighter control of operations at their largest manufacturing plant, Chestnut Ridge. Among the changes being contemplated or underway was the conversion from small batch to assembly line production and the replacement of autonomous production groups by functional product lines headed by business managers. As Kanter relates, these segmentalist (and innovation stifling) changes would lead to specialized and deskilled jobs, less team group identity, more bureaucratic levels, and a generally depersonalized work culture. In effect, the integrationist culture of Chestnut Ridge was being threatened.

The growing employee discontent about these changes led the Chestnut Ridge personnel manager, "Roberta Briggs" (a pseudonym) to propose a social innovation which would attend to these problems. Her Production Project was designed to minimize the disruptive impact of planned segmentalist change, develop the capabilities of its lower-level production supervisors while enhancing grass root employee involvement and innovation. Following acceptance and funding of her proposal by a central R&D committee specializing in people projects, Briggs proceeded to establish a plant-wide managerial steering committee and a set of subsidiary task forces to focus on identified problems. The Production Project proceeded through five stages: "initial education and support building, information gathering and diagnosis of needs, team formation and action planning, implementation, and integration and diffusion of results within the system" (Kanter, 1983, p. 186).

As a social innovator, Briggs employed a wide range of collaborative political strategies to ensure the success of the project. Foremost was *developing champions* and *building coalitions* of support among Chipco's senior managers, Chestnut Ridge line management and her functional counterparts elsewhere in Chipco. In turn, these alliances helped her as she *bargained* for resources to implement the project. Briggs effectively *used experts* by hiring external consultants to conduct management seminars (in-plant and off-site) about the merits of the Production Project. The consultants' action research survey also helped to open communication lines to the grass roots and institutionalize their participation on project action groups (*building consensus*).

Four years later, the Production Project remains in Chipco as a successful model of worker involvement. It should be noted that Briggs' collaborative political approach was also assisted by the use of deep structure tactics of *naturalization* and *socialization* to obtain support for her project. By presenting the Production Project as a continuation of the integrationist spirit of Chipco's organizational culture, existing forms and privileges were not as vulnerable to challenge or resistance (*naturalization*). By adopting an incremental approach to implementation which involved the presentation and discussion of the Production Project in multiple forums by all those affected, and by also engaging external consultants to conduct management training to reinforce project principles, Briggs was able to direct and shape the attitudes and values necessary to make the project work (*socialization*). In summary, by introducing an innovation which was consistent with Chipco's integrationist philosophy and culture, Briggs was successful in fending off the forces for segmentalism at Chestnut Ridge.

The Trials of Product Champions and Sponsors—NASA Moonlander Monitor. The case of the development of the NASA Moonlander Monitor is one which illustrates the integral role an innovation champion and his/her managerial sponsors can play in the development of a new product. It is also an example of how innovators can successfully be mavericks within an organizational culture, which while posing at the surface level a number of obstacles to such initiatives, is supportive of innovation and change in its deep structure.

As a young engineer at Hewlett-Packard, Chuck House proved to be instrumental in the development and application of oscilloscope technology for new venues (Pinchot, 1985, pp. 23–30). Initial impetus for the project was provided by the Federal Aviation Administration which identified the need for an improved airport control tower monitor. Although the Hewlett-Packard monitor did not meet the FAA's specification for a high resolution picture and subsequently lost out to competitors, there were features of their prototype which struck House as worthy of further investigation. House believed that the size (smaller and lighter than other models), speed (20 times as fast), energy efficiency and brighter (but fuzzier) picture of his group's monitor was a significant technological breakthrough—although one which had yet to find its niche in the marketplace.

In the course of his efforts to demonstrate the merits of his team's model, House proved to be a political gamesman who operated as a maverick by violating a number of organizational rules and boundaries. His first foray into the political arena involved conducting his own market research on potential applications. To gather such information, House personally showed the monitor prototype to 40 computer manufacturers and potential customers in an organizationally unsanctioned trip from Colorado to California. In doing so, not only was he violating functional organizational boundaries by circumventing the marketing department but he was also violating a cardinal Hewlett-Packard security rule which forbade the showing of prototypes to customers. However, based on the marketing information collected during his trip, House was able to gain a temporary reprieve from senior management for his project. During the next 18 months, the project team continued development work in the lab and on-site with customers.

The next obstacle to the continuation of the project came during the annual division review by senior management. This review was influenced to a large degree by a marketing department telephone survey which projected that there was only a total demand for 32 monitors. The resistance and lack of creative initiative of the marketing group (perhaps motivated by House's previous incursion into their territory) was evident in the manner in which the survey was conducted. As Pinchot (1985, pp. 26–27) reports: "Chuck argued that marketing had failed to understand his strategy for marketing the product. They had called only upon oscilloscope customers, the only customers they knew. New applications required new customers, Chuck explained. Besides, the device was difficult to describe: because it was new, only demonstrations could uncover its salability." Marketing's forecast of demand for the monitor prevailed over House's group's projections which were based on direct operating feedback from customers (and were, to some extent, obtained through organizationally illegitimate means). Not only was House's project threatened by the lack of administrative innovation by the marketing group, his project did not have the support of the chief corporate engineer who favored an alternate technology. Thus, the fledgling project was being threatened by two competitive intraorganizational political games over competitive control— *line vs. staff* and *rival camps.*

The conclusion of the divisional review was that, in light of the apparent lack of market demand and technological support from others in the organization, the only rational action was to abort the project. In corporate founder David Packard's words: " 'When I come back next year I don't want to see that project in the lab!' " (Pinchot, 1985, p. 27).

It is at this point that House's political gamesmanship was put to the test. Unwilling to accept this decision, House "chose" to reinterpret Packard's pronouncement to mean that the project would be out of the lab in one year's time but in production, not on the scrapheap (*selective use of objective criteria*). With the covert support of his boss Dar Howard (*developing management sponsors*), the games of *covering up* development costs of the project from *budget restrictions* started in earnest as House's team raced to complete the project in one year when the normal length of time would be two. In the face of continuing opposition from the marketing department, House gained additional support by convincing interested potential customers to personally call on his superiors and argue for the project (an example of *coalition building* with external parties).

Fortunately for House and his team, they made their deadline and when Packard returned one year later, the monitor was indeed in the marketplace. Packard was reported to be both amused and impatient with this obvious reinterpretation of his order but perhaps indicative of his own maverick origins, he now supported the obviously successful project. Rather than being punished for their insubordination, House and his team were now given permission to continue to develop additional applications, among them the eventual use of the oscilloscope monitor for the NASA Moon Mission, the medical monitor used in the first artificial heart transplant, and a large-screen oscilloscope which was used as part of an Emmy award winning special effects system. Without the committed championship of House and the sponsorship of his immediate superiors, these landmark innovations could have easily been the victims of opposing political forces.

Designing Political Battles to Build a New Computer. In his Pulitzer prize winning book, *The Soul of a New Machine,* Tracy Kidder (1981) treats us to a detailed account of the trials of the design engineer in the highly competitive computer industry. He also gives us an inside look at how competitive political contests can be surreptitiously orchestrated by senior managers to promote innovation.

Data General prided itself on its maverick culture—a culture which could be directly traced back to its founding members, three young computer engineers who left DEC in 1968 to set up shop in a former beauty parlor. Within ten years, Data General was on the Fortune 500 list and had carved out its niche in the minicomputer market. However, by 1976, Data General was also sorely in need of a new product, namely, a 32-bit minicomputer which was comparable, but better, than those recently introduced by their competitors.

The political stage was set by senior executives headed by CEO Ed de Castro when they announced that Data General would build a new research and development facility in North Carolina. It was here, they publicly announced, that major research would be conducted to develop the needed 32-bit minicomputer. The important Fountainhead Project (FHP) was transferred to the new location along with 50 of the most talented DG engineers and technicians. Meanwhile, among those who remained behind in Westborough, Massachusetts were Tom West and his small Eclipse group. Their previous project had been canceled in favor of the FHP—Data General could not afford to fund two major competing projects. Instead, West was assigned to revamp the lower priority 16-bit Eclipse. Although de Castro never put it in writing, West received tentative approval to transform the Eclipse into a 32-bit minicomputer as the rechristened Eagle project. Technically, the Eclipse group was not to do any groundbreaking developments—that was the territory of North Carolina's FHP. How West and his managers were able to do just that in record time is a testament to skillful team building and political acumen.

The first priority was to keep a low profile so as not to appear to be in competition with FHP. This political strategy of *impression management* was justified by West as follows:

> You gotta distinguish between the internal promotion to the actual workers and the promoting we did externally to other parts of the company. Outside the group I tried to low-key the thing. I tried to dull the impression that this was a competing product with North Carolina. I tried to sell it externally as not much of a threat . . . It was just gonna be

a fast, Eclipse-like machine. This was the only way it was gonna live. We had to get the resources quietly, without creating a big brouhaha, and it's difficult to get a lot of external cooperation under those circumstances (Kidder, 1981, p. 47).

Part of this low profile strategy was physical. The Eclipse group was located in the cramped basement quarters of Westborough headquarters where even the air conditioning didn't work properly. This resulted in both physical and social isolation from the rest of the company, all the better to facilitate *covering up* their real agenda for the Eagle project. The Eclipse group's low profile was also facilitated by the type of engineers recruited for the project. West and his lieutenant Carl Alsing hired recent engineering graduates not only for their excellent academic credentials but also for their willingness to work long hours and their unbridled enthusiasm for computer design work. By doing so, the group was ensured a low profile—there were few who would see them as competition for the higher priced and proven talent at North Carolina.

One example of the lengths to which Eclipse group members went to avoid appearing to be in competition with FHP or encroaching on their territory is how computer architect Steve Wallach got his job done. If there was a computer instruction which deviated from the approved parameters of the Eagle project and might be construed as infringing on the FHP project, Wallach would work with his friends in System Software (*networking*) on the item. When finished, he would then ask his friends to write a memo requesting inclusion of the controversial instruction into the Eagle—thus avoiding any charges that the Eclipse group was going outside of approved project parameters (*covering up*).

Throughout the project, team members were constantly negotiating with support groups for their assistance. The competition for resources was difficult for the Eclipse group as Kidder (1981, p. 112) relates: "The game was fixed for North Carolina and all the support groups knew it." Through personal contacts and persuasive skills they were able to gain the needed resources.

What is particularly interesting in this case is that many of the engineers on the Eclipse team were unaware of the full extent of West's role in ensuring survival of the project. It was all part of his managerial style which was to stay separate from the team and to run interference with other corporate bodies in order that his engineering team could be creatively free. West also benefited from having a management sponsor in Vice-President of Engineering Carl Carman who authorized the project and the money to recruit staff. Fortuitously, the FHP reported to a different Vice-President so there was no internal organizational conflict for Carman.

Finally, in a classic David vs. Goliath scenario, the small Eclipse group overcame all organizational and technical obstacles to deliver the 32-bit minicomputer ahead of North Carolina. This was a tale of a maverick group operating effectively within a maverick culture. For de Castro, it was a relatively low cost exercise in creative insurance so that Data General would have the desired product.

Organizational Development in a Hostile Environment: The Case of ICI. Given that political action in the deep structure is grounded in the corporate and/or societal culture, what happens when the innovation itself is an attempt to change the foundations of those very same political games? Organizational Development (OD) is one social innovation which attempts just such a change through the use of *socialization* techniques to effect a deep structural transformation. In his book *The Awakening Giant,* Andrew Pettigrew (1985) presents a detailed analysis of the OD initiatives undertaken in ICI, a large diversified petrochemical conglomerate in Great Britain. Essentially, Pettigrew reports on a natural experiment of strategic change undertaken in five separate units within the same organization—each being charged with effecting similar strategic changes within the context of very different corporate cultural and external market environments. OD programs were initiated to facilitate the strategic redirections in technological change, labor productivity improvement, market refocussing and management culture and organization. Comparisons of the nature and fates of these forays into cultural transformation illustrate how, when there is a lack of deep structure support, social innovations are particularly vulnerable to adversarial political tactics.

Of the four functional divisions and corporate headquarters group, perhaps the most successful OD initiative was at the Agricultural Division. Part of the success of this program can be traced to the implementation process guided by George Bridge, Divisional Personnel Director, and Noel Ripley, OD resource person. These innovation champions proved to be skillful in a number of political games which included the *development of management sponsorship,* the *use of outside experts* (they extensively used the services of external behavior scientists, including the late Douglas McGregor, to conduct in-house training sessions and T-groups), and *covering up* their social innovation program until it was fully developed and ready for implementation. As part of this last strategy, Ripley established the "Swallow Group" of internal OD advocates who met off-site in order to hone their OD skills and develop a cohesive group philosophy and approach.

Another feature of the Agriculture Division which was supportive of innovative change was its "integrationist" culture. In contrast, the OD initiatives in the other four areas of ICI were attempted in more hostile segmentalist cultures which stressed hierarchical authority, segmentation, scientific rationality and conflict—all anathema to humanistic OD principles. In the

Petrochemicals, Plastics, and Mond Divisions and the corporate headquarters, perhaps the greatest obstacle to the effective implementation of OD was the absence of skilled champions to guide the innovation through the political obstacles created by those who opposed the change. Additionally, the OD implementation process was more likely to involve top down directives and top management task forces which only served to reinforce the segmentalist tendencies of these organizations to sabotage any radical changes. Those who tried to implement OD in its true spirit were also less likely to have sufficient organizational power (positional, expert or normative) to garner the necessary resources and widespread commitment to their new programs.

In addition to the recognized need for strong change leadership (provided by either an influential management sponsor or a committed innovation champion), Pettigrew also identifies another factor which proved to be instrumental to an organization's receptivity to change, namely, the felt need for change. In the absence of a crisis situation (either in the external context or within the organization), there is no impetus to embark on new social directions. Thus any cultural change can easily be resisted by segmentalist-type organizations. As was illustrated in the four areas operating in contexts of incremental change where OD programs were effectively nullified, this situation is particularly amenable to the deep structure political game of *naturalization* which denies the need for any change to the status quo. In contrast, the Agriculture Division was in the midst of significant technological and organizational change thereby creating a readiness to accept help from Bridge's group. Furthermore, when the Mond Division experienced its own crisis in 1979, the OD change agents who had quietly operated at the lower levels of the organization came to the fore to assist senior management with the necessary strategic, organizational and cultural changes. This was the exception though, for the other divisions, including the Agricultural Division, when severe economic difficulties later arose, the OD groups were among the first victims of budget cutbacks and organizational downsizing.

An Outsider doing Battle with the Deep Structure: The Dvorak Simplified Keyboard. As related in the introduction of this paper, the case of the Dvorak Simplified Keyboard is one which clearly demonstrates how self-interested political actors can effectively forestall a demonstrably beneficial technological change. When invented in 1873, the current universal "QWERTY" typewriter keyboard was designed to prevent typists from striking two adjoining keys in quick succession. Otherwise, the keys would "jam" together in the basket of a machine which relied on the forces of gravity to pull the keys back to their original positions. Technological improvements to the typewriter (the introduction of spring-loaded keys at the turn of the century and later, the invention of electric typewriters) overcame the jamming problem but the original keyboard remained. Enter Dr. August Dvorak, education professor, who through scientific time and motion studies developed a new keyboard configuration which would enable typists to work faster, more accurately (50 percent fewer mistakes) and with less physical strain to gain productivity improvements ranging from 35 percent to 100 percent (Dvorak et al., 1936). Additionally, Dvorak proved that typists could learn their skill in one-third of the time it took to learn the QWERTY keyboard. Why then, aren't we all (present authors included) typing on this technologically superior invention?

Perhaps the chief culprits in resisting this technological innovation were the typewriter manufacturers who had considerable financial interests in retaining the traditional keyboard (Parkinson, 1972). During the 1930s when Dvorak introduced his invention, there was little incentive for typewriter manufacturers to convert over to a keyboard which would increase typist productivity thereby conceivably resulting in fewer sales. Furthermore, they would be required to pay royalties on Dvorak's patented invention.

Rejected by the manufacturers, Dvorak then reasoned that publicity at the World Typewriting Championships would help generate public demand for his invention. From 1934 to 1941, DSK-trained typists did indeed win the top typing awards at these competitions. However, the championships were sponsored by the manufacturers who, faced with these embarrassing outcomes, worked to deny Dvorak the publicity he sought. When publishing contest results, they only listed the names of the winning typists, not the machines they used in competition (*covering up*). An attempt by contest officials to ban DSK typists from competition (*terminating*) was aborted when Dvorak threatened to advise the newspapers. Dvorak was even forced to hire security guards to protect his machines during the contests when it was discovered that they had been *sabotaged*. (Parkinson, 1972).

The manufacturers were also skillful in *networking* with the American National Standards Institute. As members of the ANSI Keyboard Committee, they were able to prevent inclusion of the DSK into the national standards manual (*gatekeeping* and *managing committees*).

Dvorak's attempts to gain a government contract for his typewriters were also unsuccessful. Despite the demonstrated superiority of the DSK in experimental tests conducted in the U.S. Navy and the General Services Administration, both rejected the possibility of a conversion. The rationale was that the measurable costs of replacing obsolete equipment and retraining typists outweighed the intangible future benefits of productivity improvements. This was a surprising conclusion since the trial results showed an average productivity increase of 74 percent with retraining costs being amortized over 10 days. Then in the ultimate *covering up* political tactic, the U.S. Navy assigned the DSK test results a security classification.

It is no wonder that, after 30 years of political battles to fulfill his dream, a frustrated Dr. Dvorak told Parkinson:

> I'm tired of trying to do something worthwhile for the human race. They simply don't want to change! (Parkinson, 1972, p. 18)

But as this account of innovation politics suggests, it is not all humans who resist change but rather those interest groups who stand to lose their financial stake if the innovation is implemented.

The Power of Vested Interests to Frustrate New Ideas: Helping Autistic Children. As related by Graziano (1969) in his account of a mental health innovation, the realm of interorganizational innovation is often the scene for political action at the deep structural level. Set in the 1960s, this account shows how the entrenched interests of a medical establishment (expert in the psychoanalytic treatment of such patients) actively resisted acknowledging or experimenting with a new technique (behavioral modification) to treat autistic children. The power of the professional elite is demonstrated by their ability to effectively maintain the status quo of local mental health services while circumventing efforts of an opposing group to gain local funding for an alternative treatment. At a fundamental level, the two opposing interest groups were aligned into one which was supported by the medical profession versus one which was community-based. On the side of the entrenched power elite in the mental health community were the private-practice psychiatrists who operated the local clinics and dominated the local Mental Health Association. How they were able to parlay their position to influence other institutional actors (the local university and the "United Agency" fund-raising organization) is particularly interesting in this drama of innovation. In opposition to this *coalition* for the status quo was the Association for Mentally Ill Children (ASMIC) which was a lay group comprised of the parents of those autistic children who had not been helped by the psychoanalytic methodology (either because they had not responded to the course of treatment or had parents who could not afford the expensive private clinics). The ASMIC had employed a psychologist skilled in this new approach (remember that the time was the early 1960s when behavior modification was still a relatively radical new theory) to assist them in their attempt to change the system. However the integral role in which organizational politics plays in the course of innovation is highlighted by Graziano's (1969, p. 10) comment that:

The *conception* of innovative ideas in mental health depends upon creative humanitarian and scientific forces, while their *implementation* depends, not on science or humanitarianism, but on a broad spectrum of professional or social politics.

Although both groups initially worked together for four years in a local clinic offering both methodologies, the subsequent struggles over the resources to be allocated to each program and evaluation of the therapeutic effectiveness of each led to their separation.

Operating independently, the ASMIC tried repeatedly to gain financial support for their alternative approach. Once outside the mainstream of the medical establishment though, they encountered political resistance orchestrated by the local private clinics at both the surface and deep structure levels. An ASMIC proposal to the local university to try an experimental pilot project testing the merits of the behavioral modification methodology was rejected on two counts—it was too radical and it was not supported by the local mental health community.

Attempts to gain independent funding for their project from the local community funding agency ("United Agency") were first delayed and finally rejected after three years of efforts by the ASMIC to comply with the agency's demands. The influence of the established clinics (which were also funded by the United Agency) could be surmised to have played a role in the construction of these obstacles to implementation. Even though the ASMIC had garnered enough funds (from the parents of the autistic children and latterly from the State Department of Mental Health) to operate at a minimal level of service, the United Agency's rationale for withholding funds proved to be innovative in their own right. First there was the criticism that the program was first only a "paper proposal"; then after six months of operation, the United Agency contended that the program had been in operation "too brief a time on which to base a decision." After another year, the funding application was rejected because it had not been "professionally evaluated"; with a positive State Department of Mental Health evaluation in hand, the ASMIC program was then deemed to be a "duplication of services"; with state endorsement that it was a nonduplicated service, the United Agency declared that state financial support was required; and finally, with a state grant in hand, the United Agency rejected the application outright because the ASMIC had been "uncooperative" by not providing confidential information on clients' names, addresses and fathers' places of employment.

At each juncture in this case we see how the surface political games of *reasoning* and *assertiveness* played by the ASMIC in the quest for altruistic and pragmatic goals were effectively countermanded by a wide range of political games in both the surface and deep structure of the interorganizational domain. In seeking self-interested and self-perpetuating goals, the local dominant coalition (the medical establishment) was particularly skillful in the surface game of *networking* with related institutions. For example, one protagonist was both the director of the leading mental health agency and a leading member of the local mental health planning group which reviewed funding applications. However, the major strength of those opposed to this innovation lay in the deep structure of the mental health profession. As members of an elite profession in our society, the mental health psychiatrists were able to draw first on the game of *neutralization* to promote the perception by others that theirs was an unbiased scientific position. Secondly, as demonstrated by the rationale given by the United Agency in rejecting ASMIC funding applications, the existing structure of mental health services was supported by the deep structure game of *naturalization* which denies the validity or utility of any envisioned change. The effectiveness of these combined tactics and strategies by those in opposition is substantiated by Graziano's report that after six years the ASMIC had achieved financial self-sufficiency independent of local agencies—they were entirely funded by the state.

Automatically Controlled Machine Tools—An Object of Deep Structure Politics. That class conflict and the ideology of progress inform the institutions, ideas and social groups which determine the design and use of a particular technology is the basic thesis of Noble's (1984) analysis of machine tool automation in manufacturing production. This case illustrates how deep structure politics were used to preserve and extend the control and power of the sectional interests of the owner/managerial, scientific technical and military communities at the expense of those of workers. The capacity of a societal ideology to influence not only the choice of a technology but also to frame (in a pre-emptive manner) that decision in terms of the criteria and assumptions which are used, demonstrates the covert and subtle nature of deep structure power games.

Following World War II, there were two viable avenues by which machine tool automation could proceed. The first was Record Playback (R/P) which built on the skills and knowledge of machinist craftsmen thereby enhancing their traditional power base in the production process. In R/P, automatic control of a machine tool was achieved via a taped program which recorded the movement of the machine operator. It required a skilled machinist to make the initial program and any subsequent changes and adjustments to it. The second option was Numerical Control (N/C) technology in which the tape was programmed not by repeating a machinist's movements but by using scientific engineering methods. This in turn resulted in the assignment of machine programming responsibilities to staff engineers and technicians.

At a fundamental level what did each technological approach represent? By

removing the critical programming function from the shopfloor, N/C extended managerial control over production start-up, pace and maintenance. In
contrast, the R/P approach would be a continuation of the current sharing of
production control with the skilled workers on the shopfloor. As Noble (1984)
and Wilkinson (1983) both relate, the overwhelming choice of industrial
management was to pursue the N/C technological approach. The primary
motive for this managerial decision was that it enabled management to regain
control over production for:

> . . . in the larger firms where NC was first developed and applied, management sought to
> remove the 'intelligence' involved in production from the shopfloor to the office in order
> to gain control of production processes from what was considered a problematic work-
> force" (Wilkinson, 1983, p. 21).

This impetus for the assertion of managerial control was only reinforced by
the growing unionization of the American blue-collar workforce during the
1950s which (when coupled with the union movement's ideological alliance
with Communist ideals) served to elevate managerial perceptions of threat.
Support for this observation can be found in the fate of R/P systems which
were developed in a number of large firms such as General Electric and the
Ford Motor Company. Despite positive preliminary test results (based on
production efficiency and cost criteria) corporate management consistently
canceled these experiments in favor of more complex engineer controlled N/C
systems. Significantly, the decision at GE was made during a period of labor
union unrest.

Managerial interests were also influenced and supported by the actions of
other societal interest groups which preferred the N/C technology. The power
of the scientific and military communities in channeling the course of machine
tool automation should not be underestimated. The military underwrote much
of the research and development costs of N/C projects in the university labs.
MIT, at the forefront of computer microelectronic research, was an early
advocate of N/C technology. Not only did N/C research provide MIT with a
promising venue for applications of their new-found computer technology, but
it also was consistent with an ideological bias for the superiority of formal
educational expertise (needed to program N/C tapes) over layman experience
(the basis of R/P technology).

Noble argues that the selection of a technology is a function of the magnitude of the power which chooses it and the dominance of cultural norms which
sanction that power. Examining the relative power bases and tactics of each of
the major interest groups involved in machine tool automation provides support for Noble's contention. On the side of those in favor of or who would
potentially benefit from the R/P approach were the workers on the shopfloor

and their unions. Given the demonstrated efficiency of R/P, management/ownership would also be able to reap the benefits of this technology—based on purely objective economic criteria. However, as an interest group, workers were passive parties in the crucial decisionmaking process. Noble and Wilkinson both report that workers and their unions did not become involved in labor-management negotiations or discussions regarding the introduction of technological change. It was only during the implementation stage that they became involved.

Alternatively, in support of the N/C approach we see that there was a powerful ideological compatibility among the capitalist owner/managers, the military and the scientific technical communities. They shared a common ideology based on scientific technocratic principles which stressed the need for control, continuity and predictability through the minimization of human error or influence. In terms of power, each had significant control over the necessary resources (people, money and materials) needed to develop and implement a desired option. Thus, they were able to, and did, utilize a number of surface political games involving the control of resources. The U.S. Air Force only funded N/C technology research efforts. MIT limited their expert knowledge resources to N/C research projects. This assembly of interest groups were also able to effectively engage in a number of deep structure political games. The first was *neutralization* in which the management community was able to posit the neutrality of N/C technology by citing the "value free" proofs provided by the scientific community's research studies. However as Noble points out, MIT attempts to provide economic justification for N/C were conducted by economists unfamiliar with the production process and whose marginally supportive conclusions were based on incomplete data. Nevertheless, they concluded that N/C was the most economically viable technology. Secondly, management was able to use the *naturalization* tactic to deflect any challenge to management's "right" to organize work. In this game, workers need not be involved in the critical decisionmaking process used to choose a technological change. The power of this deep structure game is substantiated by both Noble's and Wilkinson's observation that workers and their unions (by choice and design) only became involved once the innovation was in place.

However, despite the intentions of management to extend their control over the production process through technological change, Wilkinson's case analysis of the implementation of N/C in batch process manufacturing yields several interesting insights into the informal power of workers to alter or sabotage an innovation. These political contests revolved around controlling outcomes and line vs. staff rivalries. Workers in those firms which had relatively successful transitions were able to force negotiations on work practices and obtain compensatory adjustments for the loss of some degree of control (either through altered pay practices or job rotations). However, in none of the cases studied by Wilkinson were the projected increases in production efficiency fully attained.

The Power and Politics of Innovation

In reading these accounts, one sees how innovation is very often a political process. The evident patterns in the scope and nature of political activity lead us to forward the following propositions regarding the politics of the innovation process.[9]

Proposition 1.   Product innovation success within organizational settings requires a combination of both product *and* administrative innovation.

There is an evident need for *both* product and administrative innovation in the quest for innovation success. A good idea or product is simply not enough to guarantee successful implementation and diffusion within and outside an organization. For example, Hewlett-Packard's NASA Moonlander Monitor was a technological innovation which was almost terminated by a lack of administrative innovation. The information House gained from hands-on development with customers enabled him to modify the monitor to meet their needs while generating demand for the end-product. In this case and others, reliance on standard operating procedures are often insufficient to meet the unique requirements of new products or ideas.

Galbraith (1982) goes so far as to assert that within any organization there are two parallel organizations with different functions, roles and components. Whereas the role of the "innovating" organization is the generation of new ideas and products, the role of the "operating" organization is to efficiently implement them. He further states that it is at the point of transference of an idea from the innovating organization to the operating one that new transition processes of a social administrative nature are essential. The need for administrative or managerial innovation which is complementary to technological innovation is one supported by Li (1980, p. 81) in his study of technological innovation in industrial settings: "The evolution of a successful, industrial enterprise focusses on the transfer from technological to managerial innovation; managerial innovation embraces both professional management and professional engineering and is interlaced with technological innovation."

In terms of directionality of impact between an organization's technical and social systems, Damanpour and Evan (1984) found that the adoption of innovative change in the social system has a positive impact on the technical system and not vice versa. This conclusion is further supported by the case of social innovation at Chipco where the power of social innovation to facilitate technological innovation was demonstrated.

Proposition 2a. When a proposed innovation is congruent with the organizational and societal deep structure, political activity remains primarily on the surface, is benign or at a low level. Consequently, the probability of the acceptance and diffusion of such an innovation is enhanced with the support of the deep structure.

Proposition 2b. A proposed innovation which threatens power relationships at the deep structure level evokes the full breadth and depth of opposing political forces, strategies and tactics. Consequently, the probability of acceptance and diffusion of such an innovation is significantly reduced.

These propositions focus on the type and range of political tactics which emerge or are elicited when a proposed innovation either confirms or threatens existing power relationships. As evidenced in the cases of the Dvorak Simplified Keyboard, the mental health innovation and those areas of ICI which resisted OD initiatives, when those interests which benefit from maintaining the status quo perceive an innovation to be a threat, the politics of change are both numerous and powerful. What results is a mismatched contest where the deep structure frames the rules of the game and to a large extent preordains the outcome. The metaphor of a "corporate immune system" is a useful one in understanding the dynamics of this response. As Pinchot (1985, p. 189) relates:

> When you start something new, the system naturally resists it. It is almost as if the corporation had an immune system which detects anything that is not part of the status quo and surrounds it. If you are to survive, you will have to lull this immune system into ignoring you. You will have to appear to be part of the corporate self, rather than identified as a foreign body.

Although Pinchot focuses on the intraorganizational arena, we believe that the same "immune system" can be activated in the interorganizational and societal realms. As outsiders or newcomers to the arenas in which they were trying to introduce their changes, Dvorak and the ASMIC were easily allocated the role of unwanted invaders by a system which perceived few, if any, benefits to influential system members through effecting a change to the status quo. As we have seen, if this is the case, an innovator's *reasoning, rational logic* and *assertiveness* are weak tools of influence in the face of deep structure political games of *neutralization, naturalization, legitimation* and *socialization* and the numerous surface political tactics which they engender.

At ICI, the OD change agents were also perceived to be outsiders to the production process. However the success of Ripley and Bridge's program in the Agricultural Division could be traced to their strategy of first developing a strong, coherent program for change independent of the corporate system before attempting to enter it and then, to work within the system in a non-threatening manner. They started low in the organizational structure and built support in an incremental way. In contrast, the OD programs in the other areas were more visible and did not have the strength of unity in either philosophy or personnel to withstand the opposition.

When the proposed innovation or change is consistent and/or supports existing power relationships, the politics remain at the more manageable surface level. The contests at Hewlett-Packard and at Data General were against a backdrop of a unity of interests between innovators and the corporate ethic. These innovators were secure in the knowledge that the organizational mission was to be at the forefront of their technology—a deep structure which desired technological change for competitive purposes. They also benefitted from cultures with a deep structure mythology of hero-founders who were mavericks in their own right. By acting as mavericks themselves, they were only continuing the organizational tradition and could count on a degree of understanding of their actions at the highest corporate levels. Opposition to these product innovations were of a more traditional and restricted nature in terms of internal power plays, managing line vs. staff territories and gaining the necessary resources for development. As corporate insiders, these innovators could draw on their past experience and that of others in the organization to gauge how best to proceed—which political tactics had succeeded in the past, which had failed, the relative risks involved, who were the power players and who were not.

For administrative innovations, political gamesmanship played a major role in the eventual success or failure of the proposed change. Success often hinged on the innovator's ability to marshall a wide range of supportive political tactics at both the surface and deep structure levels. Briggs at Chipco used deep structural tactics in presenting the Production Project as being consistent with Chipco's integrationist corporate culture. Her all-inclusive collaborative strategy focussed on gaining support of Chipco and Chestnut Ridge senior management (managing upward), functional counterparts within and outside the Chestnut Ridge plant (managing laterally) as well as the workers in the plant (managing downward). Ripley and Bridge at ICI's Agricultural Division also proved to be politically adept at numerous influence tactics. Review of these successful administrative innovations reveals that there was a minimal number of opposing political games, either at the surface or deep structure levels.

Administrative failures at ICI present a contrasting picture. The tactics of *higher authority appeals* and *reasoning* proved to be ineffective against the deep structure games of a resistant organization. These OD change agents were effectively pre-empted by divisional managements which denied that any change to the status quo was needed (*naturalization*) and rejected the claim that these staff persons had a right to be involved in any change process (*legitimation*).

Proposition 3a. Within organizations, the political strategy of "asking for forgiveness" is limited to only the initial phases of the conception and development of a product innovation. For the adoption and diffusion of a new product, the innovator must "seek and secure permission" of the organization.

Proposition 3b. For social and administrative innovations, the only viable political strategy is one of "seeking and securing permission."

We note in these case studies of innovation there are two distinct types of political strategies—that of "asking for forgiveness" and that of "seeking permission." "Asking for forgiveness" occurs when an innovator proceeds to the point of adoption without official organizational knowledge and/or sanction. It is an independent course of action often marked by secrecy and the furtive seconding or transfer of corporate resources. Alternatively, the strategy of "seeking and securing permission" usually encompasses the political strategies of developing champions and sponsors and of building networks and coalitions. Neglecting to do so may threaten the long term viability of an innovation.

In our view, asking for forgiveness is a viable strategy when pursuing product innovation. Seeking and securing permission is a more viable strategy when pursuing administrative innovations. It is possible to hide a product innovation from potential naysayers in the important fragile early phases of that innovation. Social and administrative innovations, on the other hand, depend more immediately on corporate interdependencies for their successful implementation. Thus it becomes important for the innovator to both seek *and* secure permission from organizational actors in a variety of positions and levels to ensure success. In the long run, product innovations move from the laboratory to implementation and thus to integration with other organizational routines and procedures. This entails a shift to a greater emphasis on the permission rather than the forgiveness strategy. (See Frost & Egri, 1988, 1990c, for a fuller discussion of this argument.)

These accounts of innovation demonstrate the integral role political strategy plays in both promoting and suppressing innovation. If the proposed change threatens the self-interests of a powerful dominant coalition (as in the mental health innovation, the Dvorak keyboard, and machine tool automation), we find that the emergence of a technological innovation is a tenuous one. In these cases, the full breadth of deep structure and surface politics is elicited to preserve prevailing power relationships. Apparently, rationality is subsumed in these high stakes interorganizational and societal level battles for survival of the fittest. On the other hand, if there is no perceived fundamental threat, the political activity remains on the surface and can be more readily managed by prospective innovators.

THE HUMAN AGENT IN INNOVATION

So far, we have discussed the innovation process in terms of the political dynamics involved. Such dynamics at the surface and in the deep structure involve human agency. As Mintzberg (1983) observed so cogently, it takes will *and* skill to successfully enact political action. Rather than focus solely on the political tactics and strategies engendering or blocking innovation, we attend also to the contribution of human agents who emerge in these accounts as product and management champions. These are the widely acknowledged *heroes* of innovation who play out the contests for change in tales which parallel the cultural myths of the hero.

Joseph Campbell has often written about the universality of myths in cultures as "public dreams." Central to many myths is the "hero or heroine who has found or done something beyond the normal range of achievement and experience" (Campbell in Flowers, 1988, p. 123). Part of the hero's lot is to overcome many trials or adventures on a journey of achievement. Campbell observed that,

> A legendary hero is usually the founder of something—the founder of a new age, the founder of a new religion, the founder of a new way of life. In order to found something new, one has to leave the old and go in quest of the seed idea, a germinal idea that will have the potentiality of bringing forth that new thing (Flowers, 1988, p. 136).

The hero's deed is "to face the trials and to bring a whole new body of possibilities into the field of interpreted experience for other people to experience . . ." (Flowers, 1988, p. 41). On a cultural level, Gilfillan (1935) focussed on the need for a mythology of great inventors:

The mythology of heroes or demigods is built up, 1, by the interest of any group in having an heroic origin or history, so that the members may feel flattered by psychologicly (sic) identifying themselves with something great, and, 2, by their interest in having a common cult and symbols to increase the cohesion of the group and its loyalty to its living leaders, all of which is very helpful to these last. Thus each monastic order promptly has its Founder made a Saint (pp. 77–78).

The notion of archetypal heroes is no stranger to the culture school of organization theory which has long recognized the importance of stories in the development of a unique, cohesive corporate culture (Deal & Kennedy, 1982; Frost, Moore, Louis, Lundberg, & Martin, 1985). And we find that many of those stories concern the corporate heroes—the founders and the leaders who guide the organization to success.

Taken together, these stories constitute the corporate mythology. In this context, myths are not defined in the pejorative sense as "falsehoods" but rather as accounts of organizational distinction. The tales of innovation are analogous to the myths of founding and rebirth which, if brought to the surface, can serve as a revitalizing force for organizational members (McWhinney & Batista, 1988). Drawing from the Jungian theory of psychology, a number of authors have explored the archetype of corporate heroes (Deal & Kennedy, 1982; Mitroff, 1983). Mitroff (1983) notes a direct application of the archetypal myth of the hero to the inventor/innovator.

In many ways this is the story of the creative inventor—he who has seen a new vision of what 'might be', not 'what is', and is faced with the tremendous obstacles and frustrations of conveying his strange, terrible, and bewildering images to those who lack his powers of imagination. To achieve his new insights, he must deliberately separate himself from the ordinary ways of seeing and of doing. But to effect change, he must reconnect himself with society and attempt to convince those who have not 'seen' what he has of the truth of his visions . . . (p. 110).

A significant subset of corporate mythology relates the stories of innovators in their quest to implement change. The parallels in these accounts to the archetypal hero myth are striking. First, there is the hero (inventor, innovator) who has a vision. He/she then sets out on a journey to realize this vision. However during this quest, the hero encounters numerous obstacles or trials which threaten his/her purpose. In corporate stories, these are often identified as organizational barriers to innovation on organizational structural and process, group and individual levels. "Slaying the dragon" of inertia or territoriality, the innovator uses weaponry from his/her political arsenal. It is in these political battles that we observe the political games necessary to achieve one's goals.

Proposition 4.   The heroic vision is in the human agent and motivates and
sustains him/her whether innovation success occurs or not.

The Champions of Innovation.   Two heroes in the mythology of innovation—the *Product* champion and the *Management* champion—have been the
focus of a number of studies. We turn now to a more detailed analysis of their
role in the process of innovation. A *product champion* has been defined as:
"A member of an organization who creates, defines or adopts an idea for a
new technological innovation and who is willing to risk his or her position or
prestige to make possible the innovation's successful implementation" (Maidique, 1980, p. 64). The need for product champions (and we would assert the
same for process champions) for innovation success is one which is widely
recognized in the literature (Cox, 1976; Daft & Bradshaw, 1980; Galbraith,
1982; Kanter, 1988; Peters & Waterman, 1982; Pinchot, 1985; Schon, 1963).
Indeed, there appears to be little difficulty in identifying these individuals.
Their contributions are highly visible and widely recognized by all involved in
the innovation process (Howell & Higgins, 1988; Smith et al., 1984). In our
accounts of innovation, we have noted how these corporate heroes have
operated in the quest for innovation success.

    Often the role of the product champion is equated to that of an entrepreneur
(Quinn, 1979, 1985; Schon, 1967). However, as argued by Hill (1987), the
dynamics of entrepreneurship can vary significantly from the corporate intrapreneurship role. For example, entrepreneurship generally occurs within a
smaller organization with relatively fewer corporate controls on activities or
processes to contend with. It is a relatively higher personal risk endeavor
where the ultimate stakes and rewards are greater for the individual. In contrast, intrapreneurs operate above a cushion of longer term corporate continuity and of procedural requirements for approval and support. The most
that the intrapreneur can lose is his/her job or future career advancement
which, although not inconsequential outcomes, do not approach the threat of
personal bankruptcy which the independent entrepreneur may face. Furthermore, the personal rewards for success are more often diffused and/or assumed by the corporation. Given the different corporate cultures in which both
operate, direct transfer of findings from entrepreneurship studies to corporate
intrapreneurship activities should be done with caution.

    An innovator is often described in terms analogous to those used to describe
heroes. The innovator is venturesome, eager to try new ideas, knowledgeable
and creative. He/she is a risk taker with a healthy irreverence for the status
quo. The innovator also has generally higher socio-economic status, has a
varied experience, is more cosmopolitan, and has a high need to achieve
(Amabile, 1988; Galbraith, 1982; Rogers, 1983). On a cognitive level, studies
have shown innovators to be rational, intelligent and able to deal with ab-

stractness. Studies of the personality characteristics of product champions use near-heroic terms in their descriptions of product champions. They are self-confident, persuasive and tenacious risk takers (Cox, 1976; Howell & Higgins, 1988; Keller & Holland, 1978, 1983). Thus innovators are uniquely qualified individuals who are suited to operating within the ambiguity and uncertainty inherent to innovative change. Additionally, product champions have been shown to be particularly proficient on the dimension of interpersonal skills. Not only do they exhibit a willingness to work with others (Keller & Holland, 1978, 1983), they are also politically astute (Chakrabarti, 1974; Mohr, 1969; Schon, 1967). This innovator is not one content to operate in isolation but rather one who uses his/her imagination to visualize new possibilities and proactively guide the innovation idea to fruition (Kingston, 1977). The strategy of developing lateral support (coalitions, consensus) in other areas of the organization has often proven to be critical to innovation success. For example, in the case of 3M Post-It Notes, chemist Spence Silver continually "shopped" his adhesive around various departments at 3M informally and at in-house technical seminars. Later, Art Fry, the chemist who discovered the ultimate application for Silver's temporarily stickable glue, got internal support by distributing samples of Post-It Notes to secretaries in the executive suites of 3M. (Nayak & Ketteringham, 1986)

There is a fundamental duality in the innovator/champion role as he/she is often placed between the creative inventor and the applied world, for as Schumpeter observed:

> It is not the knowledge that matters but the successful solution of the task *sui generis* of putting an untried method into practice . . . Successful innovation . . . is a feat not of intellect, but of will. It is a special case of the social phenomenon of leadership (as cited in Kingston, 1977, p. 23).

This leadership component is one confirmed by Howell and Higgins (1988) in their study of product champions and non-champions. They found product champions to be rated higher than non-champions on transformational leadership behaviors (charisma, inspiration, individualized consideration and intellectual stimulation) as well as on contingent reward transactional type behavior.

How then does a product champion rally commitment to his/her cause in the absence of substantive hierarchical power? Studies of the communicative patterns of product championship indicate that innovation pioneers and early adopters hold positions of centrality in sociometric networks (discussion, advice and information, friendship) of influence (Becker, 1970). As Astley and Sachdeva (1984), Brass (1984), Hickson, Butler et al. (1986), Hickson, Hinings et al. (1971), and Pettigrew (1972) have demonstrated, individual centrality in communication networks is one significant source of intraorganizational power and influence. It is our observation from the cases we analyzed that product champions not only are centrally situated in such networks but also appear to be particularly adept at utilizing this source of power to their advantage. Therefore, it is not surprising that product champions have been found to rely most often on highly communicative type strategies such as coalition formation and reasoning to create support for their innovations (Howell & Higgins, 1988).

Proposition 5.   Product champions are typically centrally situated in sociometric and communication networks and have both the will and the skill to use this centrality to promote their innovations within their organizations.

Management Champions.   Another critical role in the innovation process involves the *management* or *executive champion* of new products or directions. Several authors argue that the most important way to facilitate innovation is to develop senior managers as champions of innovation ideas (Nayak & Ketteringham, 1986; Peters, 1987; Pinchot, 1985). Empirical research by others (Blau & McKinley, 1979; Hage & Dewar, 1973; Kelley, 1976) confirms the critical importance of managerial elite support in innovation implementation. Without the protective umbrella shielding the innovative work in progress, many of the breakthroughs could easily have been terminated prematurely. Without senior support, the innovator could have been a victim of the most frequent anti-innovation game—budget cuts and resource limitations.

Armed with both strategic power in terms of control over resource allocations as well as formal organizational status and hierarchical power, the management champion appears to be one of significant influence. These management champions are not necessarily CEOs but rather persons at executive levels within the organizational hierarchy who themselves are often involved in intraorganizational contests with their counterparts. In the SAPPHO project which compared successful and unsuccessful innovations, the presence of a "business innovator" or executive champion was the principal factor in product innovation success. (Note however that the presence of product champions was also a significant discriminator of success.) (Rothwell et al., 1974) These individuals were especially instrumental in innovation success in organizations which were diversified with decentralized divisional structures and multiple product lines (Maidique, 1980).

The role of the management champion is somewhat different from that of the product champion. As illustrated in the case of the NASA Moonlander Monitor, management champions such as Dar Howard serve to buffer the innovation process and the activities of the product champion from outside interference as well as procuring the needed time and resources for product development. Although the most effective management champion is the CEO (by virtue of his/her greater degree of hierarchical power), he/she can also be a suitably powerful member of the top management team. The role of the top executive sponsor has been shown to be a critical one in facilitating and ensuring the success of an innovation (Blau & McKinley, 1979; Nutt, 1986). Unlike in the traditional bureaucratic sense of order giving, the most beneficial results occur when he/she acts at a level of altering expectations to motivate or prompt change. With the commitment of the top executive, the course of implementation may be smoother in that formal hierarchical power can be used to access the needed resources for development, especially since the lack of resources is often the primary cause of failure identified in many studies of innovation (Delbecq & Mills, 1985).

Proposition 6. Social and administrative innovations have a fragile permanence in that they are closely tied with the continuing presence of their innovator(s) and/or the support of the organizational deep structure.

Executive champions need to stay with an administrative innovation for a long period of time, not only to ensure that what was novel does in fact become routine and taken for granted (thus entrenched), but also to buffer the changes from assaults originating in the deep structure which may have long half-lives and thus play out over a protracted period of time. For example, the continued success of Chipco's Production Project can be attributed to the supportive integrationist corporate culture which it reflects. In contrast, at ICI's Agricultural Division, the departure of OD champions Ripley and Bridge placed this social innovation in jeopardy. Pettigrew reports that OD practices were either cut back or abandoned during the subsequent periods of fiscal difficulties experienced in this and other ICI divisions.

As with product innovation, the success and failure of an administrative innovation appears to be hinged on the political skills of the innovator. In successful social innovations, the innovator was shown to use a wide range of political and communication tactics at both surface and deep structure levels. Also, champions of successful innovation initiatives appeared to be cognizant of the long term implications of these changes. In contrast, the failed administrative innovations were ones in which the innovators focussed more on short term success—neglecting to lay the groundwork for fundamental change. Subsequently, the deep structure politics worked to limit and eventually to discard these attempts at social change.

How is the Hero Treated Afterwards?   In Campbell's analysis of the archetypal myth of the hero, the moral objective of heroism "is that of saving a people, or saving a person, or supporting an idea" (in Flowers, 1988, p. 127). However, as Mitroff (1983) elaborates, it is the return from the heroic journey that is perhaps the most difficult. Following the successful completion of an innovative project, what happens to the innovators and the inventors? How are they treated by their organizations? Does it make a difference to the treatment whether the innovation is a product or a social intervention? Does success as an innovator in the organization lead to more opportunities to innovate? Or is the individual promoted out of, for example, the R&D arena to an administrative post which may be more financially rewarding but less stimulating to his or her creative capacities?

For the product inventors, the scientists who pursue an idea or theory for its own sake, success has proven to be a mixed blessing. In the case of the 3M Post-It Notes, Silver has escaped widespread public recognition and continues as before, experimenting in his research labs. On the other hand, Fry now has his private lab, but works in isolation. He also has become a company spokesman and must endure public scrutiny—not all of which is flattering. Life has been transformed for Fry while Silver continues exploring new scientific avenues (Nayak & Ketteringham, 1986).

Chuck House of Hewlett-Packard continues on in his course of intrapreneurial success (Pinchot, 1985). Michael Phillips of the Bank of California MasterCard fame lost the protective umbrella of his sponsors and was subsequently fired. He now is a successful author and advocate of honesty and openness in business (Pinchot, 1985, pp. 63–64).

For other innovators, the rewards of innovation have included a career change within and outside their organizations. Richie Herink, innovator of IBM's employee training center, was a victim of his own success (Pinchot, 1985). When demand outstripped the center's ability to provide service, it was shut down. Herink subsequently headed a small department called Technology Management Education in IBM and continues to break new ground.

For Data General's Eclipse group, success brought different outcomes for team members. Tom West was promoted higher into executive management to new challenges involving a Japanese computer company which Data General had partially acquired. The Eclipse group itself was disbanded a year after the Eagle project was completed. Several in the Eclipse group had received promotions, stock options and the freedom to pursue pet projects. However by that time, the rest of the managers in the Eclipse group had left Data General to join other companies. The excitement was no longer there for them and as Wallach reflected, he now felt "unappreciated" by the company.

For innovators of administrative programs, the long term benefits of success are less clear or encouraging. In his review of six case studies of successful process innovations, Brimm (1988) found that the innovation sponsor's career did not benefit. In fact, four of these innovators were subsequently passed over for promotion. The hazards of the product and process champion roles are also confirmed by Smith et al. (1984) who found that if the innovation was successful, the rewards were plentiful. However, if it failed (especially if accompanied by significant conflict and confrontation with other organizational members), the champion's career was harmed.

Proposition 7.   Champions of social administrative innovations often sacrifice their careers as a result of the animosities created during their quest for organizational change.

Explanations as to why there is a less positive record for social innovators are fourfold. During the championing process, the innovator may have alienated and/or antagonized a number of individuals who would be able to influence subsequent career moves. Secondly, in that social innovations are less amenable to standard organizational evaluation procedures (in that the evaluation is largely subjective and has experimental status), opponents' claims of biased results gain more credence. Thirdly, in that social innovators often display a humanistic orientation (necessary for the implementation of such initiatives), charges that they are "too soft" and "not tough enough" to operate at higher organizational levels often surface (Brimm, 1988). Fourth, there is the trap that awaits all innovators who come to behave unquestioningly in the "heroic" dimension of their lives and are unable to let go of the trappings of the role. In other words, there is a danger facing innovators who are successful that lies in the accolades that often accompany their work. If they come to believe and accept unquestioningly the hero worshipping, the celebration by others of their accomplishments, and the "greatness" that others attribute to them, innovators can be seduced into overrating their own contribution and forget how much such success depends on others and on organizational processes. The unreflective innovator then spends more time playing and enjoying the "Hero" role than focussing on the creative and organizational processes that make innovations work. What dies is the creative ingredient of the individual, what remains is the mythic shell and an actor whose energies are primarily devoted to sustaining and embellishing those externalities (Sonnenfeld, 1988). Thus, the long term career hazards of being a pioneer are ones which should not be ignored by those embarking on a reformer course.

Proposition 8.   A designation as Hero can, in the long run, impede future innovative action. One major impediment will be the individual's uncritical acceptance of the trappings of the heroic role.

When There Is No Hero.   What happens to an innovation when there is no hero to champion it through the obstacles? In the case of either administrative or process innovations, this is probably the most critical component in the eventual success or failure of an innovation. Unlike a technological innovation which can be seen or touched, with social innovation there is a critical need for someone to translate and interpret the vision for others. A social innovation is one of process and relationships—one that relies even more than product innovation on the interaction of persons for its existence. In many ways it requires substantially more nurturing than a technological innovation in that its form is only that which is perceived by others—a social or administrative innovation ceases to exist once out of the minds of its champions. There is a need for the innovation to endure long enough to move from a political reality to a "technical" one which is taken for granted.

The tinkering or experimentation with social innovations is especially prone to political games. Since the actual costs or benefits are only future projections, it is very difficult, if not impossible, to conduct a cost-benefit analysis on a forgone social innovation. Meanwhile the costs of not proceeding with a technological innovation may confront one if a competitor presents it first.

While it is possible to evaluate OD, it is rarely done. What one must more typically rely on is interaction, a feel for how much better an organization is due to the change. Therein lie many of the problems encountered in the OD forays into ICI. As demonstrated in those divisions where commitment to OD principles were low or non-existent, where there was no champion, it was a short-lived experiment. The social innovation needs to be made tangible and personified in the champion in order to survive. This was demonstrated in the ICI Agricultural Division where OD was introduced in a bottom-up process. However, once the heroes left, OD efforts disintegrated. Thus we see how the following propositions play out in reality.

Proposition 9a.   Without dedicated champions, ideas for social innovations do not proceed beyond the initial idea or proposal stage.

Proposition 9b.   Without dedicated champions, ideas for product innovations may remain dormant for future development and implementation. Alternatively, a product innovation can proceed unobtrusively through the development stage until the need for an organizational decision to adopt or reject its implementation.

The Villains of Innovation. If there are heroes of innovation, are there also villains? And if so, what are the scripts for these actors in the myths of innovation? Working within the conventional view of the innovation process, the acknowledged villains of innovation are those who oppose the proposed changes. One can consider individuals as embodiments of a larger cultural or corporate ethic of resistance to change. In that virtually every innovation has or meets resistance, the interplay of political maneuvering within the organizational context can be viewed as a struggle between change and the status quo. Focussing on the struggle itself, those who resist change are seeking to preserve and protect existing privileges and benefits derived from existing arrangements (Bright, 1964). Thus, any innovation which cannot be framed as serving to enhance their self-interests would be viewed as a threat to be resisted.

A psychological approach would assert that resistance to change is simply a symptom of the human need for stability, continuity and conformity (Schon, 1967). Anything which threatens this fragile state of equilibrium is therefore viewed as suspect.

At an organizational level, the same argument also holds true for social groups, however on a larger scale. Rather than talking of threats to personal welfare, the rationalization of resistance to change is in terms of protecting professional and functional territories, minimizing the disruptive influence of change on existing systems, minimizing the financial risks necessitated by change. Given that costs are relatively known while benefits are at best future projections, the reluctance to engage in "risky" ventures is a strong impediment to change.

Thus in these tales of innovation, we are encouraged to view those who oppose innovation as the villains, the nonbelievers who do not see the potential benefits (to individuals, organizations and society) of innovative change and whose motives are felt to be self-interested and narrow. Their responses and action are cast as irrational barriers to the ultimate good which the innovation promises. In fact, this scenario has proven to be an accurate representation of the surface reality in many of the accounts we have reviewed in the literature. It is a scenario informed by a technological paradigm founded on the following principles (Fujimoto, 1978, pp. 172–173):

Principle 1. Pro-Innovation Bias: "any knowledge that can be applied should be applied. To hold back is to hold back progress."

Principle 2. The Technological Fix: "any problem created by technology can be solved by technology."

Principle 3. Elitism: only a select group or stratum of people (experts) should be permitted to "handle" technology.

For example, the principles of the technological fix and elitism have both been addressed by Perrow (1984) in his study of accidents in high-risk technologies (e.g., nuclear industry, petrochemical plants, among others). Perrow details how the technological fix has led to a knee-jerk type reaction of designing systems to fix systems thereby compounding the complexity and propensity for failures of sometimes catastrophic proportions. The propensity for systems failure is further compounded by the dominance of a technological elite (scientists, engineers) whose over-reliance on mathematical models and narrow risk-benefit analyses has led to an over-circumscribed (and potentially dangerous) approach to technological development. Schumacher (1973) has also challenged economic cost benefit analysis as being fragmentary and incomplete in that it relates only to the surface of society without delving into the natural and social facts that lie behind them.

Proposition 10.   The principles of the technological paradigm of innovation (pro-innovation bias, technological fix and elitism) create the attribution of villain for anyone(s) who resists and/or questions a proposed change.

However, what if we were to search beneath the surface of this technological paradigm to discover its bases of power? What if we were to examine innovation as it is currently constructed in light of the deep structure games on which it is founded? In other words, if we assume that the current attitudes and beliefs about innovation have political origins, then we can see how the unquestioning evaluation of innovation as "good" may itself be a social or paradigmatic construction resulting from prior deep structure political games. Seen in this light, the notions of heroes and villains become constructions that emerge out of particular contests which have their origins in more fundamental assumptions about what is right and wrong, what is good and bad in the realm of innovation. It is to this end that we focus on the key principles of the pro-innovation bias, the technological fix, and elitism which support the currently dominant technological paradigm of innovation.

DISTORTIONS OF INNOVATION AS SCIENTIFIC PROGRESS

The positive valuation of innovation in and of itself has been noted by a number of other authors (Downs & Mohr, 1976; Kimberly, 1987; Knight, 1967; Rogers, 1983; Schon, 1967; Van de Ven, 1986). This underlies the prescriptions of many to enhance the generation of new ideas, products and processes (Kanter, 1988; Quinn, 1979, 1985) and to facilitate the development, implementation and diffusion of innovations (Rogers, 1983).

The pro-innovation bias which permeates the empirical literature on innovation in organizations and in society is one which equates newness with goodness in an unquestioning way. We are encouraged to promote innovation for its own sake. We are challenged to find more and faster ways by which to guide an innovative idea to fruition. And finally, in the name of "progress," we are entreated to strike down those barriers to change.

However, as historical accounts reveal, this interpretive frame has not been the only conceptualization of scientific progress in Western civilization. During the "Enlightenment" period starting in the eighteenth century, there was another agenda for progress. As Leo Marx (1987) relates, the transition from earlier beliefs to current ones has the vestiges of political action.

> The initial Enlightenment belief in progress perceived science and technology to be in the service of liberation from political oppression. Over time that conception was transformed, or partly supplanted, by the more familiar view that innovations in science-based technologies are in themselves a sufficient and reliable basis for progress. The distinction, then, turns on the apparent loss of interest in, or unwillingness to name, the social ends for which the scientific and technological instruments of power are to be used (p. 71).

Toynbee (1972) relates how the founders of the Royal Society of London in seventeenth century England, recoiling from the turbulent religious controversies of earlier times, set about to establish a scientific doctrine which would be separate from "traditional Christian intolerance and animosity." To do so, they promoted a factual, rather than religious, study of nature but one which was itself grounded in theological philosophy.[10] Thus this new scientific doctrine promoted the dominance of man over nature and others and the subjugation of the forces of nature for the service of mankind. It is a worldview which more closely reflects the Chinese Taoist term *wei* which compared to *wu wei* is as follows: "*Wei* meant the application of force, of will-power, the determination of things, animals, or even other men should do what they are ordered to do; but *wu wei* was the opposite of this, leaving things alone, letting Nature take her course, profiting by going with the grain of things instead of going against it, and knowing how not to interfere" (Needham, 1964, p. 142).

Despite the lofty intentions of the founders of "Enlightenment," sociological observers of innovation have noted how technology has not been used for socially neutral ends but instead, reflects the human needs and interests of those involved (Benson & Lloyd, 1983; de Bresson, 1987; Schon, 1967). The process of innovation within this definition of "scientific progress" has proven not to be a neutral one of incremental evolution in the

Darwinian sense. Adopting a philosophy of technological determinism denies the critical human role of social choice in innovation. Thus in separating science from religion, the Royal Society founders set the stage for the playing out of several deep structure games. By asserting that science is morally neutral and above governmental or religious animosities, they were is a position to engage in the game of *neutralization* which hides secular value positions. By placing science above human interests, they set in motion the practice of *legitimation* tactics to justify their existence and actions. Furthermore, by separating out scientific inquiry as the domain of an esteemed and select group (comprised of "properly accredited" scientists and scholars), this newly created elite was now in a powerful position to *socialize* those who sought to gain entry. Given that the founders of the Royal Society were also powerful members of the clergy (which at that time was closely intertwined with governing interests), there remained less of a transformation but more of a reinforcement of existing forms and privileges (*naturalization*). Societal hierarchies were not abandoned; new and complementary ones were created.

This technological paradigm has proven to be a resilient one in promoting an illusion that science is separate from and above secular interests. For individuals working within this paradigm, it offers refuge from the disturbing questions about the social effects of their discoveries and inventions. But it is a refuge which leads to a false sense of security for:

> The manufacture, and the use for genocide, of two atomic bombs in 1945 made it impossible for us to shut our eyes any longer to the truth that technology is a morally neutral instrument for enhancing human power, and that, like the jinn, who was the slave of Aladdin's lamp, it can be put to work either for good or for evil, according to the will of its human master (Toynbee, 1972, p. 141).

Despite Toynbee's caution about the potential abuses of technological innovation, the study of innovation has revealed a continued subscription to these technocratic principles of scientific progress. For example, the pre-occupation with numerical indices of the number of innovations, rates of diffusion, and proportions of adoption underlie the premise of growth—more is better and quick action is preferred over inaction (Kimberly, 1987; Rogers, 1983). The language of mathematics carries with it the vehicle for legitimation of research results. Within this approach: "The talk about resistance to innovation tends to come from within the framework of official approval of innovation. It suggests, moreover, that the resistance is somewhat mechanical (inertia, foot-dragging, sand-in-the-gears) and can be removed by mechanical means (motivation, lubrication)" (Schon, 1967, p. 56). Thus the study of innovation can easily fall into the "trap" of concentrating solely on the surface of activity without delving into the underlying forces and interest groups who structure the course of innovative activity.

Another "trap" is a disregard for those phenomena that are less amenable to objective scrutiny and quantitative analyses. As observed by Huxley (1946, p. 35): "Confronted by the data of experience, men of science begin by leaving out of account all those aspects of the facts which do not lend themselves to measurement and to explanation in terms of antecedent causes rather than of purpose, intention, and values." Perhaps even more poignant is the observation of van der Post (1965) that:

> . . . the world appears to have lost the sense of the importance of the small in life. Obsessed with mere size and number, we have been deprived of the feeling for the immense significance of the tiny, tentative first movements in the individual heart and imagination. Although our neglect of these impulses is destroying one system after the other around us, we go on ardently giving our allegiance to the great established order, as if its continuance were assured. One look at the identical towns we are building all over the world ought to be enough to show us that this kind of progress is like the proliferation of a single cell at the expense of the rest, which produces the cancer that kills the whole body (pp. 124–125).

Technology and Nature: The Case of Innovation in Agriculture. One can see how the technological paradigm plays out in the modern world through the course of innovation in agriculture. At its core, agriculture represents the inextricable linkage between humans and nature in that we all depend on the fruits of nature for our survival.

What is most riveting about agricultural innovation is the outcomes engendered by a technological scientific paradigm which asserts the preeminence of mastery over nature (Devall & Sessions, 1985; Doyle, 1985; Jackson, Berry, & Colman, 1984; LeVeen, 1978). It reflects the ideology of mastery of nature which has resulted in the increased capital intensive nature of food production and distribution; the introduction and application of man-made substances such as petro-chemically based fertilizers, pesticides and herbicides into the production process; the introduction of U.S. patent legislation in 1930 and extensions in 1970 and 1980 which granted ownership rights to living organisms. Perhaps the most controversial arena for agricultural innovation has been the development of biogenetic engineering technology (gene-splicing through recombinant DNA techniques) to accelerate the natural processes of mutation and selection of crops as well as the development of new microorganisms to combat the natural hazards of agriculture (pests, weeds, and climate conditions). This avenue is a new extension of the "Green Revolution" which promised to solve world hunger problems through the introduction of new strains of dwarf wheat and rice.

The fundamental themes of these inter-related technological and biological innovations has been the pursuit of control over the vagaries of nature. Paradoxically, agriculture which is based on the production of organic matter has adopted many of the characteristics of the mechanistic metaphor (as opposed to an organic-system metaphor) with its emphasis on the control over nature in the interests of gaining predictability and uniformity of food production.

To take an alternative or critical approach to evaluating these developments, one need only look at the vulnerabilities created by this course. One outcome of the increased mechanization of farming has been the selection of produce which can endure mechanical harvesting. Thus we see the emphasis on the development (through biogenetic engineering and other means) of food varieties for qualities of hardiness, appearance and uniform maturity dates rather than for taste or nutritional value.

Another outcome of capital-intensive production methods has been the emphasis on increasingly higher yields from the same area of land. In order to rationalize the cost of the machinery (and repay loans taken to purchase equipment), farmers have turned to man-made petro-chemical fertilizers and pesticides to enhance production.

Fundamental to this shift has been the development of strains of crops which will meet the primary criteria of high yields. As learned during the Green Revolution though, these elite "superseeds" could fulfill their promise only if coupled with intensive irrigation and massive chemical inputs. One result has been a dramatic increase in yields but at the price of the creating a barren earth for future generations through depletion of the topsoil,[11] dependence on non-renewable petroleum resources as inputs to production, and declining net farm income due to increased costs of production (Commoner, 1978; Gillingham, 1978). Another outcome has been the increased genetic vulnerability to natural pests and diseases which has resulted from the development of only limited strains of seeds (Kloppenburg & Kleinman, 1987). This outcome was most clearly demonstrated in the 1970–71 Southern Corn Leaf Blight epidemic in which a new strain of fungus had found a "genetic window" to threaten 43 percent of the U.S. corn acreage which had been seeded with six inbred seed lines (Doyle, 1985).

One view of agricultural innovation would focus on the surface results of increased volumes to meet the needs of a growing population. However, searching below and behind these developments with a focus on the power dynamics of innovation, one gains a less neutral perspective. In close accompaniment with the increased vertical integration of producers and distributors of food in the hands of corporations rather than independent farmers has been the large scale entry of chemical companies (traditional suppliers of the chemical inputs to farm production) into biotechnology and agricultural genetics research.[12] Rather than pursue traditional ends, the incentive is now there to use the genetic engineering of seeds to complement other corporate products. For example, integrated firms are now developing herbicide resistant crops so that farmers may use *more* of a herbicide to combat weeds (Benbrook & Moses, 1986). Another trend that is emerging is the development of seeds which are resistant *only* to selected herbicides (thereby reducing the utility of competitors' herbicides) (Doyle, 1985, pp. 217–218). Thus with genetic engineering, a wider range and more chemicals can be utilized. However, the question remains whether this is also a prudent innovation from an ecological or public health perspective—a concern which has recently resulted in some farmers seeking alternative methods to chemical inputs (Hill & Ott, 1982; Schneider, 1989; Zakreski, 1989).

Focussing on developments within the biogenetic engineering arena, one sees how the technological innovation paradigm has played out. One also sees how challenges to this paradigm are emerging as potent forces in guiding the course of such innovation. There is developing a fundamental contest over the basic assumption that mastery over Nature is possible and to the benefit of humankind versus the environmentalist perspective which asserts the need for control over biotechnology. Whereas the microbiologists focus on the projected benefits to be reaped from their scientific discoveries, the environmental scientists focus on the potential and as yet unknown risks associated with introducing man-made organisms into the environment. Thus we see within the scientific community a chasm developing. The stakes are high for those proponents of the merits of biotechnology. In addition to the projected increases in food production, estimates as to the sale of biotechnology products in agriculture and in human health care range from $10 to $15 billion ($30 billion worldwide) over the next two decades (Schneider, 1986).

Operating within the technological paradigm, microbiologists assert that introduction of any new organisms would be subject to the natural Darwinian laws of selection and retention—if they fail to be beneficial and hardy enough to survive, the new organisms will die. As stated by Dr. Bernard D. Davis, professor of bacterial physiology at Harvard Medical School: "If an organism has an advantage over its neighbors it will spread . . . If it is at a disadvantage, it will die, no matter how large the number of organisms released" (Schneider, 1986, p. 48). In opposition, the environmentalists adopt a systemic viewpoint which asserts that once introduced into the environment, control over the diffusion and effects of new micro-organisms will not be practically controllable. The need for caution is reflected in the statement by Dr. Patrick W. Flanagan, microbial ecologist and director of the ecology program at the National Science Foundation who states: "The question of whether recombinant organisms can spread their genes throughout the soil and waters of the world, and possibly cause a problem, has not been answered" (Schneider, 1986, p. 48).

Two specific examples of how these contesting viewpoints of scientific progress have played out in practice are the proposed testing of two products of biogenetic engineering: a microbial organism to minimize frost damage in California (Doyle, 1985; Betz, 1988); and a natural insecticide developed to kill cutworms that feed on corn (Schneider, 1986). In both cases, based on scientific tests conducted in controlled environments, the U.S. Environmental Protection Agency initially granted approval for field testing. Approvals for both were rescinded prior to field testing as a result of environmental activist group publicity over the validity of these scientific experiments and the potentially disastrous outcomes which could occur. However, in the case of the microbial organism designed to inhibit frost formation on plants, this proved to be only a temporary reprieve for environmentalist opponents in that the EPA has subsequently approved and supervised field testing of this genetically engineered organism (Betz, 1988).

Concomitant with the evolution of the scientific debate is an organizational phenomenon it is engendering. The challenge against biogenetic engineering has been found to be not only from within the scientific community but also as a countervailing force from external environmental activist groups such as the Sierra Club, the Friends of the Earth, and Jeremy Rifkin and his Foundation for Economic Trends. As detailed by Douglas and Wildavsky (1982), the debate over technology has become politicized due to the emergence of "border groups" based on a sectarian worldview which focusses on the interrelatedness between the ecosystem, production system and the economic system. They trace the growing power of these groups to mobilize public concern for the environment and the risks associated with new technology to the cultural changes in American education, industry and politics. The net result has been an institutionalized distrust of corporate America with "engagement of the population in the political arena" (Chomsky, 1988, p. 763) in not only governmental politics but also in the economic institutions which control society. Thus, in organizational terms, there is emerging a complexity within the organizational domain corresponding to the systemic complexity of the environmental issues which surround such innovations.

Douglas and Wildavsky observe that the selection of technological and environmental dangers is a collective construct in that there is a cultural predisposition to select out some risks for attention while downplaying others. It is a contest over diametrically opposed viewpoints of nature and different risk perceptions for the present and for the future. It is a political contest at a deep structural level which pits the established scientific community against outside interest groups. Thus we see the proliferation of deep structure games such as *legitimation* played out when biological scientists reject the assertions of those lacking the "proper" scientific credentials to understand their experimental results. We see the operation of the game of *naturalization* with the established scientific community seeking to maintain their traditional role in the evaluation and introduction of new technology against those who would challenge their assumptions and results. We also see the process of *neutraliza-*

tion in that biological discoveries are presented as solely the outcome of an unbiased quest for knowledge and progress when, indeed, there is a close alignment with the economic benefits to be derived for the institutions which fund biological research. This latter development of increased corporate sponsorship of basic research in universities and "independent" research laboratories has itself led to a debate over the ownership, dissemination and repression of research results—abuses have occurred in the past thus contributing to the public's distrust of the neutrality of science (Kenney, 1986).

Proposition 11. The deep structural foundation of the mechanistic-technological paradigm is being challenged by individuals, groups and organizations which subscribe to an organic-systems worldview.

Essentially, these developments highlight the contest arising out of the fundamentally different assumptions held by the players about how the world functions. Many of the current conflicts focus on the problems engendered by the prevailing paradigm based on a machine metaphor which is founded on a (hidden) political base. However, one can question the purity of the altruistic claims of those who subscribe to the organic-systems metaphor for in any technological and social program, human interaction is integrally political. As illustrated in Table 2, taken separately, the machine, political and organic-systems metaphors are complete at the surface level but incomplete as accurate representations of reality in the deep structure. In actual practice, we have seen throughout this paper how there are political undertones to both the machine and organic-systems metaphors. That is, because of the human agency involved in sustaining the way they are framed and used, neither the mechanistic *nor* the organic-systems metaphors are free from the impact of power. We are, essentially, advocating that there is a political basis for the enactment of these metaphors. And as has been illustrated in the example of the innovation in the agricultural sector, we also see how there are changes in Western society which are forcing a transition from the mechanistic-political model to one which is more closely approximated as systemic-political. The question for those in the organizational sciences then is how this transition can be accomplished for a more complete conceptualization of innovation as being for the enhancement of the social good.

Proposition 12. The surface of both the mechanistic and organic systems metaphors of innovation rests on the foundation of the political processes of human interaction.

Table 2. Alternative Conceptualizations of Innovation

	Machine Metaphor	Political Metaphor	Organic-Systems Metaphor
Basic Assumptions	Rationality Control Technological Determinism	Pluralistic Self-interested Action Nonrational	Systemic interrelatedness Complexity Requisite variety Chance
Values/Principles	Pro-Innovation Bias Technological Fix Intellectual Elitism	Social Conflict Competition inevitable Self-determinism	Social and Technical cooperation and integration
Role of Human Actors	Minimal-inconsequential Passive dependence on technical interests	Primacy as heroes, victims, villains Active	Coupling of social and technical interests Passive and active
Focus	Linear causality Efficiency Means to engender innovation for its own sake	Process at surface and deep structure levels Means to control the course of innovation	Search for patterns within and between interrelated systems Means to minimize the dysfunctional or destructive impact of innovations
	Ends	Means	Ends and means
Preferred Avenues of Study	Quantitative Mathematical models Observable behavior and outcomes	Qualitative Subjective inference and observable action (motives are inferred)	Quantitative and Qualitative Longitudinal analysis
Time Span	Past and present	Past and present	Past, present and future

ORGANIZATIONAL SCIENCE'S CONTRIBUTION TO INNOVATION

What has our treatment of innovation as a political phenomenon added to an understanding of innovation? First of all, it is clearly evident that innovation is a *process* which is a function of human agency and social interaction. To treat innovation as a neutral and inevitable enterprise of only material dimensions denies its essential nature as an arena for the interplay of individual, organizational and societal interests in the quest for innovative change.

By addressing innovation as a social and political process, we can more readily understand how the failure or delay of innovation can be due to the failure of influence strategies as well as the tangible deficiencies of an innovation. We also see how the contests over innovation and change are not necessarily negative but serve as the "trials by fire" for improvements. In overcoming the political obstacles to change, the innovator is forced to justify the merits of proposed change as well as perhaps adapting the innovation to meet the needs of a wider constituency, thereby enhancing its potential benefits. At the surface, we have seen how the course of innovation is often a function of the will, skill and power of change agents and the availability of certain influence strategies. For example, individual innovators are often limited by their very position or role in an organization or society to tactics which lack formal authority. It also explains why new innovative organizational arrangements to meet certain societal goals (such as the interorganizational systems studied by Cummings (1984) and by Gray & Hay (1986)) are limited to normative influence strategies to effect change by virtue of the relative power equality of the parties involved. The nature of these systems and their voluntary co-dependent relationship creates a frame which biases their actions toward participation. The players need each other to get something done, but their choices of political action are limited due to the fragile nature of their alliances.

By focussing on the political dynamics of the change process, we can see how the prescriptions for decentralized organizational structures offer vehicles for collaboration to overcome barriers to communication (as per Kanter, 1988; Van de Ven, 1980a, 1980b; and others). Another less recognized effect of such prescriptions is that these structures also create a different climate for political conflict. By empowering those lower level players to engage in new technical and social directions, the conflict over means and ends is ostensibly pushed further down the organizational hierarchy. This is not an inconsequential outcome in that the debate over the course of innovation also frames the perspective and content of any subsequent acceptance/rejection decision. In the end though, the power to decide remains with those at the top of the organizational hierarchy who have themselves created the cultural framework for the debate through prior decisions on organizational structural and processual arrangements. This dynamic was especially evident in the case of Data General's Eagle computer innovation.

Examining the deep structure of political influence, we see how innovation is itself a social construction process reflecting the power of entrenched interests in resisting change and in promoting change which does not threaten existing relationships. Unlike incremental innovations, radical innovations which posit a much more visible challenge to existing frameworks and interests contribute to an escalation of the stakes of the political contests for all concerned. The dissimilar dynamics incurred by incremental versus radical innovations can be reinterpreted in a different light.

Using a political perspective, one sees why incremental innovations are more numerous in that they are less likely to engage the "organizational immune system" against change (Pinchot, 1985). In writing of social innovation, Karl Weick argues for the promise of a strategy which is a series or cadre of "small wins" as opposed to one which focuses on major changes. As Weick (1984, p. 44) explains "A series of small wins is also more structurally sound than a large win because small wins are stable building blocks." In light of our findings, we note that a small wins approach can be intentionally a political strategy for overcoming resistance to change—albeit one which is necessarily lengthy and fraught with uncertainty. A small wins strategy is also supported by the proposition that outcomes of current political activity form the basis of the future deep structure of interaction. Rather than focussing solely on the immediate results of surface political activity in innovation success or failure, a more fruitful avenue of inquiry may be attending to the longer term implications of such pursuits.

Learning A New Approach to Innovation. In many respects, the current technological paradigm has served humankind well in providing a standard of living and health which are beyond the expectations of those founders of the Royal Society of London. What we are proposing is a wider agenda for innovation to minimize the dysfunctional side-effects which threaten those very gains at the level of survival. How can organizations *learn* a new way of functioning which will recouple technological and social progress in a complementary way?

The contributions of organizational science regarding the processes of organizational learning offer some guidance in that innovation is essentially learning to do new things in new ways. In his typology of approaches to organizational learning, Shrivastava (1983) sees three separate avenues for inquiry. First is organizational learning as adaptation and response to new information.

This system structural perspective would focus on the surface politics used to influence behavior and to develop attention and search rules for adjustments among different parties in the innovation process (Astley & Van de Ven, 1983; Cyert & March, 1963; Daft & Huber, 1987).

A second approach is organizational learning as assumption sharing (Argyris & Schon, 1978; Bateson, 1972). Using this interpretive perspective, we see how single-loop learning is explained by surface politics whereas the underlying assumptions and framework of deep structure politics help explain the dynamics of double-loop learning which focusses on the development and surfacing of less observable assumptions which guide interaction.

However, it is organizational learning as the development of a knowledge base that we see the most fruitful line of inquiry for a new agenda for innovation. It is an approach which Lundberg (1989) posits to be transformational learning where attention is directed towards changing the core values of the organization. The questions to be addressed are now: who is to guide the process? and will it serve only to reinforce existing dilemmas or paradoxes? As such, it is always a political process in which one won't or can't avoid contests. It is also, at its core, a sense-making process which goes beneath the surface to gain knowledge about action-outcome relationships and beyond the current sphere to look at the impact of these on the interactions between organization and its environment. This approach has been used by Utterback and Abernathy (1975) in explaining the diffusion of innovations and technology. It was also integral to Jelinek's (1979) study of how Texas Instruments successfully institutionalized innovation.

In practice, how might organizational learning at this deep level be conducted? The insightful prescriptions of McWhinney and Batista (1988) regarding remythologizing prove to be particularly relevant to this process of going to core assumptions in an effort to "recapture(s) the original source energy of organizations and communities" to guide organizational innovation towards a new expanded and integrative agenda. The process of re-mythologizing involves surfacing the founding or origin on which the culture is based and reviving those myths of founding for their subsequent re-interpretation to reflect current realities rather than out-moded and/or destructive ones. The primary focus is not on the wholesale discarding of myths but rather on the recommitment to a revitalized myth which is more rewarding and beneficial for all concerned. One can posit that this process is one which is needed on a large scale throughout our society as it seeks to deal with the problems, threats and challenges of modern technology. We need to retain the positive aspects of prior history which is contained within the traditional cultural and corporate myths of innovation and transform them into a new mythology which embraces social as well as technological progress in a fruitful way. One might also ask—who will guide this process of re-mythologizing? Would it only become a potent vehicle for the reinforcement of existing privileges and interests? As we have seen, this process of surfacing basic assumptions and reformulating directions has been initiated to some degree by those self-appointed watchdogs in the environmental sphere. Working from outside, these public interest groups have indeed demonstrated significant influence in changing the course of corporate decisionmaking to include consideration of the effects of their products on the health of individuals and the environment (Nader, Brownstein, & Richard, 1981). However, we have also seen in the course of this chapter that working against organizations from the outside also results in defensive adversarial relationships which lead to short-term gains and animosity among the parties. To achieve proactive and more positive outcomes, the mode of engagement which offers the most potential is one which stresses collaboration rather than confrontation.

To guide such a course, it is here that perhaps organizational scientists can be of much use as ones who share the interests and concerns of both camps. There are two fundamental tasks for organizational scientists in facilitating innovation. The first is *researching* the process of innovative change for a better understanding of its foundations, dynamics and outcomes. The second task is *assisting* organizational decisionmakers to work with the process of innovation in a more beneficial way for all concerned. It is as the reflective enablers of change that organizational scientists can work *with* rather than *against* organizations to achieve a balanced perspective on the role of innovation in organizations and in society. However, given the major arguments of this chapter, a fundamental characteristic of successful organizational scientists is that they are not only technical experts but also possess an understanding of the nature of the political dynamics that are involved in the innovation process.

To facilitate the inclusion of social goals in innovation, we can assist in the recapturing of the vision of a non-dominator approach to innovation which reflects the holistic inter-relationship between nature and humankind for the present and for the future. In a world which is growing increasingly interrelated and chaotic (Gleick, 1987), organizational management needs to abandon mechanistic-technological assumptions about the role they and organizations play in society. As Vaill (1989) observes, absolute managerial control is not possible in a world which more closely resembles turbulent "permanent white water." In turn, organizational science needs to learn new ways to engage in research which is both diverse, self-reflective and politically aware in order to assist organizational management to navigate through this turbulence. For without self-reflectiveness, one compromises one's ability to question fundamental assumptions thereby risking uncritical acceptance of traditional assumptions (Quinn, 1988; Torbert, 1987).

Does this mean that all technological innovation must be stopped? (Assuming this was possible, in the first place.) Emphatically the answer is NO! We need new technology to guide us out of our current technological problems, not by unilaterally laying over more technological fixes (a response, as Perrow's "normal accidents" illustrate, which may have significant harmful consequences) but rather by using these in concert with social programs which would address the fundamental problems involved. The positive benefits of innovation have been numerous and promise to assist in this agenda for social progress. What is needed is a return from our detour into a strictly technocratic interpretation of the role of innovation in society for an incorporation of the lessons learned there to forward a more holistic approach to change.

> The way to solve the conflict between human values and technological needs is not to run away from technology. That's impossible. The way to resolve the conflict is to break down the barriers of dualistic thought that prevents a real understanding of what technology is—not an exploitation of nature, but a fusion of nature and the human spirit into a new kind of creation that transcends both (Pirsig, 1974, pp. 261–262).

Innovation is a central process in the journeys humankind undertake on this planet. We have argued that innovation is a political process and thus can be more fully understood as such. It is also a process that has consequences, which when not evaluated systematically, systemically and reflectively, can lead to a diminished quality of life for all. It is a worthy arena, in our view, for the attention of the best minds in organizational science. They have a contribution to make. We also have much to learn. We believe that our models of organization and our methods of investigation will likely be found wanting in some aspects as we tackle the concept of innovation in its fullest meaning. That is all to the good. *We* will be forced to innovate and in so doing, the iterations between the practice of our craft and this domain of inquiry may serve to significantly enhance our understanding, practice of and benefits from the innovative process.

ACKNOWLEDGMENTS

We would like to express our sincere appreciation to Larry Cummings, Mike Cavanaugh, Dev Jennings, Craig Pinder and Barry Staw for their thoughtful contributions to the preparation of this manuscript.

NOTES

1. See Rogers (1983) and Rogers and Shoemaker (1971) for the definitive work on the diffusion of innovations.
2. Note that Rogers (1983) and Zaltman, Duncan and Holbek (1973) propose that there are

two stages in the innovation process: (1) initiation (information gathering, conceptualizing and planning for adoption); and (2) implementation (putting an innovation into use).

3. Evan and Black (1967) suggest that the adoption of innovation differs on the product—administration process dimension. Daft's (1978) "dual core" model of directionality of the adoption process has also received significant confirmation by others (Aiken, Bacharach & French, 1980; Damanpour, 1987; Kimberly & Evanisko, 1981; Meyer & Goes, 1988; and others).

4. The degree to which an innovation is *perceived* to be either an incremental or radical change to existing organizational processes impacts on the duration and nature of the implementation stage. Both types of innovation are necessary for long-term organizational success, however, it remains a debatable point whether managerial implementation strategy and/or organizational structure should be different depending on the degree of innovation radicalness. For both sides of the debate, see Nord and Tucker (1987), Ettlie, Bridges and O'Keefe (1984), Freeman (1982), Gobeli and Brown (1987), Knight (1967), Wilson (1966).

5. Organic organizational structures are generally perceived as instrumental in promoting innovation (Aiken & Hage, 1971; Burns & Stalker, 1968; Cummings, 1965; Kanter, 1983, 1988; Shepard, 1967; Thompson, 1965) whereas mechanistic-bureaucratic structures are beneficial during the adoption and implementation stages (Daft, 1982; Nord & Tucker, 1987; Pierce & Delbecq, 1977; Rogers, 1983; Sapolsky, 1967; Wilson, 1966; Zaltman et al., 1973).

Communication as the acquisition, channeling and utilization of internal and external information is regarded as instrumental to the innovation process. For studies on communication patterns, networks and roles (information gatekeepers), see Allen (1977), Becker (1970), Ebadi and Utterback (1984), Fidler and Johnson (1984), Keller and Holland (1978, 1983), Tushman (1977), Roberts (1988).

The impact of the organizational environment and product life cycle on the innovation process has been studied by Meyers and Marquis (1969), Moore and Tushman (1982), Strebel (1987), Utterback and Abernathy (1975).

6. Causes for innovation failure have been attributed to managerial mistakes in assessing market needs and problems (Gobeli & Brown, 1987; Myers & Sweezy, 1978; Utterback et al., 1976). However, the most extensive comparative study of product innovation successes and failures was Project SAPPHO which found that accurate communication and key individuals (sponsors, champions and gatekeepers) rather than organizational structural or process variables were the keys to innovation success (Freeman, 1982).

7. Prescriptions for engendering innovation generally focus on enhancing communication within organic organizational structures coupled with the development of an organizational culture which supports rather than resists innovation and change (Delbecq & Mills, 1985; Feldman, 1988; Galbraith, 1982; Kanter, 1983, 1988; Kasper, 1986; Kimberly, 1980; Knight, 1967; Quinn, 1979, 1985; Sayles, 1974; Souder, 1988; Van de Ven, 1980a, 1980b).

8. A number of these cases draw from and build on previous analyses contained in Frost and Egri (1988, 1990b, 1990c) and Egri and Frost (1989).

9. The range of political strategies and tactics employed in the previous section's case studies of innovation plus others in the literature (notably from Pinchot, 1985; Kanter, 1983; Nayak & Ketteringham, 1986) form the foundation for these propositions. However, it should be noted that not all cases within each category of innovation type and success/failure exhibited the same set of political tactics. A more extensive list of cases and tactics can be found in Egri and Frost, 1989 and Frost and Egri, 1988.

10. The uncritical acceptance of a theologically inspired conceptualization of the relationship between man and nature is elaborated on by Toynbee (1972, p. 142) who states:

" . . . in combatting intolerance and violence, the pioneers of the "Enlightenment" were not challenging the Christian doctrine about the relations between God, man, and nature.

This doctrine is enunciated in one sentence within one verse in the Bible. "Be fruitful and multiply and replenish the Earth and subdue it" (Genesis, i, 28)."

11. As Gillingham reports (1978, p. 93), given the continuation of current agricultural practices: "By the year 2000, twenty-five percent of all the energy consumed in the world in 1973 will be required just to produce nitrogen fertilizer. Soil depletion in the form of microbial life, nitrate and salt accumulation and loss of organic matter and plant nutrients are other factors which often accompany present practices."

12. Of the 1200 seed patents issued in the United States, over half are held by subsidiaries of only 15 companies (Doyle, 1985, p. 311).

REFERENCES

Aiken, M., Bacharach, S. B., & French, J. L. (1980). Organizational structure, work process, and proposal making in administrative bureaucracies. *Academy of Management Journal, 23*(4), 631–652.

Aiken, M., & Hage, J. (1971). The organic organization and innovation. *Sociology, 5,* 63–82.

Allen, T. J. (1977). *Managing the flow of technology.* Cambridge, MA: MIT Press.

Amabile, T. M. (1988). A model of creativity and innovation in organizations. In L. L. Cummings & B. M. Staw (Eds.), *Research in Organizational Behavior,* Greenwich, CT: JAI Press, *10,* 123–167.

Ansari, M. A., & Kapoor, A. (1987). Organizational context and upward influence tactics. *Organizational Behavior and Human Decision Processes, 40,* 39–49.

Argyris, C., & Schon, D. A. (1978). *Organizational learning: A theory of action perspective.* Reading, MA: Addison-Wesley.

Astley, W. G., & Sachdeva, P. S. (1984). Structural sources of intraorganizational power: A theoretical synthesis. *Academy of Management Review, 9,* 104–113.

Astley, W. G., & Van de Ven, A. H. (1983). Central perspectives and debates in organizational theory. *Administrative Science Quarterly, 23,* 245–273.

Bachrach, P., & Baratz, M. S. (1970). *Power and poverty: Theory and practice.* New York: Oxford University Press.

Baldridge, J. V. (1971). *Power and conflict in the university.* New York: John Wiley.

Bardach, E. (1977). *The implementation game: What happens after a bill becomes a law.* Cambridge, MA: The MIT Press.

Barnard, C. (1938). *The functions of the executive.* Cambridge, MA: President and fellows of Harvard University.

Bateson, G. (1972). *Steps to an ecology of mind.* New York: Ballantine.

Becker, M. G. (1970). Sociometric location and innovativeness: Reformulation and extension of the diffusion model. *American Sociological Review, 35*(2), 267–282.

Becker, S. W., & Whisler, T. L. (1967). The innovative organization: A selective view of current theory and research. *Journal of Business, 40,* 446–469.

Benbrook, C. M., & Moses, P. B. (1986). Engineering crops to resist herbicides. *Technology Review, 89*(8), 54–61+.

Benson, I., & Lloyd, J. (1983). *New technology and industrial change: The impact of the Scientific-technical revolution on labour and industry.* New York: Nichols.

Betz, F. S. (1988). Genetically engineered microbial pesticides: Regulatory program of the Environmental Protection Agency and a scientific risk assessment case history. In P. A. Hedin, J. J. Menn, R. M. Hollingworth (Eds.), *Biotechnology for crop protection,* Washington, D.C.: American Chemical Society, 437–449.

Blau, J. R., & McKinley, W. (1979). Ideas, complexity, and innovation. *Administrative Science Quarterly, 24,* 200–219.

Boisjoly, R. P., Curtis, E. F., & Mellican, E. (1989). Roger Boisjoly and the Challenger disaster: The ethical dimensions. *Journal of Business Ethics, 8,* 271–230.

Boulding, K. E. (1989). *Three faces of power.* Newbury Park, CA: Sage.

Brass, D. J. (1984). Being in the right place: A structural analysis of individual influence in an organization. *Administrative Science Quarterly, 29,* 518–539.

Bright, James R. (1964). *Research, development, and technological innovation: An introduction.* Homewood, Ill.: Richard D. Irwin.

Brimm, I. M. (1988). Risky business: Why sponsoring innovations may be hazardous to career health. *Organizational Dynamics, 17* (Winter), 28–41.

Brown, R. H. (1978). Bureaucracy as praxis: Toward a political phenomenology of formal organizations. *Administrative Science Quarterly, 23,* 365–382.

Burawoy, M. (1979). *Manufacturing consent: Changes in the labor process under monopoly capitalism.* Chicago: The University of Chicago Press.

Burke, J. (1989). "Goodbye Descartes! Information and change." A public lecture by James Burke, October 1, 1989, Vancouver, B.C., Canada.

Burns, T., & Stalker, G. M. (1968). *The management of innovation* (2nd Edition). London: Tavistock.

Carroll, J. (1967). A note on departmental autonomy and innovation in medical school. *Journal of Business, 40,* 531–534.

Chakrabarti, A. K. (1974). The role of champion in product innovation. *California Management Review, 17*(2), 58–62.

Chomsky, N. (1988). *Language and politics.* Cheektowaga, NY: Black Rose Books.

Clegg, S. (1981). Organization and control. *Administrative Science Quarterly, 26,* 545–562.

Commoner, B. (1978). Freedom and the ecological imperative: Beyond the poverty of power. In R. C. Dorf & Y. L. Hunter (Eds.), *Appropriate Visions: Technology, the environment and the individual.* San Francisco: Boyd & Fraser, 11–49.

Conrad, C. (1983). Organizational power: Faces and symbolic forms. In L. Putnam & M. Pacanowsky (Eds.) *Communication and organizations: An interpretive approach.* Beverly Hills, CA: Sage, 173–194.

Corwin, R. G. (1972). Strategies for organizational innovation: An empirical comparison. *American Sociological Review, 37*(3), 441–454.

Cox, L. A. (1976). Industrial innovation: The role of people and cost factors. *Research Management, 14*(2), 29–32.

Crozier, M., & Friedberg, E. (1980). *Actors and systems.* Chicago: University of Chicago Press.

Culbert, S. A., & McDonough, J. J. (1985). *Radical management.* New York: The Free Press.

Cummings, L. L. (1965). Organizational climates for creativity. *Academy of Management Journal, 8* (3), 220–227.

Cummings, T. (1984). Transorganizational development. In L. L. Cummings & B. M. Staw (Eds.), *Research in Organizational Behavior,* Greenwich, CT: JAI Press, *6,* 367–422.

Cyert, R. M., & March, J. G. (1963). *A behavioral theory of the firm.* Englewood Cliffs, NJ: Prentice-Hall.

Daft, R. L. (1978). A dual-core model of organizational innovation. *Academy of Management Journal, 21*(2), 193–210.

Daft, R. L. (1982). Bureaucratic versus nonbureaucratic structure and the process of innovation and change. In S. R. Bacharach (Ed.), *Research in the Sociology of Organizations,* Greenwich, CT: JAI Press, *1,* 129–166.

Daft, R. L. (1983). *Organizational theory and design.* St. Paul, MN: West.

Daft, R. L., & Bradshaw, P. J. (1980). The process of horizontal differentiation: Two models. *Administrative Science Quarterly, 25*(3), 441–456.

Daft, R. J., & Huber, G. P. (1987). How organizations learn: A communications framework. In S. R. Bacharach (Ed.), *Research in the Sociology of Organizations*, Greenwich, CT: JAI Press, 5, 1–36.

Dahl, R. (1957). The concept of power. *Behavioral Science, 2,* 201–215.

Damanpour, F. (1987). The adoption of technological, administrative, and ancillary innovations: Impact of organizational factors. *Journal of Management, 13*(4), 675–688.

Damanpour, F., & Evan, W. M. (1984). Organizational innovation and performance: The problem of "organizational lag." *Administrative Science Quarterly 29,* 392–409.

Deal, T. E., & Kennedy, A. A. (1982). *Corporate cultures.* Reading, MA: Addison-Wesley.

deBresson, C. (1987). *Understanding technological change.* Montreal, Quebec: Black Rose Books.

Deetz, S. (1985). Critical-cultural research: New sensibilities and old realities. *Journal of Management, 11*(2), 121–136.

Delbecq, A. L., & Mills, P. K. (1985). Managerial practices that enhance innovation. *Organizational Dynamics, 14* (Summer), 24–34.

Devall, B., & Sessions, G. (1985). *Deep ecology: living as if nature mattered.* Salt Lake City, Utah: Peregrine Smith Books.

Douglas, M., & Wildavsky, A. (1982). *Risk and culture: An essay on the selection of technological and environmental dangers.* Los Angeles: University of California Press.

Downs, G. W., Jr., & Mohr, L. B. (1976). Conceptual issues in the study of innovation. *Administrative Science Quarterly, 21,* 700–714.

Doyle, J. (1985). *Altered harvest: Agriculture, genetics, and the fate of the world's food supply.* New York: Penguin Books.

Dvorak, A., Merrick, N. L., Dealey, W. L., & Ford, G. C. (1936). *Typewriting behavior: Psychology applied to teaching and learning typewriting.* New York: American Book Company.

Ebadi, Y. M., & Utterback, J. M. (1984). The effects of communication on technological innovation. *Management Science, 30*(5), 572–585.

Egri, C. P., & Frost, P. J. (1989). Threats to innovation; roadblocks to implementation: The politics of the productive process. In M. C. Jackson, P. Keys, & S. A. Cropper (Eds.) *Operational research and the social sciences,* New York: Plenum, 585–590.

Ettlie, J. E., Bridges, W. P., & O'Keefe, R. D. (1984). Organizational strategy and structural differences for radical versus incremental innovation. *Management Science, 30*(6), 682–695.

Evan, W. M., & Black, G. (1967). Innovation in business organizations: Some factors associated with success or failure of staff proposals. *Journal of Business, 40,* 519–530.

Feldman, S. P. (1988). How organizational culture can affect innovation. *Organizational Dynamics, 17* (Summer), 57–68.

Fidler, L. A., & Johnson, J. D. (1984). Communication and innovation implementation. *Academy of Management Review, 9*(4), 704–711.

Flowers, B. S. (Ed.) (1988). *Joseph Campbell with Bill Moyers: The power of myth.* New York: Doubleday.

Freeman, C. (1982). *The economics of industrial innovation*. (Second edition). London: Frances Pinter.

Frost, P. J. (1987). Power, politics and influence. In F. M. Jablin, L. L. Putnam, K. H. Roberts, & L. W. Porter (Eds.), *Handbook of Organizational Communication*, Beverly Hills, CA: Sage, 503–548.

Frost, P. J. (1988). The role of organizational power & politics in human resource management. In A. Nedd, G. R. Ferris & K. M. Rowland (Eds.), *International human resources management*, Greenwich, CT: JAI Press.

Frost, P. J., & Egri, C. P. (1988). Is it better to ask for forgiveness than to seek permission? The influence of current and past political action on innovation in organizations. Paper presented at the National Academy of Management Meetings, Anaheim, California, August 1988.

Frost, P. J., & Egri, C. P. (1990a). Appreciating executive action. In S. Srivastva, D. L. Cooperrider and Associates, *Appreciative management and leadership: The power of positive thought and action in organizations*, San Francisco: Jossey-Bass, 289–322.

Frost, P. J., & Egri, C. P. (1990b). Influence of political action on innovation. Part I. *Leadership and Organization Development Journal, 11*(1), 17–25, Bradford, England: MCB University Press.

Frost, P. J., & Egri, C. P. (1990c). Influence of political action on innovation. Part II. *Leadership and Organization Development Journal, 11*(2), 4–12, Bradford, England: MCB University Press.

Frost, P. J., Moore, L. F., Louis, M. R., Lundberg, C. C., & Martin J. (Eds.) (1985). *Organizational culture*. Beverly Hills, CA: Sage.

Fujimoto, I. (1978). The values of appropriate technology and vision for a saner world. In R. C. Dorf & Y. L. Hunter, (Eds.), *Appropriate visions: technology, the environment and the individual*. San Francisco: Boyd & Fraser, 170–176.

Galbraith, J. R. (1982). Designing the innovating organization. *Organizational Dynamics, 11* (Winter), 5–25.

Giddens, A. (1981). *A contemporary critique of historial materialism*. London: MacMillan.

Gilfillan, S. C. (1935). *The sociology of invention*. Cambridge, MA: The MIT Press.

Gillingham, P. (1978). Appropriate agriculture. In R. C. Dorf & Y. L. Hunter, (Eds.), *Appropriate visions: Technology, the environment and the individual*. San Francisco: Boyd & Fraser, 92–105.

Gleick, J. (1987). *Chaos: Making a new science*. New York: Penguin Books.

Globe, S., Levy, G. W., & Schwartz, C. M. (1973). Key factors and events in the innovation process. *Research Management, 16*(4), 8–15.

Gobeli, D. H., & Brown, D. J. (1987). Analyzing product innovations. *Research Management, 30*(4), 25–31.

Gray, B., & Hay, T. M. (1986). Political limits to interorganizational consensus and change. *Journal of Applied Behavioral Science, 22*(2), 95–112.

Graziano, A. M. (1969). Clinical innovation and the mental health power structure: A social case history, *American Psychologist, 24*(1), 10–18.

Guth, W. D., & Macmillan, I. E. (1986). Strategy implementation versus middle management self-interest. *Strategic Management Journal, 7*, 313–327.

Hage, J., & Dewar, R. (1973). Elite values versus organizational structure in predicting innovation, *Administrative Science Quarterly, 18*, 279–290.

Hayes, R. H., & Abernathy, W. J. (1980). Managing our way to economic decline. *Harvard Business Review, 58* (July-August), 67–77.

Hickson, D. J., Butler, R. J., Cray, D., Mallory, G. R., & Wilson, D. C. (1986). *Top decisions: Strategic decision-making in organizations*. San Francisco: Jossey-Bass.

Hickson, D. J., Hinings, C. R., Lee, C. A., Schneck, R. J., & Pennings, J. J. (1971). A strategic contingencies theory of intraorganizational power. *Administrative Science Quarterly, 16,* 216–229.

Hill, I. D. (1987). An intrapreneur—turned—entrepreneur compares both worlds. *Research Management, 30*(4), 33–37.

Hill, S., & Ott, P. (Eds.) (1982). *Basic technics in ecological farming. Papers presented at the 2nd International Conference held by IFOAM. Montreal, October 1–5, 1978.* Boston, MA: Birkhauser Verlag.

Howell, J. M., & Higgins, C. A. (1988). Personality characteristics, leader behaviors, and influence strategies of champions of technological innovations. Working Paper, The University of Western Ontario, Canada.

Huxley, A. (1946). *Science, liberty and peace.* New York: Harper.

Jackson, W., Berry, W., & Colman, B. (Eds.) (1984). *Meeting the expectations of the land: Essays in sustainable agriculture and stewardship.* San Francisco, CA: North Point Press.

Jelinek, M. (1979). *Institutionalizing innovation: A study of organizational learning systems.* New York: Praeger.

Kanter, R. M. (1983). *The change masters.* New York: Simon & Schuster.

Kanter, R. M. (1988). When a thousand flowers bloom: Structural, collective, and social conditions for innovation in organization. In L. L. Cummings & B. M. Staw (Eds.), *Research in Organizational Behavior,* Greenwich, CT: JAI Press, *10,* 169–211.

Kasper, H. (1986). Organisational-cultural aspects of the promotion of a favourable climate for innovation. In H. Hubner (Eds.), *The art and science of innovation management,* Amsterdam: Elsevier, 47–58.

Keller, R. T., & Holland, W. E. (1978). Individual characteristics of innovativeness and communication in research and development organizations. *Journal of Applied Psychology, 63*(6), 759–762.

Keller, R. T., & Holland, W. E. (1983). Communicators and innovators in research and development organizations. *Academy of Management Journal, 26,* 742–749.

Kelley, G. (1976). Seducing the elites: The politics of decision making and innovation in organizational networks, *Academy of Management Review, 1*(3), 66–74.

Kenney, M. (1986). *Biotechnology: The university-industrial complex.* New Haven, CT: Yale University Press.

Kidder, T. (1981). *The soul of a new machine.* New York: Avon Books.

Kimberly, J. R. (1980). Managerial innovation. In P. C. Nystrom & W. H. Starbuck (Eds.), *Handbook of organizational design,* New York: Oxford University Press, 84–104.

Kimberly, J. R. (1987). Organizational and contextual influences on the diffusion of technological innovation. In J. M. Pennings & A. Buttendam (Eds.), *New technology as organization innovation: The development and diffusion of microelectronics,* Cambridge, MA: Ballinger 237–259.

Kimberly, J. R., & Evanisko, M. J. (1981). Organizational innovation: The influence of individual, organization, and contextual factors on hospital adoption of technological and administrative innovations. *Academy of Management Journal, 24*(4), 689–713.

Kingston, W. (1977). *Innovation: The creative impulse in human progress: Industry—art—science.* London: John Calder.

Kipnis, D., Schmidt, S. M. & Wilkinson, I. (1980). Intraorganizational influence tactics: Explorations in getting one's way. *Journal of Applied Psychology, 65*(4), 440–452.

Kloppenburg, J., Jr., & Kleinman, D. L. (1987). Seeds of struggle: The geopolitics of genetic resources. *Technology Review, 90*(2), 47–62.

Knight, K. E. (1967). A descriptive model of the intra-firm innovation process. *Journal of Business, 41*, 478–496.

LeVeen, E. P. (1978). The prospects for small-scale farming in an industrial society: A critical appraisal of "Small is Beautiful." In R. C. Dorf & Y. L. Hunter (Eds.), *Appropriate visions: Technology, the environment and the individual*. San Francisco: Boyd & Fraser, 106–125.

Li, Y. T. (1980). *Technological innovation in education and industry*. New York: Van Nostrand Reinhold.

Lukes, S. (1974). *Power: A radical view*. London: Macmillan.

Lundberg, C. C. (1989). On organizational learning: Implications and opportunities for expanding organizational development. In R. W. Woodman & W. A. Pasmore (Eds.), *Research in Organizational Change and Development*, Greenwich, CT: JAI Press, *3*, 61–82.

McClintick, D. (1982). Boardroom politics at Wall Street and Vine. *Esquire*, September, 41–56.

McWhinney, W., & Batista, R. (1988). How remythologizing can revitalize organizations. *Organizational Dynamics, 17* (Autumn), 46–58.

Maidique, M. A. (1980). Entrepreneurs, champions, and technological innovation. *Sloan Management Review, 21*(2), 59–76.

Mansfield, E. (1971). *Technological change*. New York: W. W. Norton.

Marquis, D. G. (1972). The anatomy of successful innovations. *Managing Advancing Technology*, 1, 35–48.

Marx, L. (1987). Does improved technology mean progress? *Technology Review, 90*(1), 32–41, 71.

Meyer, A. D., & Goes, J. B. (1988). Organizational assimilation of innovations: A multilevel contextual analysis. *Academy of Management Journal, 31*(4), 897–923.

Meyers, S., & Marquis, D. G. (1969). *Successful industrial innovations*. National Science Foundation, NSF 64–17, Washington, D.C.

Mintzberg, H. (1983). *Power in and around organizations*. Englewood Cliffs, NJ: Prentice-Hall.

Mitroff, I. I. (1983). *Stakeholders of the organizational mind*. San Francisco: Jossey-Bass.

Moch, M. K., & Morse, E. V. (1977). Size, centralization and organizational adoption of innovations. *American Sociological Review, 42*(5), 716–725.

Mohr, L. B. (1969). Determinants of innovation in organizations. *American Political Science Review, 63*(1), 111–126.

Moore, W. L., & Tushman, M. L. (1982). Managing innovation over the product life cycle. In M. Tushman & W. L. Moore, (Eds.), *Readings in the management of innovation*. Boston, MA: Pitman, 131–150.

Morgan, G. (1988). *Riding the waves of change: Developing managerial competencies for a turbulent world*. San Francisco, CA: Jossey-Bass.

Myers, S., & Sweezy, E. E. (1978). Why innovations fail. *Technology Review, 80*(5), 40–46.

Nader, R., Brownstein, R., & Richard, J. (Eds.) (1981). *Who's poisoning America: Corporate polluters and their victims in the chemical age*. San Francisco: Sierra Club Books.

Nayak, P. R., & Ketteringham, J. M. (1986). *Break-throughs!* New York: Rawson Associates.

Needham, J. (1964). Science and society in East and West. In M. Goldsmith & A. Mackay (Eds.), *The science of science: Society in the technological age*. London: Souvenir Press, 127–149.

Nelkin, D. (Ed.) (1984). *Controversy: Politics of technical decisions*. (2nd Edition), Beverly Hills, CA: Sage.

Noble, D. F. (1984). *Forces of production*. New York: Knopf.

Nord, W. R. & Tucker, S. (1987). *Implementing routine and radical innovations*. Lexington, MA: Lexington Books.

Nutt, P. C. (1986). Tactics of implementation. *Academy of Management Journal, 29*(2), 230–261.

O'Day, R. (1974). Intimidation rituals: Reactions to reform. *Journal of Applied Behavioral Science, 10,* 373–338.

Parkinson, R. (1972). The Dvorak simplified keyboard: Forty years of frustration. *Computers and Automation, 21*(11), 18–25.

Pelz, D. C. (1983). Quantitative case histories of urban innovations: Are there innovating stages? *IEEE Transactions on Engineering Management, EM-30*(2), 60–67.

Pelz, D. C., & Munson, F. C. (1982). Originality level and the innovating process in organizations. *Human Systems Management, 3,* 173–187.

Perrow, C. (1984). *Normal accidents: Living with high-risk technologies.* New York: Basic Books.

Peters, T. J. (1987). *Thriving on chaos: Handbook for a management revolution.* New York: Alfred A. Knopf.

Peters, T. J., & Waterman, R. M. (1982). *In search of excellence.* New York: Harper and Row.

Pettigrew, A. M. (1972). Information control as a power source. *Sociology, 6,* 187–204.

Pettigrew, A. M. (1985). *The awakening giant.* New York: Basil Blackwell.

Pfeffer, J. (1981a). Management as symbolic action: The creation and maintenance of organizational paradigms. In L. L. Cummings & B. M. Staw (Eds.), *Research in Organizational Behavior,* Greenwich, CT: JAI Press, *3,* 1–52.

Pfeffer, J. (1981b). *Power in organizations.* Marshfield, MA: Pitman.

Pierce, J. L., & Delbecq, A. L. (1977). Organization structure, individual attitudes and innovation. *Academy of Management Review, 2* (1), 27–37.

Pinchot, J. III (1985). *Intrapreneuring.* New York: Harper and Row.

Pirsig, R. M. (1974). *Zen and the art of motorcycle maintenance: An inquiry into values.* New York: Bantam Books.

Porter, L. W., Allen, R. W., & Angle, H. L. (1981). The politics of upward influence in organizations. In L. L. Cummings & B. M. Staw (Eds.), *Research in Organizational Behavior,* Greenwich, CT: JAI Press, *3,* 109–149.

Pressman, J. L., & Wildavsky, A. (1973). *Implementation: How great expectations in Washington are dashed in Oakland: or, Why it's amazing that federal programs work at all.* Berkeley, CA: University of California Press.

Quinn, J. B. (1979). Technological innovation, entrepreneurship, and strategy. *Sloan Management Review, 20*(3), 19–30.

Quinn, J. B. (1985). Managing innovation: Controlled chaos. *Harvard Business Review,* May-June, 73–84.

Quinn, R. E. (1988). *Beyond rational management: Mastering the paradoxes and competing demands of high performance.* San Francisco: Jossey-Bass.

Ranson, S., Hinings, B., & Greenwood, R. (1980). The structuring of organizational structures. *Administrative Science Quarterly, 25,* 1–17.

Reppy, J. (1984). The automobile air bag. In D. Nelkin (Ed.), *Controversy: Politics of technical decisions.* (2nd Edition), Beverly Hills, CA: Sage.

Roberts, E. B. (1988). Managing invention and innovation. *Research Management, 31*(1), 11–29.

Roberts, N. C. (1986). Organizational power styles: Collective and competitive power under varying organizational conditions. *The Journal of Applied Behavioral Science, 22*(4), 443–458.

Rogers, E. M. (1983). *Diffusion of innovations.* (Third edition). New York: The Free Press.

Rogers, E. M., & Shoemaker, F. F. (1971). *Communication of innovations.* New York: The Free Press.

Rothwell, R., Freeman, C., Horsley, A., Jervis, V.T.P., Robertson, A. B., & Townsend, J. (1974). SAPPHO updated-project SAPPHO phase II. *Research Policy, 3.*

Rowe, L. A., & Boise, W. B. (1974). Organizational innovation: Current research and evolving concepts. *Public Administration Review, 34* (May/June), 284–293.

Sapolsky, H. M. (1967). Organizational structure and innovation. *Journal of Business, 40,* 497–510.

Sayles, L. R. (1974). The innovation process: An organizational analysis. *Journal of Management Studies, 11,* 190–204.

Schein, E. H. (1987). *Organizational culture and leadership.* San Francisco: Jossey-Bass.

Schilit, W. K., & Locke, E. A. (1982). A study of upward influence in organizations. *Administrative Science Quarterly, 27,* 304–316.

Schneider, K. (1986). Biotech's stalled revolution. *The New York Times Magazine,* 16 November, 42+.

Schneider, K. (1989). Fear of chemicals is turning farmers to biological pesticides. *The New York Times,* 11 June, Sec. 1, 12 Y.

Schon, D. A. (1963). Champions for radical new inventions. *Harvard Business Review, 41*(2), 77–86.

Schon, D. A. (1967). *Technology and change: The new Heraclitus.* New York: Pergamon Press.

Schumacher, E. F. (1973). *Small is beautiful: A study of economics as if people mattered.* London: Cox & Wyman Ltd.

Shepard, H. A. (1967). Innovation-resisting and innovation-producing organizations. *Journal of Business, 40,* 470–477.

Shrivastava, P. (1983). A typology of organizational learning systems. *Journal of Management Studies, 20*(1), 7–28.

Smith, J. J., McKeon, J. E., Hoy, K. L., Boysen, R. L., Shechter, L., & Roberts, E. B. (1984). Lessons from 10 case studies in innovation—I. *Research Management, 27*(5), 23–27.

Sonnenfeld, J. (1988). *The hero's farewell: What happens when CEOs retire.* New York: Oxford University Press.

Souder, W. E. (1988). *Managing new product innovations.* Lexington, MA: Lexington Books.

Strebel, P. (1987). Organizing for innovation over an industry cycle. *Strategic Management Journal, 8,* 117–124.

Thompson, J. D. (1967). *Organizations in action.* New York: McGraw-Hill.

Thompson, V. A. (1965). Bureaucracy and innovation. *Administrative Science Quarterly, 10*(1), 1–20.

Torbert, W. R. (1987). *Managing the corporate dream: Restructuring for long-term success.* Homewood, Ill.: Dow Jones-Irwin.

Toynbee, A. (1972). The religious background of the present environmental crisis: A viewpoint. *International Journal of Environmental Studies, 3,* 141–146.

Tushman, M. L. (1977). Special boundary roles in the innovation process. *Administrative Science Quarterly, 22,* 587–605.

Tushman, M. L., & Katz, R. (1980). External communication and project performance: An investigation into the role of gatekeepers. *Management Science, 26*(11), 1071–1085.

Utterback, J. M. (1974). Innovation in industry and the diffusion of technology. *Science, 183,* 658–662.

Utterback, J. M., & Abernathy, W. J. (1975), A dynamic model of process and product innovation. *Omega, 3*(6), 639–656.

Utterback, J. M., Allen, T. J., Hollomon, J. H., & Sirbu, M. A., Jr. (1976). The process of innovation in five industries in Europe and Japan. *IEEE Transactions on Engineering Management,* EM-23(1), 3–9.

Vaill, P. B. (1989). *Managing as a performing art: New ideas for a world of chaotic change.* San Francisco, CA: Jossey-Bass.

Van de Ven, A. H. (1980a). Problem solving, planning, and innovation. Part I. Test of the program planning model. *Human Relations, 33*(10), 711–740.

Van de Ven, A. H. (1980b). Problem solving, planning, and innovation. Part II. Speculations for theory and practice. *Human Relations, 33*(11), 757–779.

Van de Ven, A. H. (1986). Central problems in the management of innovation. *Management Science, 32*(5), 590–607.

van der Post, L. (1965). *The heart of the hunter.* London: Penguin Books.

Van Maanen, J. & Schein, E. (1979). Towards a theory of organizational socialization. In B. Staw (Ed.), *Research in Organizational Behavior,* Greenwich, CT: JAI Press, *1,* 209–264.

Weick, K. E. (1984). Small wins. *American Psychologist, 39*(1), 40–49.

Wilkinson, B. (1983). *The shopfloor politics of new technology.* London: Heinemann.

Wilson, J. Q. (1966). Innovation in organization: Notes toward a theory. In J. D. Thompson (Ed.), *Approaches to organizational design,* Pittsburgh, PA: University of Pittsburgh Press.

Yin, R. K. (1977). Production efficiency versus bureaucratic self-interest: Two innovative processes? *Policy Sciences, 8,* 381–399.

Zakreski, D. (1989). Growing pains. *Canadian Business,* August, 37–41.

Zaltman, G., Duncan, R., & Holbek, J. (1973). *Innovations and organizations.* New York: Wiley.

THE RISE OF TRAINING PROGRAMS IN FIRMS AND AGENCIES:

AN INSTITUTIONAL PERSPECTIVE

W. Richard Scott and John W. Meyer

ABSTRACT

While previous approaches to training programs in firms and agencies have emphasized their consequences for individuals and organizations, this paper explores the determinants of such programs. Training programs are viewed as a sub-form of a more general institutional pattern, instruction, that includes both education and training. Similarities and differences between these patterns are discussed. Four general types of explanations are offered to account for the growing size, expanding content, and the structural controls that characterize training programs in organizations. Training programs are explained, variously, by *technical* views emphasizing the increasing complexity of tasks performed by workers and managers; by *social control* arguments that stress that, on the one hand, organizations gain control from having participants internalize com-

Research in Organizational Behavior, Volume 13, pages 297–326.
Copyright © 1991 by JAI Press Inc.
All rights of reproduction in any form reserved.
ISBN: 1-55938-198-1

mitments while, at the same time, participants who gain control over organizational resources demand training benefits; by *polity* arguments noting that training is viewed as a right of membership and a requisite for movement to elite positions; as well as by more specific institutional arguments. One cluster of these arguments stresses the role of *institutional agencies,* collective actors, such as agencies of the state or professional associations, that promulgate rules or standards encouraging organizations to provide training. A second cluster emphasizes *institutional processes* which point to the effects of increasingly widespread beliefs about the desirability if not the necessity of training in modern organizations. As such beliefs become more prevalent, organization-specific predictors of training are weakened.

INTRODUCTION

Modern organizations contain all sorts of components beyond those once considered essential. There are specialized structures to manage safety, environmental impacts, personnel benefits, research, and many other functions.

Training programs in employment organizations are a prevalent structural feature that has been neglected by organizational sociologists. Such programs were once rare but are now very common. They were once limited in scope, but now cover many sorts of training—from remedial education to technical job skills to very broad human relations and management training. Organizations devote substantial resources to the training of personnel. Setting aside informal training, which occurs in all work contexts, and even excluding the semi-formalized practices of on-the-job and apprenticeship training—types of training that are clearly the dominant mode within organizations[1]—formal training is very extensive and is growing in magnitude.

In this paper, we examine organizational training, focusing on two general questions. First, why have training programs expanded so much in modern organizations? Second, what accounts for the broadened focus of organizational training?

To answer the first question, we review in the latter half of this paper, four general types of arguments. First, modern organizations have complex work requirements that call for workers trained in specialized technologies and for managers who can cope with more complex internal systems and external environments. Second, modern organizations obtain increased social control from having participants who carry their own internalized commitments; at the same time participants have increased their control over organizational resources, and one of the benefits they claim is training. Third, in modern organizations, as in modern nation-states, training is increasingly viewed as a right of membership and as a requisite for elevation to an elite position. All of these lines of thought provide explanations for the expansion of training programs and suggest specific hypotheses about organizational settings that are more likely to generate training of one type or another.

Finally, we offer two types of institutional arguments. The first focuses on institutional agencies, such as the state and professional associations, that create legal requirements and professional ideologies that make training seem necessary and rational. The second form of institutional argument stresses a process explanation. Institutional processes operate to diffuse beliefs in the desirability of training so that, increasingly, over time, the value of training in modern organizations is taken for granted. Rules and practices supporting training have become value-laden and widely accepted. More specific lines of argument are ensconced as ideologies in modern organizational belief and practice. As such beliefs diffuse, training spreads throughout organizations over and above the impact of specific causal factors characteristic of particular organizational settings. Considered altogether, the four arguments make up a multilayered explanation of and justification for training.

Institutional arguments are also employed, in the first half of the paper, to explain the broadening of focus and the reduction in direct controls over training programs. Training programs are viewed as a sub-type of a more general, institutionalized form: instruction. The social forms and cultural patterns associated with instruction are widely diffused in modern societies and operate in a wide array of settings. Although there are some distinctive features associated with each of these contexts, the broader institutional pattern exerts strong effects.

Most contemporary perspectives on organizational training emphasize the differences between corporate training and traditional educational programs, seeing the former as a product of specific technical or organizational-level requirements, and as being tightly controlled. There are, to be sure, differences between traditional education and corporate training programs. Chief among these is that educational programs devote more attention and energy toward making their processes and products appear comparable so that the values attained in educational settings can be more easily transferred to other contexts. Corporate training programs are less concerned to insure—indeed, may take steps to resist—the transferability of their products.

While there are some discernible differences between the organization of educational and training programs, our observations suggest that the appropriate contrast is not between an institutionalized framework in the traditional educational sector versus organization-specific controls in the corporate settings. Rather, there appear to be two distinct institutional forms: the one supporting education, the other, training. Though distinct from traditional educational systems, training is itself becoming institutionally stylized and legitimated. Corporate training programs appear to be developing their own distinct institutional bases, linked to modern theories of organizational, rather than to societal purposes, and creating somewhat distinctive professional norms, practices and justifications. The focus of training has been broadened from more specific to more diffuse areas and they rely on more professionalized controls rather than on arrangements of close inspection and evaluation. As it becomes institutionalized, organizational training has become more extensive, broader in scope and more indirect in its organizational controls.

THE INSTITUTIONALIZATION OF TRAINING

The Magnitude of Corporate-Agency Training

Little accurate data exists about the pervasiveness of training programs in American organizations. It is difficult to know how to count students (since most are part-time) or courses (which differ greatly in format and duration). Estimates of employer expenditures on training thus vary widely—from two billion to one hundred billion dollars per year (See Carnevale & Goldstein, 1983; Eurich, 1985; Wagner, 1980). Higher estimates extrapolate from data on expenditures from the largest companies and include trainee wages and foregone production costs. Lower estimates are based on survey data from a wider range of firms and exclude all but direct costs. Still other estimates are based on surveys of individuals who report their involvement in adult education provided or paid for by employers.

Carnevale and Goldstein (1983) provide a relatively well-grounded estimate of number of employees and size of expenditures. They employ data from an industry survey, conducted by Lusterman (1977) for the Conference Board in 1974–75, that surveyed firms employing 500 or more employees. Carnevale and Goldstein adjust their estimates for company size, add information on training within governmental agencies, and update the estimates to 1981. They conclude that

industry and government provided about 17.6 million courses or training programs to 11.1 million workers—nearly one of eight employees. About 12 million courses, or 68 percent of the total, were given in-house and the remainder in outside institutions such as schools, colleges, professional organizations and companies in the training business. In-house training alone was roughly estimated to cost between $5 billion and $10 billion, with a most likely estimate at around $7 billion. Adding a rough estimate of the wages and salaries of trainees while in training, one gets a range for total in-house expenditures of $12 to $17 billion, with a most likely figure of about $14 billion. To these figures for in-house training should be added the cost of the 32 percent of courses that were given by outside institutions. If we were to assume the same cost per course, the totals [for both in-house and external training] would be $10 billion, excluding trainees' wages and salaries, and $21 billion including these items (Carnevale & Goldstein, 1983, p. 36).

By comparison, at roughly the same time all U.S. universities and four-year colleges, public and private, enrolled approximately 7.6 million full time students and spent just over $60 billion.

In short, it appears that by any criterion training conducted by U.S. work organizations is a sizable enterprise, involving in any given year more than half again as many students as are enrolled in four-year colleges and universities and consuming from a quarter to a third of all resources expended on traditional higher education programs. Moreover, the evidence is strong that while conventional higher education programs have been and are expected to remain relatively stable, corporate training programs have been expanding.

Previous Approaches to Corporate Training

Corporate training has been examined from several social science perspectives. Far and away the dominant view is one justifying training in terms of its contributions to productivity. This technical or instrumental view of training has been in ascendance since the work of Taylor (1911) and Munsterberg (1913), both of whom emphasized the importance of worker selection and training. Taylor viewed training as critical for replacing the inefficient, casual work habits that employees developed on their own with efficient, parsimonious procedures. This general view of training is embodied in the approaches of most economists and industrial and organization psychologists.

Specifically, human capital theorists, primarily labor economists, have examined the relation between education and productivity. They posit that education contributes to human productivity (Becker, 1964) and, more often than not, have "confirmed" their predictions by noting the positive association between education and individual earnings (Schultz, 1961) or between aggregate indices of education and economic development (Denison, 1974). More recent analysts have been skeptical of the direct contribution of education to productivity. They argue that the association reflects primarily the "signaling" or "credentialling" value of education (Berg, 1970; Collins, 1979; Spence, 1973; Thurow, 1975). While some studies in this tradition have attempted to distinguish between the effects of basic and vocational training, there has been little research attention devoted to examining the direct effects of corporate training programs on productivity.[2]

Also embracing a technical view of training is the large body of work amassed by industrial and organizational psychologists (See, e.g., Goldstein,

1986; Laird, 1985; Latham, 1988; Nadler, 1984).[3] Their focus is primarily applied, with much attention given to techniques for assessing the need for training, determining the utility of alternative training techniques, and developing methods for ascertaining the effectiveness of training.

A closely related body of literature on training has been developed by researchers and practitioners in organization development (OD) and applied change (See, e.g., Bennis, Benne, & Chin, 1985; Woodman & Pasmore, 1987). Training is viewed by these analysts as one lever among many others (e.g., survey feedback, team building) for stimulating and supporting change. The primary emphasis in these approaches is on influencing motivations rather than affecting job skills or knowledge—on nonrational rather than rational sources of change (See Chin & Benne, 1985).

Two other approaches to training are more sociological in emphasis. There is, first, a small literature on socialization in organizations (See, e.g., Van Mannen & Schein, 1979; Rohlen, 1978; Van Mannen, 1978). While this work addresses the question of how individuals learn to acquire organizational roles, studies have emphasized primarily informal and apprenticeship-type training rather than more formalized training programs. Also, like the OD literature, this work has focused primary attention on the motivational aspects of socialization, stressing the development of commitment to the organization and changes in identity and self-conception.

A second body of sociological theory and research that has emerged in recent years focuses on organizational learning (See, e.g., Argyris & Schon, 1978; Duncan & Weiss, 1979; Hedberg, 1981; Levitt & March, 1988). The work exams whether, how, and under what conditions organizations learn. Learning sometimes refers to the outcomes of adaptive processes in organizations and sometimes to the processes themselves: to the ways in which organizations generalize from their own and others' experiences in the development of rules and practices. Most discussions stress the distinction between organizational and individual learning: the former emphasizing learning as structurally encoded in organizational procedures and rules such that the "lessons of experience are maintained and accumulated within routines despite the turnover of personnel and the passage of time" (Levitt & March, 1988: 326). Training conducted by organizations would appear to qualify as one important mechanism linking organizational and individual learning, but few discussions of organizational learning pursue the topic in a systematic fashion.

In sum, there exists very little in the way of a sociological analysis of why training is a prominent and pervasive feature of modern organizational structure. Dominant models are psychological and economic and either assume that training is beneficial to productivity or are involved in assessing and improving its contributions. Most of these analysts argue that training improves the knowledge and skills of performers contributing to their increased productivity. Others have broadened the argument to encompass motivation and commitment as well as technical skills and know-how; but the focus remains largely on the consequences of training for workers and worker performance.

There has been little interest in examining the determinants of training programs in organizational settings, in viewing training as a dependent rather than an independent variables. By contrast, we seek to explain the pervasiveness of training and to ascertain what accounts for its recent rapid growth. In what types of organizations is training likely to develop? Has the definition or scope of training become more diffuse over time, and if so, why is this the case? These and related questions are not adequately addressed by the current literature.

An Institutional Approach to Corporate Training

Institutional Environments and Education.   Organizational analysts in recent years have expanded their conceptions of organizations as determined by their technical work environments to include an examination of the impact of wider institutional settings (Meyer & Scott, 1983; Scott, 1987b). Early research emphasized the effects of technical factors, market forces, and uncertainty on organizational forms (e.g., Woodward, 1965; Hickson, Lawrence & Lorsch, 1967; Thompson, 1967; Pugh & Pheysey, 1969; Child and Mansfield, 1972).

More recently, thinking has shifted to focus on the importance of institutional forces shaping organizations (e.g., Meyer & Rowan, 1977; DiMaggio & Powell, 1983; Zucker, 1983). Two kinds of institutional arguments have emerged (See Scott 1987a). The first emphasizes institutionalization as a *process*: the construction over time of a social definition of reality such that certain ways of acting are taken for granted as the "right" if not the only way to do things (Selznick, 1957; Berger & Luckmann, 1967; Zucker, 1977; Meyer & Rowan 1977). The second emphasizes institutions as a distinctive class of *agencies*: the existence of collective actors empowered to create cognitive and normative symbolic systems that support and constrain organizational behavior through a variety of mechanisms, including coercive sanctions, normative pressures and mimetic influences. (DiMaggio and Powell, 1983). Both types of arguments appear to be relevant to explaining training programs, and both are employed in constructing our arguments.

The shift from technical to institutional perspectives has been particularly influential in the analysis of educational organizations—an arena to which we have devoted much of our own efforts (See, for example, Meyer et al., 1978;

Meyer et al., 1979; Meyer, Scott, & Strang, 1987; Meyer et al., 1988; Scott & Meyer, 1988). We view educational organizations as controlled and sustained primarily by institutional forces. Instructional activities and programs are rarely supported and rewarded directly in response to the quality of their educational outputs; rather, they receive legitimacy and material resources by conforming to widely shared cultural beliefs—concerning, for example, curriculum and instructional practice—and by meeting the requirements of regulatory structures—for example, accrediting bodies and licensing agencies.

In our previous work, we have examined how changes in the institutional environment of education—for example, changes in funding sources or regulatory controls—have affected the range and types of organizations in this arena. Now we ask how educational activities—more broadly conceived— vary depending on the context within which they are conducted. Specifically, what changes occur when education takes place in a business setting rather than within the traditional educational context? To pursue this question, it is necessary to broaden our purview of educational activities.

Instruction as an Institutional Pattern. Education may be usefully viewed as a sub-type of a more general institutional pattern: *instruction.* Instruction connotes a set of activities, arrangements, categories, and cultural forms that supports activities across a wide array of contexts. Whereas "learning" is something one does, "instruction" is something that is done to one. Thus instruction calls up the clear notion of differentiated roles: teacher or instructor vs. student or trainee. It suggests a set of activities distinguished from "work" or "play". It implies an outcome—the learning of subject matter or the acquisition of skills—that is expected to occur, an output different from any tangible product that may result from performing the activities. This outcome is often socially constructed to appear to be more tangible: it may be accompanied by the assigning of scores or grades, the specification of credit units, the granting of certificates or other tangible evidence of successful completion.

Moreover, if we restrict our attention to the more formally structured programs of instruction—vs. informal teaching or on-the-job training—then additional features appear. They include: the erecting of explicit temporal and spatial boundaries that define and protect the activity; the systematic structuring of program content in the form of some type of curriculum or "program of instruction"; and the utilization of a limited set of instructional techniques, such as lectures, discussion, hands-on practice, and exercises.

Such "schools" or instructional programs constitute a set of institutionalized beliefs and practices that have become compulsory for children and adolescents and are universally found in all developed and developing societies (see Meyer, 1977). Virtually every individual in the modern world has experienced this cultural form, is able to readily identify its distinguishing elements, and is likely to quickly adapt to its prescriptions.

The generic schooling or instructional form is found (and created) in the traditional educational sector, where basic socialization and general education are expected to take place. But it is also utilized in many other social contexts. Restricting attention to adult instruction, organized programs of instruction can be observed to operate in many major societal domains, as is illustrated in Figure 1. (For another categorization that emphasizes the wide distribution of educational forms, see Wagner, 1980).

Four social domains are depicted within which the instructional pattern operates: the traditionally defined arena of education, business, the military, and religion. Others (for example, health, leisure) could also be identified. We observe that instructional programs have developed at varying "levels"—depicted on the vertical axis—in all four domains. There are multiple, somewhat vague criteria for determining levels, but differentiated clusters of programs sharing common features exist in all the domains. In particular, two broad categories of instruction are widely recognized: *education* and *training* (See, e.g., Eurich, 1985; Nadler, 1984).

The top tier of programs depicted in Figure 1 is generally labeled the realm of "education;" the middle and, particularly, the lower tiers are more likely to be described as "training." Figure 2 lists a set of contrasting features commonly thought to be associated with each mode of instruction. Note that differences described relate to ends or goals, to cognitive frames or orientations, to teacher-student roles, and even to student-student relations. The contrasting features associated with the two models are not necessarily assumed to be empirically correct, but are of interest because they suggest that the institutional frames underlying different levels of instruction vary. Indeed, they suggest the possibility that training may represent a distinctive pattern of instruction, different from education.

A major difference between the higher and the lower tiers of instruction—between education and training—is in the extent to which the learning involved is expected to be generalizable across settings. Broadly speaking, education is represented as being less context dependent while training is more embedded in context. This difference in turn gives rise to some of the most important distinguishing features of the institutional context of the conventional education sector: the emphasis on degrees and all the attendant concern with graduation requirements, including credit units, grades, and standardized curricula and major fields of study.

For education to be of value outside of the context in which it is acquired, it must be made palpable, possessable, and portable. Grades and credit units

LEVEL	TRADITIONAL EDUCATION		BUSINESS	MILITARY	RELIGION
	PUBLIC	PRIVATE			
Degree Programs	Colleges & Universities	Colleges & Universities	Corporate Colleges, e.g. Wang Institute, Rand Graduate Institute	Military Academies, e.g. West Point, Annapolis	Religious Colleges, e.g. Notre Dame
Certificate, Vocational Programs	Community Colleges & Vocational High Schools	Private Training Schools	Company-run Vocational Programs	War Colleges	Seminaries
Non-Degree Programs	Adult Education Programs	Specialized Training	Corporate Training	Basic Training	Church Schools, Catechism Classes
GOAL	Self-improvement	more selective and specialized	Productivity, Human Capital	Discipline	Belief Commitment

EDUCATION → Training

Figure 1. Adult Instruction: Context and Level

Figure 2. Contrasting Education and Training

EDUCATION	TRAINING

Goals

Learning as an end in itself	Learning as a means to an end
Future utility	Present utility
Understanding	Results

Cognitive Frames

Theoretical	Practical
Subject oriented	Problem oriented
Concepts emphasized	Skills emphasized

Teacher–Student Relation

Teacher active; students passive	Both teacher and students active
Students dependent	Students independent
Student differences minimized	Student differences emphasized

Student–Student Relation

Cooperation forbidden	Cooperation encouraged
Learning only from teacher	Learning from each other

render education ownable; they transform it into a commodity that can be possessed and accumulated in a manner that can be counted and accounted (verified). Accreditation systems allow education to be portable: they act to standardize curricula and requirements sufficiently to enable students to transfer from one educational institution to another and to expect to have their transcripts and diplomas accepted by employers or other educational organizations as evidence of specific work accomplished. These types of mechanisms perform the same function for the educational sector that monetization performs for the economy. Such elements, however, are less crucial for training within organizations, since instruction is expected to have more immediate utility, and portability is not an issue. Indeed, corporations express concern that employees *not* transport skills acquired in their settings, and at their expense, to other potential competitors.

The values and belief systems associated with instruction appear to vary across the four sectors—depicted along the horizontal axis in the bottom row of Figure 1. The principal dimension of variation appears to echo one of the distinctions already noted between education and training; namely, whether the learning involved is viewed as itself an end or as being instrumental to some more ultimate value. In this sense, even the "higher" and more generalized levels of instruction are more likely to be considered as "training" when they operate in the business, military, and other "non-educational" sectors. Thus, education is more likely to be linked to and justified by its contribution to productivity in the business domain or by its contribution to deepening faith and commitment in the arena of religion. Although instructional programs are found in abundance in a great variety of domains, it appears that their meaning and the justifications employed to sustain and motivate participants vary significantly by context.

We turn now to briefly describe the nature of instructional programs in business.

Instructional Programs in the Business Arena

As Figure 1 suggests, instructional programs exist at all levels within business settings. One of the most interesting developments in recent years has been the rapid growth of corporate colleges. A survey conducted by Eurich reveals that 18 corporate colleges existed in the United States in 1985 with several more in the planning stages. These degree-granting, accredited educational organizations have developed almost entirely since World War II. Although founded by individual companies or by trade associations, all of these programs have "moved toward increasing independence, added academic degree work, broadened the curriculum and programs, and widened their clientele" (Eurich 1985: p. 97).

Just as we would expect to observe, as these organizations have attempted to survive in a niche largely occupied by traditional colleges and universities, they have, over time, become more isomorphic with these forms. With the attempt to create a more "portable" product, these organizations have shifted away from a training toward an educational pattern. Both ecological arguments emphasizing competition and institutional arguments stressing the memetic processes of modeling, the normative pressures of professional culture, and the coercive forces of accreditation would predict these results (See Hannan & Freeman, 1989; DiMaggio & Powell, 1983).

Our primary interest, however, is on those instructional programs that remain closely tied to employment settings: on corporate and agency training programs. We have already noted the general magnitude of these programs and now turn to consider their structure and content.

Much of the prevailing discourse concerning organization training programs emphasizes the differences between them and conventional educational programs. Training in employment settings is described as being closely related to the technical and managerial tasks to be performed, conducted by persons experienced in carrying out these tasks, and closely evaluated and controlled. The tone of these accounts is illustrated by Eurich's (1985: pp. 48, 53–54) description of company training:

> The ambiance is very different from the collegiate setting; there is no leisurely chatting and loitering about campus. Behavior is purposeful, the atmosphere intense and concentrated . . .
> Instructional efficiency characterized corporate training, but it is not obtrusive in a learning atmosphere that offers variety and flexibility. . . . Time is determined by purpose.
> Teaching in the corporate classroom is by objective, like management by objective: a planned and stated goal, controls, and measurement of performance. Course development . . . follows careful procedures, starting with assessment of need for the instruction. Given that, close collaboration then follows with operational personnel who know what they want and help determine clear objectives . . .

Eurich gives illustrations of such practices, but does not attempt to assess their prevalence. Most empirical surveys as well as our own observations of training programs in a diverse sample of organizations[4] suggest, by contrast, that evaluations of individual learning, instructor performance, or course effectiveness on any basis other than student's satisfaction or self-reported improvements are extremely rare (See Chmura, Henton & Melville, 1987; Saari et al., 1988). Surveys also reveal that rather than being drawn from the work place and having experience in performing the specific tasks for which training is offered, a large and growing number of organizational trainers have educational degrees and backgrounds (See Lee, 1985, 1986). A movement is underway to develop certification procedures for trainers. The American Society for Training and Development, the leading professional association of trainers, is supporting efforts to raise standards and to standardize practice by certifying trainers (American Society for Training and Development, 1983; Galbraith and Gilley, 1986).

Inspection of courses offered indicates that a high proportion are not narrowly technical but more broadly oriented to prepare persons to become better organizational members and leaders. Much of what goes on in organizations relates to the management of people and the management of information. Typical course titles are Time management; Improving communication skills; Motivating subordinates; and Leadership. Such courses involve skills that are readily transferable across organizations.

Thus, there is evidence to suggest that while corporate training programs exhibit some distinctive characteristics, they also draw on and embody many of the features of contemporary educational systems. Notions of professionalized teachers, standardized curricula, and transferable skills are appropriated from and legitimated by this source. Contrary to the notion that corporate training operates in a manner quite distinctive to instruction in more conventional educational settings, survey results reveal many similarities as well as some differences.

We consider, then, some of the factors which may account for both these general and distinctive characteristics.

EXPLAINING THE EXISTENCE, NATURE AND VARIETY OF ORGANIZATIONAL TRAINING PROGRAMS

Four general types of theoretical approaches can be identified that are intended to account for corporate training programs. The four types of explanations are not necessarily incompatible, although they may produce some inconsistent predictions.

Technical Explanations

The most obvious, widely accepted, and historically earliest explanation for the existence and expansion of training in corporate organizations is a technical or instrumental one; technological advances and environmental challenges require informed decisionmaking and skilled attention. Training is expected to contribute to such qualities in both production workers and managers. Training programs are supported because of their contribution to organizational effectiveness. Arguments and explanations along this line developed with the rise of modern organizational structures and theories and were highly developed by the early decades of this century. They were closely linked to the rise of the personnel profession (See Jacoby, 1985). More recently, they have been reinforced by the development of human capital theory.

These types of arguments can be extended to apply to all levels of the organization and to many if not most types of training. Thus,

1.   Organizations forced to employ employees lacking basic educational skills are more likely to establish remedial training programs than organizations confronting better qualified labor pools.

Whereas technical or instrumental arguments were originally used to account for the development of courses designed to provide specialized, advanced skills and knowledge, they have more recently been employed to also explain the development of remedial training.

2. Organizations operating in environments undergoing rapid technological change are more likely to establish (re)training programs for production and sales workers.

Training programs for production workers are common in organizations confronting rapid technological change—such as the computer industry—and often include not only technicians and sales persons but customers. In some types of environments it is difficult not only to make but also to sell and to buy products without technical training.

3. Organizations with managers that confront diverse employees performing complex tasks are more likely to establish managerial training programs.

4. Organizations with more decentralized decision-making structures are more likely to establish managerial training programs.

The argument here is that in organizations in which discretion is more widely distributed throughout the organizations, training provides a means not only to enhance skills and transfer information but also a mechanism for instilling a shared conception of objectives.

5. Organizations confronting more complex and turbulent environments are more likely to establish executive training programs.

Complex and changing environments reward organizations that increase the information seeking and processing skills of their executives.

6. Organizations routinely evaluate the adequacy and appropriateness of their training programs, including content, methods, and personnel, by assessing the effectiveness of training on personnel skills and knowledge and on work performance and outcomes.

A technical model of corporate training requires that performance and outcome assessment be an integral part of the system. Technical explanations of the existence and nature of such programs are difficult to sustain in the absence of clear assessment and feedback mechanisms. (For an elaboration of the requirements of such a technical model of training, see Eyre, Dahl & Shively, 1986.)

Although considerable attention is devoted in the literature to the discussion of techniques for evaluating programs, courses, teaching personnel, methods, and students (e.g., Goldstein, 1986; Kearsley, 1982; Latham, 1988; Phillips, 1983), survey results examining actual practice in organizations, as already noted, document their infrequent use. Such findings suggest that technical explanations for organizational training do not fully account for training programs and need to be supplemented.

Control Explanations

For many years, instrumental or rational explanations for prevalent features of organizations were unchallenged. Recently, however, alternative arguments have developed to undermine existing consensus. Neo-Marxist theorists argue that many aspects of organizations are better explained by power or control considerations than by efficiency concerns. For example, analysts such as Braverman (1974) and Marglin (1974) propose that the emergence of a division of labor is better explained as a strategy by managers to increase their control over workers—by, for example, deskilling workers or by increasing the need for coordination—than as a device for improving efficiency. Creating, maintaining, and augmenting hierarchal controls are viewed as valued ends in themselves rather than as means to assuring effectiveness.

Edwards (1979) has proposed a general model of the evolution of control systems in organizations. He suggests that early forms of simple, direct personal systems of subordination are replaced in many organizations by technological controls—controls built in to the design of machines and the flow of work. These, in turn, give way in some organizations to bureaucratic control: control that

> is embedded in the social and organizational structure of the firm and is built into job categories, work rules, promotion procedures, discipline, wage scales, definitions of responsibilities, and the like. Bureaucratic control establishes the impersonal force of "company rules" or "company policy" as the basis for control (Edwards, 1979: 131).

Bureaucratic control represents the formalization of the power structure: the creation of a complex system of rules governing roles, promotions and rewards, the development of an internal labor market (See Doeringer & Piore, 1971; Althauser & Kalleberg, 1981).

Training programs in organizations appear to conform to and complement these bureaucratic systems. They provide a systematic basis for distributing responsibilities, wages, and promotion opportunities differentially among employees. Training may be viewed either as a logical component and an extension of existing bureaucratic controls or as a new form of control—the evolution of a fourth level or type of control system. The argument for the latter view is that, to the extent that training is successful, we are no longer dealing with the exercise of external controls regardless of how formalized their manifestation, but with *internalized* controls that are expected to operate in the absence of surveillance or sanction. In interpreting modern organizational mechanisms in this way, neo-Marxian arguments become "critical" versions of the human relations theories they have long challenged.

Irrespective of which view of training is taken, we expect it to flourish under the same kinds of conditions that give rise to more highly bureaucratized systems (or to more highly developed internal labor markets). Following arguments developed by Doeringer and Piore (1971), Williamson (1981), and Pfeffer and Cohen (1984), among others, we would expect to find these associations:

1. Organizations operating in core industrial sectors are more likely to develop training programs than organizations operating in peripheral sectors.

2. Irrespective of sector location, larger organizations are more likely to develop training programs than smaller organizations.

One interpretation of this association is that large organizations are more likely to be formalized, and formalization is associated with bureaucratic controls. However, a second interpretation is that organization size is associated with the development of a differentiated personnel department, and that such a unit is more likely to establish a variety of personnel control mechanisms, including training programs. Thus:

3. Organizations having personnel departments are more likely to develop training programs.

Williamson (1981) argues that the more specific the skills possessed by employees are to their organizations, the greater the costs to the organization of losing those employees and, therefore, the more inducements firms provide to reward those who remain.

4. The greater the extent of firm-specific skills among employees, the more likely organizations will provide training.

This type of hypothesis is consistent with technical as well as control arguments.

Students of bureaucratic personnel systems have observed that Marxist views emphasize some functions of these systems but overlook others. From many vantage points, training is not just an obligation imposed on employees but an important individual benefit. Whether viewed as adding capital value to employees' labor, as enhancing the development of their capacities, or as enabling them to be eligible for advancement—training opportunities are desirable and sought-after benefits under many circumstances. From this perspective, we would expect:

5. Organizations employing more highly educated or more highly skilled workers will offer more training.

6. Organizations confronting more competition in the recruitment of qualified workers will offer more training.

7. Organizations that are more highly unionized will offer more training.

More generally, these predictions are consistent with Tannenbaum's (1968) observation that organizations vary not only in the distribution of power among participants but in the total amount of power exercised. Some organizations are characterized by high levels of power exercised by both superiors and subordinates: high levels of interdependence and reciprocal controls.

8. Organizations characterized by higher levels of power that is broadly distributed will have more extensive training programs serving multiple levels of participants.

Polity Explanations

In an important but neglected discussion of organizations as political systems, Selznick (1969) argues that organizations are not simply economic or production systems; they are governance structures. Selznick asserts that the concepts of law and the legal order apply to private associations as well as to public structures. Both are systems of governance, that "rely for social control on formal authority and rule making" (1969: 7). Both are marked by pressures for expanding "legality": developing mechanisms to "reduce the degree of arbitrariness in positive law and its administration" (1969: 12). Selznick argues that these concerns give rise—in both public and private governments—to the creation of due-process procedures (See Dobbin et al., 1988).

But more than specific due-process protections are at issue. Selznick argues that individual participants in private associations may not only be said to have acquired *property* rights by virtue of their participation—the sorts of rights that call up due-process considerations; they also possess *membership* rights. These rights are defined by and most fully developed in the public sphere. "Citizenship," Selznick (1969: 249) notes, "is a special kind of group membership." When applied to private organizations, membership rights, according to Selznick (1969: 117–18) ideally should include the following:

a. Employees should be treated as competent participants in a civic order.

b. As a condition of civic competence, employees need organizational support.

Such general arguments become of special interest in relation to education and training. Meyer (1977: 66) has emphasized the special functions which educational systems perform for the nation-state in rationalizing "the nature and organization of personnel and knowledge in modern society." Mass education makes national citizenship meaningful.

> Beyond defining and extending national culture, mass education defines almost the entire population as possessing this culture, as imbued with its meanings, and as having the rights implied by it. . . . It allocates persons to citizenship—establishing their membership in the nation over and above various subgroups. And it directly expands the definition of what citizenship and the nation mean and what obligations and rights are involved.

Mass education is now quite widespread among nation-states of all types, so that there is little variance to be explained by characteristics of regime (See Meyer et al., 1979; Boli, Ramirez & Meyer, 1985). But such characteristics may still explain differences in the prevalence and type of corporate training across national boundaries.

1. Organizations operating in societies that emphasize pluralism, individualism, and democracy are more likely to develop training programs than organizations operating in less democratic societies.
2. Organizations operating in more democratic societies are likely to develop more training programs that emphasize non-technical, more diffuse forms of employee training (e.g., courses in leadership and human relations skills) than organizations operating in less democratic societies.

Meyer identifies a second, different function of education in the modern state. It not only creates and validates citizens; it also creates and validates elites. Elite cultural knowledge is expanded by education; elite positions are defined and legitimated by education; and persons are allocated to elite positions based on educational attainment. While certain membership rights are available to all, others are differentially allocated. Mass education legitimates the former; specialized and restricted education legitimates the latter.

These conceptions and arguments may apply to training in corporations. There is considerable evidence to suggest that there has been an expansion in membership rights—e.g., from employment security to participation in decisionmaking—and, conversely, in corporate responsibilities for membership welfare. These concerns have expanded from relatively narrow, contractually defined rights to more diffuse notions of entitlements..

We would expect public organizations to lead the way in these developments. They are more likely to embrace an expanded conception of their members and to seek ways to insure more equal access to elite roles within their administrative structures.

3.   Organizations located within the public sector or that are more closely connected to it are more likely to develop training programs.

Some support for this proposition comes from a study by Collins (1974) of a sample of over 300 organizations in the San Francisco Bay area, although Collins focused on educational requirements rather than on training programs within organizations. Collins reports that "public trust" organizations—those which offer a public service or rely heavily upon public confidence in the standards they uphold—exhibited higher educational requirements than "market" organizations.

4.   Organizations located within or near the public sector are more likely to link training programs to promotion to elite positions and are more likely to stress broad access to such positions and programs.

In his analysis of the Federal Civil Service System, DiPrete (1989) emphasizes the continuing efforts of designers and reformers of this System to insure that opportunities to secure education necessary for promotion be available to all members.

The expanded conception of the facets, needs and rights of employees is reflected by the widened conception of the role of organizational officials charged with personnel functions. Their responsibilities are being broadened from recruitment, selection, compensation, and dismissal to overseeing a wide variety of benefit packages and programs intended to develop and expand the capacities of employees. Such changes in functions are often accompanied and signaled by a change in the name of the responsible administrative unit.

5.   Organizations that have created Human Resources departments are more likely to develop training programs than organizations that lack departments with such labels.

6.   Organizations that have Human Resources departments are likely to offer more diffuse, non-technical training than organizations lacking departments with such labels.

Institutional Arguments

Two related and separable types of arguments emphasize, respectively, the role of institutional agencies and the effect of institutional processes on the rise of training programs.

Institutional Agencies. The first strand of institutional analysis directs attention to the effect on organizational forms and activities of the actions of institutional agencies. These agents have the capacity to generate and enforce more general symbolic frameworks—both cognitive and normative belief systems—having the power to shape organizations. We include here those collective actors having the power to formulate or influence rules and regulations or to promulgate norms and standards governing practice. Principle among such actors in modern societies are agencies of the state, various legal entities, and professional associations. Organizations are rewarded for conforming to requirements generated by such actors irrespective of whether they support improved performance. (In some cases, compliance by the organizations to the demands of the external agent may serve a technical function in the sense that it leads to improved outcomes. But the outcomes have been defined by and are of interest to the external agency rather than the host organization.)[5]

Institutional agencies operate through a variety of mechanisms (see DiMaggio & Powell, 1983; Scott, 1987a): legal rules backed with sanctions, material incentives, moral suasion. Some types of training requirements are directly imposed by governmental bodies. The Occupational Safety and Health Administration (OSHA), for example, requires that training in safety procedures be regularly provided by employers for selected personnel. Other types of training are directly paid for by federal or state funds. Examples include programs such as the earlier Comprehensive Education and Training Act (CETA) or the current U.S. Job Training Partnership Act that provide incentives to employers to provide basic or remedial training or retraining to unemployed or underemployed workers. The federal government also provides tax incentives to encourage training of all employees by defining training as an appropriate business expense. And, since the 1964 Civil Rights Act, the linkage between training and selection and promotion decisions has been recognized, and access to training affirmed as a right to be upheld by the courts (See Latham, 1988).

1.   Organizational training increases with the availability of public funding and tax concessions and with the proliferation of regulations relating to training.

Other types of demands are supported primarily by normative pressures. Professional bodies may lack the power of legal enforcement for their preferred arrangements but command the loyalty of their members—often key participants in organizations—and the respect of client or constituency groups. Professional networks are often observed to stimulate and support innovations in organizations that may not necessarily improve performance. Much training occurs in response to requirements and standards promulgated by professional bodies. While much of this training targets professionals— e.g., training required for licensure renewal—some is imposed on ancillary personnel—e.g., medical technicians—who work under the direction of professionals.

2.   Organizations employing professionals are more likely to provide training for their participants, including non-professional members, than organizations lacking professional participants.

Trainers within organizations are themselves increasingly organized as a professional community. The largest and most influential association representing training interests in the United States is the American Society for Training and Development (ASTD).[6] With a current membership of over 46,000 affiliated with either national or local chapters, ASTD has served as a stimulus for expansion of the training arena and of professional development. Although the ASTD hosts national conferences and workshops, more decentralized activities are emphasized: local chapters of the Society exist in more than 125 cities; and a number of professional practice area networks operate to connect individuals with related interests (See Chalofsky, 1984).

3.   Organizations having participants who are members of professional training associations are more likely to develop training programs than organizations lacking such participants.

Recognition of the influence of groups such as ASTD calls attention to the effects occasioned by other suppliers of training. These include educational organizations such as community colleges who, increasingly, are adapting their services to meet the training needs of corporations, and companies who are in the business of retailing training—sometimes producing packaged educational materials and sometimes providing standardized or tailorized educational services. Little systematic data exist on these external training units, but informed observers estimate that between 35 and 45 percent of all corporate training is "contracted out" to external providers (Carnevale & Goldstein, 1983).

4.   The larger the number of training firms operating in a particular sector or industry, the more likely that organizations in that sector will offer training to their employees.

An institutional perspective emphasizes that much of the stimulus for training arises in structures and interests external to any given organization. As described, the number and variety of such sources in contemporary societies such as the U.S. is quite large. Training nodes will arise in varying locations within an organization in response to these diverse external influences.

5. The more diverse and complex the organization's institutional environment, the larger the number of training programs it will offer.

The diversity of sources will also have effects on the coherence or integration of training programs within a specific organization.

6. The more an organization's training programs have developed in response to different external stimuli, the less informed will any organizational respondent be about such programs and the less integrated will these programs be.

Institutional Processes. The second strand of institutional theory emphasizes the processes by which, over time, beliefs and attitudes develop such that certain arrangements and activities come to be taken for granted or valued as ends in themselves. Two variants of this perspective have developed. The first, stemming from the work of Berger and Luckmann (1967) stresses the processes by which interacting individuals construct certain interpretations or "typifications" which become depersonalized over time, appearing to be externalized and objectified. Emphasis is on cognitive processes that construct a shared definition of social reality. The second, emphasized by Selznick (1957) focuses on the processes by which arrangements or procedures which are devised for their instrumental value come over time to be valued ends in themselves. This process by which mechanisms become infused with value emphasizes the motivational aspects of institutionalization: the social construction of value.

Our observations of training programs in firms and agencies lead us to assert that these programs are undergoing institutionalization in both senses. As they become more widespread, they also become more conventional and taken for granted; and as they develop over time, they become more infused with value. Thus, technical training, by virtue of its historical success, does not have to be invented or demonstrated over and over again, but becomes a standardized organizational response to changing circumstances. This suggests:

1. As technical training becomes more routinized and legitimate, such training programs will be found in more diverse work settings.

As modern organizations come under a regime in which technical training is a routinely available and valued institution, training itself may become less technical in format and less predictable by technical factors.

Similarly, control and political theories and their justification of training have become standard parts of the modern ideology of organizing. It is widely believed that participants possess multiple capacities and needs and that organizations benefit if participants bring more than a contractual obligation and develop more diffuse commitments to their goals and values.

2.   As models of organizations stressing the ideological commitment of participants become more widely held, training programs will expand over time in diverse organizations.

Modern organizational ideologies, given their high legitimacy, may create control-related training programs in varied enterprises, little related to the specific need for strong controls.

These arguments suggest a more general proposition about the changing determinants of training. They imply that as training programs become more highly institutionalized, the types of organization-specific features we have proposed as accounting for training programs—features such as the complexity of work, location in a core industry, publicness—will become less predictive over time.

3.   With the rise of the legitimacy of training as an institutional form, organizational characteristics will become less significant as predictors of amount and type of training found in a given setting.

To the extent to which such institutional forms and beliefs are growing in significance with the passage of time, we should also expect to observe differences in training programs related to time of founding. Following Stinchcombe (1965), who was the first to argue that organizations are imprinted with distinctive structural properties at the time of their creation reflecting wider societal beliefs and patterns, we would expect:

4.   Organizations that operate within more recently founded industries will offer more training programs to participants than organizations within older industries.

5.   Within a given industry, younger organizations will offer more training programs to participants than older organizations.

6.   Organizations in newer industries and younger organizations in all industries will offer more non-technical courses than organizations in older industries or older organizations.

7.   Organizations in newer industries and younger organizations will link training and promotion more tightly than organizations in older industries or older organizations.

We noted earlier in this paper that the prevailing rhetoric of organizational training emphasizes the differences between training and conventional educational programs. The development of training as a profession, however, appears to push in the opposite direction. There is increasing impetus, as discussed, for certification of trainers. Descriptive accounts of training acknowledge that most organizations do not attempt to systematically evaluate the effectiveness of their training by examining its effects on productivity or outputs. Other criteria—primarily, employee satisfaction or attendance—predominate. The curriculum of work organizations tends to expand to include more generalized—less work specific—skills.

In all of these ways, the schooling model presses against the work model: employee development is separated as a differentiated and legitimate interest from employee training geared exclusively to improving current productivity. The goals of training become more diffuse; the competencies identified become less context specific, the time-line within which relevant effects are expected is extended.

We believe that these trends in training reflect the continuing influence and power of the institutional beliefs and patterns associated with the traditional educational sector. We have already pointed to these same influences operating to affect the evolution of corporate colleges. Although there is some evidence of attempts to differentiate training from educational models, training programs in corporate organizations still tend to draw support and legitimacy from modeling more traditional educational practices. We expect:

8. Training programs in organizations that adopt more of the characteristics associated with conventional educational programs will be more stable—more likely to persist.

CONCLUSIONS

We conclude by emphasizing two themes that underlie most of our arguments. The first comes from our descriptive and theoretical examination of the nature of training programs in work organizations. It appears to us that organizational training is already a distinctive and rather highly developed institution. Its ideology, structure, and foci are considerably impacted by the strength of the traditional models of education (themselves highly involved in organizational life and used in many ways), which provide a source of personnel, instructional patterns, and much content. But training is itself an institution and as such readily available to modern organizations as a set of taken-for-granted practices. It exhibits stability and coherence distinct from and independent of the credentialling rules and accreditation devices of the main educational system. It is seen as linked to organizational purposes rather than to societal or individual development; it has distinct content of its own, and it is organizationally and professionally controlled in distinctive ways.

Precisely because training is so heavily institutionalized, however, its structure differs from the rigorous technical model that is widely touted by its advocates. The tightly controlled training system, closely linked to very specific organizational tasks and purposes, is rarely to be found. Organizations tend to copy generally valued models, only loosely linked to their specific tasks and purposes. And they copy them as institutionalized forms, with loose controls and evaluation systems, in ways that are in many respects directly analogous to the operation of the traditional educational system.

A second conclusion follows from our analysis of the factors giving rise to training in modern organizations. Forces ranging from specific task performance demands to requirements for organizational and political control to general societal pressures to develop participants' capacities have cumulated to make for a generalized and multilayered set of pressures and justifications for training. They have not only cumulated, but become institutionalized, so that the multiple virtues of training come together to support a general package of forms and processes, and also to make this package seem reasonable and appropriate in all sorts of organizational contexts and not just those to which the original justifications and explanations most forcefully applied. We thus argue that, increasingly over time and with institutionalization, training programs can be expected to develop and flourish across the wide and diverse array of organizations that are to be found in contemporary society.

ACKNOWLEDGMENTS

We are happy to acknowledge the assistance of a large number of graduate student collaborators who have worked with us as we have developed our theoretical ideas, constructed research designs, and collected data relevant to testing and amplifying our arguments. Participating in one or more stages of our work have been: Nitza Berkovitch, Patricia Chang, Rene Fukuhara Dahl, Dana P. Eyre, Jingsheng Huang, Karen Lussier, Kelly Massey, David Miyahara, Susanne Monahan, Amy Roussel, JoEllen Shively, and Marc Ventresca.

Scott presented early versions of this paper at the Texas Conference on Organizations held outside Austin Texas, April 15–17, 1988; and at a Conference on Computers and Learning sponsored by the Social Science Research Council held in Tortola, British Virgin Islands, June 26—July 1, 1989. Participants at these conferences made useful comments, some of which have been incorporated into the paper. For all of this assistance, we express our gratitude.

Support for this program of research has come principally from the Spencer Foundation. In addition, this paper was completed while Scott was a Fellow at the Center for Advanced Study in the Behavioral Sciences. He is grateful for financial support provided by the John D. & Catherine T. MacArthur Foundation.

NOTES

1. A study by Carnevale (1986) reported that over 80 percent of the training taking place in industry was in the form of on-the-job training.

2. An exception is the recent study by Carnevale (1984) who examined the consequences of workplace learning on growth in economic output, the latter measured by variation in lifetime earnings. However, Carnevale placed primary emphasis in his study on "informal training" defined broadly as including: supervision, observation of fellow workers, learning from one's mistakes, reading, self-study, and other unstructured ways of acquiring work skills in the course of doing one's job.

3. In addition, much work of this type is published in two journals: *Training;* and *Training and Development Journal*.

4. We are currently conducting a survey of training programs in a diverse sample of for-profit firms and public agencies, including local, state and federal branches, in a county in Northern California.

5. A familiar example is provided by the economists' notion of an externality: a (usually undesirable) outcome produced by an organization for which it does not incur costs—e.g., pollution by a chemical plant. In such a case, representatives of those affected may impose regulations to insure that the organization will take steps to correct the problem or be sanctioned. The pollution control devices installed may serve to improve the technical performance of the plant, but only in terms of the new goals imposed by the external agency.

6. Other professional associations operating in this arena include: the American Society of Personnel Administrators; the National Society of Performance and Instruction; the American Association for Adult and Continuing Education; the Association for Educational Communications and Technicians; the Organizational Development Network, and the Human Resources Planning Society. Many of these associations contain one or more subgroups focused specifically on corporate training.

REFERENCES

Althauser, R. P., & Kalleberg, A. L. (1981). Firms, occupations, and the structure of labor markets: A conceptual analysis and research agenda. In I. Berg (Ed.), *Sociological perspectives on labor markets,* (119–149). New York: Academic Press.

American Society for Training and Development (1983). *Models for excellence: The conclusions and recommendations of the ASTD training and development competency study.* Washington, DC: ASTD.

Argyris, C., & Schon, D. (1978). *Organizational learning.* Reading, MA: Addison-Wesley.

Becker, G. (1964). *Human capital.* New York: Columbia University Press.

Bennis, W. G., Benne, K. D., & Chin, R. (Eds.) (1985). *The planning of change.* New York: CBS College Publishing, 4th ed.

Berg, I. (1970). *Education and jobs: The great training robbery.* New York: Praeger.

Berger, P. L., & Luckmann, T. (1967). *The social construction of reality.* New York: Doubleday.

Boli, J., Ramirez, F. O., and Meyer, J. W. (1985). Explaining the origins and expansion of mass education, *Comparative Education Review, 29,* 145–170.

Braverman, H. (1974). *Labor and monopoly capital: The degradation of work in the twentieth century.* New York: Monthly Review Press.

Carnevale, A. (1984). *Jobs for the nation: Challenges for a society based on work.* Alexandria, VA: American Society for Training and Development.

Carnevale, A. (1986). The learning enterprise, *Training and Development Journal, 40* (1).

Carnevale, A. P., & Goldstein, H. (1983). *Employee training: Its changing role and an analysis of new data.* Washington, D.C.: American Society for Training and Development Press.

Chalofsky, N. (1984). Professional growth for HRD staff. In L. Nadler (Ed.), *The handbook of human resource development,* (13.1–13.18) New York: John Wiley.

Child, J., & Mansfield, R. (1972). Technology, size and organization structure. *Sociology, 6:*369–393.

Chin, R., & Benne, K. D. (1985). General strategies for effecting change in human systems. In W. G. Bennis, K. D. Benne, & R. Chin (Eds.), *The planning of change.* New York: CBS College Publishing, 4th ed.

Chmura, R. J., Henton, D. C., & Melville, J. G. (1987) *Corporate education and training: Investing in a competitive future.* Menlo Park, CA: SRI International.

Collins, R. (1974). Where are educational requirements for employment highest? *Sociology of Education, 47,* 419–442.

Collins, R. (1979). *The credential society: An historical sociology of education and stratification.* New York: Academic Press.

Denison, E. (1974). *Accounting for United States economic growth, 1929–1969.* Washington, D.C.: Brookings Institution.

DiMaggio, P. J., & Powell, W. W. (1983). The iron cage revisited: Institutional isomorphism and collective rationality in organizational fields, *American Sociological Review, 48,* 147–160.

DiPrete, T. A. (1989). *The bureaucratic labor market: The case of the federal civil service.* New York: Plenum.

Dobbin, F. R., Edelman, L., Meyer, J. W., Scott, W. R., & Swidler, A. (1988). The expansion of due process in organizations. In L. G. Zucker (Ed.), *Institutional patterns and organizations: Culture and environment* (71–98) Cambridge, MA: Ballinger.

Doeringer, P. B., & Piore, M. J. (1971). *Internal labor markets and manpower analysis.* Lexington, MA: Heath.

Duncan, R., and Weiss, A. (1979). Organizational learning: Implications for organizational design. In B. Staw (Ed.), *Research in organizational behavior, 1,* (75–123). Greenwich, CT: JAI Press.

Edwards, R. (1979). *Contested terrain: The transformation of the workplace in the twentieth century.* New York: Basic Books.

Eurich, N. P. (1985). *Corporate classrooms: The learning business.* Princeton, NJ: Carnegie Foundation for the Advancement of Teaching.

Eyre, D. P., Dahl, R. F., & Shively, J. (1986). The organization of schools outside the traditional educational sector: An exploratory study. Project Report No. 86-SEPI-10. Stanford, CA: Stanford Education Policy Institute, Stanford University.

Galbraith, M., & Gilley, J. (1986). *Professional certification: implications for adult educational and HRD,* Information Series No. 307, ERIC Clearing House on Adult, Career, and Vocational Education, Ohio State University.

Goldstein, I. L. (1986). *Training in organizations: Needs assessment, development and evaluation.* Monterey, CA: Brooks/Cole, 2nd ed.

Hannan, M. R., & Freeman, J. (1989). *Organizational ecology.* Cambridge, MA: Harvard University Press.

Hedberg, B. L. T. (1981). How organizations learn and unlearn. In N. D. Nystrom and W. H. Starbuck (Eds.), *Handbook of organizational design, 1:*3–27. Oxford: Oxford University Press.

Hickson, D. J., Pugh, D. S., & Pheysey, D. C. (1969). Operations technology and organization structure: An empirical reappraisal, *Administrative Science Quarterly, 14,* 378–397.

Jacoby, S. M. (1985). *Employing bureaucracy: Managers, unions, and the transformation of work in American industry, 1900–1945.* New York: Columbia University Press.

Kearsley, G. (1982). *Costs, benefits and productivity in training systems.* Reading, MA: Addison-Wesley.

Laird, D. (1985). *Approaches to training and development.* Reading, MA: Addison-Wesley, 2nd ed.

Lawrence, P. R., & Lorsch, J. W. (1967). *Organization and environment: Managing differentiation and integration.* Boston: Graduate School of Business Administration, Harvard University.

Latham, G. P. (1988). Human resource training and development, *Annual Review of Psychology, 39,* 545–582.

Lee, C. (1985). Trainers' careers, *Training, 22* (10), 75–80.

Lee, C. (1986). Training profiles: The view from ground level, *Training, 23* (10), 67–84.

Levitt, B., & March, J. G. (1988). Organizational learning, *Annual Review of Sociology, 14,* 319–340.

Lusterman, S. (1977). *Education in industry.* New York: The Conference Board.

Marglin, S. (1974). What do bosses do? The origins and functions of hierarchy in capitalist production, *Review of Radical Political Economics, 6,* 60–112.

Meyer, J. W. (1977). The effects of education as an institution, *American Journal of Sociology, 83,* 55–77.

Meyer, J. W., Ramirez, F. O., Rubinson, R., & Boli-Bennett, J. (1977). The world educational revolution, 1950–1970. *Sociology of Education, 50,* 242–258.

Meyer, J. W., & Rowan, B. (1977). Institutionalized organizations: Formal structure as myth and ceremony, *American Journal of Sociology, 83,* 340–363.

Meyer, J. W., Scott, W. R., Cole, S., & Intili, J. K. (1978). Instructional dissensus and institutional consensus in schools. In M. Meyer (Ed.), *Environments and organizations,* (233–263). San Francisco: Jossey-Bass.

Meyer, J. W., & Scott, W. R. (1983). *Organizational environments: Ritual and rationality.* Beverly Hills, CA: Sage Publications.

Meyer, J. W., Scott, W. R., and Strang, D. (1987). Centralization, fragmentation and school district complexity. *Administrative Science Quarterly, 32,* 186–201.

Meyer, J. W., Scott, W. R., Strang, D., and Creighton, A. (1988). Bureaucratization without centralization: Changes in the organizational system of American public education, 1940–80. In L. G. Zucker (Ed.), *Institutional Patterns and Organizations: Culture and Environment,* (139–167). Cambridge, MA: Ballinger.

Meyer, J. W., Tyack, D., Nagel, J., & Gordon, A. (1979). Public education as nation-building in America: Enrollments and bureaucratization, 1870–1930. *American Journal of Sociology, 85,* 591–613.

Munsterberg, H. (1913). *Psychology and industrial efficiency.* Boston: Houghton Mifflin.

Nadler, L. (Ed.) (1984). *The handbook of human resource development.* New York: John Wiley.

Pfeffer, J., & Cohen, Y. (1984). Determinants of internal labor markets in organizations, *Administrative Science Quarterly, 29,* 550–572.

Phillips, J. J. (1983). *Handbook of training evaluation and measurement methods.* Houston: Gulf Publishing Co.

Rohlen, T. P. (1978). The education of a Japanese banker. *Human Nature,* 22–30.

Saari, L. M., Johnson, T. R., McLaughlin, S. D., & Zimmerle, D. M. (1988). A survey of management training and education practices in U.S. companies, *Personnel Psychology,* 731–743.

Schultz, T. (1961). Investment in human capital, *American Economic Review, 51,* 1–17.

Scott, W. R. (1987a). The adolescence of institutional theory, *Administrative Science Quarterly, 32,* 493–511.

Scott, W. R. (1987b). *Organizations: Rational, natural and open systems.* Englewood Cliffs, NJ: Prentice Hall, 2nd ed.

Scott, W. R., & Meyer, J. W. (1987). Environmental linkages and organizational complexity: Public and private schools. In T. James and H. M. Levin (Eds.), *Comparing public & private schools: Institutions and organizations, 1,* (128–160). New York: Falmer Press.

Selznick, P. (1957). *Leadership in administration.* New York: Harper & Row.

Selznick, P. (1969). *Law, society, and industrial justice.* New York: Russell Sage Foundation.

Spence, M. (1973). Job market signaling. *Quarterly Journal of Economics, 87,* 355–374.

Stinchcombe, A. L. (1965). Social structure and organizations. In J. G. March (Ed.), *Handbook of organizations,* (142–193). Chicago: Rand McNally.

Tannenbaum, A. S. (1968). *Control in organizations.* New York: McGraw-Hill.

Taylor, F. W. (1911). *The principles of scientific management.* New York: Harper.

Thurow, L. (1975). *Generating inequality.* New York: Basic Books.

Thompson, J. D. (1967). *Organizations in action.* New York: McGraw-Hill.

Tolbert, P. S., and Zucker, L. G. (1983). Institutional sources of change in the formal structure of organizations: The diffusion of civil service reform, 1880–1935, *Administrative Science Quarterly, 28,* 1–13.

Van Maanen, J. (1978). People processing: Major strategies of organizational socialization and their consequences. In J. Paap, (Ed.), *New Directions in Human Resource Management,* Englewood Cliffs, N.J.: Prentice-Hall.

Van Maanen, J., and Schein, E. H. (1979). Toward a theory of organizational socialization. In B. Staw (Ed.), *Research in organizational behavior, 1,* 209–264. Greenwich, CT: JAI Press.

Wagner, A. P. (1980). An inventory of post-compulsory education and training programs in the U.S. and sources of support. Stanford, CA: Project Report No. 80-A14, Institute for Research on Educational Finance and Governance, Stanford University.

Williamson, O. E. (1981). The economics of organization: The transaction cost approach, *American Journal of Sociology, 87,* 548–577.

Woodman, R. W. and Pasmore, W. A. (Eds.) (1987). *Research in organization change and development, 1.* Greenwich, CT: JAI Press.

Woodward, J. (1965). *Industrial organization: Theory and practice.* New York: Oxford University Press.

Zucker, L. G. (1977). The role of institutionalization in cultural persistence, *American Sociological Review, 42,* 726–743.

Zucker, L. G. (1983). Organizations as institutions. In S. B. Bacharach, (Ed.), *Research in the sociology of organizations, 2,* 1–47. Greenwich, CT: JAI Press.

THEORY IN ORGANIZATIONAL BEHAVIOR:

CAN IT BE USEFUL?

Arthur P. Brief and Janet M. Dukerich

ABSTRACT

Usefulness (defined as a theory's worth to organizational practitioners in terms of prescribing the means to some end-state they desire) often is raised as a criterion for evaluating theory in organizational behavior. By drawing on a variety of literatures concerned with philosophy of science and generalizability, a case is made against the usefulness criterion. In addition, it is suggested that attempts to create theories which meet the usefulness criterion may obstruct theory development. On a more positive note, it then is argued that theory in organizational behavior has practical value even though it may not be useful in a more narrow sense. Finally, organizational behaviorists are urged to consider whether the current mix of roles in the field (e.g., theory builders and action researchers) is appropriate.

THEORY IN ORGANIZATIONAL BEHAVIOR:
CAN IT BE USEFUL?

"Employees should have hard, specific goals . . ." (Robbins, 1989, p. 216). This is the sort of advice that makes many of us in organizational behavior

Research in Organizational Behavior, Volume 13, pages 327–352.

proud. It is a course of action we can prescribe to management with confidence. It is a prescription rooted in theory (Locke, 1968) which has withstood the test of rigorous empirical scrutiny (Locke, Shaw, Saari, & Latham, 1981).

Is this rosy picture of usefulness, in fact, warranted? Our answer is, perhaps not. Just six years after Locke et al. (1981) told us that "The beneficial effect of goal setting on task performance is one of the most robust and replicable findings in the psychological literature" (p. 145). Wood, Mento, and Locke (1987) alerted us that "Interest is now turning to identifying the theoretical limits of goal setting" (p. 416); and, even more recently, Earley, Connolly, and Ekegren (1989), based upon the results of three laboratory experiments, warned "specific, difficult goal setting may be harmful" (p. 31).

This essay is not about the usefulness of goal setting theory per se. Rather, it is about the usefulness of theories in organizational behavior in general. By "theory" we mean a set of logically related propositions that describe and explain a range of observations. By "usefulness" we mean a theory's prescriptive value in terms of the degree to which it contains actionable solutions to "real world" problems. In this essay we differentiate between usefulness and practicality and, as we will contend later, we believe that a theory's practicality lies in its ability to sensitize one to what *may* be, and not to predict firmly what *will* be (c.f., Gergen & Gergen, 1986). That is, we will argue that theories in organizational behavior can serve those in applied settings as lenses, helping them to see things a little differently; but that, our theories are not useful as prescribed courses of action to remedy applied problems.

Given the intimate relationship between theory and research, our concern necessarily is not only with the usefulness of a theory but also with the body of empirical evidence which purportedly supports it. Nevertheless, it is not our contention that a particular piece of research cannot be useful. Indeed, our essay will close with a discussion of the circumstances when this may be the case. However, we will contend that exhorting organizational behaviorists to construct useful theories, in fact, may impede theory development. Now, we turn to a discussion of the meaning of the "usefulness" concept and how it has been advocated in the organizational behavior literature as a criterion for evaluating theory.

Usefulness as a Criterion

Usefulness is a standard against which theories in organizational behavior often are judged. This is evidenced by the numerous articles which critique the field for not being useful and prescribe how it can become more so (e.g., Beyer, 1982; Boehm, 1980; Cheng & McKinley, 1983; Cummings, 1978; Gordon, Kleinman, & Hanie, 1978; Hakel, Sorcher, Beer, & Moses, 1982;

Kilmann, 1979; Kilmann, Slevin, & Thomas, 1983; McKelvey & Aldrich, 1983; Miner, 1984; Susman & Evered, 1978; Thomas & Tymon, 1982; Van de Val, Bolas, & Kang, 1976; Waters, Salipante, & Notz, 1978). But, what does the concept of "usefulness" mean?

In his analysis of a number of established theories in organizational behavior, Miner (1984) examined each of them in terms of their estimated scientific validity and estimated usefulness in application. Miner construed a "useful" theory as one which has "clear implications for practice and application in some area of management or organizational functioning" (p. 297). Operationally, in his analysis, a theory was rated highly useful if it had generated an application which was shown to produce the intended results. Although there may be agreement among scholars in the field concerning the concept of validity (c.f., Cook & Campbell, 1979), the concept of usefulness seems more open to individual interpretation (Beres, 1983; Louis, 1983). When we exhort theorists to construct "useful" theories, that is, theories with "clear implications," what do we mean? Does usefulness mean that good theories inform practitioners about concepts that may aid them in their organizational roles, or, more narrowly, do good theories prescribe specific courses of action? We contend that the latter interpretation often is seen as more valuable; and, in the present essay, we focus on this more constrained definition of usefulness. That is, we are concerned with so-called prescriptive or normative theories (Filley & House, 1969). The purpose of these types of theories is to do more than explain or describe; they explicate how some problem in an applied setting should be solved. Hackman and Oldham's (1976) job characteristic model of work motivation is an example of such a theory, for Hackman (1977) claims "the model is specifically intended for use in planning and carrying out changes in the design of jobs" (p. 128).

In order to assess the usefulness of various theories, Miner sought the opinions of fellow scientists. We, however, along with Thomas and Tymon (1982) and others (e.g., Dubin, 1976; Lindblom & Cohen, 1979; Mitroff, Betz, Pondy, & Sagasti, 1974), see the practitioner as the judge of the degree to which a theory's prescribed course of action is authoritative (i.e., entitled to credit or acceptance). This is so because managers and scientists do not always agree on what is useful (Haire, 1964). Thus, to us, the usefulness of a theory in organizational behavior refers to its worth to organizational practitioners in terms of prescribing the means to some end-state they desire. As we have suggested, this emphasis on practitioners and action in construing usefulness is common in the organizational behavior literature (Beres, 1983). It is with this constrained definition of usefulness that we ask the question, can theory in organizational behavior be useful.

Our intent is to stimulate debate and discussion on the criterion of usefulness. As researchers in the field of organizational behavior, often considered an "applied" field (as distinct from base disciplines such as psychology, sociology, political science, etc.), we, at times, have encountered pressure to construct theories which will provide practitioners steps toward solving their real world problems. It seems to us, at least, that the word, "applied" is considered synonymous with the word, "useful." Because we are skeptical of the field's ability to develop prescriptive theory, we wish to raise several issues concerning the usefulness criterion.

The remainder of the essay unfolds as follows. First, the problematic nature of the usefulness criterion is addressed by demonstrating that often espoused views of philosophy of science are incompatible with the concept of a prescriptive theory. Next, the usefulness criterion is questioned on the grounds that empirical findings obtained in one or more situations, which show a theoretical prescription to hold, afford a weak basis for generalizing to other situations. That discussion is followed by one which argues that attempts to construct useful theories may obstruct theory development (e.g., by focusing on those variables thought to be manipulatable by practitioners, the theorist's vision may become too narrow). The essay concludes with a distinction being drawn between usefulness and practicality and a brief analysis of how good theory can influence practice without being considered useful, in a narrow, prescriptive sense.

Philosophy of Science Concerns

As a long time participant observer of the social sciences, Meehl (1986) claims that social scientists generally agree that logical positivism won't wash. Alternatively, he also states that he has "never met any scientist who, when doing science, held to a phenomenalist or idealistic view" (p. 322). That is, Meehl rejects viewing science as entailing (a) the accurate description of observable events from which laws specifying natural regularities may be extracted and used to predict future events and, ultimately, to control nature or (b) the reporting of phenomenon in ways that are dependent on openness to and trust in the experiential accounts of others. Thus, he appears to adopt a realist view of science. Such a realist view, often employed with various prefixes (e.g., critical realist), seems in vogue in philosophy of science (e.g., Bhaskar, 1986; Hare, 1986; Miller, 1987). Here, we will use it as a basis for critiquing the usefulness criterion. To do so, we begin below by elaborating the realist perspective. In our brief portrayal of the realist view of science, we intend for it to become evident that "realists, unlike many positivists, do *not* identify explanation with prediction; a successful prediction is a welcome addition to a successful explanation rather than something intrinsically related to it." (Outhwaite, 1983, p. 324). This is an important point because, for a theory to be useful, its application *must* produce the intended results; in other words, if one were *not* able to predict the results of applying a theory in "some finite, well-defined population at a given point in space and time" (Kruglanski, 1975, p. 105), then it cannot be concluded the theory is useful in that context. Thus, a useful theory is one whose results are known a priori; and, as will be shown, the realist perspective tells us this cannot be for theoretical knowledge is fallible knowledge.

A tenet of the realist view is captured in the following quote from Miller (1987):

> . . . an explanation is an adequate description of the underlying causes bringing about a phenomenon. Adequacy, here, is determined by rules that are specific to particular fields at particular times. The specificity of the rules is not just a feature of adequacy for given special purposes, but characterizes all adequacy that is relevant to scientific explanation. The rules are judged by their efficacy for respective fields at the respective times—which makes adequacy far more contingent, pragmatic, and field-specific than positivists allowed, but no less rationally determinable (p. 6).

In addressing the implications of the realistic view for the social sciences, Manicas and Secord (1983) state the idea in a way that moves it closer to the point at hand:

> The practices of the sciences generate their own *rational* criteria in terms of which theory is accepted or rejected. The crucial point is that it is possible for these criteria to be rational precisely because on realist terms, there is a world that exists independently of cognizing experience. Since our theories are constitutive of the known world but *not* of the *world*, we may always be wrong, but *not* anything goes (p. 401).

As can be inferred from the above quotations, the realist position can be seen to fall somewhere between a strict logical positivist perspective and the view that scientific knowledge is socially constructed. According to the realist position, therefore, although science is governed by rigorous rules of logic (as defined by its accepted criteria), it cannot be considered infallible because these rules are socially constructed by the community of scientists. Given this fallible nature of the scientific enterprise, the extraction of prescriptive statements from theory which hold across different times and places is problematic.

Perhaps the most operational form of the realist position is reflected in Cook and Campbell's tentative philosophy of social sciences which they call a critical-realist perspective (e.g., Cook & Campbell, 1979). For example, Cook (1983, p. 89), in recognizing the "inevitable fallibility of knowledge of the external world," asserted that "public discussion usually determines the degree of temporary legitimacy that is conferred on claimed findings through a process to which the methods of science have usually contributed by rendering implausible some alternative interpretations that might have been offered and by focusing the discussion on the major unresolved issues." Thus, we see an organizational behavior theory as a system which "floats, as it were, above the plane of observation and is anchored to it by rules of interpretation" (Hempel, 1952, p. 36). The truth of a theory's propositions, in any absolute sense, is and always will remain an unknown. Cook and Campbell (1979, p. 23), likewise conclude that the process available for establishing a scientific theory "is inevitably a rather unsatisfactory and inconclusive procedure."

The idea of fallible knowledge is evident in other aspects of a realist philosophy of science. For instance, it can be seen in how realists describe scientific growth. Prior to World War II, few philosophers would have questioned "the cozy picture of science growing remorselessly, sedately accumulating knowledge in a serenely monistic manner, leaving truth-values and meanings undisturbed, on soil nurtured by common experience" (Bhaskar, 1986, p. 50). The seeds of change were planted, in part, by the 1934 publication in Germany of Popper's *The Logic of Scientific Discovery*. Popper's theme, in that and his later works, is depicted in the following quote: "It is not the accumulation of observations which I have in mind when I speak of the growth of scientific knowledge, but the repeated overthrow of scientific theories and their replacement by better or more satisfactory ones" (Popper, 1965, p. 215). Although one route to replacement is the accumulation of observations, accumulation alone does not necessarily lead to growth.

A complementary view was provided by Kuhn (1970, p. 121) when he stated "though the world does not change with a change of paradigm, the scientist afterwards works in a different world." As a final example, Bhaskar (1986, p. 60) stated "The cumulative character of scientific development forcefully indicates that theories are *fallible* attempts to describe the real structures of nature, as they complement, succeed and situate one another in offering fuller, deeper, more comprehensive accounts of reality." Thus, it can be seen that a realist perspective on scientific growth is dependent on the idea of fallible theories. We are aligned with Harre (1986, p. 37) who stated "Since, in the end, all current theories are likely to be abandoned or modified there can be no place in science for a sure catalogue of facts of the matter fixed forever by *the* way the world is."

Given this conclusion, we assert it would be illogical to accept that an organizational behavior theory could contain authoritative rules of action for practitioners. That is, although we may think we have the "truth" today, it may be refuted tomorrow. Therefore, as we asserted earlier, the usefulness criterion is problematic philosophically. Application of scientific rules of interpretation, which are socially constructed and only temporarily efficacious, yields information about the theory that is fallible, not in a probabilistic way but in an uncertain one. For example, since the theoretical limits of the prescription, "employees should have hard, specific goals," are unknown, how can it be predicted, with any degree of certainty, that its application in some "new" context will produce the intended results? That is, when asked if this prescription would work in a new context, it would be inappropriate to assign a probability (e.g., "we are 95% confident it will work"); rather, we would need to state our uncertainty. As addressed further in the section below, such a warning, in fact, always is required unless the particular context is known to exhibit no "critical differences" (Fromkin & Streufert, 1976) from those settings in which the prescription has been tested and shown to produce intended results. [In other words, the caveat would not be required for attempts at "literal replication" (Lykken, 1968).]

Concerns with Generalizability

If it is presumed that a theoretical prescription has been observed to hold in one or more situations, then questions arise regarding the generalizability of those findings. For instance, Folger and Konovsky (1989, p. 128), based upon findings obtained from a sample of production workers and a sample of clerical workers, stated, "to be maximally effective in sustaining employee commitment to an organization and trust in its management, those making allocative decisions—and other organizational decisions generally—must take procedural justice into account." If one was interested in applying the Folger-Konovsky prescription to a sample of investment bankers, physicians, or professors, for example, then the issue of generalizability most assuredly would surface. We contend such questions of generalizabilty make dubious the application of usefulness as a criterion for evaluating organizational behavior theories. [That is, we construe the application of a prescription as an attempt at "constructive replication" (Lykken, 1968).] The concerns with generalizability to be raised are tied to such issues as divergence, obsolescence, and sampling as described below.

We have noted that the growth of scientific knowledge is marked by theories being overthrown and replaced. Why is this so? The answer, in part, may entail recognizing that, in time, empirical observations divergent with a theory will be obtained. Meehl (1986) suggests eight methodological factors for such divergence:

(a) experimental design, (b) inherent construct validity of measures, (c) reliability of measures, (d) properties of statistical power functions, (e) presence and size of higher-order interactions, (f) verisimilitude of auxiliary theories relied on in deriving empirical predictions, (g) differential submission rate of manuscripts reporting significant versus non-significant findings, and (h) editorial bias as to the same (p. 325).

Some of these factors more narrowly pertain to generalizability as conceived conventionally as the reproducibility of findings, obtained in one or more situations, across other situations. (A situation refers to a setting, people, or time, or combination of such characteristics.)

Given this more narrow view of the divergence issue, the methodological factors identified by Cook and Campbell (1979) are particularly salient. They state that a failure to generalize may be attributable to one or a combination of the following statistical interaction effects: selection and treatment, setting and treatment, and history and treatment. Essentially, these three interactions reflect that the results of a treatment (e.g., a manager doing x) may be dependent on the category of persons treated (e.g., on their social, geographical, age, sex, or personality classification); on the setting in which a treatment is applied (e.g., on the setting being a military camp, university campus, factory, retail establishment, or office); and on time (e.g., on short-term historical circumstances). Although we may be alerted to the possibility of these potential interactions (i.e., through the literature), the probability of these sorts of interaction effects is not knowable in advance when seeking to ascertain if a finding obtained in one or more situations holds in some other situation. For example, in a recent article examining studies which employed organization development techniques to affect satisfaction and other attitudes, Neuman, Edwards, and Raju (1989) concluded:

These findings suggest that the outcomes that result from OD interventions are in most instances situationally specific and are, therefore, subject to the need for local validation (p. 481).

Thus, the finding one seeks to generalize, in part, may be the product of unknown and, therefore, unmeasured situational characteristics. More strongly put, the circumstances surrounding an intervention are part of the cause (Cronbach, 1982; Mackie, 1974). While such a claim may not be germane to the development of basic theories (e.g., Berkowitz & Donnerstein, 1982; Kruglanski, 1975; Mook, 1983), it most certainly would appear salient to applying a theoretically prescribed course of organizational action (Campbell, 1986; Hakel et al., 1982). This is so, as will be elaborated upon later, because for basic (or theoretical) research, as contrasted with applied (or particularistic) research, a universal scope of generality is implied by the theorist for findings across all sorts and varieties of *theoretically irrelevant* conditions (Campbell, 1969; Kruglanski, 1975). For applied research, however, these "theoretically irrelevant" conditions may have profound effects which cannot be ignored or delayed to future theorizing.[1]

Obsolescence implies more than the problem of time as it was raised in the preceding paragraph. That is, the issue refers to more than the interaction between short-term historical circumstances and a treatment. For instance, Lindblom and Cohen (1979) in attempting to depict obsolescence as the irreproducibility of findings across time, offer the following:

> Contrary to the general assumption that valid scientific knowledge cumulates, much of the mid-twentieth century investment of American political science in survey research on voting, a body of generalization to which the profession pointed with pride when claiming a new scientific status, is already obsolete. There are even signs that some of the general propositions of macrotheory in economics, once among the most secure holdings of social science, have become obsolete in a changing society that now displays inflation and depression simultaneously (p. 51).

More directly, Rescher (1970, p. 156) has stated that social science conclusions "are rooted in *transitory regularities,* deriving from the existence of temporally restricted technological or institutional patterns." Since these regularities do exist, one may believe that discernible patterns can be used to guide applications; however, the uncertain stability of the patterns again leaves one unable to make probabilistic predictions.

Gergen (e.g., 1973, 1976, 1982) has emerged as the most vocal advocate of the obsolescence argument (Greenberg & Folger, 1988; Rosnow, 1981). The essence of his position is that while social scientists are capable of providing "a systematic account of contemporary affairs" (Gergen, 1973, p. 316), such knowledge suffers from "historical perishability" (Gergen, 1976, p. 373). This position partially rests on such observations as the variables that successfully predicted political activism during the early stages of the Vietnam War are unlike those which successfully predicted activism during later periods (Gergen, 1973). Even though Gergen's claims have been attacked vigorously (e.g., Schlenker, 1974), to us it seems his position is relevant to the conduct of theory development in organizational behavior to the extent one accepts the notion that the social systems we study are open. As Katz and Kahn (1978) tell us, open systems maintain a dynamic rather than a static balance which implies the nature of the relationships within an open system are alterable. Thus, a prescription which might have "worked" in a given setting at a point in time may not hold in the future because the nature of the relationship in the setting has changed. For example, in organizational behavior, Wagner and Gooding (1987), based upon a meta-analysis of the participation-outcome research published between 1950 ad 1985, have shown a relationship between societal issues in the United States and the magnitude of reported effects. That is, as societal issues change over time (e.g., American's concerns about economic conditions and social order), effect sizes change.

Generalization, at least in a statistical sense, also can be described as entailing sampling. Simply, assume a theoretical prescription is observed to hold for a sample of a population; to seek to extrapolate that finding to another sample of the population is an attempt to generalize. Generalization occurs if the relationship observed in the first sample, in fact, is found in the second sample. How likely is this to occur? Not very according to Cronbach (1982) who has stated:

> The strength of a quantitative relationship in a subpopulation will usually differ from that in the parent population and from some other subpopulation. Karl Pearson established that principle before 1910, but only recently have social scientists awakened to the message of his mathematics for their work. The story has now been told in various forms by statisticians, econometricians, and psychometric specialists in education (Cochron and Rubin, 1973; Heckman, 1976; Reichardt, in Cook and Campbell, 1979). (p. 68)

One basis for Cronbach's statement is the recognition that an observation in a sample only provides an estimate of what some true value might be of a population; thus, the estimate obtained across two or more samples will correspond, in part, to the degree to which each of the samples are representative of the population. However, Kruskal and Mosteller (1981, p. 9), for instance, argue that a representative sample, as a miniature or mirror of the population, "is rarely appropriate or achievable in statistics." In addition, based upon a cursory examination of the literature, it appears that in organizational behavior few attempts even are made at drawing so-called representative samples; rather, convenience seems to be the selection criterion most often used. That is, while researchers occasionally may seek to draw a representative sample from an organization, one rarely observes a sample drawn to facilitate generalizing results across organizations. Thus, even in the few instances where some form of representative sampling is used, the organization(s) it is taken from generally is a matter of convenience; and, Kruskal and Mosteller (1981, p. 22) also note that it is "extraordinarily difficult for even expert observers purposively to choose observational units without introducing selection bias." More importantly, the reliance on convenience may be explained by the practice of not defining the population of interest in terms of persons, settings, or times. In sum, therefore, one is left with a weakened statistical basis for expecting findings in organizational behavior to be reproduced consistently across organizations; and, it is such generalizability that is salient in applying a prescription in a particular context.

The overlapping issues of divergence, obsolescence, and sampling consistently suggest that a theoretical prescription observed to hold in one or more situations may not generalize to some other situation. Stated more strongly, Cronbach (1982) has asserted:

> . . . sheer empirical generalization is doomed as a research strategy. Extrapolation to new circumstances apparently has to rest on a rhetorical argument, one that relies on *qualitative* beliefs about the process at work in the old and new situations (Campbell, 1974; Meehl, 1971). (p. 70)

Thus, usefulness as a criterion for evaluating organizational behavior theories would appear to be threatened by such failure to expect generalizability or, at least minimally, by the inability to specify a priori, in any certain way, the likelihood that a prescription will hold in a given context. That is, qualitative beliefs are seen as insufficient for demonstrating the usefulness of a theory; but, this is all we have available to us as a basis for asserting if the intended results of applying a theory in a particular context, in fact, will be produced. What *might* work is different from saying it either will work or should work in a probabilistic sense.

Obstructing Theory Development

Attempting to build a theory to serve the needs of managers has implications other than those associated with philosophy of science and generalizability; in this section, we argue it may obstruct theory development in organizational behavior. This obstruction may occur as a result of limiting the scientist's focus on the phenomenon to be explained. The case might be made that attempts to build managerially relevant prescriptive theories are problematic for theory development purposes, in part, because phenomena which are thought to be of concern to mangers (e.g., productivity) are chosen to be explained, thereby, a host of potentially interesting phenomena (i.e., dependent variables) may be excluded from examination by organizational behaviorists (e.g., Staw, 1984). Indeed, a prescriptive theory which does not have demonstrable effects on the "bottom line" may not be considered "useful" by managers. No less problematic is a potential limited consideration of explanatory variables. In the discussion to follow, attention primarily is focused on issues pertaining to the explanatory concepts contained in the prescriptive theory or, more operationally, the independent variables included.

It has often been asserted that for a theory to be useful, its independent variables must be able to be controlled (i.e., manipulated) by the practitioner (e.g., Gouldner, 1957; Thomas & Tymon, 1982; Tichy, 1974). While this may be true, it surely limits the vision of the applied theorist and, thereby, increases the likelihood of excluding potentially potent explanatory concepts which happen to be beyond the control of managers. Thus, theories in organizational behavior, more often than not, exclude variables beyond the workplace (Brief & Aldag, 1989). For instance, Staw, Bell, and Clausen (1986, p. 186) noted the field is not "as interested in what individuals bring to the work setting in terms of behavioral tendencies, traits, and personality (now commonly subsumed under the rubric of personal dispositions) as in how the organization can externally prod the individual to evoke more positive job attitudes and behavior." If one's purpose is to develop theories which explain job attitudes and behaviors, it becomes apparent, therefore, that exclusion of variables not thought to be readily manipulated or changed by managers, in fact, does obstruct the theory development process.

The usefulness of theory also has been tied to the degree to which its independent variables are nonobvious to managers (e.g., Gordon et al., 1978; Lundberg, 1976; Thomas & Tyman, 1982). The idea apparently is that for a theory to be useful it must go beyond the common sense of the intended user. But, it is quite plausible that lay explanations of organizational phenomena may enrich scientific ones. And, in fact, the findings of a recent study by Barley, Meyer, and Gash (1988) seem to indicate that practitioners within the field influence research more than research influences the field. Of course, however, if practitioners were the sole source of theory, then science could provide no alternatives to lay explanations.

A potential obstruction to theory development tangentially concerned with the issue of independent variable selection is the need to be timely. That is, usefulness requires that a theory be available to managers in time for them to apply it to solve a problem they are experiencing (e.g., Helmreich, 1975; Summer, 1959; Thomas & Tymon, 1982). We suspect, however, that theory construction by the clock has adverse effects. In the haste to formulate an answer to a manager's question, we are fearful, for instance, the sort of errors of omission discussed above become more probable. Moreover, consistent with the previously introduced ideas of Gergen (e.g., 1973), the extent to which the manager's problem is timebound may indicate that any explanation of the phenomenon also will be temporally limited.[2] Simply, the phenomenon, in the near future, may not exist and, therefore, not be of interest in organizational behavior. [Our treatment of the time pressure issue should in no way be construed as a failure to recognize temporal context as a potentially important theoretical construct in its own right. On this point, see, for example, McGuire (1973), Smith (1976), as well as McGrath and Rotchford (1983) and McGrath (1988).] These views about time echo the concerns expressed by Talcott Parsons in his 1949 presidential address to the American Sociological Association:

> . . . it is only by systematic work on problems where the probable scientific significance has priority over any immediate possibility of application that the greatest and most rapid scientific advance can be made. (p. 15)

and by founding editor of *Administrative Science Quarterly,* James Thompson, in 1956:

> The focus of attention on results with immediate utility limits thought and perception and thereby reduces the ultimate contributions of the research to administrative sciences. (p. 110)

Dubin (1976) has observed that because managers are concerned with what needs to be changed to obtain a desired outcome, process knowledge is irrelevant to them. That is, *why* a variable has the effect that it does often is not a managerial concern. Yet, Bergmann (1957) has argued that process knowledge stands at the center of scientific explanation. This notion of process knowledge as central to scientific explanation is consistent with the realist philosophy of science school. Recall, from our previous discussion of the realist perspective, that a successful prediction is not intrinsically related to a successful explanation. Indeed, the importance of prediction to realists is that it is *one* way of supporting a postulated explanation; moreover, to them, the criterion for choosing a theory is, in principle, explanatory rather than predictive (Outhwaite, 1983). Thus, in attending to the needs of managers, organizational behaviorists may run the risk of constructing models which potentially are predictive of outcomes of interest to managers but supply little in the way of explanation. Of course, not all managers are uninterested in process, however, given their need to focus on the "bottom line," attention to process may be sacrificed to outcomes that are desired.

Finally, theory development may be obstructed by attempting to serve the needs of managers because of the diversion of seemingly scarce resources. Applied researchers have been instructed on the necessity of "selling" their ideas (e.g., Boehm, 1980) and on how to do that successfully (e.g., Hakel et al., 1982). To the extent such successes, in fact, are realized, resources may be allocated to the building of supposedly useful theories rather than to developing theories with greater explanatory potential. For example, both kinds of theories require organizational sites in which to be tested; and, the theory builder holding out the carrot of utility is likely to squeeze out the investigator more interested in explanation per se.

In sum, the field's ability to explain any given organizational phenomenon may be hampered by attempts to build managerially useful theories. It was argued this is so because prescriptive theory building tends to (a) narrow the theorist's vision, (b) create unrealistic time constraints, (c) de-emphasize process knowledge and (d) draw resources away from more scientifically productive activities. Although the construction of "useful" theories may, in fact, obstruct theory, we do not intend to imply that theories in organizational behavior cannot be of service to managers. Indeed, in the following section, we try to show how the practicality of organizational behavior to managers, as well as others, might be enhanced.

Towards Practicality

In opening this paper, we defined the usefulness of an organizational behavior theory as "the quality of having worth to organizational practitioners in terms of prescribing the means to some end-state they desire"; and, we proceeded with arguments against usefulness by raising issues pertaining to philosophy of science and generalizability. We even claimed that attempting to be useful may obstruct theory development. Now, we turn to endorsing the practicality of theory. In fact, we agree with Lewin (1945, p. 129) that "nothing is as practical as a good theory."

Given our attack against authoritative prescriptions, what does theory in organizational behavior have to offer in a practical sense? Foremost, if not exclusively, it can add to knowledge by reshaping and refining the ordinary knowledge students, laborers, administrators, and policy makers possess about organizational phenomenon. Lindblom and Cohen (1979) define "ordinary knowledge" as knowledge whose origin lies in "common sense, causal empiricism, or thoughtful speculation and analysis" and not in the "testing, degree of verification, truth status, or currency" (p. 12) distinctive of the social sciences.

Ordinary knowledge can be reshaped and refined through the process of qualification (Masters, 1984); that is, the aphorisms of ordinary knowledge may be divergent [for example, "Absence makes the heart grow fonder" versus "Out of sight, out of mind." (Johns, 1988)] and theory can help clarify under what conditions seemingly opposing "truths" may hold. Such an end is achieved by organizational behaviorists being educators, presenting their theoretical concepts to the uninitiated. As Cronbach (1982) has observed:

> Our main stock in trade is not prescriptions or laws or definitive assessments of proposed action; we supply concepts, and these alter perceptions (Lindblom & Cohen, 1979; Rein, 1976; Weiss, 1977). Fresh perceptions suggest new paths for action and alter the criteria for assessment (pp. 71–72).

In pounding home the same message about the benefits of such "fresh perceptions," Weiss (1977) has asserted nonproblems may come to be seen as problems and vice versa; thereby, the agenda for what requires action becomes redefined.

The above view of theory as an educational device rather than an interrelated set of prescriptions formulated to solve the problems of managers is consistent with Lindblom and Cohen's (1979) position that the social sciences are incapable of supplying solutions to problems and, at best, represent *one* of several inputs to the problem solving process. As such an input, Lindblom and Cohen tell us, the social sciences provide evidence and argument, not fact and proof. As Yorks and Whitsett (1985) note,

> Truly innovative managers can proceed without believing that their actions are supported by highly certain, scientifically verified laws. Indeed, they deal with an uncertain world all the time. What is required is that they develop approaches applicable to their own situations (p. 29).

This theme also is evident in Staw's (1983) discussion of the experimenting organization. He stated a "realistic view is to acknowledge the uncertainty present in the social sciences and to accept the science of innovation at the more local level" with managers appraising our finding "in terms of *best guesses*" (p. 426).

The debate over usefulness obviously is not limited to theory in organizational behavior. Leff (1988), in evaluating the reasons for the nonuse of policy research (in particular, social benefit-cost analysis research) at the World Bank notes:

> The presumption . . . is apparently that work located more toward the 'applied' end of the spectrum provides a relatively sure and high return in terms of usefulness to practitioners. The case we have considered suggests that such an approach may in fact not be helpful (p. 401).

By providing evidence and argument, the organizational behaviorist as educator, can supply a vision for the future and challenge imagination. But, as Yorks and Whitsett (1985) warn, imagination and vision must not be converted into self-delusion about the conclusiveness of one's evidence and arguments. It is incumbent on the organizational behaviorist to be self-critical and not allow "what might be" to be taken by others as "what will be." Of course, we really have no other choice given the fallible nature of our theories and their predictions.

As depicted in Table 1, the line between what we have called the useful and the practical is not a thin one; it is the difference between being prescriptive versus descriptive, between supplying factual answers versus posing provocative questions, and between advocating a particular solution versus promoting further deliberation. To put it simply, a practical theory is an idea generator—it is capable of stimulating practitioners to view their worlds in ways they might not otherwise have. A practical theory can suggest courses of action but, unlike a prescriptive ("useful") theory, it is *not* an advocate of one particular course of action. Obviously, we are not arguing that theory in organizational behavior should not be relevant. But, following Staw (1985:

Table 1.   Contrasts Between Usefulness and Practicality
in Organizational Behavior

Dimension	Usefulness	Practicality
Subject matter	Organizational phenomena	Organizational phenomena
Primary audience	Clients	Other scientists
Major goals	Solving clients' problems Prescribing courses of action Predicting	Developing scientific theory Explaining Describing
Nature of research questions	Ultimately concerned with outcomes	Ultimately concerned with processes
Type of research	Particularistic/context centered	Universalistic/theoretically oriented
Relationship with practitioners	Problem-solver	Educator/Question-framer

97), we see relevance as pertaining "more to our understanding of how organizations function than change efforts to improve their functioning." No matter what the organizational phenomena being attended to, we see describing, questioning, and deliberating as having educational value. However, we recognize that organizational members must make choices and may seek authoritative prescriptions the organizational behaviorist as educator cannot provide. But, our thesis is *the best a scientific theory builder can do is educate.* Where then should the organizational decisionmaker turn? After Lewin (1946), we suggest the decisionmaker look to an action researcher (if one can be found). These specialists conduct research on organizational issues that has an indirect relation to theory development or, if it does have major theoretical relevance, it is driven not by the theory but by the problem at hand. [For more on the concept of action research, see, for example, Clark (1972), Foster (1972), Rapoport (1970), and Susman and Evered (1978)].

The action researcher is an organizational scientist but one who conducts, in the words of Kruglanski (1975), "particularistic (or context- centered)" research. Kruglanski (1975) characterizes this research by:

(1) an emphasis on the *concrete* instances (e.g., of applied interest) in which a given finding would apply; (2) a foremost attention to the *accuracy* of statements rendered about

these specific instances; (3) a highly restricted scope of intended generalization, notably to contexts of particular relevance; and (4) an a priori anticipation of (and concern about) possible variability in the results across the different contexts including interaction effects between the treatments and the contexts, as well as main effects of the latter (p. 105).

He further goes on to characterize particularistic research by observing its "object is to predict how a specific group will react to specific events (e.g., will a ten minute extension of the coffee break lower the error rate of telephone operators in company X?)" (pp. 105–106). Given this goal, Kruglanski concludes:

Few things are assumed to be irrelevant a priori. Rather, maximal isomorphism is sought with respect to most identifiable dimensions of the procedure including the specific operations, the testing conditions, and the type of subjects. Accordingly, under these circumstances the representativeness of sampling is absolutely essential (p. 106).

Reinforcing Kruglanski's characterization is Susman and Evered's (1978) depiction of action research. They stated:

The action researcher knows that many of the relationships between people, events, and things are a function of the situation as relevant actors currently define it. Such relationships are not often invariant (Blumer, 1956) or free of their context, but change as the definition of the situation changes. Appropriate action is based not on knowledge of replications of previously observed relationships between actions and outcomes. It is based on knowing how particular actors define their present situations or on achieving consensus on defining situations so that planned actions will produce their intended outcomes (p. 590).

Clearly, the sort of research we have characterized is not the "meat" of the typical academic journals in the field; below, we pursue this point by somewhat sharpening the distinction between the action researcher and those of us more interested in developing explanatory or descriptive theory.

A relatively well articulated class of such context-centered research is called evaluative (for example, the evaluation of training in organizations). This sort of research stresses action in a highly specific situation and entails concretely forecasting the consequences of that action. As one moves from theoretical to evaluative research, the number of situationally contingent factors increase (Suchman, 1967). The more precise the evaluative researcher can make these contingencies of "success", the more useful his/her research results. And in fact, as Van de Val, Bolas and Kang (1976) have shown, social research conducted by an in-house researcher tends to result in a significantly higher degree of utilization than projects conducted by external researchers. [While this finding could be attributed to the research sponsor, for some reason, being more committed to the in-house investigator, we see it due to the greater situational sensitivity of the researcher who better "knows" the host organization.] Alternatively, the more situational contingencies attached to a hypothesis, the less its theoretical value. This point is analogous to the one made by Kaplan (1964) in his discussion of the scope and systematic import of theoretical concepts. [Also see Campbell (1969) and Kruglanski (1975) on the theoretical value of hypotheses.]

Several other authors, writing from a variety of perspectives, have recognized the need for and differences between more theoretically oriented scientists focused on explanation and those we have identified as action researchers who are concerned primarily with solving a practitioner's problem (e.g., Bhaskar, 1975; Boehm, 1980; Gouldner, 1957; Lindblom & Cohen, 1979; Masters, 1984; Reynolds, 1979). Secord (1986) has described these differences in particularly insightful ways. His writings suggest that an action researcher must be more than a scientist by having biographical, historical, and social structural knowledge about the specific context in which he or she is practicing. For instance, Secord (1986) has stated that the action researcher, in approaching an applied problem:

> . . . must search for and describe the structural enablements and constraints that play a part in creating the problem, and he must find a way of transforming these elements to create the kind of situation desired. Often there will be little guidance from the social sciences in general, for each applied problem has many unique features. In fact, extensive experience in similar settings may well provide more guidance than the formal body of social science knowledge (p. 219).

He attributes this state-of-affairs to "the nature of our world, and not because of the immaturity or wrongheadedness of social sciences" (p. 213).

Earlier we alluded to a possible shortage of action researchers in organizational behavior. We suspect this, in fact, is the case. In academia, there is pressure (which, again, we believe to be appropriate) to do research aimed at developing explanatory theories. While some university-based organizational behaviorists may attempt to blend the roles of theory builder and action researcher, it is well known (e.g., Simon, 1967) that this is a terribly difficult road to follow.

The work of an action researcher, done for a clearly identifiable client, obviously is not ethically neutral. In general, the value-ladenness of the social sciences is not necessarily problematic (e.g., Kaplan, 1964; Mills, 1959; Weber, 1949). It is so, however, when adherence to values translates into bias. The sort of bias we are concerned with here pertains to the organizational behaviorist's choice of a user. That is, the construction of a theory intended to be useful is preceded by the choice of a user; and, in organizational behavior, it has been discussed widely that this choice often is made in favor of those who control resources sought after by organizational scientists (e.g., Benson, 1977; Bramble & Friend, 1981; Brown, 1978; Nord, 1977; Nord, Brief, Atieh, & Doherty, 1988; Ronen, 1980; Shore, 1979).[3] Becker (1967, p. 242) has argued that researchers inevitably take "sides" (for instance, management versus labor) and that many studies are "biased in the direction of the interests of responsible officials." Frost (1980, p. 502) also has noted "we are preoccupied with what managers value and with their definitions of organizational problems"; and, two decades earlier Baritz (1960, p. 61) wrote that "the values and goals of the mangers were accepted as given" by organizational behaviorists. Thus, the theories intended to be useful are constructed to meet the needs of managers. This choice of managers as the end user, in and of itself, does not necessarily constitute bias (even though it focuses attention on certain variables at the expense of others). However, if the prescriptions derived from a theory lead to outcomes which favor management at the expense of, or to the exclusion of, subordinates for example, the ethics of the prescription may be called into question.

It has been claimed that basic researchers in the social sciences often have sought to disavow any responsibility for how their findings are put to use (Diener & Crandall, 1978); rather, they advocate an ethically neutral view of knowledge (Lambarth & Kimmel, 1981). In perhaps one of the most vicious attacks on this perspective, Gouldner (1963) stated "the value-free doctrine of social science was sometimes used to justify the sale of one's talents to the highest bidder" (p. 4). Indeed, Pfeffer (1981, p. 17) has observed "under the guise of objectivity and data, the ideological bases and premises of much of the study of organizations remain systematically submerged and ignored." If the disavowal of the basic researcher is suspect, surely any advocacy of ethical neutrality on the part of the prescriptive theory builder would seem absurd (Reynolds, 1979, 1982).

We make no suggestion that attempts at prescriptive theory building in organizational behavior is unavoidably unethical. We do claim it creates a number of ethical dilemmas not often discussed or, perhaps even recognized. Nord et al.'s (1988) analysis of the unconscious ideology those of us in organizational behavior are subject to suggests that lack of recognition, indeed, is the problem. We so closely identify with the group that has the power to enact our theories, we fail to take note of what Gordon and Nurick (1981, p. 295) have called "a basic divergence between the needs of workers and the needs of management." [On this point, also see, for example, Anthony (1977).] As noted earlier, although the basic researcher is not exempt from ethical concerns, these very issues would seem to be of paramount interest to the prescriptive theory builder since the intent of such theorists is to change behavior in such a way that satisfies the end user. Thus, issues pertaining to how a theory in the service of those in power (i.e., managers) may help to perpetuate some ethically undesirable aspect of the status quo (e.g., Mills, 1959), or reinforce the adverse stereotype of a class of persons (e.g., female managers) or treat a class as scapegoats (e.g., productions line workers as the reason for decreasing productivity), need to be addressed.

In sum, how might the field move towards the practical? First, the very limited usefulness of explanatory or scientific theory needs to be recognized *and,* correspondingly, its tremendous practical value as an educational device needs to be appreciated. The practical problem solver role belongs to the action researcher whose work primarily does not entail theory building but rather generating context specific research findings intended to aid a clearly identifiable client. Most assuredly, it is mutually beneficial for the theory builder and action researcher to communicate openly [for example, the labors of the action researcher may produce what the scientist interested in explanations sees as grounded theory (Glaser and Strauss, 1967)]. Indeed, we are not arguing that the scientist should be divorced from the "real world" of the practitioner as an interactive relationship is beneficial to both. However, it needs to be recognized that the two roles of scientific theory builder and action researcher are separable and probably desirably so.

Concluding Remarks

It is our assertion that the worth of a theory should not be judged by its ability to prescribe means-ends statements for managers. We have argued that not only may it be illogical to expect a theory to be "useful," as we have defined it, there are scientific concerns about this criterion. Returning briefly to the philosophy of science arguments discussed earlier, the point was made that an organizational behavior theory could not logically contain authoritative rules of action for practitioners since all theories are inherently fallible. It can be argued, however, that not all parts of a theory are necessarily fallible, and, at any one point in time, the present theory may be the best we have. We do not take issue with this argument; however, we must be very clear about what we intend to do with the theory. Present theory may be the best we have *to raise people's consciousness,* not to specify particular actions in particular contexts. Since we cannot be sure what specific parts of any theory may be fallible or not, we assert that it is inappropriate to make authoritative statements based on the theory.

It was noted earlier that the field is not as clear on its definition of "usefulness" as it is with "validity." One important implication of the present paper, therefore, is recognition of the need to clearly define what we mean by "usefulness." For those who accept the definition given in the present paper, hopefully we have raised some concerns about the organizational behaviorist's ability to provide prescriptive statements which generalize across contexts. Even for those who question our narrow definition, hopefully, we have made a convincing case that the field needs to agree upon what the "usefulness" criterion means.

We have painted a picture of the theory builder in organizational behavior as an educator concerned with practical matters, not as one who is capable of providing prescriptive statements for solving practical problems. Also, we have depicted the action researcher as an expert capable of formulating solutions to practical problems whose usefulness probably is limited to the specific contexts in which they were developed. We anticipate that neither of these roles, as narrowly as we have construed them, will be attractive to many organizational behaviorists. In fact, we have described only two of several possible roles that may be defined in terms of the social scientist's relationship to practical matters (Masters, 1984). In describing organizational behaviorists as educators or as practical problem-solvers our intent was not to win converts to either role. Rather, our aim was to provoke thought about what reasonably can be expected from the field given its current mix of roles. We, as should now be apparent, are uneasy with that mix. Hopefully, this paper will lead others to share our discomfort.

ACKNOWLEDGMENTS

The authors would like to express their gratitude to Rob Folger, Rick Guzzo, Walter Nord, Lance Sandelands, Tom Thomas, and the editors for their helpful comments on earlier drafts. Of course, any errors remaining in the current manuscript are the sole responsibility of the authors.

NOTES

1. It has been argued that these "theoretically irrelevant" conditions also have profound effects on the development of theoretical knowledge. See, for example, Greenwald, Pratkanis, Leippe, and Baumgardner (1986) and, in particular, McGuire (1983).

2. Gergen's assertion is not a threat to science per se as an institution but to science from a positivistic perspective.

3. There are a few notable exceptions in the literature, for example, Brett (1980) and Kochan (1980).

REFERENCES

Anthony, P. O. (1977). *The ideology of work.* New York: Tavistock.
Baritz, I. (1960). *The servants of power.* New York: John Wiley.

Barley, S. R., Meyer, G. W., & Gash, D. C. (1988). Cultures of culture: Academics, practitioners and the pragmatics of normative control. *Administrative Science Quarterly, 33,* 24–60.

Becker, H. (1967). Whose side are we on? *Social Problems, 14,* 239–247.

Benson, K. J. (1977). Organization: A dialectical view. *Administrative Science Quarterly, 22,* 1–21.

Beres, M. E. (1983). Usefulness as a research criterion: Reflections of a critical advocate. In R. H. Kilmann, K. W. Thomas, D. P. Slevin, R. North, (Eds.), *Producing useful knowledge for organizations.* New York: Praeger.

Bergmann, G. (1957). *Philosophy of science.* Madison: University of Wisconsin Press.

Berkowitz, L., & Donnerstein, E. (1982). External validity is more than skin deep: Some answers to criticisms of laboratory experiments. *American Psychologist, 37,* 245–257.

Beyer, J. M. (1982). Introduction. *Administrative Science Quarterly, 27,* 588–590.

Bhaskar, R. (1975). *A realist theory of science.* Leeds, England: Leeds Books.

Bhaskar, R. (1986). *Scientific realism and human emancipation.* Thetford, Norfolk: The Thetford Press.

Blumer, H. (1956). Sociological analysis and the 'variable.' *American Sociological Review, 21,* 683–690.

Boehm, V. R. (1980). Research in the "real world"—A conceptual model. *Personnel Psychology, 33,* 495–503.

Bramel, D., & Friend, R. (1981). Hawthorne, the myth of the docile worker, and class bias in psychology. *American Psychologist, 36,* 867–878.

Brett, J. M. (1980). Behavioral research on unions and union management systems. In B. M. Staw & L. L. Cummings (Eds.), *Research in organizational behavior,* Vol. 2. CT: JAI Press.

Brief, A. P., & Aldag, R. J. (1989). The economic functions of work. In K. Rowland & G. Ferris (Eds.), *Research in personnel and human resource management.* (Vol. 7, pp. 1–23) Greenwich, CT: JAI Press.

Brown, R. H. (1978). Bureaucracy as praxis: Toward a political phenomenology of formal organizations. *Administrative Science Quarterly, 23,* 365–382.

Campbell, D. T. (1969). Prospective: Artifact and control. In R. Rosenthal & R. L. Rosnow (Eds.), *Artifact in behavioral research,* (pp. 143–179). New York: Academic Press.

Campbell, J. P. (1986). Labs, fields, and straw issues. In E. Locke (Ed.), *Generalizing from laboratory to field settings* (pp. 269–279). MA: D.C. Heath & Company.

Cheng, J. L. C., & McKinley, W. (1983). Toward an integration of organization research and practice: A contingency study of bureaucratic control and performance in scientific settings. *Administrative Science Quarterly, 28,* 85–100.

Clark, P. A. (1972). *Action research and organizational change.* London: Harper & Row.

Cochran, W. G., & Rubin, D. B. (1973). Controlling bias in observational studies: A review. *Sankhya, 35,* 417–476.

Cook, T. D. (1983). Quasi-experimentation: Its ontology, epistemology and methodology. In G. Morgan (Ed.), *Beyond method.* Beverly Hills: Sage.

Cook, T. D., & Campbell, D. T. (1979). *Quasi-experimentation: Design and analysis issues for field settings.* Chicago: Rand McNally.

Cronbach, L. J. (1982). Prudent aspirations for social inquiry. In W. Kruskal (Ed.), *The social sciences.* Chicago: University of Chicago Press.

Cronbach, L. J., & Associates (1980). *Toward reform in program evaluation.* San Francisco: Jossey-Bass.

Cummings, L. L. (1978). Toward organizational behavior. *Academy of Management Review, 3,* 90–98.

Diener, E., & Crandall, R. (1978). *Ethics in social and behavioral research.* Chicago: University of Chicago Press.

Dubin, R. (1976). Theory building in applied areas. In M. D. Dunnette (Ed.), *Handbook of industrial and organizational psychology* (pp. 17–39). Chicago: Rand NcNally.

Earley, P. C., Connolly, T., & Ekegren, G. (1989). Goals, strategy development, and task performance: Some limits in the efficacy of goal setting. *Journal of Applied Psychology, 74,* 24–33.

Filley, A. C., & House, R. J. (1969). *Management process and organizational behavior.* Glenview, IL: Scott, Foresman & Company.

Folger, R., & Konovsky, M. (1989). Effects of procedural and distributive justice on reactions to pay decisions. *Academy of Management Journal, 32,* 115–130.

Foster, M. (1972). The theory and practice of action research in work organizations. *Human Relations, 25,* 529–556.

Fromkin, H. L., & Streufert, S. (1976). Laboratory experimentation. In M. Dunnette (Ed.), *Handbook of industrial and organizational behavior.* Chicago: Rand McNally.

Frost, P. (1980). Toward a radical framework for practicing organization science. *Academy of Management Review, 5,* 501–507.

Gergen, K. J. (1973). Social psychology as history. *Journal of Personality and Social Psychology, 26,* 309–320.

Gergen, K. J. (1976). Social psychology, science and history. *Personality and Social Psychology Bulletin, 2,* 373–383.

Gergen, K. J. (1982). *Toward transformation in social knowledge.* New York: Springer-Verlag.

Gergen, K. J., & Gergen, M. M. (1986). *Social psychology,* 2nd Ed. New York: Springer-Verlag.

Glaser, B. G., & Strauss, A. C. (1967). *The discovery of grounded theory.* Chicago: Aldine.

Gordon, M. E., Kleinman, L. S., & Hanie, C. A. (1978). Industrial-organizational psychology: Open thy ears o house of Israel. *American Psychologist, 33,* 893–905.

Gordon, M. E., & Nurick, A. J. (1981). Psychological approaches to the study of unions and union-management relations. *Psychological Bulletin, 90,* 293–306.

Gouldner, A. W. (1957). Theoretical requirements of the applied social sciences. *American Sociological Review, 22.*

Gouldner, A. W. (1963). Anti-minotaur: The myth of a value-free sociology. In M. Stein & A. Widich (Eds.), *Sociology on trial.* Englewood Cliffs, NJ: Prentice-Hall.

Greenberg, J., & Folger, R. (1988). *Controversial issues in social research methods.* New York: Springer-Verlag.

Greenwald, A. G., Pratkanis, A. R., Leippe, M. R., & Baumgardner, M. H. (1986). Under what conditions does theory obstruct research progress? *Psychological Review, 93,* 216–229.

Hackman, J. R. (1977). Work design. In J. R. Hackman & J. L. Suttle (Eds.), *Improving life at work.* Santa Monica: Goodyear.

Hakel, M. D., Sorcher, M., Beer, M., & Moses, J. L. (1982). *Making it happen: Designing research with implementation in mind.* Beverly Hills: Sage Publications.

Haire, M. (1964). The social sciences and management practices. *California Management Review, 6,* 3–10.

Harre, Rom (1986). *Varieties of realism.* New York: Blackwell.

Heckman, J. J. (1976). The common structure of statistical models of truncation, sample selection and limited dependent variables and a simple estimator for such models. *Annals of Economic and Social Measurement, 5,* 475–492.

Helmreich, R. (1975). Applied social psychology: The unfulfilled promise. *Personality and Social Psychology Bulletin, 1,* 548–560.

Hempel, C. G. (1952). *Fundamentals of concept formation in empirical science.* Chicago: University of Chicago Press.

Johns, G. (1988). *Organizational behavior: Understanding life at work.* Glenview, IL: Scott, Foresman.

Kaplan, A. (1964). *The conduct of inquiry: Methodology for the behavioral sciences.* Scranton, PA: Chandler.

Katz, D., & Kahn, R. L. (1978). *The social psychology of organizations,* Second Edition. New York: John Wiley.

Kilmann, R. H. (1979). On integrating knowledge utilization with knowledge development: The philosophy behind the MAPS design technology. *Academy of Management Review, 4,* 417–426.

Kilmann, R. H., Slevin, D. P., & Thomas, K. W. (1983). The problem of producing useful knowledge. In R. H. Kilmann, K. W. Thomas, D. P. Slevin, R. North, & S. C. Jerrell (Eds.), *Producing useful knowledge for organizations.* New York: Praeger.

Kochan, T. A. (1980). Collective bargaining and organizational behavior research. In B. M. Staw & L. L. Cummings (Eds.), *Research in organizational behavior,* Vol. 2. Greenwich, CT: JAI Press.

Kruglanski, A. W. (1975). The human subject in the psychology experiment: Fact and artifact. In L. Berkowitz (Ed.), *Advances in experimental social psychology,* Vol. 8 (pp. 101–147). New York: Academic Press.

Kruskal, W., & Mosteller, F. (1981). Ideas of representative sampling. In D. W. Fiske (Ed.), *Problems with language imprecision.* San Francisco: Jossey-Bass.

Kuhn, T. S. (1970). *The structure of scientific revolutions,* 2nd Edition. Chicago: University of Chicago Press.

Lamberth, J., & Kimmel, A. J. (1981). Ethical issues and responsibilities in applying scientific behavioral knowledge. In A. J. Kimmel (Ed.), *Ethics of human subject research.* San Francisco: Jossey-Bass.

Leff, N. H. (1988). Policy research for improved organizational performance: A case from the World Bank. *Journal of Economic Behavior and Organization, 9,* 393–403.

Lewin, K. (1945). The research center for group dynamics at Massachusetts Institute of Technology. *Sociometry. 8,* 126–136.

Lewin, K. (1946). Action research and minority problems. *Journal of Social Issues, 2,* 34–46.

Lindblom, C. E., & Cohen, D. K. (1979). *Usable knowledge: Social science and social problem solving.* New Haven, CT: Yale University Press.

Locke, E. A. (1968). Toward a theory of task motivation and incentives. *Organizational Behavior and Human Performance, 3,* 157–189.

Locke, E. A., Shaw, K. N., Saari, L. M., & Latham, G. P. (1981). Goal setting and task performance: 1969–1980. *Psychological Bulletin, 90,* 125–152.

Louis, M. R. (1983). Useful knowledge and knowledge use: Toward explicit meanings. In R. H. Kilmann, K. W. Thomas, D. P. Slevin, R. North, S. L. Jerrell (Eds.), *Producing useful knowledge for organizations.* New York: Praeger.

Lundberg, G. C. (1976). Hypothesis creation in organizational behavior research. *Academy of Management Review, 1,* 5–12.

Lykken, D. T. (1968). Statistical significance in psychological research. *Psychological Bulletin, 70,* 151–159.

Mackie, J. L. (1974). *The cement of the universe: A study of causation.* Oxford: Claredon Press.

Manicas, P. T., & Secord, P. F. (1983). Implications for psychology of the new philosophy of science. *American Psychologist, 38,* 399–413.

Masters, J. C. (1984). Psychology, research, and social policy. *American Psychologist, 39,* 851–862.

McGrath, J. E. (1988). *The social psychology of time.* Newbury Park, CA: Sage.

McGrath, J. E., & Rotchford, N. C. (1983). Time and behavior in organizations. In L. Cummings & B. Staw (Eds.), *Research in organizational behavior* (Vol. 5, pp. 57–101). Greenwich, CT: JAI Press.

McGuire, W. J. (1973). The yin and yang of progress in social psychology. *Journal of Personality and Social Psychology, 26,* 446–456.

McGuire, W. J. (1983). A contextualist theory of knowledge: Its implications for innovation and reform in psychological research. In L. Berkowitz (Ed.), *Advances in experimental social psychology.* New York: Academic Press.

McKelvey, B., & Aldrich, H. (1983). Populations, natural selection and applied organizational science. *Administrative Science Quarterly, 28,* 101–128.

Meehl, P. E. (1986). What social scientists don't understand. In D. W. Fiske & R. A. Shweder (Eds.), *Metatheory in social science.* (pp. 197–221). Chicago: The University of Chicago Press.

Miller, R. W. (1987). *Fact and method: Explanation, confirmation and reality in the natural and the social sciences.* Princeton: Princeton University Press.

Mills, C. W. (1959). *The sociological imagination.* New York: Oxford University Press.

Miner, J. B. (1984). The validity and usefulness of theories in an emerging organizational science. *Academy of Management Review, 9,* 296–306.

Mirvis, P. H., & Seashore, S. E. (1979). Being ethical in organizational research. *American Psychologist, 34,* 766–780.

Mitroff, I. I., Betz, F., Pondy, L. R., & Sagasti, F. (1974). On managing science in the systems age: Two schemas for the study of science as a whole systems phenomenon. *Interfaces, 4,* 46–58.

Mook, D. G. (1983). In defense of external invalidity. *American Psychologist, 38,* 379–387.

Neuman, G. A., Edwards, J. E., & Raju, N. S. (1989). Organizational development interventions: A meta-analysis of their effects on satisfaction and other attitudes. *Personnel Psychology, 42,* 461–489.

Nord, W. R. (1977). Job satisfaction reconsidered. *American Psychologist, 32,* 1026–1035.

Nord, W. R., Brief, A. P., Atieh, J. M., & Doherty, E. M. (1988). Work values and the conduct of organizational behavior. In B. M. Staw & L. L. Cummings (Eds.), *Research in organizational behavior,* Vol. 10 (pp. 1–42). Greenwich, CT: JAI Press.

Outhwaite, W. (1983). Toward a realist perspective. In G. Morgan (Ed.), *Beyond method.* Beverly Hills: Sage.

Parsons, T. (1950). The prospects of sociological theory. *American Sociological Review, 15,* 15.

Pfeffer, J. (1981). *Power in organizations.* Boston: Pitman.

Popper, K. R. (1965). *Conjectures and refutations: The growth of scientific knowledge,* 2nd Edition. New York: Harper & Row.

Rapoport, R. N. (1970). Three dilemmas of action research. *Human Relations, 23,* 499–513.

Rein, M. (1976). *Social science and social policy.* New York: Penguin.

Rescher, N. (1970). *Scientific explanation.* New York: The Free Press.

Reynolds, P. D. (1979). *Ethical dilemmas and social science research.* San Francisco: Jossey-Bass.

Reynolds, P. D. (1982). *Ethics and social science research.* Englewood Cliffs, NJ: Prentice-Hall.

Robbins, S. P. (1989). *Organizational behavior,* IV edition. Englewood Cliffs, NJ: Prentice-Hall.

Ronen, W. W. (1980). Some ethical considerations in worker control. *American Psychologist, 35,* 1150–1151.

Rosnow, R. L. (1981). *Paradigms in transition: The methodology of social inquiry.* New York: Oxford University Press.

Schlenker, B. R. (1974). Social psychology as a science. *Journal of Personality and Social Psychology, 29,* 1–15.

Secord, P. F. (1986). Explanation in the social sciences and in life situations. In D. W. Fiske & R. A. Shweder (Eds.), *Metatheory in social science* (pp. 197–221). Chicago: The University of Chicago Press.

Shore, R. 1979. (November 2) Servants of power, *APA Monitor.*

Simon, H. A. (1967). The business school: A problem in organizational design. *Journal of Management Studies, 4,* 1–16.

Smith, M. B. (1976). Social psychology, science and history: So what? *Personality and Social Psychology Bulletin, 2,* 438–444.

Staw, B. M. (1983). The experimenting organization: Problems and prospects. In B. M. Staw (Ed.), *Psychological foundations of organizational behavior,* 2nd Ed. Glenview, IL: Scott, Foresman.

Staw, B. M. (1984). Organizational behavior: A review and reformulation of the field's outcome variables. *Annual Review of Psychology,* Vol. 35 (pp. 627–666).

Staw, B. M. (1985). Repairs on the road to relevance and rigor: Some unexplored issues in publishing organizational research. In L. L. Cummings & P. J. Frost (Eds.), *Publishing in the organizational sciences.* Illinois: Richard D. Irwin.

Staw, B. M., Bell, N. E., & Clausen, J. A. (1986). The dispositional approach to job attitudes: A lifetime longitudinal test. *Administrative Science Quarterly, 31,* 56–77.

Summer, C. E., Jr. (1959). The managerial mind. *Harvard Business Review, 37,* 69–78.

Susman, G. I., & Evered, R. D. (1978). An assessment of the scientific merits of action research. *Administrative Science Quarterly, 23,* 582–603.

Thomas, K. W., & Tymon, W. G., Jr. (1982). Necessary properties of relevant research: Lessons from recent criticisms of the organizational sciences. *Academy of Management Review, 7,* 345–352.

Thompson, J. D. (1956). On building an administrative science. *Administrative Science Quarterly, 1,* 102–111.

Tichy, N. M. (1974). Agents of planned social change: Congruence of values, cognitions and actions. *Administrative Science Quarterly, 19,* 164–182.

Van de Vall, M., Bolas, C., & Kang, T. S. (1976). Applied social research in industrial organizations: An evaluation of functions, theory, and methods. *The Journal of Applied Behavioral Science, 12,* 158–177.

Wagner, III., J. A., & Gooding, R. Z. (1987). Effects of societal trends on participation research. *Administrative Science Quarterly, 32,* 241–262.

Waters, J. A., Salipante, P. F., Jr., & Notz, W. W. (1978). The experimenting organization: Using the results of behavioral science research. *Academy of Management Review, 3,* 483–492.

Weber, M. (1949). *The methodology of the social sciences.* Glenco, IL: Free Press.

Weiss, C. H. (Ed.) (1977). *Using social research in public policy making.* Lexington, MA: D. C. Heath.

Wood, R. E., Mento, A. J., & Locke, E. A. (1987). Task complexity as a moderator of goal effects: A meta-analysis. *Journal of Applied Psychology, 72,* 416–425.

Yorks, L., & Whitsett, D. A. (1985). Hawthorne, Topeka, and the issue of science versus advocacy in organizational behavior. *Academy of Management Review, 10,* 21–30.

Research in Organizational Behavior

An Annual Series of Analytical Essays and Critical Reviews

Edited by **Barry M. Staw,** *School of Business Adminis-tation, University of California, Berkeley* and **L.L. Cummings,** *Carlson School of Management, University of Minnesota*

REVIEWS: ..."A new approach for the area of organizational behavior...The nine intermediate length essays presented here provide a valuable new facet...quality is variable—in this case from good to excellent...The text is highly recommended for acquisition but with the caveat that series acquisition will be required to maximize utility..."
— *Choice*

"...a number of think pieces that accurately portray the complexities involved in understanding and explaining some aspect of organizational behavior. As could be expected, many of the chapters, primarily because they reflect the long-term research interests of the writers, are quite informative and challenging. Social scientists interested in interdisciplinary and/or applied organizational issues will find the book particularly informative."
— *Contemporary Sociology*

"...this collection is a well-written, scholarly contribution to other texts because of its integration of new theoretical considerations and critical literature review. It is very well organized and may be consulted frequently by those of us teaching management and administration in schools of social work."
— *Administration in Social Work*

Volume 8, 1986, 375 pp. $63.50
ISBN 0-89232-551-8

and Size and Their Strategic Implications, *Howard Aldrich, University of North Carolina at Chapel Hill and Ellen R. Auster, Columbia University.* **Loosely Coupled Settings: A Strategy for Computer-Aided Work Decentralization,** *Franklin D. Becker, Cornell University.* **The Meeting as a Neglected Social Form in Organizational Studies,** *Helen B. Schwartzman, Northwestern University.* **A Process Analysis of the Assessment Center Method,** *Sheldon Zedeck, University of California, Berkeley.* **Applied Behavior Analysis and Organizational Behavior: Reciprocal Influences of the Two Fields,** *Judith L. Komaki, Purdue University.* **Structural Analysis of Organizational Fields: A Blockmodel Approach,** *Paul DiMaggio, Yale University.*

Volume 9, 1987, 368 pp. $63.50
ISBN 0-89232-636-0

CONTENTS: **Editorial Statement,** *L.L. Cummings and Barry M. Staw.* **Motivation Theory Reconsidered,** *Frank J. Landy and Wendy S. Becker, Pennsylvania State University.* **Behavior in Escalation Situations: Antecedents, Prototypes and Solutions,** *Barry M. Staw, University of California, Berkeley and Jerry Ross, Carnegie-Mellon University.* **Toward An Integrated Theory of Task Design,** *Ricky W. Griffin, Texas A&M University.* **Understanding Groups in Organizations,** *Paul S. Goodman, Elizabeth Ravlin and Marshall Schminke, Carnegie-Mellon University.* **Toward a Psychology of Dyadic Organizing,** *George Bearnard Graen and Terri A. Scandura, University of Cincinnati.* **Understanding Comparable Worth: A Societal and Political Perspective,** *Thomas A. Mahoney, Vanderbilt University.* **Negotiator Cognition,** *Max H. Bazerman, Northwestern University and John S. Carroll, Massachusetts Institute of Technology.* **The Predicament of Injustice: The Management of Moral Outrage,** *Robert J. Bies, Northwestern University.* **Whistle-Blowers in Organizations: Dissidents or Reformers?,** *Janet P. Near, Indiana University and Marcia P. Miceli, Ohio State University.* **Managerial Discretion: A Bridge Between Polar Views of Organizational Outcomes,** *Donald C. Hambrick and Sidney Finkelstein, Columbia University.* **Meta-Analysis Analysis,** *Richard A. Guzzo, Susan E. Jackson and Raymond A. Katzell, New York University.*

Volume 10, 1988, 408 pp. $63.50
ISBN 0-89232-748-0

CONTENTS: **Editorial Statement,** *Barry M. Staw and L.L. Cummings.* **Work Values and the Conduct of Organizational Behavior,** *Walter R. Nord, Washington University, Arthur P. Brief, Jennifer M. Atieh, New York University and Elizabeth M. Doherty, Washington University.* **Services Marketing and Management: Implications for Organizational Behavior,**

David E. Bowen, University of Southern California and Benjamin Schneider, University of Maryland. **Aviation Theory and Job Design: Review and Reconceptualization,** Donald G. Gardner, University of Colorado Springs and L.L. Cummings, Northwestern University. **A Model of Creativity and Innovation in Organizations,** Teresa M. Amabile, Brandeis University. **When a Thousand Flowers Bloom: Structural, Collective, and Social Conditions for Innovation in Organization,** Rosebeth Moss Kanter, Harvard Business School. **The Effects of Work Layoffs on Survivors: Research Theory and Practice,** Joel Brockner, Columbia University. **Taking the Workers Back Out: Recent Trends in the Structuring of Employment,** Jeffrey Pfeffer and James N. Baron, Stanford University. **Power and Personality in Complex Organizations,** Robert J. House, University of Toronto. **The Political Environments of Organizations: An Ecological View,** Glenn R. Carroll, University of California, Berkeley, Jacques Delacroix, Santa Clara University and Jerry Goodstein, University of California, Berkeley.

Volume 11, 1989, 3l0 pp. $63.50
ISBN 0-89232-921-1

CONTENTS: Preface, L.L. Cummings and Barry M. Staw. **The Expression of Emotion in Organizational Life,** Anat Rafeli, Hebrew University of Jerusalem and Robert I. Sutton, Stanford University. **"Real Feelings": Emotional Expression and Organizational Culture,** John Van Maanen, Massachusetts Institute of Technology and Gideon Kunda, Tel Aviv University. **Of Art and Work: Aesthetic Experience and the Psychology of Work Feelings,** Lloyd E. Sandelands and Georgette C. Buckner, Columbia University. **Elf Assessments in Organizations: A Literature Review and Integrative Model,** Susan J. Ashford, Dartmouth College. **Physical Environments and Work-Group Experiences,** Eric Dundstrom, University of Tennessee abd Irwin Altman, University of Utah. **Organization Birth and Population Variety: A Community Perspective on Origins,** Elaine Romanelli, Duke University. **Longitudinal Field Methods For Studying Reciprocal Relationships in Organizational Behavior Research: Toward Improved Causal Analysis,** Larry J. Williams, Purdue University and Philip M. Podsakoff, Indiana University.

Volume 12, 1990, 336 pp. $63.50
ISBN 1-55938-029-2

CONTENTS: Editorial Statement, Barry M. Staw and L.L. Cummings. **Neither Market Nor Hierarchy: Network Forms of Organization,** Walter W. Powell, University of Arizona. **Japanese Organization and Organization Theory,** James R.

**J
A
I

P
R
E
S
S**

Lincoln, University of California, Berkeley. **Organizational Decline Processes: A Social Psychological Perspective,** Robert I. Sutton, Stanford University. **On Leadership: An Alternative to the Conventional Wisdom,** James R. Meindl, State University of New York at Buffalo. **Image Theory: A Behavioral Theory of Decision Making in Organizations,** Lee Roy Beach and Terence R. Mitchell, University of Washington. **Looking Fair Vs. Being Fair: Managing Impressons of Organizational Justice,** Jerald Greenberg, The Ohio State University. **The Motivational Basis of Organizational Citizenship Behavior,** Dennis W. Organ, Indiana University. **Goal Setting and Strategy Effects on Complex Tasks,** Robert E. Wood, Australian Graduate School of Management and Edwin A. Locke, University of Maryland.

Also Available:

Volumes 1-7 (1979-1985) $63.50 each

Volume 14, In preparation.
ISBN 1-55938-242-2   Approx. $63.50

JAI PRESS INC.

55 Old Post Road - No. 2
P.O. Box 1678
Greenwich, Connecticut 06836-1678
Tel: 203-661-7602